P9-CLZ-715

ATLANTIC BONDS

ATLANTIC BONDS

A Nineteenth-Century Odyssey
from America *to* Africa

LISA A. LINDSAY

THE UNIVERSITY OF NORTH CAROLINA PRESS

Chapel Hill

This book was published with the assistance of the H. Eugene
and Lillian Youngs Lehman Fund of the University of North
Carolina Press. A complete list of books published in the
Lehman Series appears at the end of the book.

Open access edition funded by the
National Endowment for the Humanities.

© 2017 The University of North Carolina Press

*The text of this book is licensed under a Creative Commons
AttributionNonCommercial-NoDerivatives 4.0 International License:
https://creativecommons.org/licenses/by-nc-nd/4.0/.*

Set in Arno Pro
by Tseng Information Systems, Inc.

Cover illustration: James Churchwill Vaughan.
Photograph courtesy of Rotimi Vaughan.

LIBRARY OF CONGRESS CATALOGING-IN-PUBLICATION DATA
Names: Lindsay, Lisa A., author.
Title: Atlantic bonds : a nineteenth-century odyssey from America to Africa /
Lisa A. Lindsay.
Description: Chapel Hill : The University of North Carolina Press, [2017] |
Includes bibliographical references and index.
Identifiers: LCCN 2016030096 | ISBN 9781469631127 (cloth : alk. paper) |
ISBN 9781469652153 (pbk. : alk. paper) | ISBN 9781469631134 (ebook)
Subjects: LCSH: Vaughan, James Churchwill, 1828–1893. | African Americans—
Nigeria, Southwest—Biography. | Back to Africa movement.
Classification: LCC CT2528.V38 L56 2017 | DDC 966.9/201092 [B] —dc23
LC record available at https://lccn.loc.gov/2016030096

for

MATT

CONTENTS

Introduction   *1*

1   Scipio Vaughan's South Carolina   *13*

2   Leaving Home   *43*

3   The Love of Liberty   *76*

4   Troubled Times in Yorubaland   *108*

5   Reconstructions   *144*

6   Vaughan's Rebellion   *180*

7   Afterlives   *215*

Acknowledgments   *237*

Notes   *241*

Bibliography   *281*

Index   *301*

ILLUSTRATIONS & MAP

ILLUSTRATIONS

The Vaughan family tree   *xii*

Front page of "The Vaughan Family:
   A Tale of Two Continents"   *2*

Yoruba "tribal marks"   *4*

Vaughan family Bible   *6*

South Carolina, 1824   *15*

Bonds Conway house   *21*

Hagler weathervane   *26*

Millsburg, Liberia   *82*

Matilda Newport monument   *86*

Nineteenth-century Yorubaland   *112*

Sarah Omotayo   *139*

Town and island of Lagos, 1883   *151*

J. W. Vaughan House, 29 Kakawa Street   *177*

B. C. Vaughan house, Ebute Metta   *177*

Ebenezer Baptist Church, Lagos   *205*

James Wilson Vaughan and Burrell C. Vaughan   *210*

James Churchwill Vaughan   *211*

Close-up of placard, James Churchwill
    Vaughan portrait   *213*

Era Bell Thompson with James
    Olabode Vaughan, 1974   *216*

J. C. Vaughan's tombstone   *220*

Kofo Ademola   *222*

Dr. James C. Vaughan   *223*

MAP

Liberia in the 1850s   *79*

ATLANTIC BONDS

THE VAUGHAN FAMILY TREE

VAUGHANS IN THE UNITED STATES

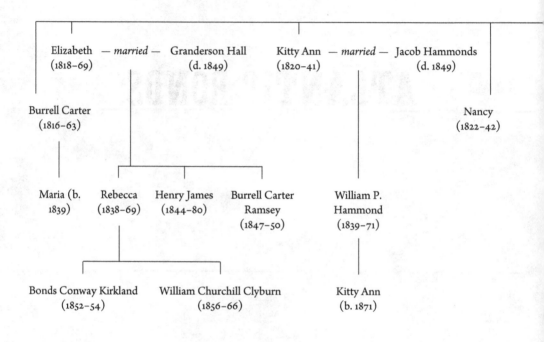

Elizabeth — *married* — Granderson Hall (1818–69) (d. 1849)

Kitty Ann — *married* — Jacob Hammonds (1820–41) (d. 1849)

Burrell Carter (1816–63)

Nancy (1822–42)

Maria (b. 1839)

Rebecca (1838–69)

Henry James (1844–80)

Burrell Carter Ramsey (1847–50)

William P. Hammond (1839–71)

Bonds Conway Kirkland (1852–54)

William Churchill Clyburn (1856–66)

Kitty Ann (b. 1871)

Harriet Conway — *married* — Moreau Naudin (1797–1854) (1800–1856)

Ellie Naomi — *married* — Andrew H. Dibble (1828–1920) (1825–74)

Eugene H. Dibble — *married* — Sallie Lee (1855–1934) (b. 1863)

Josephine — *married* — Harry S. Murphy (1887–1974) (1884–1975)

Mabel — *married* — Hugh Smythe (1918–2006) (1913–77)

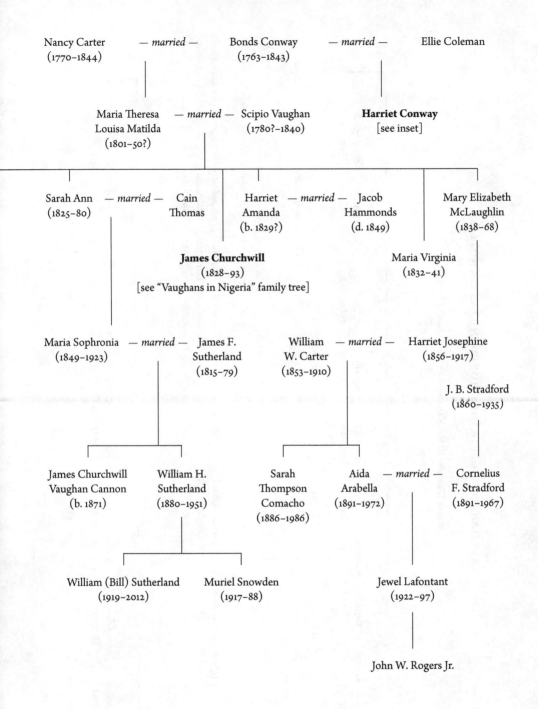

Nancy Carter — *married* — Bonds Conway — *married* — Ellie Coleman
(1770–1844)   (1763–1843)

Maria Theresa — *married* — Scipio Vaughan   Harriet Conway
Louisa Matilda   (1780?–1840)   **[see inset]**
(1801–50?)

Sarah Ann — *married* — Cain   Harriet — *married* — Jacob   Mary Elizabeth
(1825–80)   Thomas   Amanda   Hammonds   McLaughlin
                                          (b. 1829?)   (d. 1849)   (1838–68)

James Churchwill   Maria Virginia
(1828–93)   (1832–41)
[see "Vaughans in Nigeria" family tree]

Maria Sophronia — *married* — James F.   William — *married* — Harriet Josephine
(1849–1923)   Sutherland   W. Carter   (1856–1917)
                            (1815–79)   (1853–1910)

                                                                      J. B. Stradford
                                                                      (1860–1935)

James Churchwill   William H.   Sarah   Aida — *married* — Cornelius
Vaughan Cannon   Sutherland   Thompson   Arabella   F. Stradford
(b. 1871)   (1880–1951)   Comacho   (1891–1972)   (1891–1967)
                                            (1886–1986)

William (Bill) Sutherland   Muriel Snowden   Jewel Lafontant
(1919–2012)   (1917–88)   (1922–97)

                                                          John W. Rogers Jr.

VAUGHANS IN NIGERIA (MENTIONED IN TEXT OR NOTES)

James Churchwill Vaughan — *married* — Sarah Omotayo
(1828–93)

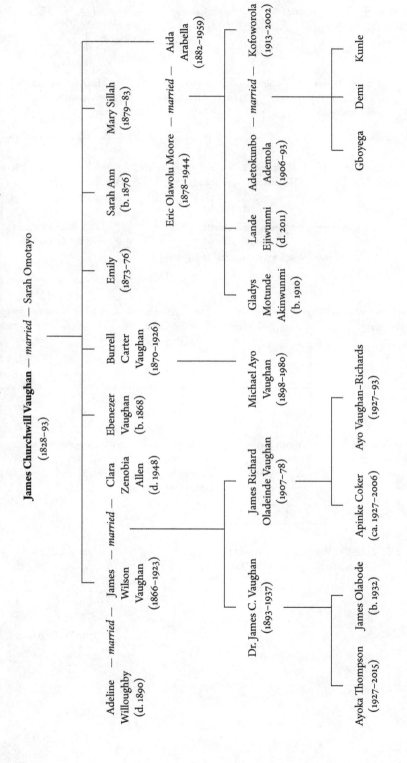

Adeline — *married* — James — *married* — Clara
Willoughby   Wilson   Zenobia
(d. 1890)   Vaughan   Allen
                          (1866–1923)   (d. 1948)

Ebenezer Vaughan (b. 1868)

Burrell Carter Vaughan (1870–1926)

Emily (1873–76)

Sarah Ann (b. 1876)

Mary Sillah (1879–83)

Eric Olawolu Moore — *married* — Aida Arabella
(1878–1944)   (1882–1959)

Dr. James C. Vaughan (1893–1937)

James Richard Oladeinde Vaughan (1907–78)

Michael Ayo Vaughan (1898–1980)

Gladys Motunde Akinwunmi (b. 1910)

Lande Ejiwunmi (d. 2011)

Adetokunbo Ademola (1906–93) — *married* — Kofoworola (1913–2002)

Ayo Vaughan-Richards (1927–93)

Apinke Coker (ca. 1927–2006)

James Olabode (b. 1932)

Ayoka Thompson (1927–2015)

Gboyega   Demi   Kunle

INTRODUCTION

On a sticky June afternoon in 2002, I stood at the front door of an elegant home not far from the University of Ibadan, waiting to meet a woman whose grandparents, I had recently read, were "an Afro-Cherokee slave of Egba descent in North Carolina and a Benin princess."[1] I had come to Nigeria on different business, but I was intrigued by the American origins of this well-known local family. A friend helped me locate some of its members, and despite transportation difficulties, side trips, delays, and all of the usual impediments of bad infrastructure and few working telephones, we had actually arrived to find the person we sought, Lande Ejiwunmi, at home. She graciously welcomed us into her sitting room, where I hoped to learn about her family's history.

Mrs. Ejiwunmi did not relate much herself, although she did put me in contact with two of her cousins, whom I soon visited as well. Curiously, I had the same experience with both of them as I did that day with Mrs. Ejiwunmi: after a nice chat and cup of tea, they asked me to wait while they rummaged through some dark cabinet stuffed with papers. Finally, each of them in turn emerged with a timeworn copy of *Ebony* magazine—the black American glossy—from 1975. In it was a feature story entitled "The Vaughan Family: A Tale of Two Continents." This, they each announced, would tell me everything I wanted to know.[2]

Sure enough, the article told a remarkable tale. It began with a man named Scipio Vaughan, a "member of the Egba family of the Yoruba tribe" taken captive and shipped to South (not North) Carolina around 1805. There he became the slave of a Camden planter who gave him his American name. One day a Cherokee woman whom Scipio encountered outside of

1

Great, great, granddaughters of patriarch Scipio Vaughan, Ayo Vaughan-Richards (l.), and Jewel Stradford Lafontant, first met in 1950 when Nigeria's principal nursing officer visited Chicago cousin, first woman U. S. deputy solicitor general. Mrs. Lafontant has visited African relatives several times. Her mother wrote only biography of Scipio.

THE VAUGHAN FAMILY: A Tale Of Two Continents

African and American descendants of former slave have kept in touch for more than a century
BY ERA BELL THOMPSON

MORE than two decades before the Emancipation Proclamation, an ex-slave named Scipio Vaughan lay dying in Camden, S. C. Calling two of his sons to his bedside, he made them promise that they would leave the South and its "oppressive laws against colored men" and go to Yorubaland (now Western Nigeria), their ancestral home.

Burrel Churchill and James Churchill Vaughan carried out their father's wishes. A prosperous merchant, James later returned to Camden to see his family. From that reunion began a trans-Atlantic communication between the African and American branches of the Vaughan tree that has continued uninterrupted for more than 100 years.

While other black families delve into genealogy in search of identity,

the descendants of Scipio know who they were, where they are and enjoy each others company.

The great-great-grandchildren of Scipio, like Ayo (pronounced eye-oh) Vaughan-Richards of Lagos, and Jewel Stradford Lafontant of Chicago, take their kinship seriously.

"We've kept in touch through the years," says Mrs. Vaughan-Richards, principal nursing school officer. "But I have a commitment to persuade all of our relations in the States to come home. Those who have visited us had tears in their eyes when I showed them the graves of their ancestors."

"Mother was always talking about our African relatives," recalls

Continued on Next Page   53

Front page of Era Bell Thompson, "The Vaughan Family: A Tale of Two Continents," *Ebony* (1975). Courtesy of Johnson Publishing Company, LLC.

town offered him a drink of water. Later she became his wife and bore him thirteen children, including James Churchwill (J. C., or Church) Vaughan. On his deathbed years later, Scipio urged his descendants to return to his ancestral homeland.

Eventually J. C. Vaughan and his brother did set out for Africa, with help from the American Colonization Society. His brother remained in Liberia, but J. C. Vaughan proceeded to Yorubaland (now southwestern Nigeria), employed as a carpenter by Southern Baptist missionaries. There, he met people bearing the same "tribal marks" (ritually cut facial scars) as those on his father's face, confirming that he was indeed in the land of his relatives.

Though he faced setbacks, Vaughan ultimately prospered in Yorubaland, and he founded an influential family. Together with the missionaries, Vaughan "played a leading role in establishing the Baptist church in Nigeria," despite the violence of continued slave raiding and "tribal conflict." Twice he was plundered of his property: first during a brutal war in which thousands were captured and enslaved; and again when Christians were expelled from the town of Abeokuta, where Vaughan and his wife, who was from the nearby Kingdom of Benin, had settled. Taking refuge in Lagos with his spouse and young son, Vaughan established himself again. Ultimately he became a successful merchant under early British colonialism, with children and grandchildren who were wealthy, educated, and politically active. Vaughan also returned to South Carolina for visits, fostering connections with American relatives that some of his descendants maintained to the present.[3]

Wow!

James Churchwill Vaughan had evidently accomplished a feat that no other African American of his time had done: he traveled to Africa and actually found his father's people, reestablishing ties broken by the Atlantic slave trade.[4] The crucial evidence was the facial scars he saw in Yoruba country, which matched those of his father. "Tribal marks" (or "country marks"), as I knew, had typically been cut into children's skin in nineteenth-century Yorubaland to show their affiliation to specific political and geographic communities.[5] Such facial scars were especially important in the era of the slave trade, and in fact it was usually free-born members of communities, not slaves, who were marked. One observer wrote that "tribal marks" allowed people to trace those carried away into slavery.[6] So in Vaughan's story, country marks did what they were supposed to do: they allowed kin and community members dispersed by slaving to find each other again. The tale seemed almost too perfect to be true — and in a way, it was.

A couple of years after that Nigerian trip, after I had already begun to confirm many aspects of Vaughan's extraordinary life story, the poignant tale of ancestral ties remembered in America and reconnected in Africa began to unravel. In Columbia, South Carolina, I visited the home of a genealogist distantly related to the Vaughan family. She generously shared with me some of her sources, including a heavy, frayed Bible first owned by J. C. Vaughan's niece Maria Sophronia Lauly. In 1869, Mrs. Lauly began compiling an exten-

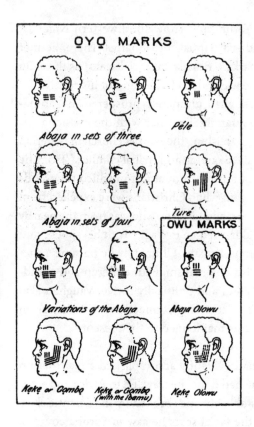

OYO MARKS

Abaja in sets of three

Pélé

Abaja in sets of four

Turé

OWU MARKS

Variations of the Abaja

Abaja Olowu

Kękę or Gombo   Kękę or Gombo (with the Ibamu)

Kękę Olowu

Facial marks as depicted in Samuel Johnson, *History of the Yorubas* (1921). "The facial marks are for the purpose of distinguishing the various Yoruba families."

sive family history in its front pages, probably copying entries from an older family Bible. Her listing commenced under "Marriages" with the 1815 union of her grandparents (J. C. Vaughan's parents), Scipio Vaughan and Maria Conway. On the next page, under "Births," Lauly wrote of her grandfather, "Sippio Vaughan was born March the 26th in Richman [*sic*] Virginia 1780." The handwriting was faded but its message was clear: J. C. Vaughan's father had been born in America, not Africa. Like other African American enslaved people, he was unlikely to have been given "country marks."[7]

At first, the revelation of Scipio Vaughan's birthplace was terribly disappointing. I tried to imagine ways that the country marks story could still be true: the Bible entry could have reflected misinformation; or the story could have been about Scipio's own father or grandfather rather than himself. (Later, when I shared what I had learned about Scipio's origins with Vaughans in Nigeria, they incredulously offered the same scenarios.) But further evidence removed any doubt.[8]

It began to dawn on me, though, that J. C. Vaughan's story was even more intriguing now than before. If the country marks version had in fact been

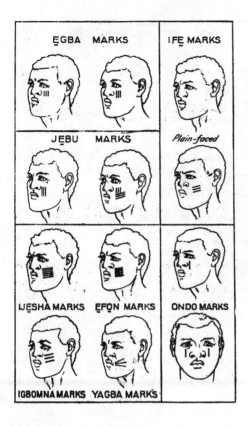

EGBA MARKS   IFE MARKS

JEBU MARKS   Plain-faced

IJESHA MARKS   EFON MARKS   ONDO MARKS

IGBOMNA MARKS   YAGBA MARKS

true, then the Vaughans would represent a fascinating but utterly unique and specific back-to-Africa journey. Without the country marks, however, their story opened up new ways of viewing connections between Africa and America, new glimpses of mobility and affiliation in the nineteenth-century Atlantic world. If Scipio Vaughan had not originally come from Yorubaland, then why did his son go there? If J. C. Vaughan was in fact an outsider in what is now southwestern Nigeria, how did he integrate so well that his descendants became important leaders? And if the story of Scipio's putative Yoruba scars was not literally true, then where did it come from?

My efforts to follow J. C. Vaughan wherever he led, and to uncover the layers of meaning in his life history, eventually took me to archives, libraries, museums, private houses, churches, graveyards, ruins, cities, and villages in the United States, Britain, Nigeria, and Liberia. Although it has been possible to recover his story, Vaughan did not lead the kind of life best suited for conventional biographies, with direct written evidence of his thoughts and interests. He left in the historical record exactly one signed letter — written to a missionary society in 1872 — along with a handful of other documents

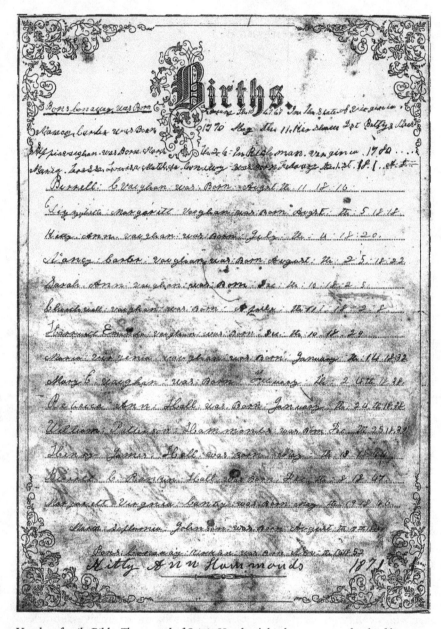

Vaughan family Bible. The record of Scipio Vaughan's birth appears on the third line from the top.

suggesting that he collaborated in their production. Yet our understanding of the world and its inhabitants remains woefully lopsided if we only concern ourselves with those who left evidence of their perspectives within easy reach. Just as social historians in the 1970s pioneered new techniques for peering into the lives of ordinary people, historians today are using a range of sources and tools to recover and interpret the experiences of those caught in the snares of slavery and its aftermaths, even when these historical subjects moved across national, imperial, or oceanic borders.[9] The narrative of Vaughan's life recounted in this book emerged from a wide variety of sources, including early Lagos newspapers and administrative and commercial records in the Nigerian National Archives; accounts from American Baptist missionaries in the archives of the Southern Baptist Convention; information on Scipio Vaughan and his family in South Carolina archives, personal papers, and privately held family Bibles; American Colonization Society records; as well as from the generous contributions of Vaughans currently living in Nigeria, the UK, and the United States.

Like a collection of discrete marks that merge to form a recognizable image, these sources together have enabled me to reconstruct Vaughan and his actions as well as the broader contexts in which he lived. Not surprisingly, Vaughan emerges more clearly in some parts of his life than in others. His encounters with missionaries, for instance, are well documented. On the other hand, I read Vaughan's relative absence from historical records during his sojourn in Liberia as itself indicative of his experience there. Even as Vaughan's presence becomes stronger or fainter in particular moments, *Atlantic Bonds* illuminates the social, political, and even physical landscapes around him to reveal the opportunities, pressures, dangers, and possibilities for local people as well as newcomers.

The result is a tale ultimately more authentic and illustrative than the version offered up in 1975 and repeated as authoritative since then. It is, like the *Ebony* account, a story of unexpected journeys, unlikely encounters, deadly perils, bold escapes, and — almost incredibly — ultimate success, in a place where one might not expect an African American to fare so well. James Churchwill Vaughan (or Church Vaughan, as he was known during his lifetime) did in fact heed his father's deathbed request and travel to Africa (without his brother), arriving in Liberia in 1853. What he saw there, however, gave him little incentive to stay. He accepted an offer of employment in Yorubaland, twelve hundred miles to the east, with missionaries from the Southern Baptist Convention, a religious denomination founded on its support of American slavery. Over the next forty years in today's southwestern

Nigeria, Vaughan was taken captive, served as a military sharpshooter, built and rebuilt a livelihood, led a revolt against white racism, and founded a family of activists. He witnessed wars that fed the Atlantic slave trade, the effects of foreign antislavery initiatives, the beginnings of missionary Christianity, the expansion of Lagos as a commercial metropolis, and the imposition of British colonialism. And he kept in touch with his relatives in America, who were embroiled in their own struggles for survival, prosperity, and dignity in South Carolina and elsewhere. Politicians, diplomats, entrepreneurs, and educators, the Vaughans of modern Nigeria and the United States have maintained contact with one another over the past century, remembering their forefathers in ways attuned to their own times.

These family members are extraordinary for the odyssey of their ancestor and the endurance of their transcontinental ties. In spite of their distinctiveness, however, the Vaughans also lead us to histories much wider than those of their family. Church Vaughan's life story forms one thread in a larger fabric of interconnections during a transformative period in Atlantic history: when slavery was abolished in the United States and colonialism began in West Africa, and when black people in both places confronted challenges to their security and autonomy. Following Vaughan's journeys from South Carolina to Liberia to several parts of Yorubaland enables a view of linkages across the nineteenth-century Atlantic world as well as a comparison of related and similar phenomena in various settings.

Fundamentally, Vaughan's odyssey reveals the pervasiveness of slavery and slavelike conditions in multiple Atlantic world locations. With every move he made, Vaughan left one slave society only to arrive in another. This was not simply bad luck, but rather the result of deep transoceanic connections. By the nineteenth century, as many historians have detailed, linked processes of empire building, trade, and migration had produced an integrated Atlantic world.[10] This world was built on a foundation of slavery and racial terror that developed colonial economies in the Americas, transformed politics in Africa, and channeled profits to Europe.[11] Moreover, slavery in any one place was reinforced by slavery elsewhere, with effects reverberating across long-distance circuits including those that Vaughan traveled. While slaving in Africa had peopled upcountry South Carolina, for instance, New World demand for captive labor fueled violence and expanded slavery in Africa itself.[12] Similarly, former American slaves sought refuge in Liberia even as slave exports from its shores to the Americas persisted.[13] Despite these linkages, Atlantic world slavery took various forms, shaped by local contexts.[14] As a young man, Vaughan may have assumed—as some still do—that its form in the American South defined slavery, both in nature and extent. But Vaughan's travels broadened his perspective. Through Vaughan's eyes, we can observe the contours of slaving and slavery in antebellum South Carolina, newly independent Liberia, and politically volatile Yorubaland, while taking account of the linkages between them.

Further, as his story shows, an evolving range of power relations blurred distinctions between slavery and freedom on both sides of the Atlantic. Church Vaughan was technically free his entire life, but *freedom* was not clear-cut for people of African descent anywhere. In each place he lived, Vaughan's security, autonomy, and livelihood had to be carefully guarded. In South Carolina, free African Americans could be sentenced to slavery or simply spirited away, and they needed the support of white patrons in order to own property or pursue a decent living. In Liberia, settlers confronted international slavers while depriving indigenous people of their own liberty. And in Yorubaland, political wars and kidnapping raids generated thousands of slaves destined for Brazil and Cuba as well as servitude within Africa. In fact, as the war that would eventually end slavery in the United States began, Vaughan himself was held prisoner in a devastating conflict between two Yoruba city-states.

Even emancipation did not result in clear-cut freedom, on either side of the Atlantic.[15] The British takeover of Lagos in 1861 was justified as an antislavery intervention. But a generation later, most residents of Vaughan's adopted home remained slave owners, slaves, or bonded dependents of some kind or other.[16] And as British colonial control over Yorubaland was consolidated—a process begun and largely completed during Vaughan's four decades there—even elite, free people were increasingly unable to participate in politics, trade, and social life as they had before. Meanwhile, Vaughan's relatives and others in the post-Reconstruction South were facing their own struggles for autonomy, safety, and citizenship, despite the abolition of slavery. Labor exploitation and white supremacy took different forms in different places, but by the end of the nineteenth century, they shaped both Jim Crow America and colonial West Africa.

Vaughan and some of his fellow Lagosians were well aware of the similarities. He had left South Carolina, as an inscription on his tombstone put it, "owing to the oppressive laws then in force against colored men in the Southern States."[17] His migration, in fact, anticipated the mass movements of African Americans after the Civil War and, on an even larger scale, in the early twentieth century.[18] But Vaughan was not only *departing from* an oppressive American South; he was *going to* Africa. Like a range of other

African Americans from the eighteenth century to our own time, he looked to the continent where his ancestors had lived as a refuge from the horrors and aftermaths of American slavery. If part of the trauma of enslavement was being taken away from kin and community, relocation to the African "motherland" promised to mitigate the damage for captives' descendants. Yet many African American sojourners to Africa have been disappointed by what they found there: not so much the comfort of literal or psychological kinship but a reminder of the differences in experience and outlook between people raised on different shores of the Atlantic Ocean.[19] The family legend about Church Vaughan's encounter with long-lost relatives bearing his father's country marks, in fact, suggests that he did not stay with them because they did not accept his Christianity.[20] The story thus encapsulates the broader dilemmas of an African diaspora conceptualized as family but differentiated by nationality and background.[21]

Though scholars writing from an American context have considered the meaning of "return" to Africa for African Americans, Vaughan's story also illuminates the diaspora from a perspective grounded in Africa. In the nineteenth century, refugees from slavery arrived in various parts of West Africa through multiple pathways, generating important effects in Africa itself.[22] Southwestern Nigeria was home to an indigenous population (itself significantly altered by warfare and political upheaval) as well as "repatriates" from Sierra Leone, Brazil, and Cuba.[23] Liberia attracted thousands of African American settlers, some of whom—like Vaughan—struck out for other parts of Africa.[24] How did these transnational migrants—the "reverse" African diaspora—affect African societies? Even as slavery persisted, white supremacy flourished, and colonial rule intensified, diasporic Africans proved remarkably adept in gaining, and also challenging, various types of authority. In Nigeria, numerous "repatriates" and their descendants prospered under British administration as merchants, professionals, and government employees. Later, this same group produced many of the first generation of anticolonial critics and Nigerian nationalists—Vaughan's grandchildren among them.

How were they able to achieve such success and influence? Black Atlantic migrants often could draw on lessons learned in multiple contexts as well as dispersed practical networks in their struggles for security and dignity.[25] When Vaughan led a rebellion against white missionaries in colonial Lagos, for instance, he and his allies—some with diasporic or enslaved backgrounds and others without—linked colonial racism to the history of Atlantic slavery. This "diasporic consciousness" went beyond the level of analysis and discourse, however, to something more concrete.[26] The rebels' strategy of separation from the mission church paralleled the contemporaneous development of all-African American religious and educational institutions, which Vaughan and some of his allies knew about from their contacts in the United States. Thus, Vaughan's links to America shaped his own life as well as broader developments in West Africa. In fact, the remarkable achievements of Vaughans on both sides of the Atlantic have likely been at least a partial result of their wide-ranging vision and connections.

Finally, one of the lessons of Vaughan's story as a "micro-history set in motion"[27] should be obvious: African and American history unfolded simultaneously. Contemporaries and historians have tended to imagine that African developments have transpired in a different temporal context than those in the United States or Europe.[28] The African diaspora concept, in fact, has often rested on two approaches to time: looking back, to a moment in which the enslaved were forcibly separated from their African communities; and looking forward, to a hoped-for restoration.[29] Early studies of African American cultural "origins" risked casting Africa as temporally frozen, with little change after the enslaved left its shores.[30] Similarly, twentieth century approaches to international development conceptualized Africa as "backward," chronologically behind the so called West in its attainment of economic growth and personal liberties.[31] Vaughan's journeys show us, though, that struggles over slavery and autonomy both spilled over national borders and occurred simultaneously in disparate places. Moreover, by the time he was well established in Lagos and continuing through the era of his grandchildren, Vaughan and his family on both sides of the Atlantic knew that West Africa was not *behind*. In fact, their prospects were arguably better there than in the United States.

This book recounts a story of survival, prosperity, and activism against a seemingly endless series of obstacles. It reveals an Atlantic world in which slavery was nearly ubiquitous and freedom was ambiguous. In that way, *Atlantic Bonds* is about ties of servitude and their legacies. But the title also invokes different types of bonds: of kinship lost, sought, or maintained across the ocean; of new communities created or joined in the aftermath of migration; and of political, ideological, and personal networks that connected far-flung locations. With his transatlantic outlook, Church Vaughan could compare the particular forms of oppression for black people in the American South and different parts of West Africa like almost no one else in his time. In his adopted homeland, Vaughan's transcontinental perspective opened up new possibilities and critiques as well as alliances beyond those evoked by mythical country marks. Despite dangers of enslavement, limits on freedom, and constraints on citizenship, some determined, savvy, or lucky refugees from slavery and white supremacy were able to find shelter, and even make their own marks, in nineteenth-century Africa. One of them was Church Vaughan.

one

SCIPIO VAUGHAN'S SOUTH CAROLINA

In 1840, a dying Scipio Vaughan gathered his family together and imparted his final wish: that they should leave South Carolina for Africa, the continent of their ancestors. Although he had spent most of his life as a slave, Scipio was by then a free man, proprietor of his own carpentry business, and owner of land and houses. His wife and their many children had never carried the burdens of slavery. They did not have to fear being sold away from one another, worked to death on a plantation, or abused by a master or overseer. Scipio and Maria Vaughan's adult offspring were settled in their own households, making a living and raising their own families; their younger ones were learning to read and write. How had a son of Africa, a slave in South Carolina, managed to achieve this? And having given them such a foothold in life, why then did Scipio want his loved ones to leave?

Scipio Vaughan's story forms one trickle in the vast river of nineteenth-century American history, flowing together with the forced removal of Native Americans from the Southeast and the expansion of plantation societies into what was formerly the frontier of European settlement. Scipio came to Kershaw County, South Carolina from Virginia as a slave around 1800, the year before his future wife, Maria Conway, was born to an Anglo-Catawba mother and a free black father. Though the numbers of white settlers and black slaves increased steadily, it remained possible for some Africans and African Americans to maintain degrees of autonomy and even attain their freedom. The pathways out of slavery were always limited, though, and they narrowed as planters became increasingly powerful and, paradoxically, fearful of threats to their dominance. Scipio barely slipped through, but even as a free man his safety and livelihood had to be guarded. Whenever white southerners felt threatened, free people of color suffered. Scipio's children, including his second son James Churchwill Vaughan, grew up in a society convulsed by a series of panics over slavery and race, officially free from slavery but not from violence and insecurity.

Echoes of that anxiety persist in Camden, South Carolina, even now. The seat of Kershaw County, Camden is South Carolina's oldest inland town, located twenty miles northeast of Columbia along what used to be the Catawba Path, a native trading route linking Charleston to the deep interior. These days its ten square miles hold seven thousand people, a bit more than half of the town's nineteenth-century population peak. A visitor to Camden is struck by the public nostalgia for a lost antebellum era: some thirty historic sites are marked with placards and annotated in a text and map published by the Chamber of Commerce. Most are former plantation houses, largely restored to grandeur, and some have been transformed into bed and breakfasts. Yet in a less grand part of town, small, mostly dilapidated dwellings house African Americans whose per capita income is one-third that of Camden's whites, and whose unemployment rate is three times as high.[1] Though they comprise 40 percent of the population, African Americans in Camden barely impinge on its public presentation; only two of the historic markers have anything to do with their forebears. The cemetery where the town's early black inhabitants are buried is difficult to find, despite its location next to the historic graveyard for whites. When I asked for directions, a white lady told me the place was dangerous.

There is no sign of Scipio Vaughan in Camden's old African American cemetery, though headstones for some of his relatives are there. He presumably lies in an unmarked grave, his leave-taking no better documented than his early years. Scipio was born on March 26, 1780 in Richmond, Virginia.[2] Of the first two decades of his life, we know only that he was a slave, and he learned carpentry. He came to Kershaw County with his master Wylie Vaughan (1775–1820), one of many thousands of white Virginians seeking their fortunes to the South and West as soil depletion and land scarcity undermined the old tobacco-based economy of the Tidewater region.[3] Wylie's father and older brother both died when he was a young man, and his father's plantation did not continue in the Vaughan name. Scipio may have been the only member of the estate not transferred to another owner when it was liquidated. This, his training for a trade that would spare him from agricultural labor, the singular status he later held among Wylie Vaughan's

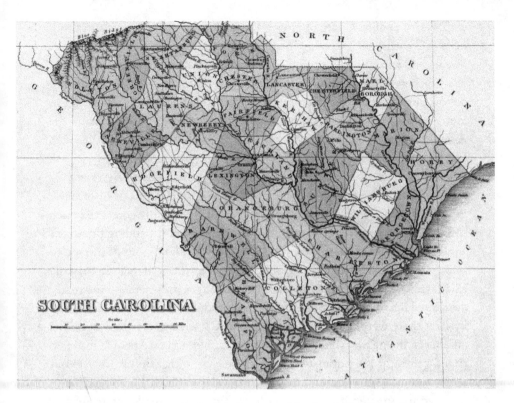

South Carolina and its counties in 1824. Courtesy of the South Caroliniana Library, University of South Carolina, Columbia, South Carolina.

slaves, and the five-year age difference between them all raise the possibility that Scipio and Wylie may have been half-brothers. No written records refer to Scipio as "mulatto," however, and it may be that the two men forged whatever bond was between them through lifelong association and the shared experience of leaving home for a new life in South Carolina.

Wylie and Scipio Vaughan arrived as Kershaw County was rapidly changing from a frontier to a plantation society. The earliest English settlers had come to what was then known as Camden District in the first half of the eighteenth century from Charleston, mostly to trade with native peoples. In the 1740s, the Indian trading path from Charleston was linked to the Philadelphia Wagon Road, opening the Carolina backcountry to settlers who trickled in over the next decades from Pennsylvania, Virginia, and North Carolina, joining others from the coast. Some brought slaves with them or purchased laborers from dealers in Charleston. The settlers planted wheat and tobacco and raised livestock, selling their surplus to coastal merchants and trading with native people. Camden grew as a transfer point for hinterland products, with a grist mill, tavern, general store, and a main street (today's Broad Street) laid out over part of the old Catawba Path.[4]

Kershaw County's real prosperity, however, came after Eli Whitney's cotton gin was patented in 1793. In spite of steady demand for cotton in industrializing Britain, the short-staple variety that grew well in most of the American South was previously unprofitable because it required so much labor to extract the seeds from the fiber. The cotton gin performed this task fifty times faster than an individual person could—effectively removing all limits on cotton profits, as long as there was land and labor to produce the crop. In the South Carolina upcountry, farmers rapidly converted open land and existing slaveholdings to cotton production, expanding the state's annual exports of the crop from less than ten thousand pounds in 1790 to some six million in 1800 and amassing personal fortunes to rival those of the Charleston-area rice planters.[5] Camden, already a commercial crossroads, developed into a bulking center for cotton produced on nearby plantations. By 1802 there were two hundred houses in Camden, more than twice the number in the nearby state capital Columbia, and enslaved people made up about a third of the population.[6] "The discovery of the cotton crop is but a new thing in Carolina & Georgia," a traveler through Kershaw County reported in 1806, yet it "has within these fifteen years made the fortune of half the great landholders whose estates now bring them in from $10,000 to $50,000."[7]

Wylie Vaughan quickly joined the ranks of cotton planters. Around the time that he moved to South Carolina, he married into the family of Richard Champion, an immigrant from England who possessed thousands of acres of land and some thirty-six slaves in Kershaw County as well as a small fortune invested in a Charleston-based mercantile company. Champion had been a Bristol merchant and owner of a pottery factory, with strong interests in North America not only through political sentiment—in the 1780s he had published proindependence pamphlets—but through a trade and shipping partnership with his brother-in-law John Lloyd of Charleston. Champion and his family had immigrated to Camden and acquired a plantation at Rocky Branch, eight miles away, in 1784. He and his wife both died in the early 1790s, however, and their estate was divided equally among their five surviving children. One of these was Sarah (born in 1774), who married Wylie Vaughan. As a wife, Sarah Vaughan could not hold property in her own name, so her considerable assets belonged by law to her husband.[8] These he augmented with land grants in Kershaw District totaling nearly twenty-five hundred acres, along with some three thousand acres in nearby Richland and Fairfield Districts.[9]

Like other land "opened up" to American settlement, Vaughan's holdings previously bore the footprints of Native Americans. By the mid-eighteenth century, Catawba communities had incorporated various native peoples living on South Carolina's northwestern frontier. Speakers of a Siouan language, Catawbas hunted in the fall and winter and farmed corn, beans, and squash in the spring and summer; they were also known as fierce warriors. Even after absorbing other peoples, however, they faced a series of crises: hostilities with rival native groups like the Cherokees to their west, incursions of white settlers, and imported diseases. From a reported population of about 1,500 warriors and 6,000 total in 1683, their numbers dropped to some 400 warriors 60 years later. A smallpox epidemic in 1759 reduced their population again, from perhaps 1,500 inhabitants to roughly 500. Under such threats, they formed strategic alliances with the English, solidified by a cordial relationship between Catawba King Haglar (who reigned from 1749 to 1763) and Samuel Wyly, a prominent settler of Camden. His people devastated by illness, and seeking to avoid the kind of bloody encounter then being waged between Anglo-American settlers and nearby Cherokees, Hagler agreed in 1760 to a treaty by which the Catawba gave up claims to Kershaw County lands in exchange for a fifteen square mile reservation forty miles north of Pine Tree Hill, as Camden was then called. In the following decades, the Catawbas began leasing most of that land, so that by 1800 nearly every acre of it was rented to Anglo-American settlers.[10] Meanwhile, the state government began granting the Catawba lands taken earlier to settlers such as Wylie Vaughan.

The new arrivals wanted labor to work the land. In the early 1700s, Indian traders had offered their prisoners of war for sale as slaves, but that trade was replaced by increasing numbers of captives from a different source: Africa. From its slow beginnings in the mid-1600s, the Atlantic slave trade to the territory that became the United States carried nearly four hundred thousand forced migrants away from Africa. Initially, their primary North American destinations were the Chesapeake Bay area, where they toiled in tobacco fields, and the rice-producing lowcountry around Charleston. Over the next century, American settlement and slavery expanded together. In the 1760s, nearly one in five backcountry South Carolina settlers was black, nearly all of them enslaved farm and other laborers. Four decades later, Baltimore merchant Robert Gilmor traveled through Kershaw County en route to Charleston and observed three hundred to four hundred slaves toiling in the fields of the district's largest slaveholder, Colonel John Chesnut. Cotton had made them valuable, he noted, "and on enquiring I find that $250 to $280 is given for new Negroes at Charleston, say for boys & $300 to $350 for grown persons."[11]

Shortly thereafter, Gilmor witnessed the source of some of these "new Negroes": slave ships from Africa docked at Charleston. Gilmor's visit there took place during the frantic, final year of legal slave importation to the United States from Africa. During the colonial period, approximately ninety thousand foreign slaves had arrived in South Carolina, first via the West Indies and then as of the 1720s directly from Africa. But rebels had closed American ports to Atlantic slaving during the Revolution, not out of solicitude for liberty but rather a general embargo on British commerce. By then, the slave population of the mid-Atlantic was reproducing naturally, if slowly, while tobacco planters were moving into less labor-intensive enterprises.[12] With the dramatic new investment in cotton, however, came a revitalized demand for enslaved labor. In 1803 state legislators reopened the African slave trade to South Carolina. Over the next five years, until Americans were prohibited from Atlantic slaving once and for all, Charleston imported 95 percent of the roughly 66,000 Africans entering the United States. This new trade re-Africanized slavery in a state where American-born slaves had predominated for decades. By 1810, captives from Africa comprised more than 20 percent of South Carolina's slaves. Most of them came from West Central Africa (in and around present-day Angola), though many also originated in Sierra Leone, modern Ghana, Senegambia, and elsewhere in West Africa. The Bight of Benin, where Church Vaughan spent most of his life, accounted for only about 1 percent of the Africans forced into Charleston in the early nineteenth century.[13]

Regardless of where they had last set foot on African soil, these forced immigrants arrived in the United States after a voyage of several hungry, thirsty, sickly, and violent months. After sailing past the Charleston bar, Africans were required to proceed to the "Pest House" at James Island (formerly on Sullivan's Island), where they were confined on their ships until declared free of contagious diseases. If the weary captives were sick, their onboard ordeal continued for another month or two, or until they died. After being released from quarantine, slave ships proceeded to the eastern edge of Charleston and docked at Gadsden's Wharf. There, as many as a thousand slaves would spend several more weeks trapped on their putrid ships while sales were advertised and transacted. Visiting in 1806, Robert Gilmor was "shocked with the sight of 400 on board of one ship, all stowed away separately, in places which almost suffocated me."[14] Eventually, many of the "new negroes" were purchased by Charleston agents who then transferred them upcountry, including to Camden. Wylie Vaughan purchased at least one African man, and probably more.[15] Their country marks, plaited hair, unfamiliar languages, and African memories distinguished them from the enslaved African Americans who had been born in South Carolina, even as they worked and lived side by side.

Joining them were other captive newcomers. Between 1780 and 1810, slaveholders from Virginia and Maryland sent or brought an estimated 115,000 slaves south and west in what was known as the "Georgia trade," which in fact reached from the Carolinas through Kentucky and Tennessee and south to the lower Mississippi Valley. Some white migrants from the Upper South brought their slaves with them when they themselves moved. Other slaveholders sold their human chattel to dealers who marched them south for sale in cotton country. This domestic slave trade—the "Second Middle Passage" as historian Ira Berlin calls it—was not yet as massive as it would become in the middle decades of the nineteenth century, but for those forcibly separated from the people and places they had known all their lives, as well as the loved ones they left behind, it was devastating.[16] Runaway ads placed in the *Camden Journal* testify to enslaved people's fierce desire to return to their families in the Upper South: according to his owner John Whitaker, the missing William Carter, for instance, "was raised in Virginia and may attempt to return there."[17]

Family lore tells nothing of Scipio Vaughan's move from Virginia to the South Carolina Piedmont. But around the same time, an enslaved man from Maryland roughly the same age as Scipio named Charles Ball was sold to a dealer, placed in irons, and forcibly transferred south. "I was now a slave in South Carolina," he recounted decades later, "and had no hope of ever again seeing my wife and children. I had at times serious thoughts of suicide so great was my anguish. If I could have got a rope I should have hanged myself at Lancaster."[18] What relatives did Scipio leave behind? He was a skilled carpenter, presumably needed for his master's new enterprises in South Carolina. Did Wylie Vaughan make any promises to ease the pain of Scipio's displacement? Is that how Scipio ultimately became free, though tied to the white Vaughan family?

During the early nineteenth century, as Kershaw County grew and prospered, Wylie Vaughan bought and sold land, built in-town businesses, and invested in cotton plantations. In 1811, Vaughan and his business partner Frances Lee bought two town lots in Camden; the next year, they sold a plantation north of Camden in Kershaw County. In 1813, he also became the executor of the estate of his late brother-in-law, Richard Lloyd Champion, proprietor of the Champion plantation at Rocky Branch as well as long-serving clerk of the court of Kershaw County and a major land developer in Camden. Yet Vaughan never became a planter to the extent of Kershaw County's *grandee* elite. His older brother Claiborne Vaughan had been murdered by his slaves during the American Revolution—perhaps a lesson about the dangers of slaveholding.[19] In 1816, Wylie Vaughan and two partners advertised a dry goods store in Camden; two years later he became proprietor of the town's only newspaper, the *Camden Gazette*. He also ran, unsuccessfully, for U.S. Congress. Vaughan owned more than four thousand acres of land producing cotton and other crops, as well as eight lots in Camden. But while the largest cotton planters each held more than a hundred and as many as two hundred slaves, Wylie Vaughan's slaveholdings amounted to twenty-one, including the skilled Scipio, whose carpentry services he hired out for wages.[20]

In 1812, Wylie Vaughan sold a plot of land in Camden, originally part of his wife's dowry, to Bonds Conway, a free black man and Scipio's future father-in-law.[21] A generation older than Scipio Vaughan, Bonds Conway (1763–1843) had also come to Camden from Virginia, in his case as the personal slave of a young man named Peter Conway. In 1793, after making money from carpentry and from selling ginger beer and gingerbread door to door, Bonds Conway purchased his freedom. A decade later, he paid for the liberty of his young daughter Harriet, child of Ellie Coleman, an enslaved woman with her own last name. By the early 1800s, Conway was buying land in Camden, and he eventually amassed several tracts in the center of town, including the one he purchased from Wylie Vaughan. On one of these lots he built for himself a "small Charleston type house," which in restored form now headquarters the Kershaw County Historical Society. Conway also owned at least one slave of his own, a woman named Sukey.[22]

Bonds and Harriet Conway were two of only seventy-eight free people of color in Kershaw District in 1810, amid 4,847 slaves. In South Carolina as a whole, about 2 percent of the black population was free (4,554 out of 196,365), most of them concentrated in Charleston.[23] They tended to be former personal servants or artisans who had known their masters well— sometimes very intimately, especially in the case of freedwomen—or children of mixed racial origins. The most fortunate were able to accumulate substantial property, and even to become slaveholders themselves. Because of their color, though, all free black people risked being treated as slaves,

Bonds Conway
house, Camden,
South Carolina,
2004. Photo by
the author.

especially when they traveled beyond familiar communities. After 1800, South Carolina law empowered all whites to demand the legal documents of black people claiming to be free, with the prospect of a reward if the papers were not in order. In doubtful cases, people of color were presumed to be slaves. Hence it was necessary to cultivate strategic ties with white patrons, who could offer protection as well as a clientele for free people's businesses. Free people of color like Conway rarely cast off the names of their former owners or moved to new locations where their connections would be un known. Carefully avoiding challenges to white privilege while distinguishing themselves from the enslaved, they tried to live, unmolested, in the narrow social space where race and slavery did not overlap.[24]

Some fifteen years after arriving in South Carolina, Scipio Vaughan himself gained the promise of freedom. In late 1814 or early 1815, Wylie Vaughan returned from Charleston, where he had served as paymaster of a South Carolina militia regiment sent there in case of a British invasion during the War of 1812.[25] Though he had faced no immediate danger, Wylie Vaughan followed his military service by drawing up a will. After leaving everything to his wife, he made three provisions directly relating to Scipio. First, he registered his desire "that the annual Labour of my negro man Scipio be appropriated as a fund for the education of my [younger] Children Claborn Ruffin Harry Vaughan and Eliza Hester Virginia Vaughan." Then came the better part: "Should Scipio survive the first day of January 1825, my will and desire is that he shall be freed and have the use of his time thereafter: That he shall also have his Carpenters Tools and one hundred Dollars at that time." Then finally, and seemingly in contradiction to the previous provision, "whenever William Langley shall desire to build a House in Camden He shall have the use and Labour of my negro man Scipio & the Carpenters Tools for the term of three months."[26] (William Langley was a physician, then-proprietor of the *Camden Gazette*, and owner of three slaves, presumably not a large enough workforce to build a house.[27]) Scipio continued to work for Wylie Vaughan, but now he could count on a time, eleven years in the future, when the fruits of his labor might be all his own.

Perhaps this is why he decided, at the age of thirty-five, to get married. Shortly after Wylie Vaughan made his will, Scipio wed Bonds Conway's second daughter, Maria Theresa Louisa Matilda Conway. In spite of the difference in their ages—Maria was fourteen—their descendants later cast their relationship as an intercultural romance. On his way home from a neighboring town along the Pee Dee River, the family story goes, Scipio stopped at an Indian tent to ask for a drink of water. A Cherokee maiden invited him to rest, and Scipio began to visit her regularly. She became his bride, and later they had many children, including James Churchwill Vaughan.[28]

One wonders how the daughter of the free African American Bonds Conway was also a "Cherokee maiden," but the history and geography of Kershaw County, along with a brief family record, offer some leads. First, the Pee Dee River is located some sixty miles east of Camden. Though Scipio might have traveled or been sent there to do some carpentry work, it seems more likely that the river along which he traveled was the Wateree, which winded its way north and south of Camden just to the town's west. In either direction, a traveler in the early nineteenth century might well have encountered Native Americans, though more likely living in log cabins than in tents.

Could Scipio Vaughan's wife have been Cherokee? Centered in the mountains of the western Carolinas and Tennessee, Cherokee territory once extended almost to Kershaw County, and neighboring Fairfield and Richland Counties were ceded by Cherokees to the state of South Carolina in 1775. Their relations with early English settlers were hostile, not least because of settler encroachment into Cherokee territory, and deteriorated into open war in 1760. At times the fighting came within a day's walk of the area now known as Camden.[29] By the time of Maria Conway's birth in 1801, traders and others from American settlements regularly visited Cherokee villages. The free black craftsman Bonds Conway could have been one of them; and like other foreign visitors to native communities, he could have formed a relationship and produced a child, who later offered a drink of water to another wandering African American, Scipio Vaughan.

Looking back, it can be romantic for twentieth-century families to claim Cherokee descent, especially given their tragic history of forced exile. But Maria was more likely Catawba than Cherokee.[30] A family Bible recorded by her granddaughter lists Maria's mother as Nancy Carter, born at or near Betty's Neck, South Carolina, in 1770.[31] This was an area of wetlands along a bend in the Wateree River about nine miles south of Camden: Catawba territory, though settlers were moving in. It would have been unusual for a Cherokee woman to originate here, rather than in the Cherokee region to the Northwest.

The listing in the family Bible also offers another clue about Maria Conway Vaughan's background: her mother's name. A native woman named Nancy Carter probably had a settler father herself. Before the American Revolution, Catawbas regularly encountered white settlers as they passed back and forth across Anglo-American towns and plantations, stopping in at stores, mills, and even churches. Catawba women made pottery for sale to settlers, traveling to collect clay and bartering their wares from house to house.[32] Not far from Nancy Carter's birthplace at Betty's Neck lived a large family named Carter, who had been in the area since at least the 1760s. Henry Carter listed in his will four sons (Benjamin, Robert, John, and George), along with his wife Barbara and his daughter Rachel. After service in the Revolutionary War, Benjamin Carter became a wealthy landowner in Camden. The basis of his fortune, though, was a large tannery, where leather was produced from deerskins purchased from native traders.[33] Apparently born in 1756, Benjamin was too young to have been Nancy Carter's father, though he never legally married. Instead, one of his Carter relatives may well have formed a relationship with a Catawba woman encountered while buying animal hides, as many white traders in this era did. Children of such liaisons generally took their fathers' names while remaining rooted in their mothers' communities.[34]

Thus Nancy Carter was likely the product of an Indian-European relationship in the early years of English settlement in Kershaw County. Thirty-one years later, she followed partially in her mother's footsteps, bearing a settler's child. This time, however, the baby's father was a free black man, Bonds Conway. This was not necessarily remarkable. In the eighteenth century, Catawba relations with Africans and African Americans had more or less paralleled their dealings with individual white settlers: seeing them all as foreigners, Catawbas had done business with, sheltered, or fought with black people depending on particular circumstances. Some Catawba women married black men, just as they had married white men.[35] Because Catawbas reckoned descent through the maternal line, the child Maria was considered a full member of her mother's kin group and clan. She grew up, free from the slavery that her father had escaped, in a small native community not far from settler farms and establishments. In fact, Bonds Conway may have been attracted to Nancy Carter precisely because of her separation from the slavery of settler society. With few free black women available to him as potential mates, Conway's best hope for ensuring his children's freedom was for their mothers to be Native American. Conway's third wife, whom he married when Maria was a small child, was the granddaughter of a Native woman, and the children of that marriage grew up free as well.[36]

When Maria Conway married Scipio Vaughan in 1815, then, she represented at least three generations of cultural and demographic mixing under American colonialism. Scipio probably was motivated to marry a Native woman for the same reason as Bonds Conway: to ensure the freedom of his children in a society in which slavery was inherited from their mothers and free black women were rare. By this time, however, it was more unusual than in Maria's mother's or grandmother's eras for a Catawba woman to marry a black man. Degraded by whites themselves, surrounded by manifestations of antiblack racism, observing — more than ever — black people as slaves, and determined to highlight their cultural distinctiveness, Catawba were increasingly hostile to black Carolinians.[37] Was Maria herself stigmatized as the daughter of a black man? Was she more open than her contemporaries were to marriage with an African American because of her own parentage? Or does her young betrothal to a man still enslaved speak something of her and her mother's desperation to ensure even a limited level of social and economic support in increasingly hard times? It was likely all three, along with other considerations — like her own feelings — lost in the passage of time.

Maria and Scipio raised nine children, born free by virtue of their mother's status and considered part of her Native community despite their "foreign" father. They were never enumerated among Wylie Vaughan's slaves, and neither was Maria. The Vaughan children did not bear the kind of derogatory labels often bestowed by slave owners on their human property — diminutives like Jimmy or mockingly grandiose monikers like Scipio, the Roman military commander "Africanus" who defeated the North African general Hannibal. Instead, they honored important people in their parents' lives. Daughters Nancy Carter (b. 1822), Harriet Amanda (1829), Maria Virginia (1832), and Mary Elizabeth (1838) carried the names of their grandmother, aunt, and mother. Sarah (1823) shares the name of Scipio's mistress, the woman whose cooperation was necessary for him to claim the freedom he was promised. One wonders about the other girls' names: were Elizabeth Margaret (1818) and Kitty Ann (1820) reminders of Scipio's lost relatives in Virginia? Is that where Maria Virginia's middle name came from? The names of sons Burrell Carter (1816) and James Churchwill (1828) reflected Maria's continuing ties, through her mother, to the white Carter family: both a Burrell Carter and a Churchill Carter lived relatively nearby.[38] While Scipio remained with Wylie and then Sarah Vaughan, Maria lived with her children, relying on the community she was raised in for support. The 1830 census, taken fifteen years after her marriage to Scipio, lists her as an independent householder but not as Maria Vaughan or Maria Conway, which would acknowledge her own or her mother's marriage, but as Mariah Carter, a name reflecting her ties to her mother's people.[39]

As a child walking through Camden, James Churchwill Vaughan would have seen on a weathervane perched atop the town market a gilded iron silhouette of Hagler, king of his Catawba ancestors, commemorated in 1826. Assassinated by a party of raiding Shawnees in 1763, shortly after he traded Catawba lands for a reservation, Hagler was (and still is) nostalgically remembered in white Camden as a peacemaker who unified his people and helped them coexist with South Carolina settlers. Yet Catawbas barely survived in the early American republic. Decimated by disease and dispersal, they lived on and off their reservation mostly in poverty. "Once proprietors of the piedmont," historian James Merrell wrote of the Catawba of the early nineteenth century, "they now existed only on the sufferance of people inclined to cheat them as often as protect them, mock them as readily as befriend them. It was a sad state, requiring more quiet resignation than open resistance, smiles in place of frowns, submission to the humiliations dished out."[40]

For all their differences, South Carolina's red and black populations shared this subordination to whites. Catawba were unusual in their sheer survival through the nineteenth century, as other Native groups were forced away or extinguished. Similarly, free blacks like Bonds Conway and his descendants were relatively lucky members of a group of people generally held in bondage, with no legal standing and vulnerable to arbitrary authority. Church Vaughan and his siblings were born out of the mixing of early America's three populations: African, Indian, and European. And though they entered the world free, things could easily have been different—if their mother had been the slave, they would have been someone's property, regardless of any Native American father or white great-grandfather. As they grew up, surrounded by Indians whose lands and livelihoods had been taken from them and by Africans and African Americans whose bodies and labor were claimed by others, the Vaughan children doubtless understood the preciousness, and fragility, of freedom.

Hagler weathervane atop the Camden Opera House, 2013.
Photo by the author.

Scipio and Maria Vaughan survived in Kershaw County through hard work and relations with white patrons like the Carters and Wylie Vaughan. Surely they suffered slights large and small, but their response was strategic deference and patience, looking forward to a time when Scipio's freedom would help to secure their family's welfare. A year after Wylie Vaughan drafted his will and a full nine years before Scipio was to be manumitted, however, other Camden slaves determined to seize their own freedom. Their revolt, allegedly planned for July of 1816, terrorized white society and laid bare the violence at the heart of slavery. In the aftermath, Scipio's freedom became a moving target, pulled ever farther out of reach by white lawmakers determined to make slavery a permanent condition for all African Americans.

The prevalence and violence of slaveholding had been growing in and around Camden through the first decades of the nineteenth century. The number of enslaved African Americans in Kershaw District nearly doubled between 1800 and 1810 (from 2,530 to 4,847), while the white population remained largely unchanged at nearly 5,000 and the number of free people of color declined from 104 to 78. Over the next ten years, the slave population grew by another nearly 50 percent, against much slower growth in the number of whites and a miniscule rise in the free black population. While one-third of white Camden residents owned slaves in 1800, nearly two-thirds did in 1810, and the average slaveholding increased from 9.6 to 13.3, to 15.3 in 1820.[41]

Charles Ball, who was marched as a slave from Maryland to Columbia, South Carolina in the early 1800s, later recalled that nearly all the fields around Camden were devoted to slave-grown cotton. "The horses and mules that I saw in the cotton-fields were poor and badly harnessed," he wrote, "and the half-naked condition of the negroes, who drove them, or followed with the hoe, together with their wan complexions, proved to me that they had too much work, or not enough food." Ball was appalled at the poor provisions allocated to slaves, who needed all their strength for relentless work. "It was manifest that I was now in a country where the life of a black man was no more regarded than that of an ox, except as far as the man was worth the more money in the market," he reflected. Outside of Columbia, Ball met a badly scarred man who had been brutally punished for stealing and cooking one of his master's sheep. Strung up by his thumbs and feet, he was repeatedly whipped on his back, and then a tea made from hot peppers was rubbed into the wounds. "This operation was continued at regular intervals, until I had received ninety-six lashes, and my back was cut and scalded from end to end," the man told Ball. "Every stroke of the whip had drawn blood; many of the gashes were three inches long; my back burned as if it had been covered by a coat of hot embers, mixed with living coals; and I felt my flesh quiver like that of animals that have been slaughtered by the butcher and are flayed whilst yet half alive."[42]

Such violence and terror reflected white fears of slave resistance—fears that only intensified after the United States entered another war with Britain in 1812. Slaveholders in the South worried that war would open the door to slave rebellion, as it had during the American and Haitian Revolutions. In coastal North Carolina, the American General Thomas Brown suggested readying several cavalry companies "to guard against a rebellion of the blacks, so probable, and so much to be dreaded in this section of the State." In Virginia, leading whites anticipated an insurrection in Richmond and perhaps through the whole state. Two years into the war, rumors circulated in Washington, D.C., that a slave conspiracy had been uncovered in Frederick, Maryland.[43]

No such coordinated revolt took place, and, in fact, British officers carefully avoided language that might incite large-scale slave revolt, wary of spreading rebellion in their own slavery-based colonies in the West Indies. Yet as they had during the American Revolution, British officers in the southern theater held out the promise of freedom—and this time, emigration—to slaves who would flee their masters and join the British forces. After British ships arrived to blockade the Chesapeake Bay in early 1813, enslaved Americans, including whole families, sought refuge among them. In April 1814, Vice Admiral Sir Alexander Cochrane made the British position official, proclaiming that "All those who may be disposed to emigrate from the United States, will, with their Families, be received on board of His Majesty's Ships. . . . They will have their choice of either entering into His Majesty's Forces, or of being sent as FREE Settlers to British possessions, . . . where they will meet with all due encouragement." Cochrane then authorized the formation of the Colonial Marines, fighting units made up of formerly enslaved young men, who later took part in the burning of Washington, D.C., the Battle of Baltimore, and skirmishes against American forces all along the coast. According to the British commander in chief, they were "infinitely more dreaded by the Americans than the British troops." Between those who flocked to the British and others who simply took advantage of the chaos of war, more than four thousand people freed themselves from slavery during the War of 1812, the largest emancipation in the United States until the Civil War.[44]

At least one company of volunteers from Camden took part in the war, McWylie's 2nd South Carolina Regiment, with Wylie Vaughan serving as paymaster. The regiment's captain was Camden lawyer, merchant, and state legislator Chapman Levy, a business associate of Vaughan's. Issac, an enslaved man belonging to the widow Sarah Lang, served as Captain Levy's drummer and servant for the campaign to help protect Charleston against possible British attack.[45] Enemy forces never entered South Carolina's premier city, but surely some of Charleston's enslaved heard talk of the threat they might pose not only to physical safety and American politics, but also to slavery there. Less than two years after the regiment returned to Camden, Issac was identified as a ringleader of an alleged slave revolt.

Other enslaved people were rebellious as well. Earlier in 1816, Governor David Williams ordered a military attack against a group of "runaway negroes, concealing themselves in the swamps and marshes" near the South Carolina coast, who "formed the nucleus, round which all the ill-disposed and audacious near them gathered, until at length their robberies became too serious to be suffered with impunity." Troops under the command of Colonel William Youngblood managed to capture or kill all of them, though other groups of maroons continued to harass settlements in the Carolinas and Virginia for years to come.[46]

In Camden that April, an enslaved man named Abraham publicly and violently resisted slaveholders by refusing to produce a pass and forcibly defending himself when he was apprehended on the road. John Fox, owner of some seventy slaves, challenged Abraham with a large stick; Abraham in turn brandished a knife, declaring that he had traveled all day without a pass and would not be interrupted before he reached home, which he could do in an hour and a half. Both men were injured in the scuffle before Abraham took refuge in a nearby plantation cabin. An enraged Fox and three others surrounded and threatened to kill him. When Abraham finally charged out, Fox shot him in the eye and broke his arm, while another in his party struck Abraham with a whip. As he ran, another vigilante shot him again. Pursued by a slaveholder's dog as well as the white men, Abraham was finally apprehended after he fell near some brush and was beaten with a hickory stick. According to Fox, Abraham "did not surrender to the last and looked very furious." He was charged as a vagabond slave with having committed assault and battery on John Fox with intent to murder him.[47] But as Abraham languished in the Camden jail, town officials postponed his case to deal with developments even more serious.

In mid-June, a slave of Colonel John Chesnut told him that the planter and his family were in danger. The Chesnuts, proprietors of Kershaw District's largest estate, lived near the town's gunpowder magazine. According to the informer, rebels hoped to seize the armory as the first stage of an uprising on the Fourth of July, when whites would be occupied—and their faculties dulled—with commemorations of their own liberty. As the wife of Wylie Vaughan's physician wrote to her cousin in Philadelphia, "It was their intention to have set fire to one part of the Town and while the attention of the people was taken up with that, they meant to have taken possession of the Arsenal which is filled with Arms and ammunition and proceeded to murder the men, but the women they intended to have reserved for their own purposes."[48] Colonel Chestnut informed the town's leading citizens, who, on the advice of the state's governor, devised a plan to check the conspiracy, arrest its participants, and try the accused without alarming the rest of Camden's population. On July 2, under the pretext of a fox hunt, deputies seized the alleged conspirators working in fields, many miles apart.

The town council—consisting of small to middling slaveholders R.W. Carter, John Reed, Wyatt Stark, Dr. William Langley, and Intendant (Mayor) Abram Blanding—met that day to investigate the alleged plot. They summoned a number of enslaved witnesses, calling on their masters to produce them. Wylie Vaughan was instructed to bring to court a man named George, part of an estate for which Vaughan served as executor. Most of those questioned said they knew nothing about a conspiracy, while two admitted familiarity with the plot but denied participating themselves. Two men were repeatedly implicated by others: March, owned by Chapman Levy, and Issac, the militia veteran from Levy's company. According to an arrested slave named Spottswood, Issac "said he had a notion to get a parcel of men and go and fight the white people." Issac allegedly instructed Spottswood to speak to as many slaves as he could and recruit them to the cause, but warned that "if I told he would have me killed." Several witnesses, including Issac, also implicated March, alleging that he met other men at the brickyard and asked if they "would join him to fight this country—that the black people who did not join they would kill." Both March and Issac maintained their innocence, though Issac admitted, "I thought it would be a good scheme if they could get through with it, but that Negroes were so deceitful that it would not do."[49]

After the meeting of the town council, immediate trials were set at the county jail for seventeen men, including Marsh, Issac, and Spottswood. Two justices of the peace, Thomas Salmond and John Kershaw, along with five freeholders (wealthy landowners) comprised the court, with Wylie Vaughan's business partner Frances Lee serving as sheriff. "Our Jail is filled with Negroes," reported an agitated townswoman. "They are stretched on their Backs on the Base floor and scarcely move their heads but have a strong guard placed over them."[50] In spite of these and other pressures painfully inflicted upon them, all of the accused pled not guilty to the charge of "attempting to raise an insurrection amongst the slaves [of South Carolina]."

What can we know about the alleged conspirators? All but one were American born. They worked for wealthy Camdenites, some closely related, all residing in town. Issac and two others, Cameron and Stephen, were owned by a prominent widow, Sarah Lang, whose son Thomas Lang owned the defendant Jack. Thomas Lang's father-in-law, the merchant and wealthy planter Duncan McRae, owned Spottswood. Another elderly widow, Sarah Martin, was the owner of an accused man named Ned. March and Issac were both connected to Chapman Levy, March as his slave and Issac as his former servant during the War of 1812. Two of the defendants were brothers, literate and religious. "A few appeared to have been actuated solely by the instinct of the most brutal licentiousness, and by the lust of plunder," an observer recounted years later, "but most of them by wild and frantic ideas of the rights of man, and the misconceived injunctions and examples of Holy Writ."[51]

Indeed, what little evidence we have suggests that the plotters (if there was in fact a plot) were motivated by a sense of their human rights, derived either from religion or from a more secular desire for freedom. Town council member William Langley, writing in his *Camden Gazette* as the trials were being held, reported that "those who were most active in the conspiracy occupied a respectable stand in one of the churches, several were professors [of Christianity] and one a class leader."[52] One of these religious defendants, according to another white commentator, testified that "he had only one sin to answer for and that was he had set down to the communion table with the White people when he knew he was going to cut their throats as soon as convenient."[53] Many of the condemned men refused to incriminate other slaves, and more than one white observer remarked on their stoicism. Planter and judge Henry William DeSaussure had heard that one of the accused acknowledged his guilt and even "gloried in it," but said that nothing, not even being drawn and quartered, would lead him to implicate others. "The tone & temper of these leaders is alarming, as it was of a cast not suited to their condition, and shows that they have imbibed deeply the principles of liberty & acceptance of death in pursuit of it," DeSaussure wrote as the trials continued. "And this is the most dangerous state of mind for slaves. Doubtless the detection & punishment of the leaders will repress it for a time, but I fear the spirit was sown deep into the minds of these people."[54]

Remarkably, white observers failed to comment on the most obvious sign of the rebels' "tone and temper": the plan for the insurrection to begin on the Fourth of July, when Americans celebrated the notion that all men are created equal. Camden attorney Francis Deliesseline blithely assumed that the plot was set for July 4 because at that time of year food crops would not yet have been harvested, and "famine would accomplish what force might not be able to effect." The rebels, he continued, "confidently relied, also, upon the usual indulgences among us on a day celebrated as a great national jubilee."[55] Yet throughout the early American republic, free and unfree black people called attention on Independence Day to the hypocrisy of celebrating liberty in a land of slavery. Charles Ball recalled that when he had worked as a slave in the navy yard in Washington, D.C. around the turn of the nineteenth century, "the officers sometimes permitted me to go up town with them, on the fourth of July, and listen to the fine speeches that were made there, on such occasions." In Columbia, South Carolina, on another Independence Day, waiting in the jail to be sold at auction, Ball noted with irony that "a great crowd of people gathered and remained around the jail . . . many of whom were intoxicated, and sang and shouted in honor of free government, and the rights of man."[56] Surely it is no coincidence that the Camden insurgents planned to seize their own liberty as their masters celebrated American freedom.

Instead, however, by July 4 the slave conspiracy trials were already in their second day. By the next evening, five men identified as ring leaders— March, Cameron, Jack, Issac, and Spottswood—had been found guilty and hanged. The only African among the accused, Tom, was tried but found not guilty. As the proceedings continued, Ned was found guilty and hanged, and eight others were freed (including George, whom Wylie Vaughan had brought to court). Two suffered personalized sentences. After Stephen was declared guilty, the court ordered that he "have the sentence of death passed on him at the same time that his fellows are condemned—and that his pardon of his said sentence be announced to him after all the ceremonies of execution have been made." The trial record is silent on how Stephen came to be the object of mercy, in that he was pardoned, as well as the recipient of this particular psychological torture. Did the judges relish the sight of Stephen in fear for his life? Was it intended to break him of his "wild and frantic ideas" of liberty? Finally, toward the end of the trials, Big Frank, who had been found guilty, was sentenced to one year in irons in solitary confinement, unless his master, Louis Ballard, agreed to remove him permanently from the United States.[57]

After the trials and executions, while the convicted men's friends and relatives mourned and seethed, their former owners added insult to injury by claiming compensation from the state for their lost "property." In accordance with the legal limit, Sarah Lang, Thomas Lang, Chapman Levy, Sarah Martin, and Duncan McRa received $122.43 for each of their slaves who had been executed "after being convicted of involvement in an insurrection conspiracy." The legislature appropriated nearly ten times that amount, eleven hundred dollars, to compensate John Chesnut for manumitting the slave who had initially revealed the plot and who had testified in court against some of the defendants—a man whose name, like that of Wylie Vaughan's carpenter, was Scipio. In addition to his freedom, this Scipio received a lifetime grant of fifty dollars per year from a grateful state government. Fearful of reprisals, however, he insisted on remaining anonymous. For decades Scipio continued to live on the estate of his former master, perhaps as a paid servant, even leading a graveside song at Colonel Chesnut's funeral in 1866.[58]

Meanwhile, in the aftermath of the alleged plot, fearful whites stepped up their security measures and increased their repression of slave resistance. Abraham, the renegade slave who had been arrested two months before the conspiracy trials for attacking (or rather, defending himself against) the white man John Fox, was warned about the hangings in July and sentenced to confinement until September 24. Then, his jailor took him to the gallows to "be branded publicly on each cheek and forehead with the letter v in large letters and further have one half of each ear cut off beginning at top and cutting to the bottom."[59] Beginning in December 1816 and over the next several years, the state assembly appropriated funds for improvements and an armed guard at the Camden arsenal. Wylie Vaughan served as one of the managers of the Camden artillery, along with his fellow militia veteran from the War of 1812, William McWylie. Under direction from the assembly, the Camden town council also began to organize a rotating patrol duty.[60] In 1820, perhaps haunted by the ghost of the militia drummer Issac, citizens of Kershaw District petitioned the state government to prevent slaves and free people of color from being present at military reviews or musters or from serving as musicians for military corps. The petitioners argued that these practices allowed blacks to become acquainted with firearms and war tactics.[61] The following year, an item in the *Camden Journal* mentioned the pursuit and killing of fugitive slaves in the swamps of the Wateree and Santee Rivers. The head of one fugitive was cut off and stuck on a pole as "a warning to vicious slaves."[62]

But not all whites were in favor of tightening the slave system. For some, like Wylie Vaughan's associate Dr. William Langley, slavery itself was the problem, degrading and endangering the white population. Writing in his *Camden Gazette* in December 1816, Langley argued that "The influence of slavery extinguishes the glowing spark of religious fervor and produces cruelty. . . . It begets idleness, voluptuousness and a thirst for power. It endangers our safety and destroys domestic tranquility. If it were not for slavery we should be consolidated as a people." Langley insisted that he did not favor emancipation, but instead suggested the removal or emigration of black people—a cause that would become increasingly popular in the years to come.[63] Other whites urged moderation, fearful that the aborted slave revolt and ensuing trials would encourage a spiral of violence and retaliation. A few months after the executions, David Carwell, a white man, assaulted and carried off into slavery a free black woman named Polly Horn. Camden's intendant, Abram Blanding, tried to soothe racial tensions by pressing criminal charges against Carwell, a habitual offender with numerous arrests for petty crimes. Despite Blanding's efforts, however, the all-white jury acquitted Carwell.[64] Blanding's brother and sister-in-law, who had moved to Camden from Massachusetts, determined to leave the South. "We have taken such a disgust to slavery that we cannot feel satisfied here," Rachel Blanding wrote to a cousin, "although we are sensible it will be much against our interest to remove."[65]

Scipio Vaughan surely knew some of the men tried and executed in 1816, and he witnessed the increased vigilance of white townspeople. A year after the trials, one of Wylie Vaughan's slaves, an African named Tom, ran away.[66] But Scipio carefully guarded his behavior and demeanor, careful not to jeopardize his trusted position. Wylie Vaughan continued to hire out Scipio's labor as well as that of another enslaved carpenter named Jack, for months at a time.[67] This brought Scipio some autonomy, as well as earnings that he could set aside for his future. It also, however, kept him profitable to the white Vaughan family. As circumstances both inside and outside their household changed, Scipio could not be sure that the promise of his manumission would be honored.

In 1819, his health deteriorating rapidly, Wylie Vaughan transferred ownership of all his assets to three close associates to administer on behalf of his wife. His property included some five thousand acres of land, multiple lots in the town of Camden, his share in the newspaper, horses and livestock, and various personal items. Vaughan also conveyed thirty-five slaves that he listed by name and age, including three over forty years old, eight children under five, two house servants, and the carpenters Scipio and Jack.[68] These bondspeople must have carefully noted the identities of their new owners. One was Dr. William Blanding, the New England physician who, along with his Quaker wife, had been repulsed by the aftermath of the 1816 slave revolt. Though they owned three slaves, the basis of their income was Dr. Blanding's extensive medical practice. Another was Sarah Vaughan's younger brother George Lloyd Champion, a bachelor and a lawyer, who owned no slaves in his own name.[69] But in his conveyance Wylie Vaughan identified the third trustee, Benjamin Bircham, as a planter, and in fact he had been one of the wealthy "freeholders" acting as judge in the 1816 slave conspiracy trial. Would a man so invested in the slave system, so willing to uphold it through violence, follow through on Wylie's instruction to free Scipio?

Wylie Vaughan died in October 1820, five years before Scipio was to be manumitted. By early spring, what every slave of a deceased master feared had come to pass, though it could have been worse. The widow Sarah Vaughan and her brother sold nine of Wylie Vaughan's enslaved people—two young mothers and their children, plus two adolescent house servants whose mother had recently died—to John Chesnut for three thousand dollars.[70] Scipio remained with Mrs. Vaughan, turning over his wages when he labored for hire.[71] His own family at this point included three children under the age of four; two more would be born within the next five years. He and Maria named one of these daughters Sarah, perhaps as an extra reminder to Scipio's mistress of the bonds, and the pledge, that connected them. Even as he stepped gingerly toward his future freedom, though, it seemed to move farther beyond Scipio's reach.

In 1822, an emancipated carpenter named Denmark Vesey was convicted of plotting a massive slave insurrection in Charleston. Along with a core group of African- and American-born enslaved urban craftsmen, Vesey allegedly organized some six thousand to nine thousand slaves in a plan to storm Charleston, capture weapons, and kill all whites they found before plundering the city's banks for gold and silver and setting sail for Haiti. As in Camden six years earlier, a house slave leaked the plans to his master, who notified the state governor. While militia leaders organized the protection of the city's white inhabitants and their property, other officials arrested some 131 suspected participants. Over the next five weeks, seventy-nine men were tried; thirty-five, including Vesey, were executed, while thirty-seven were banished from the state.[72] Fear-stricken whites in Charleston sought to suppress further rebelliousness among the slave population not only through terror—three black men were hanged by a white mob a month after Vesey's execution—but by passing new laws to restrict the movement of slaves and free people of color.

Though all but three of the convicted conspirators in Charleston were enslaved, Denmark Vesey stood as an example to white South Carolinians of the dangers posed by free blacks. He had been taken to Charleston in 1783 as the slave of a ship captain, who had originally purchased Vesey on the Caribbean island of Saint Thomas. In 1799, Vesey bought a lottery ticket with money earned by hiring out his labor. He won fifteen hundred dollars, purchased his freedom, and opened a carpentry shop in downtown Charleston. Over the next two decades, he used his substantial earnings to acquire property worth some eight thousand dollars. That such a successful businessman could ally with rebellious slaves suggested to slaveholders that no black person was truly "safe." With their relative autonomy and mobility, in fact, free people could organize an insurgency more effectively than slaves could. South Carolina's free black population numbered 3,185 in 1800, 6,714 in 1820, and 8,276 in 1840, the vast majority concentrated near the coast. In contrast, there were 146,151 slaves in South Carolina in 1800; 251,783 in 1820; and 327,038 in 1840.[73] In spite of their relatively small numbers, however, free people of color represented an affront to slavery because they undermined the ideology that black people, needing the protection and civilizing influence of slavery, were incapable of freedom.

Especially after the Vesey trials, South Carolina's planter-dominated government was determined to keep the numbers of free black people low. This could be achieved both by limiting manumissions and by restricting the immigration of free people of color from outside of the state. Already in 1820—the year of Wylie Vaughan's death—new state laws outlawed manumission except by legislative act, forbade immigration of free blacks on penalty of enslavement, and imposed strong restrictions on the movement of free people of color. After the Vesey trials, Governor Thomas Bennett suggested expelling all recent free black immigrants from other states. The General Assembly did not go that far, but it did prohibit the reentry of free people of color who left South Carolina, with imprisonment set as the punishment for the first offense and enslavement for the second. The law was made retroactive, leaving free black people who had already traveled outside the state stranded in exile. The legislature also imposed an exorbitant new tax of fifty dollars per year on every free black male between the ages of fifteen and fifty who was neither a native of the state nor a resident of at least five years. Finally, to help ensure that they were watched and controlled, lawmakers required free black men over the age of fifteen to have a white guardian or be sold into slavery.[74]

These new restrictions compounded those already in place. As early as 1792, just before Bonds Conway purchased his liberty, a yearly capitation tax of two dollars was imposed on every free person of color between the ages of sixteen and fifty, regardless of employment status. In addition, free black people had to pay all the same taxes that white South Carolinians did, often making their total tax burden greater than their entire income. A year after the tax schedule went into effect, twenty-three free black inhabitants of Camden protested that they were "a Poor needy people; have frequently large Families to maintain; and find it exceedingly difficult and distressing to support the same and answer the large demands of the Publick; . . . In consequence of which they conceive their Situation in life but a small remove from Slavery."[75] They were right about how close to slavery they hovered: those who failed to pay their taxes were sold at public auction for a specified period of time, during which they were to earn the required sum in forced labor. White tax defaulters, in contrast, faced a fine or more limited imprisonment.

Taxation was not the only means by which free people of color could be, and were, deprived of their liberty. Until 1821, free blacks found guilty of harboring fugitive slaves were subject to public sale if they could not pay the fine imposed on them. Even people going about their ordinary business could find themselves abducted and sold. Not only were free people of color required to carry certificates of freedom at all times or be subject to seizure by any white citizen, under South Carolina's longstanding patrol system, local militia units formed to prevent and apprehend runaway slaves could invade the homes of free black people. Camden's Patrol Ordinance of 1831 was aimed both at slaves and free people of color, mandating that companies of white men guard the town for twelve hours every day in order to "suppress any mischievous designs of free negroes or slaves authorized to carry weapons; to apprehend all slaves beyond the owner's premises under suspicious circumstances; to correct moderately with switch or cow skin those abroad without permit, lashes not to exceed twenty and to commit to jail." The early twentieth-century authors of *Historic Camden* recalled an "old negro song" (though one surely enjoyed more by whites than blacks) with the line "Run, nigger, run, or the patrol'll get you."[76] Free people of color were constantly subject to arrest, interrogation, and corporal punishment by patrolmen and others. Once apprehended, a free person could be sold as a slave, either through the court system or by unscrupulous individuals.

Only in 1837, after discussing the matter for nearly two decades, did the state General Assembly pass a bill aimed at preventing the kidnapping of free black people.[77]

January 1, 1825, the date Wylie Vaughan had stipulated for Scipio's freedom, arrived less than three years after Denmark Vesey's execution. Since manumission was then illegal except by legislative fiat, Sarah Vaughan may have simply allowed Scipio to claim his freedom informally. But his status seems to have remained as unclear as his faint paper trail. When taxes were due, as in 1826 and 1832, Scipio was counted, and charged, as a free man.[78] Yet in 1830, the federal census enumerator did not find Scipio living with his wife and children and instead listed a male slave in his age range in the household of Sarah Vaughan.[79] Four years later, a local merchant from whom a bale of cotton had been stolen alleged — without justification, it turned out — that the missing goods may have been received by "Scipio, a slave belonging to Vaughn."[80] No record of his manumission has survived, and perhaps none was ever drawn up. Over time, Scipio may simply have allocated increasing portions of his income to his own family, operated with less and less of Mrs. Vaughan's oversight, and spent more nights in the home of his wife and children. If the provision of Wylie Vaughan's will granting his liberty was known publicly, and as long as Scipio's behavior remained scrupulously inoffensive and he paid his taxes, local whites likely came to acknowledge him as *de facto* free. Without official proof of freedom, however, Scipio was always vulnerable to seizure or extortion, and sometimes it may have been safer simply to be known as a Vaughan slave.[81] Only in 1840 — fifteen years after the freedom date stipulated in Wylie Vaughan's will and a quarter of a century since the promise was made — did the U.S. census list Scipio as a free man.[82]

Scipio achieved his freedom, such as it was, in a more restrictive era than his father-in-law Bonds Conway had. Yet for both men, and freedpeople in general, it was necessary to stay connected with former masters or other whites — employers, customers, inhabitants of the same plantation, church members, unacknowledged relatives — in order to defend their security and livelihoods. In practical terms, it was virtually impossible to stake a claim to freedom without a white patron who could serve as official "guardian," who could attest in court to a freedperson's status and good character, and who could facilitate a range of economic, legal, and social transactions. White guardians were not so much concerned with free people's welfare, but were to guarantee their behavior in relation to other white people. Free people of color had to conduct their business in their guardians' names, and guardians were theoretically responsible for their debts.[83] When Colonel John Chesnut registered as guardian for his former slave Scipio in 1823, for instance, he described the freedman who had perhaps saved his life as "formerly my slave, industrious fellow and worthy of the trust and confidence of good citizens."[84]

Free people of color did have rights to private property and to enter into contracts and profit from their own labor. They could marry and form families of their choice, except when spouses were enslaved. But their rights were always limited. They could theoretically move around the state, though they risked seizure in areas where they were not well known; they legally could sue for grievances, though only through a white guardian; they had a nominal right to petition the government, though this was rarely accepted. Free people of color did not operate within the legal system for whites, but in special Magistrates and Freeholders Courts. These courts had no juries, and in them blacks were denied the right to self-defense against whites, or even to testify against whites. Free people of color faced harsher penalties for a range of given crimes than their white counterparts. "Liberty for the black was therefore hedged about by a multiplicity of qualifications," a historian of South Carolina wrote. "It was a right enjoyed only on sufferance and, as such, maintained only by a combination of vigilance, subordination and sheer good luck."[85]

On the other hand, the flexibility of legal matters in the early United States, shaped by local norms and practices as well as the personal characteristics of the people involved, could occasionally enable free people of color as well as others with limited legal rights, such as slaves and women, to transact official business or buy and sell property. For example, Bonds Conway, the most prosperous of Camden's few free black men, cultivated sufficient material and social resources that he managed to operate locally in ways generally reserved for white people. Conway conducted his legal business in the regular courts, rather than in the Court of Magistrates and Freeholders, designated for slaves and free blacks.[86] In his own name, he bought and sold several plots of land in downtown Camden, including the one from Wylie Vaughan, ultimately willing them in parcels to four of his children. In 1820, he successfully pressed charges against a white man for assault, as did his wife Dorcas on that occasion and again in 1826.[87] When it became necessary for him to register a white guardian, Conway first enlisted Thomas Salmond, Kershaw County's clerk of court. Nine years later, Conway registered as his guardian John Boykin, a member of an established planter family and aspirant politician, who described Conway as a "free black man of good habits."[88]

Doubtless the backing of these respected and influential patrons, cultivated over years of personalized interactions, helped Conway to ensure the security of his person, his family, and his property.

In contrast, James Walker, another free black man from Kershaw County, failed to secure the kind of reputation that would protect him among whites. In 1828, this fifty-year-old carpenter was arrested and put on the auction block, like a slave, for failing to pay his acreage taxes. Joseph Mickle, a prominent planter and merchant with an interest in phrenology, signed a note for $215.37 1/2 to the state of South Carolina in exchange for the next five years of Walker's life and labor. Within months, Walker escaped to North Carolina, where he had friends and relations, but he was captured and jailed in Fayetteville. Mickle sent an agent to identify and retrieve Walker, but the jailer refused to turn him over, contending that he was "a free man, and would soon be declared so by a proper authority." Mickle rallied Camden public opinion behind him, casting Walker as an individual of bad character, a suspected arsonist and thief, and "a habitual drunkard, . . . capable of any outrage for which depravity could prepare the human mind." At the very least, Mickle and his supporters urged that the state cancel Mickle's promissory note, since he no longer had access to Walker's labor.[89] The record is silent about whether Walker was eventually apprehended, but the fact that local people rallied around Mickle in opposition to him meant that he would have had a very difficult time returning as a free man to Kershaw County.

Scipio Vaughan never registered a white guardian. In 1838, however, he paid $350 through the planter, merchant, and former town intendant Henry Cook to buy three parcels of land in Camden from the estate of Richard Champion. Scipio's former mistress Sarah Vaughan, Champion's sister, doubtless played a role in the transaction, or else her son John Champion Vaughan did. The thirty-two-year-old lawyer was at that time selling his assets in Camden and moving out of town. John DeSaussure, executor of Richard Champion's estate, was facilitating John Vaughan's land sales, with Henry Cook as witness. The same two men were involved in the land sale to Scipio Vaughan.[90] With their assistance, Scipio now had the chance to build his own house on his own lot, and additional houses on the two adjacent lots. Two years later, the census enumerator counted "Sip" Vaughan as a free householder, living in Camden with his wife and four of his children, including 12-year-old James Churchwill.[91]

Church Vaughan, as he was known in Camden, had been born there on April 1, 1828, three years after his father was supposed to have become free. Somehow he was learning to read and write, although when he was six years old it became illegal for free black people to organize schools. This was one of a new set of restrictions on free people of color, milder in South Carolina than in the Upper South, imposed after Nat Turner's rebellion in Virginia. By twelve, Church must have been learning carpentry by assisting his father, his older brother Burrell, and perhaps his aged grandfather Bonds Conway. Though later, in Africa, he would be baptized, Vaughan's family did not then go to church: his mother's Catawba people had little interest in white people's religion, and his father did not join several of Sarah Vaughan's slaves at Camden's First Baptist Church. Moreover, the law prohibited "assemblies and congregations of free negroes."[92]

In Camden, Church Vaughan's family associated more with members of the town's free black population than with the few remaining Native Americans who passed through and around. The three lots his father purchased were situated within a couple of blocks of plots owned by Bonds Conway and settled by members of his large family. Two blocks to the west, Conway's eldest daughter Harriet and her common-law husband, a white man of French background named Moreau Naudin, had purchased three lots for themselves and their four children.[93] Harriet Conway was like an aunt to the Vaughan children, having stayed close to her half-sister Maria Conway Vaughan over the years. Church's two eldest sisters, Elizabeth and Kitty, had married free black craftsmen (Granderson Hall and Jacob Hammonds, respectively) and were now settled with their babies in their own households nearby. Kitty and Jacob Hammonds lived next door to Scipio's house on one of the lots he had purchased from Richard Champion's estate. Scipio probably collected rent from the inhabitants of the other lot, a free black matriarch named Sarah Cole, two of her sons, and two grandsons. Outside of town, Church's only brother, Burrell Vaughan, was farming and doing carpentry work, living with his wife and their two young children. Yet like other free people of color, the Vaughans always lived "in the shadow" of slavery, as one historian put it, surrounded by enslaved people whose predicament was sometimes not far from their own. Church's teenaged sister Sarah (and perhaps eighteen-year-old Nancy Vaughan as well) worked as a paid servant for the wealthy planter William Ancrum, face to face with enslaved reminders of her exceptional, if tenuous, free status.[94]

In the late summer of 1840, having only just been counted as a free man, Scipio's once hardy body began to shut down. His wife Maria, not yet forty years old, tended him while caring for their four younger children: twelve-year-old Church, plus Harriet (11), Maria Virginia (8) and Mary Elizabeth (2). Scipio's five other children must have gathered around him too, with their spouses and the grandchildren. As he thought about what he had endured and built in his sixty years, Scipio Vaughan had to have been pleased with his large family and their ability to keep the tax collector, the jailer, the patrol, and countless other dangers at bay. Their assets may seem meager compared to those of the white Vaughan family—some land, a few simple houses, carpenter's tools, clothing, a trunk or two—but for someone who started not only with no assets but as the embodied asset of someone else, freedom and survival were accomplishments to be proud of. As his spirit began its journey home, Scipio could know that he had given his children a precious head start in the dangerous world of slavery and white supremacy.

Scipio Vaughan left his children with something else too: advice born of bitter experience—abuses endured, promises deferred, freedom always tempered. The sources available to historians contain none of Scipio's own words, and in fact, considering the shortage of written records about individual slaves, it is remarkable that several traces of his life exist at all. But Scipio's children and grandchildren repeated to each other and to their own descendants what he told them on his deathbed, passing his sentiments, if not his exact parting words, through the generations.[95] "Don't stay in South Carolina," he reportedly told them. "Go to Africa, the land of our ancestors!"

Scipio left this earthly world on September 12, 1840. Twelve years and two months later, his son James Churchill Vaughan would begin his own journey.

two

LEAVING HOME

The *Joseph Maxwell* rocked back and forth in the brisk November breeze while it sat at anchor just south of Wilmington, North Carolina. The three hundred-ton barque had arrived three days earlier, having been newly built in Baltimore and chartered by the American Colonization Society (ACS) to transport 150 settlers to Liberia.[1] Now, on the morning of Monday, November 22, 1852, the sailing ship's passengers were arriving. Within a few hours, Captain Joshua Ferrell would give the order and deckhands would raise the four square sails on the front two masts, set the two triangular sails on the aft mast, and raise the anchor. As the wooden craft lumbered to life, its passengers–Church Vaughan among them–would gaze for the last time at the shores of the United States of America. Ahead lay the vastness of the Atlantic Ocean and, beyond that, Africa.

In small groups, men, women, and children left the steamer that had transported them just beyond the ocean bar and climbed aboard. Quinny Young, a forty-year-old carpenter from Fayetteville, North Carolina, helped his wife Clarissa and their nine children across the gangplank. Also part of the large contingent from Fayetteville were the family of ailing wheelwright William Johnson, along with his brother John and John's wife Mary, and John Andrews, a carpenter, with his wife and three young children. Two families from Chapel Hill, North Carolina included fifty-five-year-old Patsy Boon and her four children and toddler grandson, along with carpenter Charles Williams, with his pregnant wife Beda and four children. Mrs. Williams may have been too far along for traveling, but she could look forward to giving her new baby a start in a land of freedom. Old Benjamin Jacobs and his recently freed wife Milly came aboard with their nine children, including their son Peter Jacobs, who brought his wife and their five children. Robin and Patsy Waddle, at ninety and seventy, were emigrating as a condition of their emancipation from slavery. Ephraim Wilson, seventy-one, was a free man from Charleston, traveling without family on what would be his last earthly journey. The Hoopers—Marshall, Rachel, and their daughter Emily—may have been particularly emotional as they boarded the oceangoing vessel; their tragic circumstances would become known to Church Vaughan, if they were not already, over the course of their voyage together.[2]

Vaughan had said goodbye to his family nearly a month before and joined the Jacobs and Wright families when they passed through Camden on their way to the coast from Lancaster, South Carolina. Temporarily stranded in Wilmington when help from the Colonization Society was slow in coming, they took matters into their own hands and rented a house where they could wait for their Africa-bound ship, hoping that they would eventually be reimbursed. Through early and mid-November, the rest of the prospective emigrants trickled into Wilmington from other parts of North Carolina: sixty-nine from Fayetteville, thirteen from Chapel Hill, eight from near Charlotte, four from Cabarrus County, and two from New Bern, joining nine from Wilmington. Thirty-six more came from South Carolina, and seven arrived from Georgia. Twenty—including two whole families—had been slaves, emancipated only if they would emigrate. Nearly all the rest, like Vaughan, had been born free. Many could read, belonged to Baptist or Methodist churches, and practiced skilled trades. Church, Peter Jacobs, and a couple of the other men from Lancaster took advantage of their time in Wilmington to find work as day laborers, knowing that they would need all the money they could bring to Africa.[3]

When ACS agent J. W. Lugenbeel arrived in Wilmington to coordinate the sailing, the travelers took it as a signal that the voyage would begin soon. On Saturday, November 20, Lugenbeel received word that the *Joseph Maxwell* was anchored off Smithville (today's Southport), twenty-five miles south of Wilmington near the mouth of the Cape Fear River. At that point, it was already too late in the day to round up the passengers in town and take them there by steamer. "Consequently," Lugenbeel reported later, "we had to wait until Monday morning, when 'we all took a ride' to Smithville in the steamboat 'Fayetteville'—put the emigrants on board, with all their luggage in safely—threw up our hats, and bid them goodbye—all hands in fine spirits."[4]

"Fine spirits" vastly oversimplifies the outlook of these and other African Americans who left the United States for Liberia. As Church Vaughan learned before he ever set foot on the *Joseph Maxwell*, the American Colonization Society's efforts to send free people of color to Africa were fraught with racist condescension. Since its beginning, African Americans and their allies were repelled by the white supremacy inherent in the society's mission and its kowtowing to slaveholders. For some thirty years, free people of color had chosen to take their chances at home, or, if they were driven to move, elsewhere in North America, rather than cast their lot with white colonizationists. By the early 1850s, however, new developments pushed increasing numbers of African Americans, like Vaughan, to look toward the continent of their ancestors. Free people of color had always suffered when whites feared threats to their authority. Now, as sectional divisions tore at the United States, southern lawmakers devised new measures to limit free black mobility, inhibit their earning power, and generally equate them with slaves. In the past, the Vaughans and other free black southerners guarded their limited rights through hard work and the cultivation of white patrons. As Church reached adulthood, however, predatory officials threatened the family's ability to make an independent living, while the old paternalist ties that had protected them in an earlier era dissipated. Even if emigration offered the chance of a new life in which black people governed themselves, it was a hard bargain to make. Some of his shipmates had boarded the *Joseph Maxwell* under terrible duress. Vaughan almost didn't make it either.

Five years before the *Joseph Maxwell*'s maiden voyage across the Atlantic, Liberia had become the world's second "black republic," after Haiti. But while Haiti had been born in a violent slave uprising against a brutal colonial regime, Liberia's origins reflected more ambiguous sentiments about slavery and emancipation. In 1816, Virginia legislator Charles Fenton Mercer, Baltimore lawyer Francis Scott Key, Supreme Court clerk Elias Caldwell, and New Jersey clergyman Robert Finley launched the American Colonization Society with the aim of sending free black people from America to Africa. Its supporters included prominent statesmen such as Henry Clay and Supreme Court justice Bushrod Washington, George Washington's nephew and heir; white opponents of slavery, like Finley, who sought to undermine the institution by creating a settlement where African Americans could truly be free; and southern whites eager to shore up slavery by ridding the country of free black people.[5]

Today the idea of a mass, race-based relocation appears far-fetched and reeks of "ethnic cleansing." The characterization is apt, though in its time, removing black people to Africa seemed perfectly conceivable. In 1787,

British philanthropists and government officials founded the colony of Sierra Leone, on the West African coast just north of where Liberia would be, as a settlement for the "black poor" who were considered a nuisance in England. Five years later, the British sent some twelve hundred African Americans to Sierra Leone from Nova Scotia, where they had already been relocated once after joining the British on the losing side of the American Revolution.[6] In the early nineteenth century, the U.S. government engineered large-scale migrations of Native Americans, most notably the removal of Cherokee from Georgia and neighboring states to Oklahoma. Throughout the 1800s, intellectuals and lawmakers in both the United States and Western Europe increasingly believed that the ideal state reflected a "nation"—that is, a people united by a shared history, culture, and institutions. For many white Americans, there was no place in their "imagined community" for the descendants of Africa. If black people were to be freed, they had to leave the United States.[7]

Proposals to remove black people from the United States had been around since the Revolutionary era, when the question of slavery troubled those who espoused freedom from British colonialism. Thomas Jefferson wrestled with the "problem" of America's black population in his *Notes on the State of Virginia*, written in 1782. There, he argued that slavery was immoral, but that white and black Americans could never coexist. "Deep rooted prejudices entertained by the whites; ten thousand recollections, by the blacks, of the injuries they have sustained; new provocations; the real distinctions which nature has made; and many other circumstances, will divide us into parties, and produce convulsions which will probably never end but in the extermination of the one or the other race," he argued. Jefferson did not oppose emancipation, but he insisted that "when freed, he [the slave] is to be removed beyond the reach of mixture."[8] Other white Virginians such as James Madison and James Monroe agreed, even if they differed over the particulars of expatriation.

Meanwhile, in the North, fledgling emigration schemes more reflected concern for black Americans' welfare than the threat they might pose to white supremacy. In the 1780s, African Americans in Boston and in Newport and Providence, Rhode Island formulated plans to move to Africa. They had concluded that in spite of the gradual erosion of slavery in the North, black people could never achieve freedom and equality in the newly formed United States; moreover, by migrating to Africa, they could bring the benefits of "civilization" (that is, western education and above all Christianity) to those they considered backward.[9] Although their proposals went unfulfilled, African Americans continued to be attracted to Africa. In the early nineteenth century, as free blacks in northern cities and towns banded together, they called their churches "African churches," their schools "African schools," and their mutual aid societies "African benevolent societies." The first independent black church was the African Church of Philadelphia, founded in 1790; the African Methodist Episcopal Church was formed there in 1816.[10]

Such activity inspired Paul Cuffe, a Quaker merchant and ship captain and probably the wealthiest man of color in the United States, to launch his own back-to-Africa movement. Descended from a Native American mother and an enslaved black father, Cuffe had become involved in the struggle for free African American political rights in his home state of Massachusetts. Frustrated with increasing restrictions on free people of color even in the North, he turned his attention to Africa, especially the British colony of Sierra Leone, which he visited in 1811 and 1812. Cuffe believed that black American emigration to Sierra Leone would help build a black Christian nation in Africa, create commercial and political connections between black people in Sierra Leone and America, and also suppress the slave trade. In late 1815, Cuffe transported thirty-eight African Americans to Sierra Leone. He bankrolled the expedition himself, hoping to benefit from trade, but it was a financial disaster. Cuffe died in 1817 without returning to Africa.[11]

The American Colonization Society had been founded the year before. Its leaders sought to build upon black emigrationist movements and presumed that their goals were compatible. But at the inaugural meeting of the society, southern politicians made it clear that for them, colonization was not about improving conditions for black Americans, but rather deporting free people of color. Speaker of the House Henry Clay, one of the society's many vice presidents, rose to ask the assembly: "Can there be a nobler cause than that which, whilst it proposed to rid our country of a useless and pernicious, if not dangerous portion of its population, contemplates the spreading of the arts of civilized life, and the possible redemption from ignorance and barbarism of a benighted quarter of the globe?"[12]

Clay's speech, printed in newspapers throughout the country, galvanized black opposition to the American Colonization Society. Less than a month later, three thousand African Americans gathered in Philadelphia to protest it. They repudiated the notion of free blacks as dangerous, resolved not to separate themselves from the American slave population, and objected to the prospect of migrating "into the savage wilds of Africa." Instead, they floridly asserted that African Americans were "entitled to participate in the blessings of [America's] luxuriant soil, which [their ancestors'] blood and sweat manured."[13]

African Americans, especially in the North, continued to object to colonization on these and similar grounds for the next half-century. At meetings and in the emerging black press, they derided the ACS's alleged interest in their welfare and charged that the organization sought to remove free African Americans in order to reinforce the slave system. Most importantly, they challenged the assumption that free people of color did not belong in the United States. The ACS campaign to deport them, in fact, so disturbed many free black people that as of the 1820s they began to call themselves "Colored Americans" rather than "Africans" and to substitute "Colored" for "African" in the names of their institutions.[14]

Meanwhile, the colonization society's politically connected leaders managed a legislative maneuver to get their program off the ground. American participation in the Atlantic slave trade had become illegal as of January 1, 1808. Eleven years later, Congress passed an Act for Suppression of the Slave Trade, which provided for naval patrols along the African coast to intercept slave ships. Like the British, whose Navy undertook a much larger effort to clear the ocean of human traffickers, American officials faced the question of what to do with any captives who might be found on detained vessels. The British answer to the question was the crown colony of Sierra Leone, where nearly thirteen thousand "recaptives" were settled between 1814 and 1824 (and a total of nearly a hundred thousand over the course of the nineteenth century).[15] In the United States, they provided a crucial opportunity for the American Colonization Society. Charles Fenton Mercer, newly elected congressman from Virginia and one of the founders of the ACS, sponsored a bill appropriating a hundred thousand dollars for the Monroe administration to create a settlement for liberated slave ship captives on the African coast. The job was given to the newly formed colonization society, which had begun to recruit some African American settlers but lacked funds to send them to Africa.[16]

On March 2, 1820, the first ACS-chartered ship, the *Elizabeth*, landed eighty-eight African Americans and three white agents at the British colony in Sierra Leone. Ostensibly, they were to clear land and build houses to accommodate future recaptured Africans. In reality, they were settlers, nearly two-thirds of them children. Within two months, the three agents and twelve of the settlers had died. Vulnerable to tropical diseases and possessing no claim to land on their own, the survivors and a subsequent shipload of colonists remained at the British settlement until 1822. At that point, visiting U.S. Navy commander Robert Stockton and ACS agent Dr. Eli Ayers approached a Dey political leader known as King Peter in order to purchase land at Cape Mesurado, 250 miles south of Freetown, Sierra Leone. Through hours of haggling, gift-giving, and threats, the king refused. Finally Stockton held a loaded pistol to his head, and the sale was made. The colonists named their base at Cape Mesurado "Monrovia" after the president who had made it possible. The entire colony was called "Liberia" after the Latin *liber*, or freeman.[17]

Throughout the 1820s, the American Colonization Society sent eighteen voyages to Liberia, carrying a total of 1,321 emigrants.[18] Only 154 were free blacks from the North (nearly half of them on the initial voyage of the *Elizabeth*), while 720 were free black southerners and the rest were manumitted.[19] As settlers' accounts began to reach the United States from Liberia, criticisms of colonization expanded to include not only its links to slavery and racism, but the deadly conditions that emigrants faced. Nearly a third of the first decade's settlers died of malaria and other diseases, most within a year of their arrival.[20]

Even while they rejected the ACS, however, some African Americans were willing to consider emigration elsewhere, especially under black leadership. In the 1820s, Haiti's president Jean-Pierre Boyer offered to fund the immigration of black Americans in an effort to bring skilled labor to the struggling republic. Some six thousand African Americans—that is, far more than were willing to emigrate to Liberia—accepted the invitation and sailed for Haiti. They found language, religious, and other cultural barriers difficult to surmount, however, and within two years at least a third of the settlers returned to the United States. In 1825, President Boyer discontinued the travel stipends and land grants he had originally provided, and the mass movement came to an end.[21] In the 1820s and '30s, African Americans settled in Michigan, Indiana, and Ohio. Facing increasing discrimination even in the North and Midwest, other free black people looked to Canada.[22] Yet there remained virtually no free black support for Liberian colonization until the 1850s.

The only exception to this general trend was a brief surge in southern emigration to Liberia in the aftermath of Nat Turner's rebellion, as free people of color fled violent reprisals. Three months after the August 1831 revolt, the colonization society shipped 326 African Americans to Liberia from panic-stricken Southampton County, Virginia, and adjacent counties in North Carolina. It was the largest emigrant party ever assembled for passage to Liberia. In 1832, the ACS sent a total of seven ships to Liberia carrying 796 emigrants, the majority of them from Virginia—an all-time high for a single year. While most were free people escaping the threat of vigilantes, others were manumitted and sent overseas by jittery whites worried about murderous rebels within their own slave quarters. The rebellion also prompted lawmakers in the Upper South to consider once again the deportation of black Americans. In the early 1830s, legislators in Maryland, Virginia, and Tennessee appropriated funds to help relocate ex-slaves and consenting free people in Africa. The Maryland legislature incorporated its own colonization society and organized the emigration of free blacks from the state to a new settlement at Cape Palmas, south of Monrovia.[23]

After 1833, however, colonizationist activity went practically dormant. In 1834 the ACS sent only one expedition, with 127 people, and by 1839 only forty-seven people emigrated, the lowest yearly number since Liberia's founding in 1822. Part of the problem was financial: the organization had run up huge expenses with the voyages of 1831–33, yet its main source of funding, federal allocations, had gone dry. After a government investigation into ongoing support for the American Colonization Society under the provisions of the 1819 Slave Trade Act, Andrew Jackson's administration ceased making payments to it. Now the colonization program would have to be financed solely by private contributions and state appropriations, and through subscriptions to the ACS newspaper, the *African Repository*. Moreover, the parent society had to compete for donations with state colonization organizations based not only in Maryland but also New York, Pennsylvania, and elsewhere. Some financial relief came in 1847, when settlers in Liberia declared national independence. Thereafter, the ACS continued to sponsor emigration but relinquished administrative responsibility for the colony to its own inhabitants.[24]

Even with healthier finances, the colonization movement was unlikely to have fared much better, not least because it had virtually no support among its primary target, free people of color. In 1829, outspoken abolitionist David Walker, born free in North Carolina but based in Boston, published his widely distributed *Appeal to the Coloured Citizens of the World*, which challenged racism, encouraged black self-help through education and religion, and exhorted readers to actively fight their oppression. The last of its four "articles" entailed a scathing indictment of colonization, which Walker described as "a plan got up by a gang of slave-holders to select the free people of colour from among the slaves, that our more miserable brethren may be the better secured in ignorance and wretchedness, to work their farms and dig their mines, and thus go on enriching the Christians with their blood and groans." "This country is as much ours as it is the whites," he continued, "whether they will admit it now or not, they will see and believe it by and by."[25] Walker's *Appeal* infuriated southern slaveholders. It was banned in South Carolina, while officials in Georgia offered a reward of ten thousand dollars to anyone who would deliver Walker alive and a thousand dollars to anyone who would kill him. Less than a year later, David Walker was found dead in Boston.[26] His anticolonization message lived on, however. At a mass meeting in Baltimore in 1831, for instance, participants responded to the prospect of removal from the state by resolving "that the land in which we were born [is] our only 'true and appropriate home' and when we desire to remove we will apprise the public of the same, in due season." Urban free black people organized opposition so effectively that few emigrants could be found, even in the countryside. Opponents even met potential recruits at ports of embarkation, where they offered final warnings about the dangers of emigration.[27]

The American Colonization Society was only marginally more popular among white people. As national politics became increasingly polarized around the issue of slavery, the society's leaders continued to portray the organization as centrist, courting the support of both proslavery and antislavery whites. At their annual meeting in 1835, for instance, ACS delegates unanimously passed a resolution denying that they were intent upon "interfering with the legal rights and obligations of slavery," but they also reaffirmed that the organization's "operations would be productive of unmixed good to the colored population of our country and of Africa."[28] Neither side was particularly impressed. White abolitionists, many now embracing immediate mass emancipation, became frustrated with the society's gradualism and association with slaveholders. Boston-based William Lloyd Garrison, formerly a supporter of colonization, routinely denounced the ACS in the pages of his newspaper, the *Liberator*, as well as in a 240-page volume of essays entitled *Thoughts on African Colonization*.[29] In the South, proslavery whites also lost their taste for voluntary colonization, which to them resembled abolitionism, even if gradual and respectful of property rights. After 1830, white support for the ACS came mainly from the small number of southerners who manumitted their slaves and sent them to Liberia.

By the time Scipio Vaughan urged his children to go to Africa, in late 1840, only three groups of South Carolinians had ever migrated to Liberia, all in the brief colonization burst of 1832 and '33.[30] It may seem surprising, but in

South Carolina free people of color operated with relative autonomy, even as Virginia and other states tightened restrictions on their liberty. In the Upper South, changes in the agricultural economy had created a surplus of slaves by the early nineteenth century, leading both to manumissions and to slave sales outside the region. Consequently, Virginia, Maryland, and other parts of the Upper South had much larger populations of free people of color, and smaller populations of slaves, than existed in the Lower South cotton belt. While Upper South whites saw free black people as posing a real threat to racial hierarchies, Lower South whites cultivated them as a tiny middle caste between slaves and themselves. Their sense of paternalism sometimes translated into sympathy for free black people, whom they saw as hopelessly incapable of succeeding in the white world. White people in South Carolina patronized free black tradesmen, loaned them money, sold them land, and sometimes protected them from danger. Occasionally, they granted success-ful people like Bonds Conway additional rights, such as to testify in court. At the same time, they controlled free people of color in part through the sys-tem of white guardians, cloaking restrictions on autonomy in the language of protection.[31]

Scipio Vaughan had navigated this terrain with some success. As the years passed after his death, however, tragedy descended upon his survivors. Their hard-won economic autonomy, and even their physical survival, be-came precarious. Death came to the old and the young. White officials con-spired to take their property. The elite patrons who had, however partially, made it possible for Scipio to claim his freedom, earn a living, and become an independent landowner were no longer present, while new allies were few. Whatever security the Vaughans' Catawba relations may have offered also withered away in the new era of Indian exclusion. And after personal hardships in the 1840s, a new wave of persecution landed upon free people of color in 1850.

Scipio's death was the first of many that the Vaughans endured. Within months of his father's passing in late 1840, twelve-year-old Church Vaughan lost two more members of his family. It may have been influenza that struck that winter. Church's nine-year-old sister Virginia died on February 24, 1841. Two days later, their elder sister Kitty Ann, at that time twenty years old, married, and the mother of a toddler, died too. Then, as the weather turned warm, the southern United States was wracked by an epidemic of yellow fever. Remarkably, none of the Vaughans succumbed. Church's youth and that of his younger sisters may have helped them survive the virus, leaving them with lifelong immunity—in Africa as well as the American South. The next summer, however, Church's twenty-year-old sister Nancy passed away, perhaps as fever flared in Camden again.[32]

The deaths came just about every year, striking Church's grandparents next. In 1843, eighty-year-old Bonds Conway died and was buried in Camden's Cedar Cemetery. He had been a prosperous man, but he had seven surviving children besides Church's mother, Maria. His will bequeathed land and houses in Camden to four of them, but nothing to her.[33] The next year, Maria's mother, Nancy Carter, also passed away. With her went most of the Vaughans' connections to their Catawba ancestry. What remained of the tribe had ceded all their land in South Carolina to the state government in 1840, and many moved to western North Carolina. There, they expected to obtain new territory near the small group of Cherokees who had recently escaped forced removal along the "Trail of Tears" by hiding in the Appalachian Mountains. The land purchase never materialized, however. The Catawbas left the Cherokees and about half of them came back to South Carolina, negotiating the return of a small portion of their previous reservation. Soon even those had scattered, and by the end of the 1840s the Catawba Nation was considered, in the words of Governor David Johnson, "in effect, dissolved."[34]

As Church passed through his teenage years, his family struggled to maintain their livelihood and independence. His brother-in-law Jacob Hammond, widower of Kitty Ann Vaughan, shouldered much of the finances of their extended household, which included Hammond's little son, William; the widow Maria Conway Vaughan and three of her children; Church; Church's younger sister Harriet; and Harriet and Church's much younger sister Mary. In 1846, Hammond married seventeen-year-old Harriet Vaughan, securing a new wife while remaining connected to the family, whose carpentry business he kept going. Jacob Hammond was probably assisted by Church, who was becoming, in the words of a Camden merchant, "a first rate carpenter, [who] can lay out and frame any building."[35] Their good name must have assured them of some business, but clients often preferred either to hire whites, because of their color, or slaves, because the wages paid to their masters were low. Consequently, free black craftspeople like Hammond and Vaughan had to underbid whites and work on the same terms as slaves, depressing their own incomes and earning the ire of white workingmen.[36]

After four years without a funeral in the family, Jacob Hammond died in 1848, in his thirties or early forties. It was both a personal and a financial tragedy for the Vaughans. Jacob had become the official owner of one of the three plots of land that Scipio Vaughan had purchased toward the end of his life, although if the Vaughans were like other Carolina families at this time, they assumed the land would continue to benefit the family as a whole.[37] It did not. Unlike other adults in the family, Hammond had not registered a white guardian. Not all free black people did, after all; Scipio Vaughan had never enlisted one, relying instead on the fact that people in Camden generally knew him to be free. But now, taking advantage of the fact that there was no one to stop them, two town officials colluded to acquire Hammond's land and the house he or Scipio had built there.[38] Kershaw County's "ordinary" (probate registrar), John R. Joy, a Methodist minister, schoolmaster, slaveholder, and close associate of the town's planter elite, declared himself guardian of the now orphaned nine-year-old, William Hammond. In order to "provide for" young William, Reverend Joy took control of Jacob Hammond's estate. In August 1848, he filed an inventory and appraisal of Hammond's possessions, which included furniture, cooking utensils, two framed pictures, a shovel, candles, and two quilts, all valued at thirty-eight dollars, plus the house and lot. The following January, Joy petitioned the Kershaw Probate Court to allow him to sell the land and house at auction. One day later, T. W. Doby, a banker and Kershaw County's tax collector, paid $250 to acquire the Vaughans' property.[39]

The records of this transaction reek of conspiracy. Though the auction took place on January 17, 1849, the official paperwork was not filed with the clerk of court until nearly two years later, in December of 1850. There, Joy alleged that when the application to sell the real estate was filed, a summons was issued calling for the appearance of anyone who might object. No one came forward, and so the auction was scheduled for, and took place, the following July 1849. Yet it is hard to believe that the Vaughans did not mobilize to prevent this sale. Moreau Naudin, Kershaw County's clerk of court at the time, was the common-law husband of Maria Vaughan's half-sister Harriet Conway. In fact, when the sale was finally registered—long after the fact—the paperwork was noted "Left for record 21st Dec., Moreau Naudin," implying that it was filed only in Naudin's absence. Even this documentation made clear the long lag between the sale and its official registration, dating the real estate auction to February 15, 1849. This date appears to be a fabrication, but it is at least closer to the real time of sale, in January 1849, than the registration in December 1850.[40]

In spite of the apparent shadiness of this legal maneuver, the sale took effect, depriving the Vaughans of roughly a third of the assets that Scipio had worked so hard to provide them. They no longer could use that land and house as collateral should they need to borrow money for tools or taxes, or if they found themselves in legal trouble. Harriet Vaughan lost her free-of-rent housing, though as Hammond's widow she received $98.50 from the estate sale. Other sums were allocated to tax and sheriff's bills. Burrell Vaughan, Harriet's older brother, inherited from Hammond "one old trunk" valued at thirteen cents. Reverend Joy took the rest, $132.65, as "bond" for the young William. Twenty years later, after Joy had died, William Hammond was still trying to recover his inheritance from the unscrupulous probate official's heirs.[41]

The surviving Vaughans carried on, in spite of their loss. A year after Jacob Hammond died, the husband of Church's eldest sister Elizabeth, Granderson Hall, also passed away, leaving her with three young children to support by herself.[42] Still, Maria Vaughan managed to pay the taxes on the house where she and some of her children and grandchildren continued to live.[43] Twenty-year-old Harriet, Church's sister and the widow of Joseph Hammond, moved into the house two doors down from her mother's, sharing it with free black renters. A few houses away, Church's widowed sister Elizabeth Hall lived with her three children and earned money as a seamstress. Another sister, Sarah, continued to work as a servant for the planter William Ancrum and his family, as she had done since she was a teenager and would continue to do until her death in 1862 (three years after which, at the age of forty, she finally married). In 1849 Sarah Vaughan bore a daughter, Maria Sophronia, who was so light-skinned that the census taker described her as white. The little girl grew up in her grandmother's house with her mother, her uncle Church, her young aunt Mary, and her cousin William Hammond.[44]

The core of the Vaughan household was decidedly female. Maria was remarried to an enslaved man named Basken Coleman when she registered her own white guardian in 1844, though she remained in the house Scipio had built. Sometime around 1850, she married again, this time to a free man, James Johnson. They rarely lived together either: he was often found at the house next door, now owned by T. W. Doby and rented to a young white couple who may have hired Johnson to work for them. Maria's eldest son, Burrell Vaughan, now in his thirties, was not living in Camden, although he registered an official guardian with the Kershaw County Court in 1845 and 1850.[45] He may, in fact, have departed Kershaw County with the Catawbas in 1840, only to return a short time later, no better off than when he left. Raised largely by his mother and her Indian relations, Burrell may have identified more with the tribe than his younger siblings did. Like the hundred or so remaining Catawbas, he may have led a wandering life, spending part of the year in North Carolina and another part closer to home—the way their ancestors had seasonally traveled to pursue food, supplies, or ene-mies.[46] Though Burrell earned a living as a carpenter and mechanic, he had no recorded address until 1860, when he resided with his wife in Clarendon County, south of Camden. And Church only lived part of the time with his mother. Many nights he slept at the home of Joseph F. Sutherland, a married furniture maker and future judge who had come to Camden from New York in the 1830s. Two months after his twenty-first birthday, Church duly regis-tered with the clerk of court. Though records do not name his official white guardian, it may well have been Sutherland, who, many years later, fathered children with Vaughan's niece Maria Sophronia.[47]

By the late 1840s or early 1850s, J. F. Sutherland may have been Church's family's most significant white ally, since the white Vaughans, with whom Scipio had been so closely connected, had disappeared from their lives. Wylie Vaughan's son John Champion Vaughan (born 1806) had never spent much time in Kershaw County, attending school in his mother's native England before returning to South Carolina to study law at the College of Charles-ton. When he graduated in 1827, his entire class was offered employment in the governor's office, which, according to an account by his English cousin, Vaughan declined because of his growing antislavery sentiment. He returned to Camden, married, and opened a profitable legal practice with the son of his father's former business partner.[48]

If Vaughan was turning against slavery at this point, it certainly was not clear from his actions: in 1831 he advertised for the return of a runaway bonds-man named Bob, and in 1832 he listed eight slaves as his on the town tax rolls. Three years later, Vaughan attended a public meeting in Camden, called in response to the increasing militancy of abolitionist societies and publica-tions in the North, and he joined the committee of town elites that wrote the meeting's proclamation defending slavery and states' rights. "Slavery, as it exists with us," it read in part, "we deny to be an evil. . . .We shall regard any attempt on the part of Congress to abolish slavery . . . or any resolutions or Act of Congress adverse to slavery, as a reckless violation of our Consti-tutional compact, as a wicked and direct infringement of our rights and as involving the certain and speedy dissolution of this Union." Within another two years, however, Vaughan had sold his portion of his father's estate, ar-ranged for his remaining slaves to live freely, and moved to Cincinnati.[49]

Vaughan was one of thousands of whites who left South Carolina in the 1830s, but most of them went south rather than north. Though cotton production in the state had flourished in the first part of the century, intensive cultivation depleted local soils. As new land nearby became scarce and expensive, many planters directed their ambitions toward Georgia, Florida, Alabama, Mississippi, or Louisiana, which had been "opened" for white settlement by the Louisiana Purchase of 1803 and a series of Native American removals. Vaughan's law partner Thomas B. Lee, in fact, moved to Louisiana.[50] In Kershaw County, the white population dropped from 5,625 in 1820 to 5,016 in 1830 and 3,988 in 1840. The *Camden Journal* reported in 1835 that "the old and the young are preparing to emigrate, and the inquiry is not whether you are going, but when do you go." Overall, between 1820 and 1860, nearly two hundred thousand white people who had been born in South Carolina moved out of the state. The involuntary black out-migration was almost as large. In the half-century before the Civil War, an estimated 179,000 black South Carolinians were taken south and west with their owners. In spite of a net increase in the slave population of Kershaw County, unfree people could never be sure that their owners would not uproot them. During Church's childhood, he was surrounded by broken slave families—parents and children, husbands and wives separated as the young and strong were forced south in the relentless expansion of the plantation frontier.[51]

Although most migration was driven by the desire for new land, some white people who left South Carolina were also prompted by political controversies over slavery and states' rights. Dr. William Blanding, who had moved to Camden in 1807 and who, with his wife Rachel, had been repulsed by the aftermath of the 1816 slave conspiracy, left South Carolina for Philadelphia in 1835. Later they returned to Dr. Blanding's home state of Massachusetts.[52] After his move to Ohio, John Vaughan became involved in a number of reform movements, including those to promote public education, poor relief, and, in a reversal of the attitude of his young adulthood, antislavery. In 1838, shortly after leaving Camden, he traveled to Mason County, Kentucky, to act as defense attorney in the trial of John B. Mahan, an Ohio abolitionist who had allegedly helped several fugitive slaves from Kentucky make their way to Canada. By the 1840s he had replaced the practice of law with his father's line of work as a newspaperman, believing that white opinion on slavery might be swayed through the press. But he was no William Lloyd Garrison. Instead, he hoped to move other white southerners along the course he had taken himself, toward gradual abolitionism. In 1845, he took over the leadership of the *True American*, a financially troubled abolitionist newspaper based in Lexington, Kentucky, and edited by the firebrand Cassius Clay. Vaughan secured its finances through contacts with northern abolitionists and relaunched it as the Louisville *Examiner*, intended to provide a safe and calm forum in which white citizens of the Upper South might examine the issues of the day.[53]

One of these was the question of African American settlement in Liberia. The *Examiner*'s first edition featured on its front page the beginning of a three-part series on colonization by Louisville judge William F. Bullock, delivered as a speech to the Kentucky Colonization Society. Because of white racism, Bullock argued, blacks would never progress in the United States. Only by "returning" to Africa could their "intellectual and moral grandeur" flourish. His speech ended with the stirring prediction that "the time will come when the proud vessel of our Republic, freighted with the last cargo of American slavery, shall spread her canvass for the shores of Liberia."[54] Letters to the editor repeatedly praised African colonization, as did, in more subtle tones, announcements of the Liberian Republic's independence in 1848.[55]

After only a year at its helm, Vaughan left the running of the *Examiner* to associate editors and dedicated himself to promoting a national antislavery political party. He became an organizer and speaker as antislavery factions splintered from the existing Whig and Democratic parties to form, in succession, the Liberty, Free Soil, and Republican Parties. In June 1848, Vaughan was one of fifteen delegates to the Whig convention in Philadelphia who protested the nomination of slaveholder Zachary Taylor as the party's presidential candidate. He then attended a Liberty/Free Soil Party convention in Columbus, Ohio, followed by the Buffalo, New York, convention that established the Free Soil Party and nominated Martin van Buren for president. Nominated by the Liberty Party to run for senator from Ohio, Vaughan was defeated by his antislavery associate Salmon P. Chase. In July and August of 1848, Vaughan traveled through the Western Reserve of Ohio for six weeks with Chase to stump for Van Buren.[56]

Meanwhile, as John Vaughan was making a new life in the Midwest, his mother also left Camden, never to return. Wylie Vaughan's widow Sarah, who had facilitated Scipio's gradual emancipation, was now an aging matron. In the mid-1840s, she and her daughter Virginia sailed for Liverpool, where they stayed with Sarah's English sister and her family for several years. After returning to the United States, they spent a winter with friends in Mobile, Alabama, beginning their journey back to Camden in early March 1850. With nearly 150 other passengers, they boarded the steamboat *Orline St. John*, headed to Montgomery. On March 4, after two days on the Alabama River, a fire erupted and quickly engulfed the midsection of the ship. The captain

Leaving Home

ran the front of the vessel aground so that the passengers could escape, but many, including all the women and children, were trapped in the rear, surrounded by flames and deep water. Forty-one passengers perished, including six from Camden: town intendent James Robert McKain and his mother, a Mrs. Sizer and her daughter, and Sarah and Virginia Vaughan.[57] Their remains, buried next to Wylie Vaughan in the Episcopal cemetery, were all that was left in Camden of Scipio's white Vaughans.[58]

Around the time that news of the steamboat fire reached Camden, Church Vaughan and his family began to consider seriously the possibility of leaving. Church had lost his father, three of his sisters, and two brothers-in-law. His mother had seen the community of her birth dwindle and scatter, leaving its members ever more impoverished and vulnerable. His sister may well have been raped by her employer or someone in his household, but there was not much anyone could do about that. Nor had they any recourse when the probate officer seized their property and sold it to the tax collector. Under increasing stress, they may have read with interest some of the procolonization pieces in John Vaughan's newspaper, if copies circulated among his associates in Camden. What finally pushed them, though, was most likely the Fugitive Slave Act, passed by Congress and signed by President Fillmore in 1850.

Brokered by the aging statesman (and colonizationist) Henry Clay, the Fugitive Slave Act passed as part of the infamous Compromise of 1850. In exchange for southern acceptance of California as a free state and a ban on slave trading within the District of Columbia, Congress vastly expanded the power of masters and their agents to recapture escaped slaves over state lines. The law placed the courts and law enforcement officers at slaveowners' disposal, allowing "reasonable force or restraint" to be employed to return fugitives to their owners. It deprived suspected runaways of the right to testify, of habeas corpus, and of jury trials; and it imposed fines and imprisonment on anyone who impeded the apprehension of an alleged fugitive. The Fugitive Slave Act endangered both actual fugitives and legally free people of color. Anyone could charge that a black person was a runaway slave and would only have to enlist a judge or commissioner in order to reduce the accused to slavery. In a number of towns, violent defiance of the law prompted the intervention of local and federal authorities. In addition, black people fled to Canada in unprecedented numbers — 3,000 in the last three months of 1850 alone and perhaps as many as 20,000 over the course of the 1850s, increasing the British territory's African-descended population by 50 percent.[59]

The Vaughans probably did not seriously consider moving to Canada, or even to the Midwest, where states such as Ohio, Indiana, and Illinois, previously havens for free people of color, were beginning to pass new laws banning their immigration, as were some in the West. Northern states, never free from racism, now fell within the jurisdiction of the Fugitive Slave Act and thus were not safe. Yet Church and his family clearly had reason to worry that Camden was less and less hospitable for them. In 1843 Burrell Vaughan had been arrested for assault and battery, two weeks before his half-cousin Peter Conway spent a night in jail for an unspecified misdemeanor. The charges against Conway were dropped through the intervention of a white "guardian"; in Vaughan's case, charges were never even filed.[60] Free people of color had always been vulnerable to arbitrary arrest, seizure, and enslavement, and had relied on community ties to protect them, as they did when Burrell Vaughan and Peter Conway ran into trouble. After their inability to stop the sale of Jacob Hammond's land and house, though, the Vaughans must have come to the grim conclusion that they could no longer rely on sympathetic whites to defend them and their property. How much more vulnerable they must have felt when, only a year later, the Fugitive Slave Act made every black person a potential target for seizure, wherever he or she might be.

Like the Vaughans, other free African Americans now began to reconsider Liberia, whose recent independence blunted previous criticisms that colonization was entirely white-controlled. Between 1848 and 1860, some 2,167 free African Americans moved there, more than the total of free emigrants in the first seventeen years of settlement. They were joined by 3,436 former slaves who had been emancipated on the condition that they go to Liberia — again, far more than in the 1820s or '30s. In the Upper South, renewed fear of free black subversion revived interest in African removal among whites. Although state-sponsored colonization schemes had collapsed in the 1840s, every Upper South state except Delaware and North Carolina instituted a colonization plan in the 1850s. In Washington, D.C., Secretary of State Daniel Webster, a longtime member of the American Colonization Society, called for federal funding for African colonization; President Fillmore included a proposal for a colonization venture in an initial draft of his 1852 State of the Union address.[61]

In Camden, emigration prospects were shaped, like so much else, by social networks and patronage. One of the philanthropic interests of William and Rachel Blanding, the Camden couple who had moved north in the 1830s, was Liberia, and they had been raising money to support missionary activities and a school there since at least 1840. They remained closely tied to friends and family in Kershaw County, including an elderly Scottish-born merchant named James K. Douglas. In 1849, Douglas wrote to Dr. Blanding that one of his slaves, Edmund Taylor, was in the process of purchasing himself and his wife and hoped to go to Liberia as a missionary — a project Douglas encouraged.[62] Two years later, Douglas became the contact between the American Colonization Society and Church Vaughan, who lived just two blocks from Douglas's house. They may have also known each other through Church's sister Sarah, who worked as a servant in the home of Douglas's daughter Charlotte, Mrs. William Ancrum.

Douglas seems to have shared with the Vaughans the pamphlet "Sketches of Liberia," which he received from its author, ACS agent and former Liberia resident Dr. J. W. Lugenbeel.[63] In it, Lugenbeel promised that "the earnest inquirer may find the principal topics of information which he may desire, respecting the Republic of Liberia." Such topics included Liberia's geography and climate, agricultural products, the African American settlements there, and diseases. Lugenbeel did not hide potentially discouraging facts from potential emigrants. His month-by-month account of the weather indicated much more heat and rain than Americans were used to, not to mention the month-long harmattan winds that swept in from the Sahara every January. Along with crocodiles and boa constrictors, he mentioned driver ants, which marched in columns sometimes hundreds of yards long, overcoming and devouring every obstacle in their way. A medical doctor, Lugenbeel devoted two of his "sketches" to all of the ailments, many fatal, that befell inhabitants of Liberia. But on the whole, his tone was upbeat, emphasizing that with diligence and good sense, a settler could overcome all the obstacles and build a prosperous, healthy new life there. "In view of the social and political position and relations of colored persons in the United States," he concluded, "contrasted with the position and relations of the free and independent citizens of that young Republic, it must be admitted by all candid persons, that the condition of those people in Liberia who are disposed to use the necessary appliances for making themselves truly independent, is vastly superior to that of free people of color in any part of this country."[64]

Church Vaughan, well used to exhausting work and possessing a young adult's abundant self-confidence, certainly could think that he and his family had the resourcefulness to succeed in Liberia. After surviving the diseases that ravaged their household, he must have felt (rightly, it turned out) that he could live through whatever ailments came to him in the tropics. And in reading the description of Monrovia's fine houses, he may well have imagined himself and his brother making a good living as builders, or even living in such accommodations themselves. "The dwellings of many of the citizens of Monrovia are not only comfortably, but elegantly, and some of them richly furnished," Lugenbeel wrote, "and some of the residents of this little bustling metropolis live in a style of ease and affluence, which does not comport with the contracted views of those persons who regard a residence in Africa as necessarily associated with the almost entire privation of the good things of this life."[65] After two decades of watching others enjoy a standard of living that his color would always prevent him from attaining, Vaughan must have been ready to enjoy some comforts himself. He informed Douglas that he and four relatives — his brother Burrell, their mother, and two sisters — were interested in emigration, and speculated that they might be ready to sail to Liberia before the end of 1851.[66]

If Douglas could help facilitate the Vaughans' move to Africa, however, he could also thwart it. In a letter to William McLain, the corresponding secretary of the ACS, Douglas described the brothers as "two man carpenters of good character" and reported that they had money for the passage and some property to help them begin new lives in Liberia. He could not attest to the integrity of the Vaughan women, though. "There is nothing against the females," Douglas wrote, "but [i.e. except] what is lamentably too common, wherever the race exists." Did he mean to imply that, like other black women, the Vaughan sisters were morally lax? If so, he certainly was not the first or only white southerner to invoke such an image — often blaming the victims for the sexual transgressions of white men. In this case, it may have also been more personal. Douglas could well have been aware of the light-skinned baby born to the unmarried maid in his daughter's house, and he may have even wondered why his son-in-law, who owned over a hundred slaves, felt the need to hire a free black woman as a family servant. Douglas's daughter Charlotte Ancrum had died in October 1849 at the age of thirty, her sixth child not yet two years old and Sarah Vaughan's baby just two months old. A devastated J. K. Douglas visited her grave every day, on the same hour as he had visited her home daily when she was alive. He may have been gratified to imagine Sarah Vaughan and her family gone from Camden, no longer able to remind him of the injury done to his beloved daughter. Even so, when he wrote to the American Colonization Society, he did not resist disparaging her character.[67]

Within the next couple of months, Douglas supplied Church Vaughan with an application titled "African Aid Society, Paper for Intending Settlers in Africa."[68] To the first question, "Are you desiring to leave [blank] and go to the Land of your Forefathers?" Church answered yes. Question number seven, "Of what Church are you a member?" he left unanswered; and he probably had no enthusiasm for question ten, either: "Will you strive to spread the truths of the Gospel among the natives?" But he reported that he could read and write, and that he worked as a carpenter. Asked for the names, ages, and marital status of those desiring to emigrate, Church listed himself, his mother, his brother Burrell, and his two youngest surviving sisters. Earlier, Douglas had attempted to dissuade Church and Burrell Vaughan from traveling to Liberia with their mother and sisters, although he knew they were "resolved to all go together."[69] Now Church attached to his application a document entitled "Record of the Family of Scipio Vaughan, as recorded anew by James Churchwill Vaughan on March 14, 1852, at Camden, South Carolina." The entire text read:

> Scipio Vaughan was married to Maria Conway on the 15th August 1815 and had issue as follows:-
> (1) Burrell Vaughan, born August 11, 1816
> (2) Elizabeth Vaughan, born August 5, 1818
> (3) Kitty Ann Vaughan, born July 4, 1820
> (4) Nancy Vaughan, born August 25, 1822
> (5) Sarah Ann Vaughan, born December 10, 1823
> (6) James Churchwill Vaughan, born April 1, 1828
> (7) Harriatt Vaughan, born December 10, 1830 (or 1829)
> (8) Virginia Vaughan, born January 14, 1832
> (9) Mary Vaughan, born February 24, 1838
> William Hammond, born December 25, 1839
> Rebecca Ann Hall, born January 24, 1838
> Henry Hall, born May 13, 1844
> Burrell C. Rankin, born December 8, 1847.

So many years later, and separated from any contextual information, the purpose of this listing is not clear. By the time he wrote it, Kitty Ann, Nancy, and Virginia had been dead for a decade. William Hammond was the son of his deceased sister Kitty Ann and brother-in-law Jacob Hammond; the three listed last were children of his widowed sister Elizabeth. Not all the names on the list, then, were of people desiring to move to Liberia. And a copy of the list remained with Church's relatives even after he left Camden.[70] Was this his note for posterity, some kind of marker to remind his family of his place among them? It so, it may indeed have helped to keep his name alive in South Carolina: two years after Church's departure, his niece Rebecca Hall named her new son William Churchill Clyburn (her first son had been named after Bonds Conway); much later, in 1871, another niece, Maria Sophrona, named her son James Churchwill Vaughan Cannon.[71]

Events moved swiftly after Douglas submitted Church Vaughan's application to the American Colonization Society on March 16, 1852. The organization's secretary, William McLain, wrote back to inform Douglas that a vessel would sail to Liberia from Baltimore on May 1, only five weeks away. His response indicated that the Vaughan brothers had been accepted as Liberian settlers, but it said nothing about the women.[72] Douglas then provided Church with an ACS pamphlet entitled "Information about Going to Liberia." Written in question-and-answer format, the four-page booklet addressed both the passage to Liberia and what to expect after arrival. Church learned that the voyage would last about thirty-five days, and that no ACS vessel had ever been lost at sea. He read a list of suggested items to bring: woolen clothing for the rainy season, a mattress and bedclothes for the voyage and afterward, his carpenters' tools, utensils, furniture, seeds, and money. In addition to ACS support for his first six months in Liberia, he could expect to receive ten acres of land; families received twenty-five acres. Church may have been reassured to learn that "blacksmiths, carpenters, masons, brickmakers, cabinet-makers, shipwrights, etc. find employment at good wages." But perhaps what most captured his imagination was the pamphlet's concluding remarks: "The great advantage which the colored man gains by going to Liberia is not as to his eating or drinking or making money, but in his social and moral condition. He becomes a *man*. He is no longer despised as of another race, but is treated as an equal and as a brother, and secures immense advantages for his children. Those who can and do appreciate these, and go to Liberia, will never regret it."[73] As he approached his twenty-fourth birthday in a town starkly stratified by skin color and class, where he struggled to help support a family full of women but had few options for economic betterment, Church may have longed to be just such a man.

As the proposed May departure approached, however, the Vaughans were having second thoughts. Was Liberia really a haven for African Americans, where they could participate fully in civic life, as emigrationists proposed, or was it a dumping ground designed to strengthen slavery by ridding the United States of free blacks? Were African Americans better off, as abolitionists insisted, leaving Liberia to Africans and claiming the place they deserved in the United States? On a practical level, could they succeed in a colony where they started with nothing and faced tropical diseases and hostile natives? As they revisited these now decades-old debates, the Vaughans faced a momentous choice. Because the in-migration of free people of color to South Carolina was illegal, they would not be able to return once they left the state. The fate of the Catawbas, who tried to get away and then returned in penury, may have hung heavily over the Vaughans' deliberations.

A month after submitting their application to the ACS, Church Vaughan told J. K. Douglas that he and Burrell had changed their minds. According to Douglas's account, "They have a sister in Philadelphia who has written them that she had seen some 70 Liberians who had returned to this country in horror and disgust, since the battle of Fish Town, and this was enough for them."[74] Who the sister was in Philadelphia is unclear, since the Vaughan sisters were all either in Camden or deceased. Perhaps it was one of their many relatives through their grandfather Bonds Conway's third marriage. But what this sister, friend, or cousin had heard about Liberia would indeed give a prospective settler pause. Fishtown was a settlement in the Bassa Cove area of Liberia, south of Monrovia. Its initial African American settlers had been massacred by neighboring warriors in 1834, though a small Liberian outpost remained. In November of 1851, as the Liberian government was extending its authority further along the coast from Monrovia, Kru-speaking people under the leadership of a chief called Grando attacked the Fishtown settlement and killed ten settlers. Two months later, a large force of Liberian troops and local allies waged a successful retaliatory attack.[75]

The Fishtown debacle was held up as only one piece of a larger critique of colonization that continued to circulate in northern cities and towns. Frederick Douglass, a former Maryland bondsman who had become the most prominent black opponent of slavery, repeatedly lambasted the American Colonization Society, calling it "the arch enemy of the free colored citizens of the United States." Martin Robeson Delany, a Pittsburgh medical doctor, journalist, and political organizer, denounced the ACS and Liberia in his book *The Condition, Elevation, Emigration and Destiny of the Colored People of the United States*, published in 1852. Not only was Liberia unhealthy, he charged, but it "originated in a deep laid scheme of the slaveholders of the country to *exterminate* the free colored of the American continent." In spite of official self-government, Liberia was "*not* an independent nation at all; but a poor *miserable mockery — a burlesque* on government — a pitiful dependence on the American Colonizationists." To support his point, Delaney invoked the events at Fishtown: "Does king Grando, or a party of fishermen besiege a village and murder some of the inhabitants," and the "President" of Liberia "dispatches an official report to the American Colonization Board, asking for instructions . . . and war *actually declared in Liberia,* by virtue of the *instructions* of the *American Colonization Society*"?[76]

While the book was being printed, in April 1852, Delany spoke at a meeting in Philadelphia that opposed not only the American Colonization Society but emigration in general. "Believing that our destiny is to be fulfilled in this, the land of our birth," the meeting resolved, "we therefore recommend to our brethren to stand firm, and contend for 'Life, Liberty and Happiness' in the United States."[77] Church Vaughan would meet Delany a decade later, when events that neither could have predicted took them both to Yorubaland, West Africa. But in the early 1850s, Delany may have been responsible, via their relative in Philadelphia, for the Vaughan family's loss of interest in emigrating to Africa.

While the Vaughans were deliberating about whether to stay or go, others in nearby Lancaster, South Carolina, had determined to cast their lot with Liberia. Together with his son Peter, sixty-year-old Benjamin Jacobs headed a large family of skilled, literate, free people of color. The only enslaved member of the family was Benjamin's wife, Milly, who would be freed by the time they left the state. At the same time that Church Vaughan was receiving information about the ACS from James Douglas, Benjamin Jacobs was in touch with a middling, white Kershaw District farmer named Dudley Ussery, who was also part of a tiny local network of white supporters of colonization.[78] Ussery shared with Jacobs the pamphlet with information about prospective settlers in Liberia, letting him know that his family would receive free passage to Liberia, unless they could afford it themselves, plus six months' support once they arrived.[79] By late September, a total of twenty-nine free people of color, all relatives of Benjamin Jacobs and another family anchored by Elijah Wright, had applied to the ACS for emigration to Liberia. Though a few lived in the village of Lancaster, most were from the surrounding countryside. They comprised nearly all the free people of color of Lancaster District, "all highly respected," in the estimation of the society's agent.[80]

The American Colonization Society's J. W. Lugenbeel was so pleased about this large number of emigrants that he arranged to visit Lancaster himself to provide information and to help arrange their departure. In particular, he hoped that "the good citizens of the county would be willing to make a handsome contribution to help their way." The Jacobs and Wright families were instructed to make ready to sail from Wilmington, North Carolina, in mid-November.[81] By the time Lugenbeel arrived in Lancaster on October 22, however, the emigrants—now thirty-three in number—had already made their own arrangements and left for the coast. They may have been in a hurry to get away from obstructionist whites, who Ussery reported "look[ed] with a jealous eye on every movement among the colored people be the object what it may." The Jacobs/Wright party traveled first about twenty miles south to Camden, and then on to Charleston, where they would board a boat north for Wilmington.[82] They must have met Church Vaughan in Camden toward the end of October 1852.

What prompted Church Vaughan to change his mind about Liberia, even when the rest of his family was unwilling to go, is lost to history. More than forty years later, his children inscribed their understanding of his motivations on his tombstone: "He migrated to Africa in the year 1853, leaving behind a large family, owing to the oppressive laws then in force against colored men in the Southern States."[83] Some racially motivated indignity may have been the last straw; or perhaps it was political outrage combined with heartbreak over a broken engagement or even a slave sale in town. His sister Harriet, a year younger than Church but already a widow, seems to have died or moved away.[84] Perhaps Church had been planning his departure for months, or maybe he decided only when he encountered the families from Lancaster. By the time the group waited in Wilmington for their Liberia-bound ship, however, the original party of thirty-three had grown to thirty-four.

The ACS agent J. W. Lugenbeel finally caught up with Benjamin Jacobs and his party, now including Church Vaughan, at the rooming house they had rented in Wilmington in early November. Lugenbeel arrived after a month of traveling in North and South Carolina, gathering support for the American Colonization Society and recruiting emigrants. He was accompanied by a black man who posed as his servant but who, in fact, was working with him to solicit colonists for Liberia. Marshall Hooper had already lived in Liberia and was planning to travel back there when the *Joseph Maxwell* left Wilmington in late November. Vaughan may not have spoken much with Hooper during that initial meeting, in which Lugenbeel simply ascertained how many were with the Jacobs/Wright party and how they were doing. ("Take them all together, they are a very fine set of emigrants," was his assessment, "excepting the color—too much white in the paint—hardy looking, however; and very clever."[85]) But over the course of their month-long voyage to Liberia, Vaughan would come to know Hooper and his wife, the only passengers to have made the Atlantic voyage before. He would befriend the Hoopers' sixteen-year-old daughter Emily, a newly emancipated freedperson from Chapel Hill, North Carolina. And in learning their story, Vaughan would get a firsthand introduction to the hard bargains of the emigration project.[86]

Emily Hooper was deeply ambivalent about emigration to Liberia. On one level, she was grateful for the enormous sacrifice her father had made for her. On another, she was distressed about leaving her home in North Carolina. Pleased to be free from bondage, she had nonetheless heard enough about Liberia to anticipate severe hardships. Her parents, Marshall and Rachel Hooper, had gained their freedom in the 1840s, probably from his wages as a clerk in Fayetteville. With their last forty dollars, they had purchased two one-way fares to Liberia in 1849, leaving Emily and eighteen siblings or half-siblings behind in slavery. But they did not intend to part from them permanently: the Hoopers still owned a house and other property in Wilmington. After spending a couple of years getting on their feet in Liberia, they intended to return to North Carolina, sell their assets, and use the money to bring at least two of their children back with them to Africa.

For the first year or so, the Hoopers were reasonably successful, in spite of only limited ACS assistance. After landing in March 1849, they received their six months of rations and housing from the Colonization Society, though sometimes it came so late that a hungry Marshall Hooper inquired about returning home. At the very end of their term of support, they were finally granted land — during the rainy season, when it was nearly impossible to start building or planting, and with months to wait before a crop could be harvested. They survived that first rainy season in the riverine town of New Virginia, however, and they managed to build a house and plant cassava and potatoes, plus engage in some trade. Marshall Hooper also emerged as something of a community spokesman, forwarding a letter from twenty-one of his neighbors complaining about one of the society's agents. Two years after arriving in Liberia, Hooper was "doing as every enterprising and industrious man will do," a missionary wrote to the Colonization Society, "—well."[87]

From Liberia, Mr. and Mrs. Hooper managed to stay informed about their family in North Carolina, and in 1852 they learned that three of the children were about to be sold. Again using the last of their cash, Marshall and Rachel Hooper frantically arranged to get back to Fayetteville, hoping that they could come up with the money to purchase the children themselves. Arriving in North Carolina that summer, they found out that their former owner, Caroline Mallett Hooper, had not sold the children as they feared. A resident of Alabama since her marriage sixteen years earlier, Mrs. Hooper was on her way out of town, but she agreed to negotiate with Marshall Hooper for his youngest child upon her return. Meanwhile, Marshall Hooper also hoped to free his daughter Emily, who was owned by Sarah (Sallie) Mallett of Chapel Hill, Caroline Hooper's sister. Mallett agreed to free Emily in exchange for six hundred dollars, a sum Hooper hoped he could raise.[88]

Hooper seems not to have been able to liquidate his Wilmington property. Instead, his strategy drew on his roots in Fayetteville and his existing connections to the American Colonization Society. In early August, he arranged to be commissioned as an ACS recruitment agent, paid five dollars for every person he persuaded to embark for Liberia in its expedition planned for mid-November. "One thing it seemed to me would be important in your case," warned the society's corresponding secretary William McLain, "is that you should return to Liberia yourself; and that it should be known that you intended to return. Without this, it appears to me, only few would believe your account of it." Hooper assured McLain that "my whole energy is for the goals of the Colonization Society, as through my own exertions and with some aid from the Society I hope to effect the liberation of three of my children and with them and my wife expect to return and spend the remainder of my life in Liberia."[89]

Over the next three months, Marshall Hooper visited free blacks and slaves, concentrating on his home territory in eastern North Carolina and following networks of his former master's dispersed family in Fayetteville, Raleigh, Hillsborough, and Chapel Hill. In spite of his intense motivation to recruit emigrants, Hooper conveyed a realistic sense of life in Liberia. A white man who spoke with him in Lumberton, North Carolina, determined him to be "honest and perfectly sincere," but got the impression from him that "there must be a very great change in the character of both the government and people of Liberia before it can amount to much." He concluded that while colonization was "desirable to the white people" as a way of "getting rid of the free colored people with least injury to them," it represented "the least of two evils to the blacks." Perhaps in spite of his candor, by mid-September, Hooper was able to inform the secretary of the Colonization Society that he "had the promise of about 100 to go. They are mostly young people, and some of them of a superior class." This prompted ACS officials in Washington to send Lugenbeel, a medical doctor and former agent in Liberia now working for the society in Washington, D.C., to coordinate the migration from North Carolina.[90]

Lugenbeel arrived in Raleigh in early October, "considerably fatigued" and not at all happy with his food and accommodations there (he preferred the fare in Fayetteville). A few days later he met Hooper, whom he described as "a less intelligent man than I expected to find," though "very respectful and clever." Hooper described his plight to the society's agent, informing him that he was very anxious to free Emily, that he had only a fraction of the necessary sum, and that he hoped that the ACS would assist with the outstanding balance. Lugenbeel made no promises beyond assuring Hooper that his organization would honor the agreement to pay him five dollars per emigrant recruited. Meanwhile, Hooper tried to negotiate with Emily's owner, Sallie Mallett, but she would not budge on the cost. She did agree to have Emily "in readiness to be delivered to her parents, at her price," although she took the girl to Fayetteville for an extended stay with relatives.[91]

Lugenbeel and Hooper spent the next few weeks traveling together, soliciting recruits, and bucking up the nerve of those who had already promised Hooper that they would emigrate. To save money on transportation, they hired a horse and carriage "as a gentleman and his servant." Already in Raleigh, Lugenbeel had complained not only that the volunteers were a "very sorry set," but that "I very much doubt whether one half will go to Wilmington to embark for Liberia." Now in Fayetteville, local whites reported to him that many of "Hooper's people" were having second thoughts. Lugenbeel had no sympathy for the obstacles they faced in leaving everything they knew for an uncertain future: "foolish creatures," he carped, "they allow every little difficulty to thwart them. 'Can't sell my house.' 'Can't sell my lot.' 'Money owing to me, can't get it.' Etc. Etc." Hooper was no doubt more sympathetic to their problems, but his own plight made him desperate to persuade them to go.[92]

By late October, Marshall Hooper was preoccupied with the fate of his children and seemed to be making little progress. Corresponding Secretary McLain declined to write to Emily Hooper's mistress until he had a better idea of how many recruits would actually go to Liberia and thus how much the society would owe Marshall. "What on earth any man means by having *19 children* I cannot imagine!" he wrote to Lugenbeel. "You may tell Hooper so!"[93] In Fayetteville, Lugenbeel met with Caroline Hooper, the Alabama-based owner of Marshall Hooper's three youngest children, as well as with Emily's owner Sallie Mallett, who was visiting from Chapel Hill. Mallett repeated that she was willing to "hold [Emily] in readiness for him, if he can raise the money," but she insisted that the six hundred dollar price was firm. Her sister was even less cooperative. Mrs. Hooper, Lugenbeel learned, "hates him [Marshall Hooper], but for his wife's sake, she may be willing to sell the youngest child." This little boy was less than ten years old, but Caroline

Hooper wanted four or five hundred dollars for him, which Marshall did not have, especially since he lacked even the money to free Emily. He hoped to be able to raise two hundred dollars on his own in North Carolina, to add to the money the ACS would pay him for recruiting emigrants, but he would still come up short. Neither Lugenbeel nor McLain offered the Colonization Society's help with the remaining balance.[94]

The ACS had scheduled the *Joseph Maxwell* to embark for Liberia on November 20, 1852. Around November 10, Marshall Hooper handed Lugenbeel $198, all that he had been able to raise for his daughter's freedom. He had convinced sixty-nine Fayetteville African Americans to emigrate, which should have earned him an additional $345 from the Colonization Society. Lugenbeel also agreed to pay him $75 for recruiting fifteen members of a Raleigh family named Pediford, though they were traveling on a different voyage embarking from Norfolk, Virginia.[95] Thus, Hooper had $618 to his credit, more than enough for his daughter Emily, but insufficient to also free his young son. Having left her children once already, Marshall Hooper's wife was especially anguished by the prospect of setting sail without her "baby boy," as Lugenbeel wrote. But the Mistress Hooper "*hates* him [Marshall] with a perfect vengeance, and she doesn't want *him* to have the boy anyhow." Even if she were to consent to sell him, the price would be far beyond what the Hoopers could afford. "And there's another dilemma!" Lugenbeel complained. "Where's the money to come from?"[96]

Lugenbeel feared that without their youngest child, the Hoopers would not go back to Liberia after all—which might cause many of the emigrants they had recruited to back out too. In fact, a mutual acquaintance in Wilmington informed Lugenbeel that Hooper preferred not to return to Liberia. "He is in for it, however," Lugenbeel concluded, "and I shall make him toe the mark, if possible." So that Hooper would not "fly the track," Lugenbeel informed him that he intended to purchase Emily in his own name, and would only transfer the title to her father once the family was actually aboard ship. At that, Hooper "exhibited one of those wild, significant looks, which seemed to be expressive of distrust and disappointment"—furious, no doubt, that Lugenbeel was using Emily as a hostage to ensure the family's compliance with ACS plans. But his hands were tied. Should Marshall "attempt to play any trick, so that she [Emily] shall not go [to Liberia]," Lugenbeel wrote to the society's secretary, "I shall certainly advertise her as my slave."[97]

Because the Hoopers and Malletts were spread over eastern North Carolina and into Alabama, Emily Hooper must have already been separated from many of her enslaved brothers and sisters. But in claiming her freedom and departing for Liberia, she had to face the prospect of never seeing them again. As the *Joseph Maxwell* left the port of Wilmington on that blustery day in 1852, perhaps her parents consoled her, and themselves, by promising to continue with their efforts on behalf of her siblings. In fact, three years later her father again traveled to Fayetteville in another futile attempt to rescue her younger brother from slavery.[98] Meanwhile, during the voyage the Hoopers must have continued to fulminate to fellow passengers about Lugenbeel's duplicity and the painfully partial victory over slavery their family had achieved.

The *Joseph Maxwell* spent forty days "wafting over the deep blue sea," as Marshall Hooper later recounted. "We had a good time under Captain Ferrell," he continued; "he is quite a gentleman."[99] Whatever meaning might lay behind that oblique compliment, the voyage was mostly an ordinary one. After the initial activity of loading the ship and setting sail, life onboard settled into a routine, punctuated by sickness, birth, and death.

Like the other passengers, Church Vaughan was allocated a sleeping berth below deck in the large emigrants' cabin, made more comfortable with a mattress brought from home. According to the Colonization Society's rules, each adult emigrant was allowed to bring the equivalent of two barrels in bulk, or ten cubic feet, in addition to bedding for the voyage, while children were allotted proportionately less luggage space. The travelers packed clothing, tools such as axes and handsaws, farming implements like hoes, spades, and rakes, cooking utensils and tableware, and other items such as nails, cotton fabric, seeds, salted provisions, and money—the items they would most need to start their lives in Liberia. Emigrants with means could bring more—articles of furniture and boxes of goods charged as freight at $1.50 per barrel, stowed in the ship's cargo hold.[100] Though the emigrants' cabin did have some windows, it was too stuffy and nauseating to spend much time there. Consequently, Vaughan and the others mostly stayed on deck, breathing the sea air and feeling the increasingly warm rays of the sun.

With no oceangoing experience, Church must have shared with his shipmates the near-universal experience of seasickness. As a traveler on an 1856 expedition to Liberia observed, within the first day of sailing, "some dropped on deck, some slid below, some groaned, some tried to brave it out with a laugh. But all joined in a general regurgitation or casting up of accounts. . . . For three days, scarce an emigrant was seen on decks, and it was almost impossible to keep the between decks in a tolerable condition." The two water closets provided for some 150 queasy passengers must have been overwhelmed. Only gradually did most people become accustomed to the sway of the ship; and regular, if monotonous, patterns of maritime life began to take shape.[101]

Passengers well enough to eat were divided into "messes" for meals, each with a head who was responsible for distributing food and water rations. Women from each family did the cooking in the galley, producing two meals every day from the ACS-provided beef and pork, cornmeal, molasses, and other supplies. Marshall Hooper, again a self-appointed leader, took over the distribution of rations, over Captain Ferrell's objections. After breakfast, literate passengers like Vaughan offered tutoring to children and the unschooled, while others read, talked, sewed and mended, or sang songs. Hymns were popular, augmented by organized prayers twice a day. After dinner, as many as three-dozen children frolicked while even some adults danced on deck. Vaughan and the other skilled men—seven other carpenters, two wheelwrights, a blacksmith, a bricklayer, two plasterers, a cooper, and a ship-carpenter—may have undertaken some small projects, or looked with interest at the construction of the ship. Mothers with infants, seven in all, cradled their babies or strapped them on their backs. The teenaged girls—Sarah Jane Wright, Arabella Jacobs, and Emily Hooper, all aged sixteen—likely clustered together. After sunset, most passengers retreated below deck for bed, leaving the last few talking quietly while gazing at the sea.[102]

Two events brought momentous breaks from the maritime rhythm. On December 1, the ninth day since leaving shore, old Ephraim Wilson passed away. He had traveled on his own, perhaps like Church Vaughan the only one of his family willing to make the voyage. His body did not hold out long enough to breathe the air of Africa, in spite of the hopes that had motivated his trip. He was old enough to have been born there. Perhaps he told his story to Church before he died, inspiring the young man many years later to keep his name alive among his own descendants. A few more days into the voyage, the women who likely tended Old Mr. Wilson were needed to attend a passage of a different kind: twenty-seven-year-old Beda Williams, traveling from Chapel Hill with her family, gave birth to her fifth child. She and her husband Charles named their new daughter Mary Maxwell in honor of the Africa-bound vessel.[103]

Without his family, Vaughan must have felt deeply isolated on the month-long trip. Perhaps he found companionship with the two other unaccompanied men around his age, twenty-eight-year-old James Richardson from Savannah, Georgia, and twenty-one-year-old John Smith from

Charleston. Both of them were recently freed ex-slaves, though Smith was literate like Vaughan. Four of the Fayetteville passengers were unmarried and around his age — siblings Nancy and Henry Johnson, a bricklayer named James Ford, and carpenter Hales Payne — as were a brother and sister from Chapel Hill named James and Keziah Boon. He may have stayed close to the group from Lancaster, South Carolina, that he had joined when he left Camden, and in fact he probably took his meals with them. Francis Jacobs, twenty-eight, and his sisters, twenty-one-year-old Mahalia and eighteen-year-old Martha, were all around Church's age. But it may have been their younger sister Arabella Jacobs who captured Church's heart, at least temporarily. The evenings became warmer as the *Joseph Maxwell* moved toward the equator, and perhaps Church and Arabella gazed together over the moonlit waters, speculating about new lives in a place they could hardly imagine. Though he eventually lost track of her, memories of these nights may have been with Church Vaughan thirty years later, when he named his youngest child Aida Arabella.

Names mattered for the Vaughans. Church's family tree is full of re-peated first names — Burrell, Sarah, Nancy, Maria — that pay homage to im-portant people in the family's past. And so it is possible to speculate that later in his life, Vaughan carried with him the memory of several shipmates from this voyage to Liberia. For Marshall Hooper, "one thing always cast a gloom over the whole 5,000 miles" of their journey to Liberia. "It's my chil-dren, my children," he lamented. "Oh! My children!"[104] Having said goodbye forever to his family, Church must have felt keenly the Hoopers' anguish. He could take comfort, though, that his mother, brother, and sisters lived as free people, at least somewhat safe from the exactions and potential abuse of white masters. Emily Hooper and her parents had no such consolation. Only recently liberated herself, she knew more than anyone what her baby brother and other siblings were left to endure. Church may have commiserated with the girl, just two years older than his little sister Mary. He may have stayed close to her once they landed in Liberia. And some twenty years later, though there were no women with the name in his family, he called his first-born daughter Emily, perhaps in homage to this memorable fellow traveler.

In countless hours of conversation, as they attended sickness, death, and birth, the passengers on the *Joseph Maxwell* and other emigrant vessels formed bonds of sympathy and friendship akin to those forged by shipmates in the trans-Atlantic slave trade. In fact, it could not have been lost on any of the adult passengers that they were reversing the ocean crossing their enslaved African forebears had endured. Although five out of every six of the ship's passengers had been born free, they all came from states where slavery flourished, and where the color of their skin marked them as noncitizens descended from captive Africans. They may have shared the sentiment of another emigrant from North Carolina, who wrote to the Colonization Society in 1853 that the desire to go to Africa had been "abirdon [a burden] on my mind ever since I was a boy of fourteen years old hearing my mother tell aBought [about] her grandfather being kidnapped and brought from His mother country."[105] For his part, Church Vaughan probably dwelled on Scipio's deathbed advice as he sailed ever farther from home. Many years later, his descendants would say that his voyage from the United States to Africa reversed one his own enslaved father had made. When he landed in Liberia on the first day of 1853, however, it was not exactly into the warm embrace of his motherland. As Church would find out, his journey was more complicated than leaving a land of slavery for one of freedom.

three

THE LOVE OF LIBERTY

Five months after Church Vaughan arrived in Liberia, in May 1853, settlers held an election. It had been six years since Liberia had become an independent republic, its constitution largely modeled on that of the United States except for a few key provisions. Slavery was illegal, for one thing, and only "Negroes or persons of Negro descent" were eligible for citizenship, property holding, or public office.[1] Liberia's president, Joseph J. Roberts, was a former free Virginian who had emigrated in the 1820s and built up a profitable trading business. For six years before independence, he had served as the American Colonization Society's governor of Liberia; now he was standing for his fourth two-year term as president. As Vaughan could read in the *Liberia Herald*, the settler newspaper, Roberts had intended to retire from politics but had been prevailed upon by some of Liberia's leading men to stand for one more term. His opponent, chief justice of the Supreme Court Samuel Benedict, took little issue with Roberts's performance as president, but argued that Liberia's political system would benefit from a change of administration.

Church's recent allocation of land from the Liberian government entitled him to vote for the first time in his life, though it is unknown whether or not he actually cast a ballot. No one in Liberia's capital, however, could miss the celebration of Roberts's re-election that took place after the results were announced. The morning of May 20, 1853, began with a barrage of gunfire heralding the daylong postelection festival. At nine o'clock A.M., a fleet of boats and canoes, many decorated with flags and pendants, arrived from other American settlements and were met at the harbor by a delegation from Monrovia. After landing, the participants organized themselves into groups representing different towns and villages, each with its own banner, and together with a band of musicians, they marched in procession to President Roberts's residence. Hundreds of spectators were already assembled outside, cheering as the president and his vice president-elect emerged. One of the banners read, "We are happy without a change." The crowd's enthusiasm continued during several speeches, including those by President Roberts and Vice President Stephen Benson. Then, under orange trees opposite the home of one of Monrovia's prosperous traders, lunch was served at a table set for three hundred gentlemen. Meanwhile, Mrs. Roberts entertained the same number of Liberian ladies at the president's house. After lunch, the president and vice president paraded in a richly decorated carriage through the streets of downtown Monrovia to the president's mansion, "followed by the largest political concourse ever assembled in Liberia." At seven o'clock that night, the crowd was treated to a fireworks display, and they ended the evening singing patriotic songs composed especially for the occasion.[2]

If Church Vaughan had left the United States frustrated that black people there could never truly be free, he had firm grounds for optimism when he stepped foot on African soil for the first time the previous January. Two years earlier, nineteen-year-old Edward Blyden, later to become one of Liberia's foremost intellectuals, had been so moved when he landed at Monrovia that he had penned a poem, which began: "Liberia, happy land! To thee/The oppressed colored man may flee;/Thy pleasant, thy delightful shore/To him true freedom will restore!"[3] Indeed, within six months of his arrival in Liberia, Church was able to assume more of the rights and duties of citizenship than he had in his twenty-four years in South Carolina. He trained with the militia and was dispatched to military duty; he received a land grant from the government to establish his own homestead; and he was eligible to vote. Moreover, he could make a good living as a carpenter. Yet less than three years after he arrived, when presented with the opportunity to leave Liberia—for a place reputed to be roiled by warfare and slave trading, no less—he took it. Why was he not more attached to his new home?

The answer to this question does not appear in any written record, as Church Vaughan left behind scarcely a trace of his life in Liberia. He may have composed letters to his family, but if so they did not pass through the American Colonization Society's corresponding secretary, as some settlers' letters did. In fact, Church did not come to the attention of ACS officials at all. Nor is he mentioned in surviving accounts from fellow settlers, or in the Liberian press. Though it is possible to piece together his experiences based on records of those who knew him, Church himself either kept a low profile in Liberia, achieving neither spectacular success nor scandalous ruin, or he produced a paper trail that has not survived.

The latter is certainly a reasonable proposition. In 1980, the long-simmering resentment of so-called "country" Liberians (that is, those indigenous to the area) against the descendants of American settlers finally boiled over. A military coup toppled the government of President William Tolbert, whose True Whig political party had dominated Liberian politics to the benefit of Americo-Liberians for most of the country's history. Then, between 1989 and 2003, Liberians endured civil war and horrific violence, which killed some 250,000 people and displaced many thousands of others. In Monrovia, archives were looted, and most of the country's historical documents were lost. More than a decade after the end of the war, archivists and historians are only beginning the painstaking process of reconstructing, and reconsidering, Liberian history.[4]

Church Vaughan's alienation from Liberia was likely connected to the same historical process that brought about the country's devastation more than a century later. As he learned, settler society was in its own way as exclusive and exploitative as the one he had left behind in South Carolina. As in North America, colonialism in Liberia was built on land expropriated from native people. From the beginnings of American settlement, a series of military battles and lopsided treaties had either displaced local Dey, Golah, Bassa, Vai and other peoples or else brought them under the "protection" of the Liberian administration, subject to the foreigners' laws and unfavorable trading agreements. Liberia's boosters described this process as bringing civilization to savage Africans, especially since one of their goals was to stop slave trading between local leaders and transatlantic purchasers. Yet Liberians' use of indigenous labor for their own enterprises came awfully close to slavery itself, as some of Church's contemporaries pointed out. In South Carolina, Church Vaughan had been neither a slave nor a master, but he knew about labor exploitation and group prejudice. Liberia's official motto, emblazoned to this day on its official seal, proclaims, "The love of liberty brought us here." Yet Church may well have wondered — as Liberians in our own time have too — what exactly that liberty entailed, and for whom.

Church's first sight of Liberia's shores came in late December 1852, more than four weeks after the *Joseph Maxwell* left port. Rising over a thousand feet above sea level was Grand Cape Mount, a broad-based, pyramid-shaped hill jutting into the ocean forty miles northwest of Monrovia. Its plateau extends for miles to a chain of still higher and more broken hills, the whole

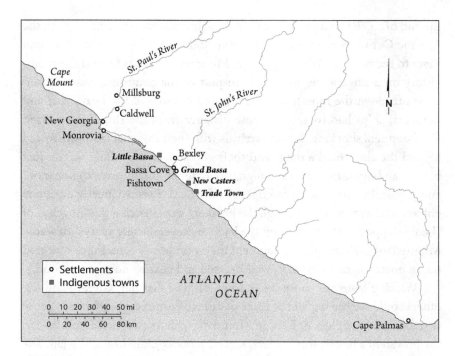

Settlements in Colonial Liberia

area covered with a thick forest. A visitor who saw it less than a year after Church did was spellbound: "The Cape and country adjoining appeared to me the most beautiful scene I ever beheld."[5] For Church Vaughan and the other passengers, the dramatic sight must have seemed like a good omen.

Three days later, on January 1, 1853, they reached their destination: Cape Mesurado, the location of Liberia's capital Monrovia. "One who has never been in the torrid zone can form no just conception of the exuberance, and I may say, intensity of tropical vegetation," wrote the missionary Thomas Jefferson Bowen—whom Church would later meet—about landing there three years previously. From the ship, Church and his fellow passengers could see the brown sand of the beach and its bubbling white foam, leading quickly to the Cape Mesurado promontory, which rises some 250 feet "like a heavy cloud of vegetation over the sea." Arriving during West Africa's dry season, the new immigrants were already feeling heat and humidity like that of the South Carolina summer, with the addition of the dusty harmattan wind blowing in from the Sahara. As they peered at the horizon through the haze, they must have pondered, as Bowen had, "what strange rivers, towns and people were there in the unknown countries to which we were going."[6]

Cape Mesurado, named centuries earlier by Portuguese explorers, forms the end of an elevated peninsula stretching northwest to southeast, with the Atlantic Ocean more or less on its south and west sides and the Mesurado River to the north and flowing inland. Monrovia itself sits behind the promontory on a ridge along the northern part of the peninsula, best reached by sea through the mouth of the river. But because of the heavy surf and sandbars, ships had to anchor some distance from the shore. Specialized Kru boatmen, shocking the new arrivals with their minimal clothing, rowed toward the ship to take them and their goods over the rolling waves. Just before landing, if the sea was rough, the Krumen might leave their canoes and physically carry their passengers to dry land. Even so, nearly everyone got wet as they ventured through the breakers, experiencing the "novelty" of "being slapped in the face, or on the back, by several white sprays" of water. Monrovians — always glad to augment their numbers — sometimes ventured out in boats to greet the ships, well-dressed and bearing flowers and food.[7]

Walking from the shore up to town on that first day, Church and the others could see the imprint of three decades of American settlement. Some two thousand people now lived in Monrovia, which contained a state house, the president's house, warehouses, stores, schools, churches, and a jail. The main thoroughfare, Broadway (these days a boulevard called Broad Street), ran parallel to the river, with cross streets at roughly equal intervals. The town was divided into spacious lots, each intended to accommodate one dwelling, though some were still empty and overgrown. Church's carpenter's eye could appreciate the many two-story houses, with lower levels built from stone and used for servants, storage, and businesses, and wooden upper floors for living spaces. But the tropical climate and dense foliage left their mark: brambles crept into every clearing, and wood softened under pressure of the elements. A disappointed contemporary of Church's grumbled, "I know places in the streets of Monrovia, in which elephants might hide in perfect safety."[8] Yet the grassy spaces meant opportunity for Church, who ultimately would make his living carving American-style buildings into the lush Liberian landscape. For now, though, he and his shipmates faced their own problem of where to live in their new environment — and indeed, if they would live at all.

The passengers on the *Joseph Maxwell* had been told all along that their new homes would be at Millsburg, a settlement about twenty miles up the nearby St. Paul's River from Monrovia, where conditions were supposed to be favorable for farming.[9] But the houses the Colonization Society had arranged to be built were not yet ready, and the task of accommodating the newcomers fell to its overworked agent, Henry Dennis. Twenty-five years old and nearly a lifelong resident of Liberia, having immigrated with his family as a child, Dennis impressed observers as "an honest, upright, faithful and attentive agent," if perhaps too forgiving of the Colonization Society for its paltry pay and disorganization.[10] He managed to arrange temporary lodging for the new arrivals in an empty warehouse owned by General John Lewis, a longtime settler who simultaneously served as commander in chief of Liberia's armed forces, secretary of state, a Baptist missionary, and a private merchant. Church Vaughan and the other passengers from the *Joseph Maxwell* made camp there while they awaited their next move.[11] Eight days later, Krumen rowed the *Joseph Maxwell* shipmates up Stockton Creek, which connects Monrovia to the St. Paul's River, and then beyond to Millsburg, where they hoped that housing awaited them.

Millsburg had been founded twenty-five years earlier when Dey leaders ceded this sparsely populated river landing for the equivalent of about twenty-five dollars. The town was intended to be a settlement of farming families and a commercial entrepôt. A road connected Millsburg to the interior town of Bopolu, bringing African-produced trade goods into the colony. Yet its distance from Monrovia and high density of deadly mosquitoes — given the river's low banks at that point — rendered Millsburg a sleepy, very small town. Though 435 immigrants had been sent there by 1844, ten years later there were only 355, spread out on both sides of the river and bordered by a "half town of natives." By then, settlers were taking up land elsewhere along the St. Paul's River. A missionary traveling along the waterway in 1851 reported that "the banks had been generally cleared, farms laid out and planted, and comfortable cottages erected — as exhibiting nature in her primitive wildness, but blended with cultivation."[12]

The immigrants from the *Joseph Maxwell* experienced more of the primitive wildness than the cultivation, since their accommodations were still not ready when they got to Millsburg. Dennis managed to rent tiny rooms for some of them, in spite of charges so expensive that he was not sure how they would be paid. The rest of the newcomers were assigned hastily built, thatched huts plastered with mud. Though each contained only a single room and a loft, whole families of up to fifteen people were crowded inside. At least it seldom rained; after about May, the huts' leaky roofs would make it impossible for inhabitants to stay dry, even in their beds.[13]

Church's shipmate Marshall Hooper, enterprising as always, tried to make the best of the situation. Though he already owned a house at New Virginia, the nearest to Monrovia of the St. Paul's River settlements, Hooper did not return there. Instead, he left his wife Rachel and daughter Emily at

Millsburg, Liberia, with a glimpse of the St. Paul's River, 2012. Photo by the author.

New Virginia and accompanied the others to Millsburg, where he applied to Dennis for a formal position as colonization subagent. Though he needed the help, Dennis was wary of hiring Hooper, who could neither read nor write and who, in the agent's opinion, had been too liberal with the immigrants' provisions on board the *Joseph Maxwell* and upon landing at the wharf. Another Colonization Society agent, Ralph Moore, had been the subject of Hooper's complaint on behalf of a group of settlers a couple of years previously. Now he chimed in that Hooper had taken advantage of his fellow *Joseph Maxwell* passengers by buying the gunpowder they had brought with them for twenty-five cents per pound on board the ship, but then selling it back to them after landing for a dollar a pound. Though he hired another subagent, Dennis arranged for Hooper to receive ACS food rations for six months, as the other newcomers did and as he had already done once, in exchange for his assistance in helping the immigrants get settled.[14]

Two months after they arrived in Millsburg, Hooper composed an anguished letter to his former traveling companion, the colonization official James Lugenbeel, now back in Washington, D.C. After invoking his heartbreak at leaving his children in North Carolina, he bemoaned the immigrants' current plight: "Twelve have died! Namely, three of Quiney Young's children died, Mr. and Mrs. Wadle is dead; Patsy Boon! Old Mr. Wright of South Carolina and Peter Jacobs of South Carolina. William Johnson who was sick before we left Fayetteville is dead and J Johnson's wife +6!! All the rest are better."[15] In Millsburg's squalid conditions, the *Joseph Maxwell* shipmates had contracted dysentery, aggravated by sickness from the voyage and new infections of yellow fever or malaria. According to J. S. Smith, the settler doctor who had been hired to treat them, two of them also showed signs of tuberculosis, while "the leg of one was bent into a bow by white swelling and large portions of bone coming away." Soon after, two others died of sunstroke.[16] Dr. Smith administered morphine and opium to treat the rampant dysentery, but his supplies soon ran out. His own contraction of the disease put a stop to even these limited efforts.[17]

Death loomed over Liberian settlers, no matter how long they had been in Africa. The main killer was malaria, whose cause and transmission were only vaguely understood, along with yellow fever and other tropical ailments. Colonization Society recruiters tried to downplay the dangers, and those who lived often attributed their survival to particular hygiene regimens, clothing, or diets. But the mortality rate was astronomical, especially in the first year of acclimation, during which nearly a quarter of all settlers died. Although 4,571 African Americans had immigrated to Liberia during the first twenty-three years of settlement, the Liberian census of 1843 reported only 2,388 people living in that year. By the time Church arrived, more than 7,300 Americans had come to Liberia, but the settler population was still estimated, with improbable optimism, at just over 6,000. Settlers' spouses, children, friends, and relatives succumbed in such great numbers that in letters home, their accounts of good health seem just as noteworthy as the death notices.[18]

The *Joseph Maxwell* contingent was sickly even by Liberian standards. Two days after they arrived in Liberia, another vessel, the *Linda Stewart*, dropped anchor off Monrovia, landing 172 passengers who had embarked in Norfolk, Virginia. Some of them were acquaintances of the immigrants from the *Joseph Maxwell*, having come from Raleigh and Fayetteville, North Carolina. In fact, Marshall Hooper had recruited one of the families onboard, that of twenty-eight-year-old carpenter Sewell Pettiford, his parents, and two other relatives.[19] While everyone rejoiced in their safe landing, the colonization agent Dennis was overwhelmed, especially because he was already working to house and provision fifty-six settlers from the ship *Oriole*, which had arrived two months earlier. With General Lewis's warehouse already full, Dennis managed to accommodate a hundred or so members of the

Linda Stewart group in the Liberian senate's chambers, loaned by President Roberts. The remaining seventy were sent to the Colonization Society's "Receptacle" at New Virginia.[20]

Later, as he and Sewell Pettiford became friends, Church probably heard about conditions in the receptacle, which were even more fetid and unhealthy than at Millsburg. Originally built in 1847 to house captives liberated from slave ships, the receptacle already looked by the 1850s like an "old, shabby brick building" of one story, with a garret on top. The main floor was divided into twelve rooms of about eight by ten feet, with entire families of up to ten people crammed into each one. Gaps between the floorboards let in mud and insects, and the smell of rotting rations and human waste permeated the air. One small window adorned the exterior wall of each room, but lacking glass, it had to be closed during rains and at night, "thus making a suitable dungeon for a murderer," in the words of one appalled observer. The only furniture provided in each room was a rough bedstead made out of saplings, which shared space with barrels, boxes, cooking utensils, provisions, and whatever else the settlers brought from America. Food stores and chamber pots sloshed together under beds where the sick lay.[21]

Yet even there, new immigrants survived better than in Millsburg. By mid-March, only one of the settlers from the *Oriole* and three from the *Linda Stewart* had died, compared to twelve from the *Joseph Maxwell*. By the end of the next month, a total of twenty-one of Church's 149 shipmates had perished. Agent Henry Dennis was unable to explain the appalling mortality, other than that *"Millsburg is not a healthy place."*[22] Most painfully, Church lost Peter Jacobs, one of his traveling companions from South Carolina and the father of his new friend Arabella Jacobs.

Church may have been spared the terrible conditions at Millsburg himself, though. When nearly all of the *Joseph Maxwell* passengers had proceeded upriver, six of them stayed in Monrovia to await more housing.[23] Historical records do not name them, but they probably were men of working age, able to earn a living in the urban economy, and traveling without families. James Richardson, a freedman from Georgia, must have been one of them, since within a year he married Matilda Lomax, a widowed, longtime settler living in Monrovia.[24] Another was probably Church Vaughan. Even after he was eventually assigned farmland along the St. Paul's River, remaining in the capital would have appealed to Church, who had spent all his life in town and had no interest in farming. In Liberia's capital he could earn a living as a builder of houses and furniture. He also could witness the fullness of settler society and begin to exercise the rights and responsibilities of citizenship, for the first time in his life.

Less than three months after Church arrived in Liberia, most of its adult male settlers were called to militia duty. The republic's legislature had authorized a punitive expedition against African leaders at Cape Mount who were reported to be ignoring Liberian authority, attacking their neighbors, and harassing Liberian traders. Though military service was new to Church, seven years later he and his friend Sewell Pettiford would be described in Yorubaland as "Afro-American sharp-shooters, who harassed [their enemies] a good deal with their rifles."[25] On this occasion or later in the military service that was compulsory for all Liberian men, Church learned to handle a gun. He also began to understand the conflicts that pitted settlers against the Africans they were displacing.

Arriving in January, Church had just missed the annual celebration of Matilda Newport Day, during which, every December, settlers reenacted their earliest battle with local Africans. Within months of the first immigrants' arrival in 1822, the Dey leader King Peter, still ruing the land sale he had been forced to make, had organized a coalition of nearby African groups to destroy the colony. Though heavily outnumbered, the better armed settlers repulsed the invasion. The tide turned, allegedly, after a woman named Matilda Newport used her pipe to light one of the cannons — an event that probably never took place but is nonetheless depicted on a monument still standing in downtown Monrovia.[26] By early 1853, as Liberians prepared for yet another battle against Africans, they must have told newcomers like Church about their military history. Settlers took pride in having extended their territory along the coast and in establishing relatively secure trade routes to the interior. They also could claim credit for their role in curtailing the slave trade from Liberia's shores, a process connected, in their view, to the expansion of Liberian authority over local people.

When the initial contingents of African American settlers and Colonization Society agents had arrived at Cape Mesurado in the 1820s, they were appalled by the trade in human beings carried on practically within their sights. Great Britain, France, and the United States had outlawed Atlantic slave trading, but New World demand for enslaved Africans remained strong, especially in Cuba and Brazil. Although most of the captives forcibly taken to the Americas in the 1820s originated elsewhere in Africa, perhaps as many as two thousand were exported per year from the less-than-one-hundred-

Matilda Newport monument, Monrovia, Liberia. Photos by William E. Allen.

mile stretch of coastline between Grand Cape Mount in the north and Monrovia in the south.[27] These war prisoners, victims of raids, and condemned criminals were supplied by African political leaders to a number of locally based, foreign-born traders who were well adapted to the illegal trade. Since slave ships could no longer linger on the African coast picking up captives as they became available, dealers like the Spaniard Don Pedro Blanco and his French-Italian agent Theophilus Conneau became semipermanent residents in Africa. From their trading "factories" at the mouth of the Gallinas River near Sierra Leone or southeast of Monrovia at New Cesters, they carried on business with African suppliers, amassed captives in jail-like barracoons, negotiated their sale with visiting ship captains, and received payment from slave importers in Cuba.[28]

African American descendants of slaves, some of them freedpeople themselves, had not come to Africa to tolerate the slave trade.[29] In a series of battles in the 1820s and early 1830s, Liberians attacked and destroyed the barracoons in their vicinity and imposed antislave trading treaties on local chiefs, though these were often ignored.[30] In 1832, the Colonization Society's administrator Joseph Mechlin refused to return a Dey king's captives who ran away to the colony while awaiting sale. After a retaliatory attack by Dey forces and their Gola allies, a force of settler volunteers marched on their enemies and burned their towns. Seven years later, Liberia's Governor Thomas Buchanan organized a force of seventy-five volunteers to attack a slave factory south of Monrovia at Little Bassa. Peyton Skipwith, a Liberian from Virginia who participated in the attack, recounted that "we went down and broke up the factory and brought away all the effects say in goods and destroyed about fifty puncheons [of] Rum . . . the effect in goods &c to the amt of ten thousand Dollars. After we had taken the goods or a part we had to contend with the natives which fought us two days very hard but we got the victory and form a treaty before we left with one of the chiefs but not with the other and only got four slaves so we cannot say that we concluded a final peace." Buchanan reported with satisfaction, however, that his forces managed not only to capture the barracoon, but also took possession of a slave ship, the *Euphrates*, and exacted from two local chiefs an agreement for colonial jurisdiction over their territory.[31]

To the great frustration of colonization agents and Liberian settlers, however, the U.S. government offered them little support in fighting the slave trade. This is not surprising, given the political volatility of slavery in America, but it contrasts sharply with the attitude of the United Kingdom. To enforce its 1808 ban on international slaving, the British government sent its navy to patrol the African coast, intercept slave ships, and land the captives they rescued at its colony in Sierra Leone. Moreover, British diplomats secured treaties by which France and other major European powers agreed to abolish their slave trades, with Portugal pledging to end slave trading north of the equator. In order to enforce those treaties, Britain exacted from France, Spain, Portugal, Brazil, and several other countries the right to search suspected slave ships and detain those found to be slavers. Between 1817 and the end of 1840, the British Navy intercepted 468 slave ships, landing approximately sixty-seven thousand "recaptives" in Sierra Leone.[32] Moreover, as the Liberian settler Peyton Skipwith reported that year to his former master in Virginia, "Within the last month . . . the Large [slave trading] Establishment of [Pedro] Blanco has been destroyed by one of his Majesties ships of war. It is said that they took one thousand slaves from that factory and destroyed and taken to the amount of one hundred thousand Dollars. Kennet [Canot's] factory, under the same firm, has been given up by him to one of the cruisers with one Hundred slave and put himself under the protection of the English. He has been since that to the Town of Monrovia and was admitted to come on shore and he has proceeded to see the ruins of that splendid slave factory at Galenas that was belong[ing to] that rich man Blanco."[33]

Lacking Britain's enthusiasm for antislavery and sensitive over the issue since even before the War of 1812, the United States government refused to allow British naval officers to search American-flagged vessels. Instead, Americans promised to send their own ships to police the Atlantic—which happened rarely and without much effect. Consequently, slavers of all nations carried the Stars and Stripes, which they ran up their masts as protection against British searches. As Liberia's Governor Buchanan protested in 1839, "The chief obstacle to the success of the very active measures pursued by the British government for the suppression of the slave-trade on the coast is the *American flag*. Never was the proud banner of freedom so extensively used by those pirates upon liberty and humanity, as at this season."[34] Settler Peyton Skipwith agreed, fulminating to his former master in Virginia that "I see daily the Star Spangled Banner unfurled on the coast of Africa as a protection for the slaver to keep the British man of wars from taking them[,] which we think as a hand full of people to that of the United States a disgrace to her Banner."[35] Under pressure from Britain, the American government agreed in 1842 to reorganize its navy's previously haphazard antislavery patrols and maintain its own naval squadron on the African coast. Over its entire eighteen-year life span, however, the American antislavery squadron never consisted of more than eight vessels, and it captured only thirty-six slavers. In contrast, the British averaged nineteen ships on patrol at any one time, and between 1843 and 1861 they captured 595 slave ships.[36]

Liberians called for a stronger U.S. naval presence off their coast not only to deter slavers but also to support their claims to political sovereignty. British traders from Sierra Leone had refused to pay customs duties on goods purchased in Liberian territory, on the grounds that the Colonization Society did not constitute a national or colonial government. When Liberians and the ACS sought reinforcement from the United States, Secretary of State Daniel Webster clarified instead that Liberia was not an American colony and U.S. armed forces would not assist in regulating Liberian commerce. Without further recourse, Liberian leaders declared independence from the American Colonization Society in 1847. As an independence gift, Britain's Queen Victoria gave the Liberian government a steamer, the *Lark*, "to assist in destroying the slave trade on our coast," the *Liberia Herald* explained, "and for the protection of our revenue." It became the sole vessel in the Liberian Navy.[37]

Shortly after independence, President Roberts arranged for the purchase from African leaders of Gallinas and New Cesters, both regions notorious for slave trading, along with territory at Cape Mount. In seeking loans from Americans and Europeans in order to make it possible, he argued that settler control over a continuous stretch of coastline was the only sure means of suppressing the slave trade.[38] Indeed, immediately after the purchase of New Cesters, the Liberian government gave notice to slave traders that they should stop their business and export no more prisoners. The next year, however, the *Liberia Herald* reported that slaves were often transported in the vicinity of New Cesters and nearby Trade Town, and that the primary slave merchant there, a Spaniard named Don Francisco, "is as deeply engaged in [the slave trade] now as he ever was." This struck at Liberian antislavery values and national pride. As the settler newspaper editorialized, "If we are able to break up that establishment [the Spanish slave fort] and yet suffer it to remain, . . . we will most certainly be accused of winking at the slave trade. Yet to say we are not able to remove a few slavers is humiliating." Over the next several months, tensions mounted at New Cesters, with attacks on Liberians and their property and chiefs refusing to deliver those whom the Liberian authorities accused of the crimes.[39]

"No insult or wrong will as soon fill their ranks with volunteers, as the suppression of slavery," the settler and missionary John Day, then based just inland of Grand Bassa at Bexley, asserted about his fellow Liberians. In

March 1849, after President Roberts returned from a trip to France, "we were all commanded to get ourselves in order for the war, as we had to contend against an African tribe, called the New Cesters tribe," one of the settlers later recounted.[40] Some 350–400 volunteers were mustered at Monrovia for an expedition accompanied by President Joseph Roberts, commanded by General John Lewis, comprised of two regiments, and transported by the French steamer *Espado*. At New Cesters, opposing African troops were no match for the Liberian onslaught and cannon fire from the French steamer. The slave trader Don Francisco fled his establishment, leaving it empty. Over the following week, the Liberian regiments proceeded to settlements known as Joe West's Town and Trade Town, where another Spanish trader surrendered and promised to release some two thousand slaves to the Liberians at a later date.[41]

The victorious Liberian forces returned to Monrovia with a renewed sense of their power and mission. Solomon Page, one of the volunteers, wrote that "We were successful during the war, something which I did not expect or anticipate before we went." Another boasted, "A great many told me when I was in America that we could not take the Spanyards. We have got them in our town waiting for tryal. It proved as in all of the wars that God is on our side & if he be for us who can be against us. We have been oppressed long enough. We mean to stand our ground & contend for our rights until we die." John Day pointed out that this victory over slave traders was also a victory for Liberian territorial expansion. Eleven new headmen had put themselves under the "protection" of the Liberian republic, he reported, and many more were talking of doing so. "Our civil jurisdiction will now extend far and wide," he concluded. The editor of the *Liberia Herald* noted the enormous cost of the expedition, but asserted that its achievements were worth the outlay. "We cannot expect peace and quietness while the slave trade is going on near us," he wrote. "Nor can we hope to exert our full influence upon the surrounding tribes until the accursed traffic is wholly destroyed. When that most desirable object is accomplished, we shall then breathe freely."[42]

Soon, in fact, the suppression of the slave trade was largely accomplished, especially from the Windward Coast. In 1850, under strong British pressure, the Brazilian government passed legislation to enforce its treaties against slave trading, effectively ending the largest section of the Atlantic slave trade in the nineteenth century and leaving Cuba as the last remaining slave importer in the western hemisphere. Just a month before Church's arrival in Liberia, British naval forces destroyed a barracoon on the southern Sierra Leone coast, forcing its director, a slave trader named Crispo, to flee in his nightshirt. Slaving from Liberian ports had ended, and in Sierra Leone it was drastically reduced.[43]

By the time Church landed in 1853, settlers' clashes with nearby Africans centered not on slaving but on access to trade routes and territorial authority. Liberians insisted that Africans under their jurisdiction trade preferentially with merchants from the republic, rather than with British or other traders, provoking resistance from those whose fortunes suffered. Before he had left South Carolina, Church had heard from a relative in Philadelphia about an attack on the Liberian settlement at Fishtown in Bassa Cove, southeast of Monrovia. Now Liberians could tell him more: in November 1851, Kru-speaking people under the leadership of a chief named Grando killed ten settlers there, perhaps with the encouragement of British traders in the area. Two months later, a company of 550 Liberians and the same number of native troops launched a retaliatory attack so successful that, in the words of President Roberts, "It will convince the aboriginal inhabitants of every part of the Republic of the ability of the Government to maintain the majesty of the laws, and punish crime wherever committed within its jurisdiction."[44] Then-journalist Edward Blyden had not accompanied the Liberian troops, but instead had been assigned to guard duty in Monrovia while they were away. Though he recounted to a correspondent that "we have to struggle sir, to maintain our liberty," he was sure, like Solomon Page, that "God is on our side."[45]

Church had only been in Liberia for two weeks when settlers celebrated "with appropriate honors" the anniversary of the battle against Grando and the reoccupation of Fishtown.[46] Six weeks later, Liberians again mobilized to enforce Liberian authority over local Africans, this time at Cape Mount. As Matilda Lomax, the widow who would soon marry one of Church's shipmates, wrote to a correspondent in Virginia, the chiefs "have been intruding upon the Republick and [are] fond of arbitrary authority, in stopping the mart from coming in & that rouse[d] the citizen[s] & at last cause[d] the officers in chiefs to make a positive conclusion and they went to war."[47] But this conflict was more complicated than simply exerting colonial domination and protecting trade, and it revealed to Church and others that the end of trans-Atlantic slaving did not necessarily mean the end of forced labor or human trafficking.

Territory at Grand Cape Mount and Little Cape Mount had been purchased by the Liberian Republic shortly after independence. Few Liberians had settled there yet, though some conducted trade in the area. (These days, the beachside town of Robertsport, named after President Roberts, sits at

Cape Mount.) Still, local Dey, Vai and Golah groups had come under the "protection" of the Liberian government, which asserted the right to adjudicate their disputes. When Boombo, one of the Vai chiefs, launched repeated attacks on his Golah neighbors, they called on the Liberians for support. President Roberts organized several meetings of the local chiefs in 1851 and '52, but Boombo continued to disregard his authority; "indeed at one time," according to the *Liberia Herald*, "his reply to the Government was insulting." In late 1852, he finally went too far: extending his raids into Dey country, close to some of the Liberian settlements, "burning towns and villages, and murdering scores of the inoffensive inhabitants," Roberts charged, "as well as robbing several factories established there, owned by merchants of this place." This the Liberians would not tolerate, and in December 1852, as Church Vaughan sailed across the Atlantic, Roberts requested that the legislature authorize a military expedition to Cape Mount in order to either convince Boombo to make peace, or to expel him from the country.[48]

President Roberts told officials of the American Colonization Society that the cause of Boombo's aggression was "a restless disposition to make war for the sake of plunder." But shortly after the legislative resolution passed, he learned that the issue was more complicated than previously thought. The Cape Mount chiefs had another motivation for their raids, "strongly intimated by some of the country people, to obtain captives for a purpose — next of kin to the slave trade."[49] Though slave trading *per se* from the Liberian coast had come to an end, New World demand for labor had not, nor had mechanisms for supplying vulnerable people to meet that demand. The same British government that was working to enforce its ban on Atlantic slave trading, and that had abolished slavery in the entire British Empire in the 1830s, was now facing a severe shortage of labor in its sugar-producing West Indian colonies. In one of a number of initiatives to replace enslaved workers, the British government had granted a London-based commercial firm called Hyde, Hodge, & Co. a contract to supply African laborers to plantations in the British West Indies. Along with Boombo at Little Cape Mount, another chief based at Grand Cape Mount, known as George Cane, was also waging attacks against Dey and Golah people. Agents of Mssrs. Hyde and Hodge had visited Grand Cape Mount and offered George Cane ten dollars — formerly the cost of a slave — for each person the chiefs there could supply. In early 1853, word reached Liberian authorities that Cane intended to sell his prisoners as "emigrants" to the British firm. A month before the expedition to Cape Mount, President Roberts issued a proclamation mandating strict observance of the law governing passports and forbidding the

The Love of Liberty

sailing of any vessel with emigrants without first landing at Monrovia, where passengers would be interviewed.[50]

When word of Roberts's proclamation reached the British government, several members of the House of Lords insisted on the respectability of Mssrs. Hyde, Hodge & Company and the care taken by Her Majesty's Government to prevent the system from becoming one of slave trading. In his very diplomatic explanation, President Roberts stressed that he would never suspect the company's agents of engaging in anything resembling slave trading, and Liberians certainly had no intention of interfering in the legitimate procurement of voluntary laborers. (In fact, the Monrovia agent for Messrs. Hyde, Hodge, & Company was none other than Roberts's brother-in-law General Lewis.) "But the government had good grounds for believing that attempts would be made, by certain chiefs, to force persons to emigrate without the facts being known to the emigration agents."[51] And indeed, it was Boombo and Cane who were the objects of the Liberian expedition, which sailed for Little Cape Mount on March 1 with 250 men, Vaughan probably among them.

This time Edward Blyden was part of the militia, and he wrote a detailed account of his week-long adventure for the *Liberia Herald*. The mobilization began with great excitement in Monrovia, as the beating of drums and assembly of soldiers with their knapsacks and muskets attracted a crowd of spectators. Some of the soldiers were new recruits such as Church and Sewell Pettiford, and they awkwardly boarded the canoes that conveyed them to the schooner *Lark*, waiting at anchor. After a northward passage in which, predictably, many suffered from seasickness, they landed at Cape Mount. President Roberts sent a messenger to Boombo's town to invite him and George Cane to meet him on the beach, suggesting that he would be unarmed. "But it is evident that they did not expect to find so large a company of armed men as they did, from the expression of surprise which the countenance of Boombo assumed as he approached the soldiers whose glittering bayonets rendered their appearance at once grand and terrible." The Liberians then accompanied the chiefs inland about three hours' march to occupy Boombo's town. Over the next two days, as President Roberts summoned and then interviewed nearby headmen about the abuses committed by Boombo and Cane, the two chiefs tried several times to escape. Only George Cane managed to do so, early the third morning as the militiamen prepared to detain them for trial. Boombo and fifty-three others were taken against their will onto the *Lark* and hauled back to Monrovia.[52] After their hearing in Monrovia, Boombo was sentenced to make restitution for property damages, pay a five hundred dollar fine, and endure two years' imprisonment.[53] Though George Cane remained at large, Roberts declared victory as he had in 1851: "They [the natives] are now convinced on all sides of the ability of the Government to maintain its authority, and to punish any who may be disposed to violate these engagements."[54]

Few Liberians were aware that Boombo and George Cane's crimes were connected to British labor recruiters. The *Liberia Herald* reminded readers that Boombo broke his promises to the Liberian government "by carrying on predatory wars, destroying towns and murdering and carrying into captivity hundreds of inoffensive men, women and children."[55] But Blyden, who as a journalist and diplomat would later advocate for better relations between Liberian settlers and local Africans, was already beginning to doubt the typical settler portrayals of African barbarism. Though he was horrified by evidence of "the cruelty and bloody deeds of Boombo," he also was impressed by the elaborate barricade surrounding the chief's town. "This fortification appeared wonderful to me," he wrote, "and as I gazed upon the massive structure, I could not but admire the inventive genius of the natives, and reflect upon the unfairness of those who represent the native African as naturally indolent, and living in a state of ease and supineness."[56] Church, too, may have already begun to suspect that reality was messier than in the standard settler depictions. As he set about making a living in Liberia, he could see that it was not only African chiefs who could credibly be accused of keeping slaves.

By mid-April 1853, three months after their arrival in Liberia and a month after the expedition to Cape Mount, nearly all of the surviving passengers from the *Joseph Maxwell*, even those who had been left in Monrovia, had been assigned land along the St. Paul's River, opposite where they were then living at Millsburg. The Pettifords and other immigrants from the *Linda Stewart*, many still quartered in the Colonization Society's receptacle, were allocated plots at New Virginia and a nearby settlement called Kentucky (which later became known as Clay-Ashland, after colonizationist Henry Clay and his Ashland plantation).[57] As in other colonial societies where indigenous people were forcibly displaced, the challenge for settler would-be farmers was not securing land. Instead, it was controlling enough human labor to make the land productive. While Church opted out of farming altogether, other members of his community rose or fell according to their access to healthy family members, hirelings, or African "apprentices" who could perform the exhausting work of bringing food or cash crops out of the tropical soil.

As a single man, Church received a town lot in Millsburg, if he chose to occupy it, as well as an allocation of ten acres of farmland, while families were assigned twenty-five acres.[58] But farming was difficult. Compared to other groups of new arrivals, who had to trudge many miles to cultivate their fields and build their houses while they were "on the public," Church and his companions were well situated, their tracts just a canoe trip across the river from where they had been staying. Still, they had to clear dense vegetation on their plots before they could even plant, a task made more onerous by the absence of draft animals because of sleeping sickness infestation. Many people were still weak or ill much of the time.[59] To make matters worse, by May, when the settlers were finally recovering from most of their initial illnesses, the rainy season began with three weeks of near-continuous torrents—hardly conducive to building or planting. Nevertheless, in June, the Colonization Society agent H. W. Dennis reported that "our emigrants per *Linda Stewart* and *Joseph Maxwell* are now doing well and making rapid improvements on the St. Pauls." Even so, they would be off the Colonization Society's six months of support by July, while it would probably be September before the earliest of their food crops—likely the local staple cassava—would be ready to harvest. Only those who had brought enough money from home to purchase food could afford to wait.[60]

For new immigrants looking for signs that they might survive and even prosper, a few who did manage to amass substantial landholdings and grow cash crops such as coffee and sugar cane stood out. Some of the immigrants from the *Linda Stewart* went immediately to live with their cousin Sion Harris, who had come to Liberia in 1830 at the age of nineteen. Now this "true and independent farmer," as a correspondent from the *Liberia Herald* described him, owned 110 acres of land on the St. Paul's River, had recently built a large brick house, and served as a member of Liberia's House of Representatives.[61] In the St. Paul's settlement of Caldwell, William W. Findley, who emigrated from Indiana with his family in early 1851, had recently acquired a forty-acre farm, on which he had built a "pretty" white two-story house, surrounded by a grove of trees. His twenty acres of coffee were said to bring in annually about one dollar per tree.[62] The "most successful sugar manufacturer in Liberia" was Abraham Blackledge, a South Carolinian who had settled along the St. Paul's in the early 1840s. Within ten years, he was producing approximately 5000 pounds of sugar and 500 gallons of syrup per year, and had planted some 2,500 coffee trees. He too had built a large brick house, as well as a hand-powered sugar mill.[63]

Pioneering a farm, on his own, in a "bush" settlement remote from the hustle and bustle of Monrovia, could have held no appeal for a young man used to living in town, however. The twenty-four-year-old Church could support himself better by selling his services as a builder than with farming, which seemed almost impossible under the circumstances. Everywhere in Liberia, people needed carpenters: to build private and commercial houses in Monrovia, to replace the thatched huts for new immigrants at the expanding settlements, and in some cases to establish substantial residences, reminiscent of those the immigrants had known in the American South, along the St. Paul's River.[64] In Monrovia, new settlers were allocated lots with the proviso that they must build a house with a shingled roof and a plank floor within two years or lose the land.[65] Schooled in carpentry back in South Carolina, Church knew how to frame houses, stack stairways, create broad front porches, and finish the kinds of buildings African American settlers wanted. He even had learned to fire bricks, a useful skill in a tropical climate so hard on wooden structures.[66] Church probably offered one of his shipmates from the *Joseph Maxwell* the use of his farmland in exchange for some of the produce. Then he must have become something like the itinerant carpenter his father Scipio had been in South Carolina, based in Monrovia where steady work could be found, but also traveling up the river for jobs, to see his friends, and to check on his land and crops near Millsburg.

One source of potential clients was Church's shipmate Marshall Hooper, who seemed to know everyone in the area. Shortly after he arrived in Millsburg, Hooper went to see an old acquaintance, perhaps a relative, now the proprietor of a prosperous farm along the banks of the St. Paul's River. Allen Hooper had been enslaved to members of the same family as Marshall Hooper, and the two knew each other in North Carolina. In fact, Allen Hooper knew a number of the *Joseph Maxwell* passengers from Fayetteville, including "Old man Robbin" and Patsy Waddle, the elderly couple who had perished soon after their arrival in Liberia, and Marshall Hooper's wife and daughter. Like Marshall Hooper, Allen had made the Atlantic crossing twice: first in 1848, and again, for a permanent stay in Liberia, in 1850. By the time Marshall came to see him in 1853, Allen had purchased two hundred acres of land and planted a hundred thousand coffee trees; he also cultivated twenty-five acres of sugar cane. As he wrote buoyantly back to North Carolina, "Tell all my colord Brother to come home and take posesion of the land of our Farthers. Tell them to come and let us Build up a great Republice to our Selfs."[67]

But who would actually work the landholdings of planters like Allen Hooper? Edward Blyden was probably the newspaper correspondent who visited several large riverside operations in 1852. He singled out Hooper's estate, christened "Iconium" (the site in modern Turkey of St. Paul's first missionary journey) as "one of the handsomest places we have ever seen," with flowerbeds, fields of coffee and sugar cane, and plots of garden vegetables. On a walk around the farm, the journalist noted favorably the "quiet manner [in which] the laborers perform their seemingly agreeable task," without specifying who the laborers actually were. Samuel Williams, a black preacher from Pennsylvania, obliquely compared Liberian planters like Hooper to those in the American South: "The St. Paul's farmers are in general, industrious and prosperous. Many very fine plantations are to be seen . . . as good sugar plantations as I ever saw in the neighborhood of New Orleans."[68] Perhaps Rev. Williams was reminded of New Orleans because of the passing resemblance between the broad St. Paul's River and the Mississippi, or because the St. Paul's area, like Louisiana (the name of one of the settlements along its banks, in fact), was becoming known for sugar cane cultivation. But one could not invoke New Orleans in 1854 without also raising the specter of slavery. As Liberians insisted, the plantation workers who grew coffee and sugar cane, as well as those who tended many settlers' food gardens, carried their loads, and worked in their households, were not in fact slaves. Yet they were not other settlers, either; and they bore more than a little resemblance to the unfree laborers of the southern United States.

Liberia had been founded, theoretically at least, to be a place of freedom for captives liberated from slave ships by American cruisers. Between 1820 and 1843, however, the U.S. Navy sent only 287 recaptured Africans to Liberia. Many settled at New Georgia, on the edge of Stockton Creek, where they farmed and sold produce to Monrovia. But in 1846, the American naval squadron captured the slave ship *Pons* and brought 756 Africans from its hold to Liberia. After enduring the receptacle at New Virginia for some time, they were placed as "apprentices" with settlers, who received an annual allocation from the U.S. government for their support and education.[69] This followed an already established pattern: when settlers had attacked nearby slave barracoons, they had also "liberated" captive people into apprenticeship. And Liberians took as apprentices local Africans as well, often children or teenagers, promising them a brighter future than they might have with their economically struggling families while putting them to work. The system was not unlike one that existed throughout West Africa, called pawnship, in which human beings served as collateral for loans with their labor functioning as the interest.[70] For Liberians, the difference was that they were offering their apprentices entry into "civilization" by assimilating them into settler society.[71]

By the late 1850s, an observer noted that just about all the settlers he saw made use of African labor, even to carry the smallest of packages.[72] Legally, however, these were neither slaves nor pawns. In 1830 the American Colonization Society had established stiff penalties for any immigrant convicted of slave trafficking, largely in response to rumors that colonists were secretly selling captives to Spanish dealers at the Gallinas River and Cape Mount.[73] Slavery itself was explicitly prohibited in the ACS charter and later in the Liberian Constitution. Moreover, from 1838, the apprenticeship system was regulated by a law requiring that apprentices be registered, provisioned, and paid, and that they have recourse to government officials in case of abuse. Yet few of those "apprenticed" were actually educated, and credible critics alleged that apprenticeship was simply a cover for slavery.[74] The settler and missionary John Day, for instance, wrote privately to his Southern Baptist Convention correspondents that his colleague A. P. Davis was keeping his receptive apprentices in chains to prevent them from running away, and that some Liberians had been convicted in court of selling slaves. "But as regards the existence of slavery among us," he insisted, "there is no such thing."[75]

Previously whispered allegations about Liberian slavery became public in 1851, when Commander Frederick Forbes of the British Navy published an account of his recent expedition to the kingdom of Dahomey, more than a thousand miles to the east of Liberia in what is now the Republic of Benin. In two pages of a book otherwise unrelated to Liberia, Forbes, who had captained one of the British antislavery patrol ships, accused Liberians of keeping and trafficking in slaves. "In Liberia there is as much, if not more, domestic slavery—that is, the buying and selling of God's image—as in the parent States of America, over which flaunts the flag of liberty," he wrote. "It is difficult to see the necessity or the justice of the negro who escapes from slavery on one side, crossing the Atlantic to enslave his sable prototype on the other; yet such is the case; . . . I doubt if many benevolent Christians in this country are aware that the model Republic is, in reality, a new name and form for slavery in enslaved Africa; and, until the system be altered, totally undeserving of the high support and liberal charity it receives from the benevolence of Englishmen."[76]

Once the accusations were reprinted in the British *Anti-Slavery Reporter* and in American newspapers, Liberia's defenders sprang into action. In the United States, James Lugenbeel and a colleague named Dr. Bacon of the

American Colonization Society quickly produced a report labeling Forbes's allegations "*utterly groundless.*" They protested that Liberians had succeeded in ending slave exports from their coast, that slavery was illegal under Liberian law, and that Liberians had imposed more than forty antislave-trade treaties on local African groups, at times backing these up with armed force. In England, longtime ACS supporters Elliott Cresson and Thomas Hodgkin addressed a letter making the same points directly to Commander Forbes, who, they added, had never even visited Liberia.[77]

In his defense, Forbes replied that though he had not visited Monrovia, he had been stationed for six months at Cape Mount and he knew many Liberians. "That the citizens of Liberia are guilty of buying and holding slaves I had ocular demonstration," he insisted, "and I know personally two Liberian citizens . . . sojourners at Cape Mount, who owned several slaves." Forbes acknowledged that though these were slaves "in the general use of the term," they were not in the strict legal sense, "as these slaves were what are termed domestic slaves, or pawns, and not intended for foreign slavery." But the distinction, to him, was moot: "These pawns, as I have stated and believe, are as much slaves as their sable prototypes in the parent States of America, and my informants acquainted me that almost all labor in Liberia was derived from a system of domestic slavery."[78]

President Roberts took issue with Forbes's reasoning, asking in a published response, "Is it not ungenerous, unkind, and unjust, in Commander Forbes, even admitting it were true that he saw two Liberian citizens at Cape Mount, at that time beyond the jurisdiction of Liberia, engaged as he states, in the slave trade, to denounce a whole community? No, sir; I thank God, the Liberians, as a people, certainly, abhor slavery in all its phases, and would no sooner engage in the nefarious traffic than Commander Forbes himself." The editor of the *Liberia Herald* went, rather unbelievably, even further: "We emphatically deny the practice of the pawn system in Liberia, or that labor is derived here from slavery in any of its phases."[79]

Yet outsiders continued to point out the similarities between Liberia's labor system and American slavery. In 1853, the year Church Vaughan arrived, a Pennsylvania African American named William Nesbit published an account of his four months' travel in Liberia, with an introduction by Martin Delany. Although his trip had been sponsored by the American Colonization Society, Nesbit became a bitter critic of colonization. According to him, forced labor within Liberia's borders was widespread. "Every colonist keeps native slaves (or as they term them servants) about him, varying in number from one to fifteen, according to the circumstances of the master," he charged. "These poor souls they beat unmercifully, and more than half starve them, and all labor that is done at all, is done by these poor wretches." Nesbit's account devoted a full chapter to slavery. Liberian slaves faced the same kinds of toil as those in America, he wrote, except that they were fed less because they were more easily replaced. A large supply of laborers was available for cheap purchase from their parents, presumably because their own opportunities for earning a living were being eroded by the expansion of Liberian settlement. Nesbit's characterization of Liberian slaveholders was stark: "They are mostly manumitted slaves themselves, and have felt the blighting effects of slavery here, only to go there to become masters." This, he scoffed, was in spite of Liberian claims about civilizing Africans. "They [the settlers] profess to have broken up the foreign slave trade, which is far from the truth; but suppose they had done so, is that *even* a blessing, under the circumstances?" he asked.[80]

Other observers acknowledged abuses in the apprenticeship system, but fell short of labeling it slavery. Rev. Samuel Williams, who arrived in Liberia shortly before Nesbit's trip, refuted his fellow Pennsylvanian in his own publication, *Four Years in Liberia*. Though he had been the one to compare Millsburg with New Orleans, Williams took strong issue with Nesbit's assertions about slavery in Liberia, reminding readers that slavery was against the law and that strict rules governed apprenticeship. "Nearly all [settlers] have natives as helps in their families, and this is as it should be; but I confess that black people are no better than white people, as many, when they have power, abuse it, and so it is with some in Liberia; wicked persons there do abuse the native youths," he wrote. Still, like President Roberts had a few years earlier, he insisted that the entire settler population should not be blamed for the transgressions of a few.[81]

Unlike Allen Hooper and other large-scale planters, Church Vaughan's surviving shipmates and new acquaintances were in no position to take on "apprentices," instead making do with family members or occasional hired labor. If death, disease, bad weather, or other misfortunes meant that they did not have enough to eat, they were left with few options. First-generation settlers were not allowed to sell land they had been allocated by the government; only their children could.[82] But it was not easy to enter the labor market either. In South Carolina, slavery depressed the wages of free black people like the Vaughans; in Liberia, cheap, quasi-free indigenous labor did the same thing. "Their is Some that have come to this place that have got rich and a number that are Suffering," wrote the settler Payton Skipwith in 1834. "Those that are well off do have the natives as Slavs and poor people that come from America have no chance to make a living for the natives do all the work." In the early 1850s, "native" labor could be hired in Monrovia for a third of the rate charged by settlers—who could not work for less and still afford to buy food. Female immigrants, many of them widows, earned only a small fraction of that. Many Liberians who had started as farmers made their way to Monrovia and turned to trade, a source of wealth for a relative few but one requiring little previous training. Countless immigrants, like Church's shipmate James Richardson and his new wife Matilda Lomax, became mired in poverty. As another of Church's contemporaries, the visiting missionary Augustus Washington, put it, "Where one succeeds [in Liberia] with nothing, twenty suffer and die, leaving no mark of their existence."[83]

With his ability to construct the kinds of houses and furnishings familiar and desirable to American settlers, Church Vaughan did not have to worry much about finding work or competing with native labor himself. If he was growing disillusioned with Liberia, it was not because he personally was in danger of poverty, but for moral and political reasons. He had left South Carolina because he no longer wanted to live in an oppressive society, yet Liberia seemed to be developing its own plantocracy. In the American South, white settlers had displaced native communities like his mother's and kept Africans and African Americans like his father in bondage. Here, as he was learning, settlers had also displaced natives and were coming close to enslaving indigenous Africans. Liberia's founders had based their Declaration of Independence and their Constitution on what they saw as the best of American traditions. Yet Liberia's settlers were also creating an American-style ethnic caste system based on land dispossession and labor exploitation. Did Church want to become a permanent member of that society?

According to letters to white correspondents and testimonials printed in the procolonization press, Liberians would rather endure terrible hardship than leave their adopted country. Susan Capart, who had emigrated from North Carolina in 1850, reported several years later that although she was unmarried and "farming on the smalls . . . doing Very mutch the same work that I did when I was in America . . . the longer that I live in Africa the better I like it." Henry Franklin, who left Virginia for Liberia with his aged mother in 1856, wrote to a doctor at home two years later that "I like the country very well indeed & have no reason to return to America, for we believe there is no Country on the Earth can Equal it [Liberia] in the world." Even "if the President were to fit out a steamship for her express accommodation," another colonist had asserted in 1853, she still would not return to the United States.[84] These stalwart assertions of Liberian loyalty, however, mask a running current of discontent. Some Liberians did in fact want to leave, but their options for doing so were limited.[85] Money had to be secured for passage, and furthermore, there were few promising places to go. Would-be immigrants only had contacts and prospects for making a living in the United States, but in many states, not just southern ones, the entry of free blacks was illegal.

Church's friends Marshall and Emily Hooper experienced such problems themselves, though in different ways. In 1855, Marshall Hooper made his second return trip to the United States, reprising the role he had played in recruiting Liberian emigrants two years earlier. As before, he hoped to secure the freedom of his youngest son; but again he was disappointed. His efforts may have reduced him to poverty, too, as he appeared in records at this point not as a farmer or trader but instead as a common laborer.[86] Three years later, Marshall's daughter Emily Hooper was so discouraged that she wrote a letter to her former owner in North Carolina, Sallie Mallett, complaining of the difficult conditions in Liberia. Mallett then requested help from the secretary of the American Colonization Society in bringing the now twenty-two-year-old back to Chapel Hill, where, Mallett asserted, she "had never been accustomed to hard work." But Emily Hooper would have to sacrifice her freedom in order to return. Since free people of color could not lawfully enter the state, Mallett successfully appealed to the North Carolina legislature to pass "A Bill for the Relief of Emily Hooper of Liberia." The act provided "that Emily Hooper, a negro and a citizen of the republic of Liberia, be and she is hereby permitted voluntarily to return into a state of slavery as slave of her former owner, Miss Sallie Mallett, of Chapel Hill." Mallett interpreted Emily's situation as an affirmation of slavery: that, as a Charlotte newspaper put it, the young woman was "sick of freedom and prefers living with her mistress in the Old North State than to being fleeced by abolition friends (?) in Liberia." Instead, however, it reveals the depth of Emily's dissatisfaction with Liberia and the dearth of options for leaving. Emily Hooper did finally return to North Carolina from Liberia, but it was not until 1871, well after slavery had ended for African Americans and immediately after the death of Sallie Mallett.[87]

Church Vaughan may well have remained in Liberia had the opportunity to leave not presented itself. His deliverance, earthly rather than spiritual, came through the Southern Baptist Church, and in particular two missionaries: an African American named Joseph Harden and the white southerner William Clarke. In spite of his first name, Church had no denominational background and probably not much Christian conviction at this point in his life.[88] But just as emigration from the United States had made unlikely bedfellows—bringing African Americans with hopes for freedom together with white colonizationists who supported slavery—so too did Church's departure from Liberia, made possible through networks of missionaries in West Africa.

Numerous evangelists were at that time scattered around Liberia, trying to bring Christianity and its accompanying cultural package of "civilization"—including western education, clothing, and household organization—to indigenous Africans and unconverted settlers. Some were Methodists and Presbyterians; about a half-dozen—all African Americans—represented the Southern Baptist Convention, which had recently separated from American Baptists over the propriety of appointing slaveholders as missionaries. Immediately after their organization, Southern Baptists created a Foreign Mission Board and sent their first missionaries to China. Aware that there had been a strong Baptist presence among Liberian settlers since the 1820s, they determined that the little republic would also be a promising site for a mission. The problem was finding missionaries. In spite of their general view that African Americans were not as capable as whites, the Mission Board directors deemed black missionaries to be more appropriate for work in Africa, and they looked for suitable black candidates both at home and already in Liberia. Their best prospect was John Day, a former cabinetmaker from Virginia who had immigrated to Liberia in 1830 and was already an ordained pastor. In 1846 the Southern Baptist Mission Board appointed Day as the superintendent of its Liberia mission, a post he held along with several Liberian government offices until his death in 1859.[89]

Church's interaction with missionaries of the Southern Baptist Convention likely began shortly after his arrival in Liberia. Joseph M. Harden, the African American charged with the Baptist mission at New Virginia, had come to Liberia two years earlier. Now, his efforts to build a suitable chapel for his growing congregation had stalled for want of materials and skilled labor. In January 1853, the *Linda Stewart* docked at Monrovia carrying nails that Harden had requested from Virginia.[90] At the same time, the carpenter Church Vaughan arrived on the *Joseph Maxwell*, along with Marshall Hooper, the well-connected denizen of New Virginia who could introduce him to one of his first new clients.

Church and Harden in some ways shared a similar background. Only two months apart in age, both were born free to parents who had known slavery, and both had received a rudimentary education. But Harden had spent most of his youth "bound," as he described his forced apprenticeship, to a gentleman in Baltimore as a house servant. At nineteen, he later told his Baptist superiors, he was introduced to religion by a black Methodist woman and baptized in that church, "my father being a Methodist preacher." Within a few months, however, he converted to the Baptist faith. For the next three years, Harden preached in a congregation later known as the Saratoga Street African Baptist Church, until in 1850 the Foreign Mission Board of the Southern Baptist Convention appointed him to be a missionary in Africa.[91]

These days it may be hard to fathom why an African American, let alone one with memories of bondage, would join and promote a church that saw slavery as part of God's plan for humanity. Yet a powerful strain of African American Christianity at this time also interpreted slavery this way, as a means for bringing black people to the one true religion, which they then could share with their benighted brethren. In this Christian cause, white-run, or even white-supremacist, church organizations could still help them.[92] Like other missionaries, Harden was convinced that Africans needed to become Christian in order to achieve both salvation and civilization, and he had come to Africa to bring it to them. In 1855, for example, he reported to the Mission Board about an African initiation ceremony he witnessed. While his contemporary Edward Blyden had at least recorded grudging respect for "native genius," Harden condemned what he saw as "a true picture of heathenism in this part of Liberia, and God alone can provide the means of bringing them out of it."[93]

Harden had come to Liberia with his pregnant wife, but she and the baby died of fever within a year of their arrival. His second wife, the Liberian-born daughter of settler parents, died in childbirth, along with the child, in October 1853. After so much death, Harden harbored a certain fatalism about his mission in Africa. "Africa is not like America," he wrote to the Foreign Mission Board secretary in 1854. "We have no paved streets or well kept roads to travel on. Vegetation is always green and rank, and having to travel through the bushes during the rains on foot, you can almost at any time wring as much water out of your clothes as if you had been washing them. And then traveling from five to ten miles in an open canoe, through a hard driving rain, will bring on sickness." But Harden was stoic about his fate: "Dear brother, do not suppose for a moment that I am complaining, far be it from me, for I have long since consecrated myself to God and the Board, and expect to die preaching the glad tidings of salvation. I shall consider it an honor to die in such a cause."[94]

Missionary work did eventually kill him, but it was not in Liberia. Through the chain of Southern Baptist missionaries stretched between Liberia, the United States, and the territory that would later be known as Nigeria, Harden would relocate to Yorubaland, some twelve hundred miles southeast along the West African coast. Harden had no idea, however, that this was in his future—or in Church Vaughan's—when in mid-1854, he received a white visitor from the United States. Rev. William H. Clarke was passing two months in Liberia en route to Yorubaland. When John Day took him on a tour of the country's Baptist stations, Clarke met Harden at New Virginia, a mission he deemed "in good condition."[95]

A young preacher from Georgia, William Clarke had been inspired to become a missionary after meeting Thomas Jefferson Bowen, the Southern Baptist Convention's first (and at the time only) white missionary to Africa. In 1852, Bowen had been granted land for a mission by the king of the inland Yoruba city-state of Ijaye, but had returned to the United States to raise funds and personnel. Already renowned among Southern Baptists as an intrepid missionary-explorer, Bowen dazzled Pastor Clarke with his stories of a verdant land where sincere, intelligent people could be lifted from barbarism through the Gospel. After Bowen returned to Africa with his new bride and two other missionary couples, Clarke resolved to follow him.[96]

In September 1854, Clarke left Liberia and reached the Bowens in Ijaye. They were on their own, the other missionaries and their wives having died or returned to the United States. Over the next year, though, Clarke's letters home expressed optimism about the prospects for spreading Christianity. "I have never yet been unkindly received or treated by a single crowd," he wrote. But like Harden had been in Liberia, he was frustrated with the building projects that formed a necessary part of mission work. "My brother," Clarke wrote to his Richmond superior about building a chapel and mission house, "you have no idea of our trouble and embarrassments in the prosecution of our labors." The missionaries' African agent in Lagos often neglected to forward supplies on time, compelling Clarke to travel to the coast to take care of business. Back in Ijaye, Clarke resented the constant need to supervise construction workers, when he had no experience as an overseer. As he and Bowen made plans for a string of mission stations stretching from the coast further to the interior, he worried about who would do the building. "I suggest," he wrote back to Richmond, "that the Board consider the propriety of connecting with their mission two, three or four good mechanics of our own denomination, worthy men such as may be obtained in Liberia or Sierra Leone whose duty it shall be to erect suitable buildings for every station." They could even help with missionary work at the proposed new stations, learning the Yoruba language and thereby being "useful to the missionaries in various ways—perhaps as teachers or preachers, thereby uniting two avocations most desirable in a Central African Mission." They could also train local builders to carry on the necessary construction work. Clarke was so confident of this idea, he reported, that he had sent for a builder from Liberia at his own expense, expecting that if he were "well pleased," the carpenter would then be joined by some of his compatriots.[97]

Meanwhile in Liberia, John Day was working on Bowen and Clarke's behalf to find a missionary for a new Baptist station in Lagos, Yorubaland's port city. In April 1855, he wrote to Bowen that he had found "an excellent man" for the job: a recently arrived, 49-year-old freedman from Virginia named Washington Johnson. Though he was booked on the next steamer, Johnson must have died or backed out. Instead, by July Joseph Harden was on his way to Lagos. Reverend Day was sorry to see him go: "He is the most studious of our preachers and has a gravity of demeanor which cannot fail to render a minister venerable and an immanence which defies the tongue of slander."[98] Two months later, Church Vaughan and another carpenter, a Vai man whose name was not recorded, followed Harden to Yoruba country, their passage paid by Clarke and Bowen.[99]

Their agreement was for a fixed term, giving Church the option to return to Liberia at its completion.[100] After nearly three years in the African American colony, however, he had seen enough to be ready to leave. Though Liberia did offer an escape from white supremacy and the opportunity for citizenship and perhaps even wealth, settlers' new lives came at the cost of local people's old ones. The Americo-Liberians decried slavery and risked their lives to suppress the slave trade, yet they had created a system disturbingly similar to the plantation societies many of them had left behind. Having seen through his family the effects of land dispossession and slavery in South Carolina, Church may have been especially sensitive to their occurrence in Liberia.

But where was he going, and with whom? All Church may have heard about Yorubaland at this point was vague rumors of warfare and slave trafficking—which he would see firsthand soon enough. The British Navy had bombarded the port of Lagos in 1851 in an attempt to suppress the slave trade from there. A few missionaries, most of them British, were endeavoring to bring salvation to African rulers and common people; they and a handful of European traders were the only foreigners in residence. Perhaps Church was intrigued by the idea of living in "real," uncolonized Africa. Maybe he had some sympathy for the missionary enterprise—though he would not become a Christian for some time — and surely he felt affection for Harden, whose family would remain in his life for many years to come. William Clarke would soon become his closest companion, and he would remember Thomas Bowen into his old age. For now, though, the missionaries served a strategic and specific purpose: they were Church's way out of Liberia.

four

TROUBLED TIMES IN YORUBALAND

Nothing in Church Vaughan's background could have prepared him for the sensory intensity of landing in Lagos. He had traveled by steamer before, on a short hop along the North Carolina coast when he first left for Liberia. This time, Church and the Vai carpenter hired along with him spent a week as passengers on a British-owned steamship that regularly connected Europe and several stops along the West African coast, servicing international traders in palm oil and other commodities. Landing at the low-lying Lagos waterfront after a harrowing canoe ride from the ship—sharks as big as horses preyed upon those who fell into the turbulent water—Church entered into a bustle of activity. Shouts rang through the air, mostly in Yoruba, but also in pidgin English and a smattering of Brazilian Portuguese. Porters, stripped to the waist and glistening with perspiration, hauled drums of palm oil to and from nearby storehouses, while canoemen labored to unload cargo from the waiting steamship. Independent traders as well as agents of European firms—some Europeans and Brazilians but mostly Africans—bargained for prices and credit and oversaw the movement of goods, supplies, and money in multiple forms—mostly South American dollars and bags of cowry shells imported from Asia or East Africa. Street venders offered ready-cooked meals of fried bean cakes or fish stew. "This city," observed the black nationalist Martin Delany prophetically when he passed through five years later, "is destined to be the great black metropolis of the world."[1]

At twenty-seven years old, Church had experienced much more than his contemporaries had back in South Carolina. He had crossed the Atlantic and survived the devastating fevers that greeted new arrivals in Africa. He spent two years among the African American settlers of Liberia, where he earned a living as a carpenter, served in the militia, and perhaps voted. Yet he still had not made his place in the world. His mobile construction business introduced him to a range of people—resulting in his current contract, in fact—but it did not help him to put down roots in or around Monrovia. When he accepted the offer of employment with Southern Baptist missionaries in Yorubaland, he knew he would be starting over yet again, in a foreign place about which he knew virtually nothing. This new adventure, though, offered him the chance to become the man he hoped to be: accomplished, secure, and even prosperous. It would also, however, put him on more than one occasion in grave danger.

Searching for a familiar face along the waterfront, Church spotted Joseph Harden, the African American missionary from Liberia who had arrived three months earlier. Now Harden was working for the Baptists in Lagos, constructing a bamboo mission house and preaching through an interpreter while he tried to learn the Yoruba language. As he led the two new arrivals into central Lagos, Harden could brief them on the city. Formerly an insignificant, low-lying fishing village and surrounded entirely by water, Lagos had grown rapidly in the eighteenth century as an Atlantic slaving port. In the nineteenth century, the export of palm oil—in demand as an industrial lubricant and key ingredient of soap and margarine in Europe—began to replace the slave trade, transforming Lagos into "the Liverpool of Africa." Its twenty thousand inhabitants made this metropolis the largest Church had ever seen—more populated than all of Kershaw County; three times the size of Wilmington, North Carolina, where he had last touched American soil; and ten times bigger than Monrovia. Yet the island occupied only about four square miles, and even less than that was dry enough to build upon. A hundred or so European-style houses had been built by foreign merchants, missionaries, and the wealthier local traders, with thousands of other dwellings tucked behind the city's thoroughfares and between its winding streets and alleyways. While the compounds of indigenous lineages clustered around the royal palace at one end of the island, new arrivals filled the rest of the city with fortune-seekers, refugees, slaves, and ex-slaves from elsewhere in Yorubaland and beyond. Some were returnees from Sierra Leone, where they or their parents had been landed when the slave ships in which they were captive were intercepted by British naval cruisers. Another group were Brazilians of Yoruba origin, returned from slavery largely by their own initiative, joined by a handful of ex-slaves from Cuba. Only the Saro, as the Sierra Leoneans were known locally, had much interest in Christianity, having been previously exposed to it, and they formed the main constituency for the three Protestant missions in town, representing the (Anglican) Church Missionary Society, the (Methodist) Wesleyan Missionary Society, and the (Southern) American Baptists.[2] "Lagos is a fine place, in a commercial point of view," was Harden's opinion, "but it is the place where Satan's seat is and wickedness abounds." People do not respect the Sabbath, he elaborated, and the women "will strip themselves naked before you and think nothing of it."[3]

In spite of Harden's exaggeration—most women thought nothing of going about topless, but only the truly poor or insane were completely un-clothed—his larger point was certainly right: no critical mass of settlers had brought Western-style dress or culture to Lagos, as they had in Liberia.[4] Lagos was firmly an African city, and those of the interior even more so. It was governed by an indigenous monarch with a council of chiefs, although a British Consul represented the interests of foreign traders and antislavery reformers. In 1851, four years before Church's arrival, the British Navy had bombarded Lagos and reinstalled a king, Akitoye, who had been deposed by his nephew and rival. In exchange for British backing, Akitoye pledged to help suppress the slave trade. But through the 1850s, ordinary people scarcely felt the British presence, which mainly took the form of the consul's support for so-called "legitimate" (that is, nonslave) commerce with European firms.

Lagos was Church's first stop on a journey that would take him inland through the town of Abeokuta and finally to Ijaye, some 150 miles from the coast. These were even larger cities than Lagos, though like the seaport, they were being built and rebuilt by newcomers—refugees, fortune-seekers, warlords, and returnees from Atlantic slavery. More so than at the coast, however, Yorubaland's inland towns were marked by violent trauma. Church Vaughan had arrived during what was known locally as the "age of confu-sion." For nearly forty years, Yoruba people had been engulfed in warfare as the formerly dominant inland polity, the Oyo Empire, cracked apart. Sol-diers and raiders seized many thousands of captives, more than a quarter million exported to the Americas in the first half of the nineteenth century through Lagos alone, along with more than 160,000 from other nearby ports. In the violence, old communities were destroyed and new ones were consti-tuted, typically under strong warrior-rulers.[5]

On a small scale, Church faced the same central questions as Yoruba people did more generally: with whom did he belong, and who would help keep him safe? In South Carolina, he had learned the strategic importance of allies and patrons, but in Liberia he had been something of a loner. Church spent his first few years in Yorubaland within the orbit of American mission-aries, who provided his livelihood and cultivated his mind and spirit. But as

Troubled Times in Yorubaland

he became more self-sufficient, and when his closest missionary companion departed, he struck out on his own, living not only separate from the Baptists but between the two major city-states of the area. In Atlantic Africa, however, autonomy often meant danger rather than freedom, and Church needed to be careful of his footing, lest he be swept into the sea with other captives. Church Vaughan and the other diasporic Africans in Yorubaland may have hoped to fulfill their dreams of freedom in the land of their ancestors, but what they found was more complicated. For them as for others, freedom as *independence* brought vulnerability, while freedom as *safety* or *prosperity* was best achieved through subordination to strong, autocratic leaders, most of whom profited from slavery and slaving themselves.

After resting in Lagos for a day or two, Church and his Vai companion set out to join their new employers at the Southern Baptist mission station in Ijaye. The roughly ten-day northward trip would take them through dense tropical forests, open grasslands, small villages, and the well-protected city of Abeokuta. It would also take Church back to living with white southerners — the kind of people he had gladly left behind in South Carolina and whom he had not missed in Liberia. Once he arrived at the mission station, he would have to conform to the missionaries' sense of propriety and racial etiquette. His association with them, however, would transform Church fundamentally and forever. Through his missionary connections, Church would receive an education in Yoruba language and culture as well as English literacy and learning. His time with the Baptists would stimulate his intellect and self-confidence, preparing Church, once he got the opportunity, to make a new bid for freedom.

Because it was the rainy season, Church and his party could travel by water most of the way to Abeokuta, their first stopping point, ninety miles up the Ogun River from the coast. At the north side of Lagos Island, they said goodbye to Joseph Harden and boarded a canoe large enough to accommodate the travelers' mattresses, with a makeshift tent of grass mats overhead for shade. By the end of the day, they and their canoemen entered a narrow, overgrown creek that connects the lagoon north of Lagos with the river running inland — an efficient route but one that struck the American missionary William Clarke, who had traveled it almost exactly a year before Church did, as "one of the most dismal, malarious, miasmic swamps the imagination could picture."[6] The scenery improved the next day, when the travelers entered the Ogun River, a thoroughfare alive with birds, monkeys, and watermen carrying trade goods between Abeokuta and the coast.

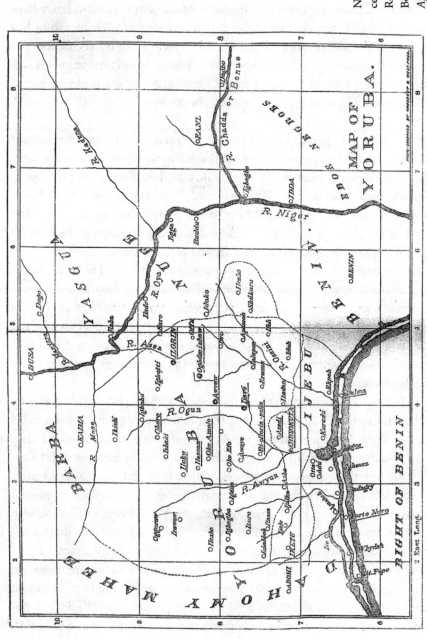

Nineteenth-century Yorubaland. Reprinted from Bowen, *Central Africa* (1857).

Church probably learned his first Yoruba phrase as he passed riverside villages and market stands over the next several days: "Ẹ kú àbọ̀!" ("welcome"), which greeted travelers and newcomers at every turn (and still does).

Finally nearing Abeokuta on the fifth day, Church and his fellow carpenter paid their canoemen and set off on foot through open farm country, where fields of corn flourished in the river valley. Perhaps, like William Clarke before him, Church had assumed that all of West Africa was flat and swampy and thus was "wholly unprepared for such a change as my eyes were continually beholding in the rolling undulating surface, the open country of sparse timber, the productive soil, the cultivated farms, the waving grass and the beautiful scenery." Soon several hills came into view, surrounded by twenty or thirty giant granite masses rising more than two hundred feet high. Among the two largest of these, on their sloping sides and around their bases, some sixty thousand people had made their homes, surrounded by a wall about fifteen miles in diameter. This was the town of Abeokuta.[7]

When Church arrived there, Abeokuta was a new city, having emerged only twenty-five years earlier out of the ruined Oyo Empire. Oyo had been the most powerful of the many kingdoms founded by people now known collectively as Yoruba. Though other Yoruba polities were situated in the forested south of what is now western Nigeria, Oyo centered on the savannah farther north. Its economy combined agriculture with control over major trade routes that brought in horses from the north—for the kingdom's formidable cavalry—and sent slaves to Atlantic ports. But by the late 1700s, as external demand for slaves reached its height, the kingdom began to crumble, strained by dissent within the ruling group and moves for autonomy from its constituent provinces. In 1830 a group of refugees from a subgroup known as Egba established a settlement among giant, protective boulders that they named Abeokuta, literally "Under the Rock." Then, seeking their own security by controlling the trade route to Lagos, they turned on the smaller polities to their south. This pitted the Egba against their western neighbor, Dahomey, a formidable kingdom once subordinate to Oyo but now seeking its own tributaries on the fringes of Yorubaland.[8]

Just a few years before Church arrived, the gates through which he entered Abeokuta had been the site of a fearsome attack by Dahomey's army. The American Baptist pioneer Thomas Jefferson Bowen had been there on his first trip to Yorubaland, stalled in his bid to establish a station further inland. A veteran of battles against Creek Indians and Texas Mexicans before his embrace of Christianity, Bowen had consulted with the Egba on war strategy, while the English missionary Henry Townsend distributed bullets received from the British Consul in Lagos. On March 1, 1851, an Egba army of more than 15,000 defended Abeokuta against a Dahomean invasion of 10,000 men and 6,000 of the kingdom's famed Amazon warriors, well-armed women who had originally formed a palace guard. "The walls were black with people," Townsend reported of the Egba defenders guarding the perimeter of the town. "A most furious discharge of muskets took place from both sides" before the Abeokuta forces were able to repel the invaders, ultimately pushing them back fifteen miles before the killing and capturing ended. Their support earned the missionaries much goodwill among a faction of the Egbas, and Henry Townsend came to exercise special influence among their leaders. Though Egba opinion certainly was not unanimous, by the time Church Vaughan stopped there in late 1855, Abeokuta was gaining a reputation in missionary circles as the "sunrise within the tropics," for its people's support of missionaries, cooperation with the British in slave-trade suppression, and openness to "legitimate" trade through Lagos.[9]

In contrast, Church's final destination of Ijaye was sixty miles more remote from Lagos and contained only a tiny missionary presence—three men on two stations (the Southern Baptists Bowen and Clarke along with Adolphus Mann of the British Church Missionary Society)—and perhaps only a handful of people besides them who could communicate in English. And as Church must have heard before he left Abeokuta, it was governed by an autocrat known both for his military valor in the Yoruba wars and his tight grip on power. Kurunmi, who held the Oyo title *Arẹ-Ọna-Kakamfo* (something like "generalissimo"), may have been "the greatest Yoruba general and tactician of the day," as the nineteenth century Yoruba historian Samuel Johnson wrote of him. But he also terrorized his people, eliminating rivals and claiming for himself, rather than distributing among subordinate chiefs, all the fines, tolls, and tributes flowing through his territory. "There is no least liberty for the people of Ijaye, with the exception of those whom he has selected to help him in his wicked deeds such as his sons, slaves etc. These are at liberty with him," an African catechist for the CMS wrote of Kurunmi. "But the others are his prey."[10]

Such a warning may have seemed overly dire as Church and his companion walked along the caravan road leading northeast from Abeokuta to Ijaye. The countryside reminded Americans of the fields of the southern United States, with sparse woods, winding streams, and occasional palm trees interspersed with cultivated farms of corn, yam, and other crops. Over the course of the four-day journey, they passed through two belts of forest, each time emerging to rolling plains and slightly higher elevations. Ijaye was smaller than Abeokuta but nonetheless huge compared to Camden or Monrovia. Some thirty-five thousand people lived there in compounds constructed of mud and thatch. The king's palace complex was the largest of these, housing at times three hundred wives and a thousand slaves, who commuted daily beyond the walls to tend the king's agricultural fields. Thousands of other farmers, slave and free, did the same, returning in the evening "in a living stream coming in for hours." In the middle of Ijaye sprawled a market of perhaps twenty acres, while smaller markets operated at each of the six gates in the town walls. Though the streets were narrow and irregular, the missionaries appreciated Ijaye's order and cleanliness — which they attributed to the firm hand of the *Are* Kurunmi.[11]

In fact, the American Baptists tended to overlook the worst features of Kurunmi's rule. "He was haughty, despotic, ambitious and cruel, yet he was just such a ruler as these people needed to keep them in order; for he was also firm, just and reasonable on most occasions," remembered Richard Stone, who arrived a few years after Church Vaughan did. Viewing white people as potentially conducive to trade with the coast, Kurunmi had recruited Reverend Bowen to establish a mission in Ijaye and granted him land for building, as he did with the English missionary Adolphus Mann. He cemented his relationship with the missions by placing two of his sons with the missionaries, one for each, as well as calling upon Bowen, who had some medical training, when he fell ill. But though Kurunmi guaranteed the missionaries' safety, he would not protect African converts from persecution, and he had no interest in Christianity himself.[12] Moreover, as the Anglican missionary Adolphus Mann and his African assistant repeatedly reported and protested, he ruled through terror, meting out often grisly capital punishments for infractions ranging from theft to adultery by the king's many wives.[13] But even they kept their criticisms mostly to themselves, dependent as all the missionaries were on Kurunmi's patronage in order to build on land in the town, preach, or even recruit workers.

Thus, when Church arrived at Ijaye, he entered into a series of ambivalent, nested relationships. His most immediate supervisors were missionaries from the Southern Baptist Convention, white men both determined to improve the lot of Africans (at least spiritually) and part of an organization founded on the defense of slavery. The missionaries, in turn, had become the clients of a fearsome local ruler, who himself operated within an unstable and insecure region nominally under the authority of the king of Oyo. In some ways the missionaries lived apart from local people, insulated from Yoruba relationships and practices. Their challenge, however, was the same as Church's would be: to make their own way while maintaining the protections that came with affiliation.

Church and his companion reached Ijaye on September 10, 1855 and proceeded to the Baptist mission. After hearing so much about him, Church must have been curious—and perhaps a bit intimidated—to meet the great explorer-missionary Thomas Jefferson Bowen. At forty-one years old, Bowen was full of frenetic energy and also wracked with physical and mental illness, a crazed genius wrestling with contradictions in his temperament and outlook.[14] Over the past five years, he had thrown himself into Yorubaland, learning the language, traveling extensively, and collecting what in academic circles today we could call ethnographic knowledge—that is, information about how people lived, communicated with the spiritual world, and governed themselves. By the end of his second tour of duty in Yorubaland he had nearly completed the book that would make him briefly famous, *Travels and Explorations in Central Africa*, as well as a Yoruba dictionary and grammar.[15] He preached on the streets or in his chapel every day, focusing his knowledge of Yoruba life on the goal of saving souls. Though he insisted that foreigners could stay healthy in Yorubaland, Bowen was constantly sick and sometimes delusional. The baby born to him and his wife during their first year in Ijaye—named, in a gesture of hope, Mary Yoruba—died in infancy. Preoccupied with his former life as a sinner, Bowen secretly medicated himself with whiskey, laudanum, and flagellation.[16]

Bowen's views on race may have been considered open-minded by some of his southern peers, but he was steeped in white supremacy, beginning with his birth on Georgia lands recently taken from the Cherokees, through his military expeditions against Indians and Mexicans, to his marriage to the former Lurana Davis, a young southern belle from a wealthy Georgia plantation. His published writings repeatedly indicate respect for Yoruba forms of government, social life, and even religion as legitimate, sometimes admirable, and rife with possibility for improvement. "At the present time," he wrote from Ijaye in 1853, "I think it would be premature to decide that any race of men is doomed to perpetual barbarism."[17] Yet Bowen also referred to uncultivated Africans as "niggers" and could not resist characterizing them according to American planters' stereotypes about "the great difference in the character" of African slaves from various geographical origins.[18] His wife Lurana even wrote a letter to her father's slaves from "the black man's country, among your own kin's people." You may not realize it, she told them, but "you are much happier, and far better off than they are," because American bondspeople had the opportunity to become Christians, while Africans

Troubled Times in Yorubaland

"worship wood and stone."[19] When Thomas Bowen met Church Vaughan, he seemed more taken with the younger man's light brown–colored skin than with the details of his biography: "He is a mulatto from N. Carolina, and a good, quiet man," Bowen recorded of his "carpenter from Liberia." Arriving with Church were "also two civilized natives, one from S. Leone, and a civilized Vy man—a good fellow. I hope that all four of them are Christians."[20] Church probably thought discretion the better part of valor and kept to himself that he was not much of a Christian, and that his copper coloring came from his Native American mother. Given how little Bowen bothered to know about them, perhaps the Vai carpenter wasn't really Vai either.

Ten days after Church arrived, the Bowens departed for a new outpost fifty miles northeast at Ogbomosho. They left the Ijaye mission in the hands of their junior William Clarke, assisted by Yoruba and Saro personnel, plus Church and the man who might have been Vai. At this point, Clarke knew scarcely more about Church Vaughan than Bowen did, though he had been the one to recruit carpenters in Liberia two years earlier. From this point forward, however, Vaughan and Clarke developed a close collaboration, living, working, and traveling together until the missionary returned to the United States nearly three years later. Clarke's memoir of his time in Yorubaland includes only one line about Vaughan, whom he called "my excellent Liberian friend." Like Vaughan, he too may have found discretion to be prudent: readers might not have countenanced his interracial comradeship. But fragments of evidence suggest that they spent much time together. Vaughan's intellectual and religious development was clearly influenced by Clarke; it may be too that Clarke's "radically liberal views" on racial difference, as a Nigerian historian has characterized them, were formed in his close association with Church Vaughan.[21]

Clarke and Vaughan were now the two lone Americans at the Ijaye mission.[22] Though Clarke preached in town every day, he also joined Vaughan in the carpenter's main occupation: finishing the mission's church and continuing to improve and furnish the compound's other structures. For their buildings, foreigners demanded more than the mud and thatch constructions local to the area. They wanted logs sawed into planks, wooden floors and ceilings, and windows and doors that could be opened and closed. Local people had no experience with this kind of building, which is why Vaughan's abilities, and those of other craftsmen from the African diaspora, were so valued. Repeatedly Bowen had complained to his correspondents in Richmond about the lack of skilled builders in Yorubaland. He had tried unsuccessfully to find a carpenter—along with an interpreter or native assistant—when he had last stopped in Sierra Leone, where British missionaries did their recruiting. "I heartily wish we had a pious colored man from home, who could do our work and instruct some natives in the use of the shipsaw and carpenters' and turners' tools," he pined. "He would be well worth his salary."[23]

At the time of Vaughan's arrival, Bowen and Clarke had already made considerable progress laying out the Baptist compound and constructing the rudiments of a four-room house, a more modest dwelling for native assistants and translators, an even smaller shelter for servants, a separate kitchen, and a stable. Outside the compound's mud wall were the foundations of an unfinished chapel and a shed intended as a builder's workshop.[24] Over the next year, Vaughan, Clarke, the Vai carpenter, and their local assistants completed the chapel, an optimistically large structure able to seat, once the benches were constructed, five hundred to six hundred people.[25] They also transformed the mission house into a model of craftsmanship. This eighty by twenty-foot rectangular building, ten feet high, with a sitting room, storeroom, and two bedrooms, was covered by a roof of poles and thatch. All around the house, the roof rested on posts so as to form a wide, airy piazza, which itself had horizontal wooden shutters rising up from a three-foot high mud wall. Closing the shutters at night secured the piazza, so that inhabitants could leave their bedroom windows open for the breeze without people or animals getting in. Though the house's exterior surfaces were made of mud in the local style, Vaughan and the others smoothed the inside walls and plastered them with a fine, blue clay. "This had been so skillfully whitewashed with lime made from oyster shells brought up from the coast that one would never suspect the coarse material underneath," raved the missionary Richard Stone after his residence there. The doors, window frames, ceilings, flooring, and some of the furniture of the house were made of hard, polished *roko* wood (African teak). Vaughan and the other carpenters from Liberia and Sierra Leone cut the logs in pits in the forest, thereby introducing board sawing into Yorubaland and teaching it to their assistants.[26]

In supervising and training local construction crews, Vaughan came to learn not only how to communicate in the Yoruba language, but also about local systems of labor. If he had disapproved of "apprenticeship" in Liberia, he may not have found Yoruba arrangements any more admirable. In Yorubaland, like elsewhere in nineteenth-century Africa, everyone was either a patron or a dependent (or sometimes both), and slavery was pervasive. As the Anglican missionary in Ijaye put it, "In reality, all a man cannot do himself or by his family is done by slaves." Though captives were still being exported from the coast, thousands were retained by kings and chiefs, or sold locally, for military, agricultural, or other kinds of service. In fact, as palm oil exports grew with European demand for industrial lubrication, this so-called "legitimate" trade—touted by antislavery reformers—expanded rather than diminished slavery.[27] Kurunmi had thousands of slaves who worked his farms, served administrative functions, fought in his army, and bore his children. When the Bowens had first moved to Ijaye in 1853, the Are provided them with some of his own slaves to clear the land of bushes and trees. Thomas Bowen found these workers to be so "uncertain and expensive"—presumably because he was expected to offer presents to Kurunmi in return—that he resolved to hire laborers by the day from then on.[28] Wage earners were practically nonexistent, though, since anyone free enough from slavery or patronage to sell his own labor would have worked on his own farm or trade instead. In fact, working for a money payment was seen as shameful, outside the realm of the normal relationships that entangled labor and personal affiliation. "There are some wicked persons who often go to the building and quarrel with the laborers, calling them the white man's slaves, trying to ridicule them and get them to leave their work," Lurana Bowen recounted of the Baptists' building projects. "Others have waited in the road and caught the girls who were bringing water, and flogged them, because 'they worked for the white man,' as they would say."[29] By the time Vaughan was supervising workers and apprentices, they mostly were Christian converts from Abeokuta or lured away from the Church Missionary Society.[30] Still, missionaries continued to make use of slave labor, encouraging workers to redeem themselves with the wages earned but also reimbursing masters when their slaves ran away on the job.[31]

After nearly a year, Vaughan's major building projects were well enough completed, and his relationship with Clarke sufficiently strong, that Clarke included him on one of his exploratory trips. Clarke frequently traveled to learn about Yoruba life and to scout out prospects for future missions. In July 1856, he set out on a five-day trip to the town of Iwo, located some forty miles northeast of Ijaye (and these days the home of a university named after Thomas Bowen[32]). "My companions," he later wrote, "were my interpreter and an excellent colored friend, a native American from Liberia, who was in our employ as mechanic, and the necessary carriers."[33]

The trip offered Vaughan a glimpse into the widespread insecurity of the region in which he lived. About six miles outside of Ijaye, the travelers encountered the ruins of the town of Abemo, which had been destroyed by Ijaye's leader Kurunmi some twenty years earlier. Later the same day, they reached "a nice little town" called Fiditi, which had "several times defeated the attacks of plunderers and robbers."[34] As they learned, the area where Clarke and Vaughan traveled fell under the competing influence of two powerful city-states that had emerged as the Oyo Empire disintegrated: Ijaye and Ibadan. Now vying for supremacy in Yorubaland, leaders of both demanded tribute and military loyalty from the towns and villages around them. Iwo, which they reached the next day via caravan road, fell under the suzerainty of Ibadan.

Shared experiences, especially extraordinary ones like travel, can create deep personal bonds. On this trip, Vaughan and Clarke rode together on horseback through dense forest and in a downpour, slept in a gatekeeper's hut as well as an Iwo compound, and perhaps laughed at each other as they experienced an especially soggy form of African transport on the way home. Because so much rain had fallen, Clarke hired a ferryman to help his little party cross the nearby Ọbà River, which they had simply forded on the outbound trip from Ijaye. But the rivers in this area were too rocky for canoes to be useful. Instead, "we were safely ferried across in the peculiar Yoruba manner—of course on a huge calabash." The "African sailing vessel," as Mrs. Bowen had previously described it to her relatives, was made by cementing together the largest cut ends of two calabashes, forming a cushion-shaped floating gourd that could support hundreds of pounds of cargo. Probably unable to swim, Vaughan had to cross the river either clutching the calabash to his chest as a life preserver or, if it were big enough, sitting in the hollowed out gourd itself, while being pushed across the river by a hired swimmer.[35]

It is impossible to know what kind of relationship Vaughan and Clarke formed as they lived, worked, and traveled together. They were both single men in their late twenties (Vaughan was one year older than Clarke) from the American South facing the same conditions in Africa, who were nonetheless separated by background and the racial ideologies of the era. Like his elder missionary Thomas Bowen, Clarke had been born and raised in rural Georgia. But when he was sixteen, Clarke's father Jeremiah moved the family to Savannah, where he became a successful merchant and active member of the Baptist church.[36] In 1849 William Clarke graduated from Mercer University, an institution supported by Baptists and dedicated to liberal education, before becoming a teacher and then a church pastor.[37] Perhaps because of his more urban background, his higher education, or his friendship with Vaughan, Clarke ultimately became much more broad-minded about race than Bowen was. Throughout his account of his four years in Yorubaland, he repeatedly contrasted stereotyped notions of Africans as savages—"so firmly rooted in my childhood"—with the productive and logical ordering of societies that he observed. He determined that people in Africa "lived and thrived as in other lands; that they were actuated by the same motives, stimulated by the same objects and ends; and impelled by the same affections and desires; and that the only difference in their commerce was that of quantity, not principle. The same life, noise, confusion, energy, enterprise, the same diversity of character, person and talent could here be found," he wrote of a stop on a caravan route, "as at a railroad depot or steamboat landing in a civilized country."[38] A century after he left Yorubaland, Clarke was remembered there as "the most humane of men, with a balanced, cultivated mind. . . . With him, religion was not an excuse for destroying human values, but for ennobling them."[39]

Clarke's strongest influence on Vaughan was through education. All along, Clarke had hoped to educate future mission teachers and preachers, and he believed that black people would make better mission personnel than whites because they could withstand tropical diseases. When he first came to Yorubaland, he brought with him a "little Liberian boy to educate, at the earnest solicitations of his parents." The youth was stricken with illness and homesickness, though, and he died shortly before Vaughan arrived.[40] The carpenter may have become Clarke's next pupil. Though he was literate when he left South Carolina, Vaughan had never received any formal education. He was later known as a voracious reader, however, and the "best geologist in the colony" of Lagos.[41] Notably, Clarke's memoir of his time in Yorubaland includes a whole chapter on geology. Moreover, both Bowen and Clarke brought extensive libraries with them to the Yoruba missions, leaving the books behind when they eventually went home.[42] After a day spent outdoors sawing boards, finishing windows, or constructing furniture, Vaughan may have passed his evenings by lamplight, making his way through works of history, philosophy, or science and discussing their contents with his educated friend William Clarke, or with Andrew Phillips, the young widower missionary—also a graduate of Mercer University—who shared the Ijaye station for several months in 1856. His love of books may be why the Anglican missionary David Hinderer, after visiting Ijaye, mistook Vaughan for a schoolmaster.[43]

In April 1856, half a year after Vaughan arrived in Yorubaland, the Bowens returned to the United States, broken in physical and mental health. Clarke took over the Ogbomosho station that September, "begin[ning] my work from the foundation," Vaughan with him.[44] Their little world of Baptist missionaries was now growing, though: over the course of about a year, Phillips had joined the Ijaye station with his wife, who died soon after; Mr.

and Mrs. John Cason followed them to Ijaye; Mr. and Mrs. Selden Trimble joined Clarke in Ogbomosho; Mr. and Mrs. R. W. Priest opened a station at Abeokuta; and Mr. and Mrs. T. A. Reid opened one at (New) Oyo.[45] Though Clarke and Vaughan had become close companions, it is not clear that the other white Southern Baptists were so willing to relax American racial hierarchies, especially in front of their wives (several of whom, however, perished fairly quickly).[46] It may have helped Vaughan that he seemed to the new arrivals to be "nearly white" and "of excellent character."[47] Still, by American classifications, he was a colored man. Vaughan may have no longer slept in the mission house with Clarke, who now took the white missionaries as his traveling companions.[48] When Clarke and the Trimbles sat at the dinner table in Ogbomosho, it may have been awkward for Vaughan to join them, but humiliating if he did not.

Vaughan could navigate the racial etiquette of the mission, however, by invoking his desire for self-improvement. The white southerners with whom he worked did not have to consider Vaughan to be their social equals in order to loan him books or discuss religion with him. Their opinion of him improved, in fact, the more he shared their knowledge and values. A year previously, Clarke seems to have been describing Vaughan when he wrote of one of the participants in a mission meeting—the only one not explicitly identified as a local: "Then I see an old traveling companion, with a pleasing countenance and benign eye. Mark him, he must be a Christian. Most even temper, scarcely ever out of humor. But long ago, he felt he was a sinner— hates sin now, and has turned away from it, says he would serve God even in a distant heathen country. He too says he loves the Saviour, while his regular attendance on church would confirm his word."[49] On October 19, 1857, as a rainstorm rolled in, William Clarke baptized Church Vaughan in an Ogbomosho stream, signifying that the carpenter had accepted Christianity into his heart. For all of its religious significance, Vaughan's embrace of Baptism also appears as an affirmation of his relationship with Clarke and a bid for inclusion as a full member of the Christian fold. Clarke seems to have seen it this way too, writing to the Foreign Mission Board secretary in Richmond that "I have had the pleasure this evening of baptizing one of our carpenters, J. C. Vaughn, who is a very good workman, has done us much service, and I hope will yet be serviceable to our mission in many ways."[50]

Two years after arriving in Yorubaland, though, Vaughan was becoming less of a dependent employee for the missionaries and more of a self-reliant contractor, tendering bills for the building he continued to do as the Baptists extended their activities. When Clarke went on a month-long tour of northern and eastern Yorubaland in late 1857, Vaughan oversaw work at Ijaye and Ogbomosho and traveled through Abeokuta to Lagos to get payments and supplies from his old friend Joseph Harden. At other times, he sat at the table of the Reverend Priest in Ijaye, tendering his invoices. Extant bills show that Vaughan earned over $300 from the missionaries in 1857 and at least $200 in each of the following two years. (In comparison, missionary salaries were $750 per year.)[51] Evidently, Vaughan reported favorably back to Liberia, because in early 1858 he was joined in Yorubaland by two other Americo-Liberian carpenters, Henry Sewell Pettiford and Richard Russell. Vaughan had known Pettiford in Liberia, where the two arrived on different ships within a week of each other. Russell had come to Liberia, like Pettiford a free man from North Carolina, a couple of years earlier. The two went to work at the new station in Oyo and in Ogbomosho, where Reverend Reid baptized Russell shortly after his arrival. Other carpenters, including two identified as Barbour and Smith, and at least one woman arrived from Liberia later and fanned out to the different Baptist stations.[52]

Vaughan became even more independent of the mission after he said goodbye to Clarke, who traveled to the United States on leave in mid-1858. Clarke expected to return to Yorubaland after he married and improved his health. He seems to have clashed with the Southern Baptist Foreign Mission Board over policies and payments, however, and he resigned in 1860, never setting foot in Africa again.[53] Meanwhile, Vaughan probably remained at the Ogbomosho mission station at first, but things were not same under the new missionary Sheldon Trimble, a Kentuckian from a hardscrabble background who, even according to a sympathetic account, "was sometimes abrupt and exceedingly severe in his reproofs."[54] At least Vaughan now had the company of Pettiford and Russell. Some months later, the Trimbles also returned to the United States, leaving Pettiford to sort out their belongings.[55]

Vaughan must have decided the time was right to move out on his own. He was not interested in remaining closely attached to any mission. The Ogbomosho station was now vacant and closed, though Reverend Reid remained at Oyo and Mr. and Mrs. Priest were based in Abeokuta. The Ijaye station had two resident missionaries, Phillips and the recently arrived Richard Stone, accompanied by his wife Sue. A Liberian was given "a sleeping place in our yard" there, but Stone poked "much fun" at the man and his "childish" response to a noise in the night — an attitude that surely would not have attracted Vaughan.[56] By this time, he could speak Yoruba reasonably well and had established local contacts through mission circles and construction work. As Stone put it, Vaughan and Russell "had lived in the country so long that they were natives in all respects except in dress and in religion."[57]

Thus, sometime after his thirtieth birthday, after building for others his whole adult life, Church Vaughan began constructing his own house. He was granted the use of some land by the *bale* ("father of the town") at Ido, a little settlement situated within the triangle formed by Ijaye in the North, Ibadan in the Southeast, and Abeokuta to the Southwest. The town had been evacuated in the warfare of the 1820s but was currently being repopulated by Egba farmers, though it was officially claimed by Ibadan.[58] In other words, it had no official ties to Kurunmi or Ijaye. Moreover, it offered Vaughan opportunities to make a good living as a builder for missionaries in the three nearby cities.

Over the next year, Vaughan achieved the kind of freedom he and his family had hoped for in South Carolina. He had his own house and was able to support himself from building and a little farming. He made his own decisions about how he worked and lived. He was outside of the oversight of white missionaries as well as Ijaye's ruler. He had no political voice like he had in Liberia; but neither did free people of color back home. As tensions mounted between the old rivals Ijaye and Ibadan, however, his situation became increasingly precarious. Ultimately, his safety depended on his choice of allegiance, and the patronage of a strong protector.

In a portentous coincidence, Vaughan made his bid for autonomy at the very moment that other African Americans determined to form their own settlement in Yorubaland. Martin Robeson Delany and Robert Campbell would go on to have illustrious careers in the military, politics, and journalism, but in 1860 they were in Abeokuta on what turned out to be a quixotic undertaking. Unlike Vaughan, who simply wanted to live on his own, these self-styled "Commissioners from the African Race" intended to lead an African American colonization movement in West Africa, and not in Liberia. "*Africa for the African race, and black men to rule them,*" proclaimed Delany, clarifying that by black men he meant those of African descent, not necessarily Africans.[59] Only later would he, Campbell, and Vaughan realize that their ideas of freedom, shaped in reaction to white supremacy in the United States, were incompatible with local dynamics and untenable to African authorities — especially as political crisis and violent conflict again exploded in Yorubaland.

Let's begin with Vaughan. To understand the peril he faced at Ido, we have to consider the aftermath of the fall of the Oyo Empire. In the 1830s, its capital at Old Oyo was sacked by warriors from the former province of Ilorin, its surviving inhabitants fleeing south. Atiba, a son of the ruler killed in the attack, constructed a less impressive imperial capital at a place that became known as (New) Oyo, about twenty miles north of Ijaye (where the Baptist Reverend Reid was later stationed). Facing continued threats from Ilorin, Atiba ensured the loyalty of the region's two principal warlords, the leaders of Ijaye and Ibadan, by conferring high Oyo titles on each of them, and by allocating to each town a specific geographic area in which to collect tribute. Atiba thus created a working alliance among his leading subordinate city-states, which managed to stop the advance of the Ilorins. But as Ibadan and Ijaye both grew in strength by the 1850s, so did their rivalry. In April 1859, Atiba died, having mandated that the Crown Prince Adelu should succeed him instead of dying with his father according to tradition. However, Kurunmi of Ijaye refused to recognize the new king. When Adelu drew on the support of the leaders of Ibadan, this set the stage for a conflict between the two longstanding rivals.[60]

Vaughan may have suspected the precariousness of his position as these tensions increased, though he still did not return to the well-protected town of Ijaye. Two months after the new king Adelu was crowned in Oyo, Vaughan applied to Andrew Phillips, one of the American Baptists, to be the missionaries' agent for Abeokuta. The mission house there was unfinished, and since the resident missionary had recently left, now was a good time to complete the work, before a new man was sent out from America. After four years of self-education under Clarke's tutelage, Vaughan must have been literate enough to serve as agent; and he could also do the building. He may have also been seeking a safer haven in case war were to break out between Ijaye and Ibadan. "I think he will be a valuable addition to our Mission," Phillips wrote of Vaughan in requesting authorization to hire him. Vaughan never got the job, however, and he remained at Ido.[61]

In late 1859 and early 1860, troops from both Oyo and its subordinate Ijaye attempted to collect tribute from some of the outlying towns that under the prevailing system had been allocated to Ijaye. The new Oyo king called for reinforcements from Ibadan, prompting an angry and insulting response from the Ijaye leader Kurunmi. The leaders of Ibadan then debated whether they should go to war against Ijaye on Oyo's behalf. It was a difficult decision, because in spite of the enmity between the two towns, their populations were closely connected through family ties. Citizens of both met for weddings, funerals, and festivals; and they bore the same facial markings and would not be able to distinguish one another on the battlefield. As one of the Ibadan chiefs put it at a public meeting, he had no less than 120 close relatives in Ijaye—was he to go and fight them?[62] Ibadan's *Balogun*, or war chief, Ibikunle favored patient diplomacy, especially since Kurunmi was an old man. However, Ibadan's Chief Ogunmola, next in rank and rival to the *Balogun*, led the younger war chiefs on a public relations campaign in favor of war. They even tied a scrawny bird to Ibikunle's house to insult his bravery, reminding onlookers of the Yoruba expression "as cowardly as a crow."[63] Ogunmola had his own reasons to favor war: when he was younger, he had been captured by Ijaye soldiers and had to be ransomed. Some observers speculated that he also looked toward a future alliance between Ibadan, Dahomey in the West, the kingdom of Benin in the East, and the proslavery former king of Lagos to expunge British influence from Yorubaland and protect the slave trade.[64]

In Ijaye, Kurunmi boasted that Ibadan would never beat him. As Anna Hinderer, an English missionary in Ibadan, recounted, both sides taunted each other with "most passionate messages": "Calabashes were presented to one and another, with the request that the chief of Ijaye desires such and such an Ibadan chief's head in that calabash; then these people send back, 'We want *Are*'s [Kurunmi's] head in this calabash first.'" As leaders in both city-states began to drill their soldiers and seek outside allies, they declared open season on kidnapping their enemies to sell as slaves. By February 1860, the roads between Ibadan and Ijaye were closed, infested by Ibadan war boys who "have been catching everybody, man, woman, or child, who ventured out in the Ijaye farms." "Whether there is to be real war we cannot tell," Anna Hinderer mused, "there are various reports, but it is an anxious time." However, the Baptist missionaries, naively, "could not see how that [the conflict between Ibadan and Ijaye] could affect the safety of a foreigner who was entirely neutral in the matter."[65]

Evidently, Vaughan could. Still avoiding Ijaye, he decided to secure some of his property with people he knew in Ibadan. As both towns mobilized for war, Vaughan arranged for some Ibadan men to come to his farm and help him move his valuables—presumably tools and perhaps some finished furniture or other goods. But whether they saw him as loyal to Ijaye or simply as a source of easy loot, they turned on him. The movers ransacked his house and took everything. One struck him hard on the head with his musket. Vaughan fought back, and leaving his assailant apparently dead, fled to Ibadan. By the next day, he was being held by Ibadan's *Balogun* Ibikunle, though whether he would be sheltered or treated as an enemy was an open question.[66]

Troubled Times in Yorubaland

Despite Vaughan's apparent determination to sidestep them, Ijaye's leader and its Baptist missionaries still viewed him as under their protection. On February 20, 1860, the *Arẹ* Kurunmi sent word to the Baptists in Ijaye that "our friend Vaughn was in great danger, and that we should warn him to come into [Ijaye] immediately." Reverend Phillips was ill with smallpox, so the duty fell to Richard Stone, a 22-year-old minister who had arrived in Ijaye from Virginia with his new wife Sue almost exactly one year earlier.[67] Stone brought out his horse, a giant white Arabian purchased from Kurunmi and known to all as "*Arẹ's* war horse," which he outfitted with a recently ordered Mexican saddle. He donned boots and spurs, but his wife convinced him to leave behind his seven-shooter. She also persuaded Richard Russell, who had served in the Liberian militia and had just arrived from Oyo, to accompany him. Both were good ideas.

Stone and Russell rode through depopulated hamlets and thick forests to reach Vaughan's farm. They found it completely deserted, his belongings destroyed and scattered over the ground. "There was every indication that the enemy was there," they later recounted, "and that something serious had befallen their friend." Riding to a nearby village to look for him, the two Americans "fell into a nest of about a thousand Ibadan warriors, and were taken for spies and roughly treated." Unlike Stone, Russell understood the Yoruba language well, and he told his companion that he expected to be killed, since their captors would not be able to sell them as slaves. But the leader of the hostile party dismissed the others and took them farther into the woods, toward Ibadan. Along the way, "they were pretty roughly used, their clothes torn and their hats stolen."[68]

The two prisoners were escorted to Ibadan and presented to the *Balogun* Ibikunle. Since he had been riding the *Arẹ* Kurunmi's horse, Stone was accused of being an Ijaye military officer, in advance of an army to attack the Ibadans. Through an interpreter, Stone explained the real reason for his mission, and he demonstrated that he was (fortuitously) unarmed. Ibikunle replied that a badly wounded white man had been brought to Ibadan and was being held in an adjoining house. The chief assumed that this was the one Stone and Russell had attempted to warn of danger.[69] Presumably, the Americans knew that the Yoruba term *òyìnbó*, generally translated as "white person," was used for all foreigners or those with European ways, regardless of skin color. Though they considered him to be black, they probably realized that the "white" person in question was indeed Vaughan. By that point, however, their main problem had become their own safety.

Not knowing what to do with the Americans, Ibikunle had Stone and

Russell brought to the house of the CMS missionaries David and Anna Hinderer, who were away in Abeokuta. There, they waited for a decision about their fate. After two days, Stone penned a letter to his missionary superiors in Richmond, Virginia. "I am quite ragged and dusty in appearance, but got some things from a young man who is here. . . . I suppose Sue is almost frantic with grief, supposing that I have been murdered, for no communication can reach Ijaye now."[70] On the fifth day of their captivity, a recently returned Mrs. Hinderer went to Ibikunle to plead for Stone and Russell's release, playing for sympathy by mentioning Richard Stone's wife. "Why can't he get another?" asked Ibikunle's messenger wryly.[71]

As the Ibadan chiefs continued to deliberate, Stone and Russell took matters into their own hands. With Anna Hinderer's assistance, they slipped away from their captors and quietly left Ibadan by the road leading north to Oyo, well east of the dangerous path directly between Ibadan and Ijaye. The next day, at the town of Iwo, they learned that Ibadan soldiers were on the road leading from there to Oyo, and the only way to avoid them would be to proceed to Ogbomosho, sixty miles north and neutral in the hostilities. Their route would thus be a giant loop, with a hundred-mile detour to get to Ijaye. Along the way, both Stone and Russell became exhausted and feverish, though Stone described his companion as "cool, sympathetic and brave in all this great trouble."[72] After spending two nights along the route, the men arrived safely in Ogbomosho.

There, Stone and Russell rested and briefly recovered in the Baptist mission house, whose missionary was on leave in the United States. But the mission's interpreter was there, as well as two foreign visitors: Martin Delany and Robert Campbell, exploring Yorubaland in their search for a proposed colony of African Americans. If Vaughan had perhaps been willfully inattentive to local developments when he tried to separate himself from Ijaye, Delany and Campbell were even more oblivious. Their understanding of the politics of Yorubaland was much shallower than Vaughan's, but they too hoped to live independently of them. Their ultimately unsuccessful mission offers a telling counterpoint to his own.

Martin Delany was one of the most colorful figures in nineteenth-century African American history.[73] Born free in 1812 and raised in Pennsylvania, Delany proudly traced his ancestry to African royalty. From 1843 to 1848 he edited his own antislavery weekly, before joining Frederick Douglass as coeditor of the abolitionist newspaper the *North Star*. After his resignation two years later, he was accepted at Harvard Medical School but forced to leave after only one term because of racist student protests. Delany became increasingly convinced that black Americans could only thrive in their own nation, although he had no admiration for the white-run American Colonization Society and its project in Liberia. In fact it had been one of his vehement anti-ACS speeches that had soured Vaughan's family on going to Liberia.[74] Delany's 1852 book, *The Condition, Elevation, Emigration and Destiny of the Colored People of the United States, Politically Considered*, included a powerful denunciation of the Colonization Society, but it did argue for emigration, under African American leadership, to Central or South America. Five years later, worsening developments in the United States — notably the infamous *Dred Scott* Supreme Court decision, which insisted that African Americans could never be citizens — pushed Delany farther in favor of emigration. Now, however, he had a new destination in mind: Yorubaland, introduced to the American public by the missionary Thomas Jefferson Bowen.

In 1857, after returning to the United States, Bowen had published *Central Africa: Adventures and Missionary Labors in Several Countries in the Interior of Africa*, and he embarked on speaking tours to promote the book, the cause of colonization, and Yorubaland itself. Bowen had always been a strong supporter of African American emigration and the American Colonization Society, but he believed that the Niger Valley offered a better destination for African Americans than Liberia because of its salubrious environment, intelligent and industrious population, and commercial potential.[75] With the support of the ACS and a number of merchants, Bowen even convinced the U.S. Senate (but not the House of Representatives) to appropriate twenty-five thousand dollars for an expedition up the Niger River ("the Mississippi of Africa"), in order to promote trade, Christianity, and emigration.[76] Though their racial politics differed dramatically, Delany found Bowen's account of the Niger Valley to be "interesting and intelligent."[77] In 1858, he set about raising support for his own exploratory venture in Yoruba country, though with limited success. Delany managed to recruit only one other traveler, Robert Campbell, a Jamaican of mixed European and African ancestry who was teaching science at the Institute for Colored Youth in Philadelphia.[78] Campbell sailed to England in early 1859 to raise funds, while Delany traveled via Liberia, his passage provided, ironically, by the American Colonization Society. They rejoined each other in Abeokuta in November.

Delany and Campbell ultimately visited several cities and towns in what is now southwestern Nigeria, retracing some of Thomas Bowen's footsteps. Abeokuta most appealed to them as a possible place for a settlement, not only because of its large population of returnees from Sierra Leone, but also because of its prospects for cotton production. For nearly a decade, some

Saro entrepreneurs connected with the Anglican mission's Industrial Institution had been working with a Manchester merchant to supply African-grown cotton to the British textile industry. In Delany's and Campbell's view, cotton production could be the means of support for African American settlers, who would profit at the same time that they undermined American slavery. (No matter whether African Americans would ever voluntarily tend cotton fields, even in Africa.) When Campbell traveled through London on the way to Africa, he had received financial backing and letters of introduction from the cotton merchant; when he arrived in Abeokuta two months ahead of Delany, his principal contact became Josiah Crowther, who had apprenticed in Manchester and ran the local cotton exporting industry, and his brother Samuel Crowther Jr., a London-trained medical doctor. The Crowthers, not incidentally, were the sons of Samuel Ajayi Crowther, probably the most famous resident of Abeokuta before the twentieth century.[79]

Samuel Crowther, the father, had been captured in the Yoruba wars as a youth, rescued from a slave ship, and taken to Sierra Leone. There and later in England, Crowther was educated by British missionaries and became a devout Anglican. Because of his great facility with languages and his religious devotion, he was recruited in 1841 to join Britain's ill-fated Niger expedition, intended to expand "legitimate" trade into the West African interior but utterly debilitated by fever among the European personnel. Two years later Crowther was ordained an Anglican minister, and in 1846 the Church Missionary Society sent him and the Englishman Henry Townsend as their first missionaries to Abeokuta. By the time Delany and Campbell arrived thirteen years later, both Townsend and Crowther wielded strong influence in Abeokuta, but Crowther's stature in the missionary society—he would become the Anglican Church's first black bishop—fostered a bitter rivalry between him and his nominal supervisor. This tension, as well as friction between the indigenous leadership and Sierra Leonean returnees, only worsened the prospects for the two visiting North Americans.

In December 1859, Delany and Campbell met with the *Alake* (king) of Abeokuta to negotiate a treaty that would allow African Americans—"select and intelligent people of high moral as well as religious character"—to settle there.[80] They were accompanied by Samuel Crowther Sr. and Jr., but the Reverend Townsend was notably absent. With the Crowthers as witnesses, the North Americans and the *Alake* signed a four-article treaty, ratified the next day by six other chiefs. Whether or not by design, the document left vague the place of the proposed American settlement in the Egba polity. On the one hand, the first article granted "on behalf of the African race in America, the right and privilege of settling in common with the Egba people, on any part of the territory belonging to Abeokuta, not otherwise occupied"— suggesting that the proposed settlers would intermingle with other residents of Abeokuta. The fourth article similarly provided "that the laws of the Egba people shall be strictly respected by the settlers." Indeed, the Baptist missionary T. A. Reid, with whom Delany and Campbell were then lodging, reported a month before the treaty was signed that "their object is not to establish a colony but for each one to come and settle where he pleases without any organization. This is the only safe and resourceful course for their purpose," he added prophetically, "because a separate government would not be allowed by the rulers and people."[81] The other two provisions of the treaty, however, left the impression that the "Commissioners" did envision a separate colony for American immigrants. According to the second article, "All matters requiring legal investigation among the settlers, [are to] be left to be disposed of according to their customs." And disputes between the settlers and the Egba, according to a provision of article four, would be adjudicated by "an equal number of commissioners, mutually agreed upon."[82] Delany and Campbell left Abeokuta a couple of weeks after the agreement was signed, in mid-January 1860, to explore Yorubaland, apparently ignorant of both the looming troubles with the treaty and the impending war between Ijaye and Ibadan.

Though the two "commissioners" would not learn this for many months, their proposed Abeokuta settlement was doomed. After they left town, Reverend Townsend convinced the *Alake*, who was already having second thoughts, to repudiate the treaty. The American settlers would be too independent, Townsend argued; they would not obey local rulers. (Not incidentally, Townsend worried that black American settlers, "full of bitterness against all white men," would not submit to his own authority either.[83]) Moreover, such outright, permanent alienation of land as suggested in the treaty ran contrary to Egba norms. After a year of arguing over the matter between the Egba leaders, the Crowthers, Townsend, and the colonial government at Lagos, the *Alake* and other chiefs finally issued a statement in February 1861 denying that they had ever signed a treaty with Delany and Campbell; rather, the two explorers had simply been assigned land for farming. So much blame was placed on Samuel Crowther Jr. for facilitating the treaty, now interpreted as a bid to swindle Egba of their land and undermine their authority, that he had to flee Abeokuta.[84]

As this controversy was just beginning to unfold, however, Campbell and Delany made their way north to Ilorin. Though they were personally unimpeded by the developing hostilities between Ijaye and Ibadan, ordinary people's attempts to take shelter and stay off the roads made it difficult to hire carriers for the travelers' voluminous luggage. In February 1860, Campbell and Delany waited for several days at the Baptist mission house in Ogbomosho. There, they encountered Stone and Russell, "two horsemen" who arrived "weary, starved and almost in rags."[85] After some food and rest, Stone took the opportunity to trade horses with Campbell, making it the Jamaican's problem to ride on Kurunmi's mount when he and Delany continued their travels the next week. Stone and Russell then resumed their journey.

Worried about his wife, Stone determined to head straight south to Oyo and from there try to get back to Ijaye. At Oyo, Stone met his fellow American Baptist missionary T. A. Reid. After a hearty welcome, Reid told his own tale of how he had heard of Stone and Russell's disappearance and, along with a British missionary, a couple of carriers, and his own Liberian recruit (probably Pettiford), set out to look for them. He had just returned from a hazardous and futile four-day trip. He also told Stone that he had heard from Ijaye that Mrs. Stone, supposing her husband had been murdered, had been prostrated by grief, contracted a fever, and was not expected to live.[86] Right away, Stone secured permission from the king of Oyo to proceed—a relief, since the monarch was allied with Ibadan—and set out for Ijaye. Ten days after attempting to warn Church Vaughan of danger, Richard Stone returned to his overjoyed wife and much celebration in Ijaye.

Meanwhile, Campbell and Delany's difficulties in recruiting porters delayed their return to Lagos by more than a month. Ultimately, they were forced to leave most of their possessions—including a collection of some of the first photographs taken in Africa—in Ijaye, where they did not survive the disaster that was then looming.[87] When the two finally departed Yorubaland in April 1860, Delany and Campbell thought that they would soon return with colonists from the United States. This never happened. Once the American Civil War began, would-be settlers as well as Delany himself focused their energies on the emancipation of American slaves. In February 1865, Abraham Lincoln commissioned Delany as a major in the Union army, making him the first African American ever to hold field rank in the U.S. military. Robert Campbell, a British subject, did return to Lagos in 1862, settling with his family and establishing an independent weekly newspaper called the *Anglo-African*.[88] Later in their lives, he would be a friend and business associate to Church Vaughan.

And what about Vaughan, wounded and detained in Ibadan? Certainly he was safer with Ibikunle than he would have been with Ogunmola, Ibadan's ambitious secondary war chief. Two years later, when the Ibadans captured Edward Roper, an Englishman from the Church Missionary Society, Ogunmola demanded money, guns, and ammunition for his release, adding that if the captive had instead been Adolphus Mann, the CMS missionary who had treated wounded Ijayes, "we should have killed him right out, for he fought us."[89] Vaughan had managed to carry some of his money with him, and he may have hoped that he could ransom himself. Even if his own money were not enough, perhaps Ogunmola would demand a payment from the missionaries, especially once Stone and Russell were also captured. Vaughan knew, however, the stretched finances of the American Baptists (because they still owed him money); and there was no reason to think that they or British missionaries would spend their precious resources on him — especially since he could be blamed for the ordeal of Stone and Russell. Indeed, the Yoruba interpreter for the Baptist missionaries at Ijaye was also captured in early 1860. Unransomed, he was kept in irons in Ibadan for three years and died soon after his release.[90]

The Ibadan leader Ibikunle must have also discussed Vaughan, however, when he contacted the CMS mission in Ibadan in connection with the other American prisoners. At that point, David and Anna Hinderer, the resident missionaries, had not yet returned from a trip to Abeokuta, and instead, responsibility for the captives fell to their assistant, a "native" catechist named Henry Johnson. Johnson was a repatriated Yoruba man from Sierra Leone, and his children went on to distinguished careers in religion and education. His son Samuel Johnson, educated by both the Hinderers and Yoruba historians, later penned the landmark *History of the Yorubas, from the Earliest Times to the Beginning of the British Protectorate*.[91] And there, in a chapter on the Ibadan-Ijaye war, the reader learns both that "the missionaries were caught and brought to Ibadan on the 20th of February 1860," and that "Mr. Vaughan had escaped back to Ijaye by another route."[92]

Vaughan's captivity may well have caused him to reflect upon the fate of his ancestors, and his own father, held against their will. Even the missionary Richard Stone connected his experience to that of American slaves. "It would require but a very short residence in this country to make anyone detest the slave trade," he wrote after his escape, "especially if they are torn from their homes and friends as I have been and as many are daily being done."[93] But perhaps it was not so much slavery but freedom that Vaughan considered in light of his harrowing experience. Vaughan, like Delany and Campbell, had sought to make a life in Yorubaland outside of its structures of power and patronage. For all of them, such autonomy — in earning a living, forming social relations, and conducting themselves without deference to a master or political superior — was part of the dignity of freedom. But this kind of freedom ran against the currents in most of Atlantic Africa, and certainly in Yorubaland.[94] For Delany and Campbell, it undermined their plans for an African American settlement; for Vaughan, it brought real danger. As devastating wars began in both Yorubaland and the United States, Vaughan and the two "Commissioners" gave up their bids for self-determination in Africa, at least for a while.

After fleeing from Ibadan, Church Vaughan needed somewhere to recuperate. His house had been damaged and looted, and all that remained of his property was some money and a few articles of value that he had secured with him.[95] Perhaps reluctantly, he returned to the Ijaye mission, where he had lived with Clarke on his first arrival in Yorubaland more than four years earlier. By the time he arrived, the search party sent to aid him — Stone and Russell — had returned, as had two Liberians that Sue Stone had sent to find them. In addition to Mrs. Stone, who had been wracked with illness and worry, Russell came out of "this unfortunate adventure" with "his nervous system . . . completely shattered," and he later died at Abeokuta.[96] If Vaughan appreciated the efforts mission personnel had undertaken to find him, their suffering still must have soured his relations with them — as did the knowledge that Vaughan had first turned to Ibadan rather than to his connections in Ijaye when the danger began. Richard Stone, who even a fellow missionary described as "rather irritable in his nature and [having] a weak constitution," may have only grudgingly granted Vaughan the use of one of the outbuildings that the carpenter had likely built himself. But Vaughan could not return to his own farm: early in March, Ibadan forces destroyed Ido and another nearby Egba hamlet as they made their way to disrupt supply lines between Ijaye and the coast. Moreover, Kuranmi now forbade people from leaving Ijaye.[97]

During and after the Ibadan-Ijaye War, Vaughan oscillated between living with Baptist missionaries and on his own. His clear preference was for the latter, but every time it seemed safe to seek autonomy, he was struck down. With city-states pitted against one another and even bystanders killed or captured, Vaughan took necessary refuge among the missionaries, who were themselves under the wing of Ijaye's king and Abeokuta's war chiefs. Later, as the war wound down and he began finally to establish a household with his own dependents, it would be Vaughan's Christian connections that rendered him vulnerable. If separating from the missionaries had proven to be perilous, so too, it turned out, was joining them.

Ibadan declared war on March 16, 1860, some three weeks after Vaughan's capture and flight to Ijaye.[98] Though they may have hoped to remain outside the fray, Vaughan and other mission personnel were soon drawn into service. The opening battles, fought in the forests between Ijaye and Ibadan, involved tens of thousands of combatants and heavy casualties on both sides. After three indecisive engagements, the Ijaye forces ran short of ammunition—because Kurunmi had forbidden subordinate chiefs from accumulating weapons that might be used against him—and retreated to within the town's walls.[99] Ijaye would have been defeated then, but for the intervention of the Egba from Abeokuta, who feared Ibadan's growing power. Some twenty thousand Egba soldiers reached Ijaye in May 1860, settling into a fortified camp south of the town. In June, the allied Ijaye and Abeokuta forces began to engage the Ibadans in massive, bloody battles. Missionaries, drawing on their basic medical skills, tended the Ijaye wounded, with the Anglican Adolphus Mann reporting that he treated between forty and sixty soldiers per day.[100] Motivated by self-preservation if not *esprit de corps*, Vaughan and Pettiford took up positions as "sharp-shooters, who harassed the Ibadans a good deal with their rifles," as the Yoruba historian Samuel Johnson later recounted.[101]

It soon became clear that the Egba were ambiguous allies at best. Ijaye women began composing songs about their military weakness, which were promptly banned. Moreover, it was said at the time that the soldiers from Abeokuta may have replenished the Ijayes' ammunition, but they exhausted their granaries. Ijaye farmland was now in the hands of the Ibadan army, so food supplies began to run out. Their livestock quickly consumed, Ijaye people planted their streets and yards with corn and greens, but hungry residents ate the unripe cornstalks.[102] The situation worsened over the next year, as Ibadan forces also attacked tributary towns that supplied food to Ijaye. Even during the first few months, desperate parents trapped inside the town walls pledged their children as pawns to the Egba warriors in exchange for food, or in hopes that the children would be fed from supplies at Abeokuta. Instead of keeping them to be redeemed by their parents later, however, the soldiers sold the pawns to slave merchants who were collecting thousands of war captives for transport to the coast. Egba troops were engaged in a "legal slave hunt," charged the Anglican missionary Adolphus Mann, who estimated that they sold over five thousand Ijaye children in the first two years of the war.[103]

This was only a portion of the widespread slaving carried out by combatants. Thousands of prisoners were added to the armies or labor forces of local elites.[104] Another thirteen thousand or so were exported to Cuba through the markets of Dahomey and the Lagos lagoon, sold by both sides largely in exchange for weapons. With Cuba the last legal importer (until 1865) of African captives, these prisoners were among the final victims of the transatlantic slave trade.[105]

Unlike most of their neighbors, Vaughan and the other inhabitants of the Baptist mission at Ijaye were relatively safe from starvation because they had cowrie shell currency with which to purchase food. The senior missionary, Andrew Phillips, determined to help as many families as possible, using their supplies to take children into the mission rather than see them sent to the Egba soldiers. Soon the Baptists had more or less adopted over a dozen children, ranging from toddlers to teenagers, and more followed.[106] Phillips then realized that they would be safer, and have better access to provisions from the coast, if they moved to Abeokuta. Several months into the war, he and most of the children at the Ijaye Baptist mission joined a caravan under Egba military escort. They left Richard and Sue Stone to operate the Ijaye mission, which increasingly fell under the protection and patronage of the Egba military commander. Vaughan, Pettiford, and Russell must have gone to Abeokuta too, as the Anglican missionary Mann reported in early 1861 that there were no carpenters remaining in Ijaye.[107]

The Baptist mission at Abeokuta, christened "Alabama" after the home state of the first missionaries who had inhabited it, quickly grew to a bustling little village. Phillips no longer did much preaching, but instead "had become a schoolmaster." Soon his forty-four pupils were augmented by an additional seventy children sent from Ijaye, the small ones carried in baskets on soldiers' heads, as well as war orphans already in Abeokuta.[108] The mission's population grew even more in early 1861, when a letter brought the news that seven southern states had seceded from the United States and established the Confederacy. The Baptists assumed, rightly, that they could no longer count on steady supplies from their headquarters in Richmond and decided for the sake of economy to close the Ijaye station. Under cover of darkness, the Stones and the last of their foster children left Ijaye for a nerve-wracking three-day journey to Abeokuta.[109]

At the Baptist compound there, Vaughan lived with Pettiford and the ailing Richard Russell, along with the missionaries and some sixty children and forty adult refugees from Ijaye. The war had stopped all new construction, but Vaughan earned his keep maintaining buildings, farming, and instructing some of the older boys in board sawing and carpentry.[110] As the Egba leaders became increasingly desperate to break the military stalemate, they conscripted all possible recruits, making it clear that Christian converts were not to be exempted. Yet the Americans remained safely in their own compound, where at times they could hear the roar of muskets from the battlefield seventy miles away.[111] Effectively, their "headman" was Reverend Phillips, who repeatedly wrote home that he had become like a father to the children in his care.[112] As the American Civil War stopped all support coming from the United States, Phillips sustained the Abeokuta mission largely through his own fund-raising in Lagos, and with $578 bequeathed by Richard Russell at his death.[113] Vaughan may have missed his previous autonomy, but he too was under the protection of the mission, as it was just too dangerous not to be.

In March 1862, two years after the outbreak of the war, Vaughan and other residents of Abeokuta learned from informants to the West that they faced yet another danger. Every dry season, the army of the kingdom of Dahomey mobilized in pursuit of slaves and tribute. With the bulk of the Egba forces occupied outside of Ijaye, Abeokuta was more vulnerable than it had been since the last Dahomean invasion over a decade ago. Yet the Egba's allies needed them desperately: Ijaye's leader Kurunmi had died the previous June, people there were starving or trying to flee, and the besieging Ibadan army outnumbered Ijaye's defenders by some three to one. On March 17 the Dahomeans advanced to within fifteen miles of Abeokuta, laying waste to the outlying town of Ishaga and carrying off five thousand captives before pulling back. That evening, the Egba abandoned Ijaye, leaving desperate inhabitants to flee in their wake. Stories trickled into Abeokuta that some Ijaye household heads put halters around the necks of their wives, children, and relatives, pretended that they were slaves, and led them to Ibadan in hopes of joining their kinfolk who lived there. Countless others were killed or taken captive by the Ibadans. Some of the Ijaye chiefs committed suicide. The following day, March 18, 1862, Ibadan forces entered an empty town, set fire to every building (including the Baptist mission house), and decreed that Ijaye should never be rebuilt.[114] Though the injunction was later reversed—it was said to have caused a smallpox epidemic in the region—Ijaye today is a small, impoverished satellite of the Ibadan metropolis.[115]

If Vaughan thought the fall of Ijaye would end the war, he was mistaken. The fighting now moved into a new phase, pitting Abeokuta directly against Ibadan, with other Yoruba allies drawn in on both sides. Most of the battles over the next three years took place at some distance from Abeokuta, though, in territory to the Southeast along Ijebu-controlled trade routes to Lagos. This created a new opportunity for Vaughan to break away from the Abeokuta mission. In early 1862, Phillips traveled to England for nine months in order to restore his health and raise funds for his orphans, leaving Richard Stone in charge of the Abeokuta mission. At the earliest possible opportunity, Vaughan tried again to establish his own homestead. He chose Atadi, some eight miles from Abeokuta, near where he had previously lived at Ido and seemingly safe from the continuing warfare. There, he resumed carpentry and board sawing as well as farming. He also constructed his own machine for extracting the juice from sugar cane and began to produce brown sugar, reportedly the first time this was done in Yorubaland. Indeed, the Anglican mission's newspaper praised his product as "equal to some bought in England at five pence a pound at one of the best London shops."[116]

On his own little homestead, Vaughan avoided any identification with Yoruba political communities, even when the Dahomean army made its periodic threats on Abeokuta. He did not come to the town's defense in March 1864, when some of the Egba forces were away in Ijebu country fighting and thousands of troops from Dahomey stormed the town gate in another attempted invasion. Other foreign and African Christians were drawn into the conflict: the King of Dahomey boasted that he was clearing a field for the execution of the white missionaries from Abeokuta, and the town's numerous Christians even formed their own fighting regiment. Vaughan's friend Sewell Pettiford manned a cannon donated by the English for the defense of the town, remaining at his post even when the weapon's platform lost a wheel and he was pinned down by Dahomean gunners. The Baptist missionaries Phillips and Reid exhorted the defenders from near the town wall.[117] But Vaughan played no part in the Egba victory, nor did he join Egba and Ijaye troops still fighting Ibadan on battlefields to the Southeast, as Pettiford did. Pettiford became renowned for his skill with a rifle, knocking several Ibadan chiefs dead from their horses, and hitting the leader Ogunmola's hat though missing his head.[118]

About a year after the Dahomey invasion, in early 1865, Vaughan married a woman named Sarah Omotayo and brought her to his place at Atadi. Remarkably little has been remembered about this woman by her descendants, other than that she came from the kingdom of Benin, located more than two hundred miles east of Lagos and at one time the island's overlord. A surviving photograph of her is not at all like the conventional portraits of prosperous, nineteenth-century West African women: she appears in a plain dress, with neither hat nor headscarf. Indeed, she looks like a mission schoolgirl, which is probably what she was, given her European first name. Certainly she

Sarah Omotayo. Photo courtesy of Johnson Publishing Company, LLC.

must have been a Baptist convert, for the baptized Vaughan would not have married someone outside of the faith. Eight years earlier, Reverend Phillips had been visited in Ijaye by a messenger from the king of Benin. It may be that Sarah arrived with the messenger, or perhaps with some of the soldiers from Benin who joined the Ibadans in their war against Ijaye, or through the Benin arms trade to Ibadan.[119] She may have been the young woman kidnapped from Benin, sold and resold, until she wound up in 1860 at one of the CMS Abeokuta missions; or, more likely, she could have been one of the young people taken in by Reverend Phillips.[120] Her parents had called her Omotayo, meaning *the child is a thing of joy*. Yet somehow they had parted with her through death or hardship. She may have grown up in the Baptist compound, learning domestic arts, a little literacy, and Christianity. Indeed it may have been Phillips who initiated the match with Vaughan, since missionaries did at times try to arrange Christian marriages as their wards became adults.[121]

At thirty-six years old, Vaughan was finally forming his own family. In Yoruba as in American conceptions, marriage — followed by the production of children — was a crucial step in attaining social adulthood. It also brought officially sanctioned female companionship, as well as help managing his household. Yet Yoruba marriage was, crucially, a process of alliance-building between two lineages. In marrying a woman without local family ties, Vaughan was avoiding entanglements with an extended family that might call on him not only for payments and gifts at the time of marriage, but every time a relative needed help. Moreover, he was maintaining his separation from any specific Yoruba community. He may have also found it difficult to marry a local woman, as he had no lineage — other than missionary stand-ins — to bring together in alliances with new in-laws. When they were unable to attract free women and their parents, men without families such as Vaughan (not so rare during the age of Yoruba warfare) in fact sometimes purchased slave wives. Vaughan's marriage thus brought together two outsiders, whose only "family" was the Baptist community. Yet Sarah could also help Vaughan be more of an insider, since she spoke Yoruba well and understood local ways of doing things. And by forming his own household, Vaughan was planting his own roots in Yorubaland, despite his determined independence. Again, however, his secure autonomy from the mission as well as from Yoruba politics did not last.[122]

Church and Sarah embarked upon married life just as the king of Oyo was brokering a ceasefire between Ibadan and Abeokuta. In fact, it may have seemed like a propitious time to form a new household. The aftershocks of war had not ended, however. Church and Sarah had scarcely begun to live together when hostilities came practically to their door. In March 1865, Ibadan forces, led personally by General Ogunmola, overran their new hometown of Atadi, destroying dwellings and farms and carrying away prisoners. The raid was in retaliation for the Egba kidnapping of Ibadans, especially women, during the king of Oyo's peace negotiations. Rumor had it that Egba authorities had known the raid on Atadi was coming but failed to intervene, hoping that this sacrifice would settle the score and restore the peace process — which it did.[123] The Vaughans thus may have been warned in time to take refuge at the Baptist mission in Abeokuta.

Church and Sarah Vaughan's first child, James Wilson Vaughan, was born at "Alabama" in February 1866. He shared the first name of his father,

James Churchwill Vaughan, though he too may have been called by a short version of his middle name instead. *Will* harkened not only to part of Church Vaughan's own name, but to that of his mentor in Yorubaland, William Clarke. But *Wilson* reached back further—not to South Carolina, where the Vaughans did not know any particularly admirable bearers of that name, but to Church's life-changing voyage to Africa thirteen years before. Seventy-year-old Ephraim Wilson, a possibly African-born free man from Charleston, had traveled with Church on the *Joseph Maxwell*. He and Church had been among the few who were unaccompanied by friends or relatives. But Wilson did not make it, perishing at sea, without family to attend to him, before reaching Africa. His determination to live out his remaining days on the continent of his ancestors may have stayed with Church, who perpetuated that memory in the name of his son.[124]

Nonetheless, Church remained apart from many elements of the society in which he lived. He and Sarah did not add a Yoruba name (or one in Edo, the language of Benin, which is closely related to Yoruba) to their child's English ones, an act that might have signaled some degree of local identification. The new family lived in their own house in the Baptist compound along with the remaining missionary Phillips, Vaughan's friend Pettiford, former orphans and refugees from Ijaye, and a small number of Saro and local Christian converts. As head of the mission, Andrew Phillips maintained good relations with local chiefs and English missionaries. However, the public image of white Christians had soured considerably since Vaughan had first come to Abeokuta a decade earlier, largely because of the actions of British officials at Lagos. Ultimately, events beyond Vaughan's control would make the missionary community no longer a safe haven.

In 1861, the British had formally annexed Lagos with the justification of fighting the slave trade but just as much to promote their own trade through the port. Since then, British administrators increasingly meddled in the affairs of the interior, in 1865 even sending troops and heavy weaponry against Egba forces who, as part of their war against Ibadan, were blocking trade routes northeast of Lagos. Abeokuta's leaders were furious at the loss of what had previously been British support and worried that their town would be annexed next. Increasingly they turned for advice to a group of educated Saro rather than Townsend and other missionaries, who complained that all white people in Abeokuta were falling under suspicion. Then in September 1867, the British commander at Lagos, Captain John Glover, stationed constables along the road to Abeokuta in order to protect traders, which the Egba authorities took as interference within their own jurisdiction. Hundreds of "war boys," restless since the end of the war with Ibadan, had to be restrained from going after the constables. Only weeks later, in a movement later known as the *Ifọle* ("breaking of houses"), they turned on Abeokuta's Christians.[125]

On Sunday, October 13, 1867, residents of the Baptist mission heard the town crier announce on behalf of the *Bashorun* (military chief) of Abeokuta that no church services should be held that morning. Not realizing the extent to which politics had shifted around them, Reverend Phillips wondered if perhaps there had been some mistake. In what he later learned was an affront to the *Bashorun*, Phillips preached that morning anyway, as did the leaders of some of the other mission stations. Early that afternoon, news began to arrive about disturbances across town at the Methodist mission and one of the CMS posts, followed by word a couple of hours later that a mob was plundering another of the CMS stations. The Baptists remained vigilant, Church Vaughan perhaps counseling his wife Sarah to keep their little son close by in case of trouble. Shortly after sunset, a group one hundred strong, "like so many fiends," arrived at Alabama and surrounded the main mission house. Phillips, Vaughan, and the rest of the mission population watched from across the yard as the mob broke window glass and shutters before carrying away everything of value: doors, boxes, beds, provisions, and $150 worth of cowry shells that Phillips had recently purchased to use as currency. All that remained by the time the looters left were bare walls and the floor, along with a chest Phillips had hidden containing his clothes and fifteen British pounds.[126]

The next morning, the Baptists learned that the same fate had befallen the Anglicans and Methodists as well. All of the town's mission stations had been destroyed except for one, which had been protected by Ogundipe, a war chief rising to prominence and following his own policies. The target of Egba animosity seemed not to be Christians *per se*, however, but European influence. The rioters had torn the hats from the heads of Christian leaders, telling one African CMS preacher that his head too would be cut off if he resisted; and they destroyed foreign traders' property, including palm oil barrels and canoes stored outside the Aro Gate. At a meeting two days later, Egba chiefs lectured the assembled missionaries on their grievances against the British administrator of Lagos, notwithstanding Phillips's insistence that the colonial government and Christian missions were entirely separate. Over the next week, as Vaughan and other mission inhabitants wondered who might be the next targets, the Abeokuta chiefs forbade further Christian preaching in the town and equivocated about returning stolen property. In early November, Phillips and the other white missionaries, convinced that they could not continue their operations in Abeokuta, reluctantly left for Lagos.[127]

With their mission leader and employer gone, the Baptists at Alabama now fell under the direct power of the Abeokuta chiefs. Right away, local authorities took charge of the refugee children Phillips had adopted during the Ijaye war, some of them now teenagers and young adults. In what Phillips considered "too painful a subject for me to write upon," an "unusually pious" young woman whom he had raised from childhood was taken as a wife of Chief Ogundipe, perhaps in connection with the protection he had given to the missionaries.[128] Egba converts and Saro pastors at all of the damaged and now headless mission stations were allowed to remain in town as long as they did not hold church services. They feared, though, that staying would make them vulnerable either to persecution by Abeokuta authorities or to suspicions of disloyalty by the missionaries, should they be allowed to return. Many local mission personnel felt betrayed that the white preachers had gone to Lagos without securing their safe passage as well. "I am also dealt with as the Europeans," fumed a Saro catechist with the CMS named William Allen. "All we can gather from the missions is that everyone can shift for himself." Over the next few months, hundreds of Christians made their way from Abeokuta to Lagos — Church, Sarah, and little James Wilson Vaughan among them.[129]

With only the clothes he wore and five pounds in his pocket, Church put his toddler son on his shoulders and walked with his wife Sarah and about a dozen others for three days until they reached Lagos, where Christians were protected by the colonial government.[130] During his twelve years in Yorubaland, Vaughan had been associated with American Baptist missionaries to varying degrees. After getting on his feet within their orbit but always being separated because of race, he had sought to live and work on his own. But as it did for all people in Yorubaland's "age of confusion," autonomy made him vulnerable to violence and capture. Rejoining the missionaries, reaffirming his status as a dark-skinned òyinbó, ultimately put him at risk as well. Vaughan was neither insider nor outsider, distinct from the white missionaries but only partially assimilated to Yoruba society. Now he was seeking freedom and safety in a British colony. Would his prospects there be better than they were under African or mission authority, or than they might be if he returned to postemancipation South Carolina?

five

RECONSTRUCTIONS

In the hot July of 1869, more than a year after Church Vaughan sought refuge in Lagos, several small canvas bags arrived in Camden, South Carolina. They had traveled thousands of miles from the coast of West Africa to England, across the Atlantic, and through parts of the American South in the luggage of Rev. Andrew Phillips, who was returning to the United States from his missionary post in Lagos. Phillips carried them to Greenville, South Carolina when he visited his old Yorubaland comrade T. A. Reid at the Baptist seminary there. From Greenville it was only a short trip by rail to Camden, where the little pouches were delivered into the work-worn hands of Church Vaughan's surviving relatives — his widowed sister Elizabeth Hall and her thirty-one-year-old daughter Rebecca Ann, his sister Sarah and her twenty-year-old daughter Maria Sophronia, his adult nephew William Hammond, and a niece named Harriet MacLaughlin, who was born after he left for Africa, now just turning thirteen.[1]

Recent times had been hard on the South Carolina Vaughans. Church's older brother Burrell had died during the Civil War at the age of forty-seven. Though Elizabeth Hall and her sister Sarah Vaughan worked as seamstresses, they did not make much money, and the family must have relied heavily on William Hammond's earnings as a carpenter. The land and homes Scipio Vaughan had bequeathed to his children were gone — perhaps having been irreparably damaged when General Sherman's troops burned a nearby block of Broad Street in 1865, or lost through unpaid taxes to the Confederacy, Kershaw County, or the state of South Carolina.[2] Sickness, perhaps compounded by hunger, took Rebecca Ann Hall's two sons, aged eight and ten, within a month in 1866. In the spring of 1868, Church's thirty-year-old sister

Mary died.[3] By the time Church Vaughan's gift reached them a year later, his relatives were barely scratching out a living. We can only imagine their reaction when they opened the pouches and saw what he had sent them from Africa: gold coins, enough to change their lives.

William Hammond took the lead. The same month that the money arrived, he hired the legal firm of Loatner and Dunlap to help claim what he should have received from the estate of his father, Jacob Hammond, who had died twenty-one years earlier in 1848. At the time, in a move of dubious legitimacy, a local official named John R. Joy had sold his father's property and kept the proceeds "in trust" for the nine-year-old Hammond. As the years went on, the money—reckoned in 1869 as $172—had never been paid. Now Hammond's lawyers petitioned the local probate judge, the Vaughans' old acquaintance James F. Sutherland, to compel Joy's heirs to settle with their client. Five months later, in January 1870, William Hammond bought three lots and houses in downtown Camden, right across the street from the old Vaughan properties, for $170.[4] Though it is possible that this all could have happened without the gold coins from Africa, it is clear that his relatives were thinking of Church Vaughan as they reentered the ranks of Camden's property holders. In June 1871, Vaughan's niece Maria Sophronia gave birth to a baby boy. In a gesture of remembrance, she named her little son James Churchwill Vaughan Cannon.[5]

It may seem surprising that Church Vaughan was in such a position to help his American relatives, given that he had been forced to reconstruct his life and livelihood—once again—when he relocated from Abeokuta to Lagos. The explanation lies in the differences between postbellum South Carolina and early colonial Lagos, two areas pulsing with dramatic change, not least the abolition of slavery. In both places, slavery had been outlawed through outside initiatives—the British Foreign Office in the case of Lagos, and the federal government of the United States for South Carolina—while officials closer to the ground equivocated. In both places, former masters worked to narrow the scope of change, while ex-slaves sought to assert their freedom through mobility, new economic opportunities, and redefined social relations.

The key difference between the two, however, was white supremacy. In South Carolina, not only did former slaveholders and their supporters endeavor to restrict the freedoms of the previously enslaved, in their vision, all people of color should be relegated to the lowest rung of the economic and social ladder, by extralegal means if necessary. For previously free people of color like the Vaughans, life may have been hard before the Civil War, but afterward it got even worse, as their distinctive status and opportunities eroded under the pressure of a generalized white war on black people. In Lagos, to the contrary, colonial rule did not bring an influx of Europeans, and white supremacy did not flourish. The expansion of trade and early colonial administration created new opportunities for indigenous and diasporic Africans—many of whom, in fact, were among the slaveholders resisting British-imposed abolition. Church Vaughan did not himself own slaves, but he could prosper in the social and economic space between Lagos's most elite merchants and its most downtrodden dependent workers. In this way, he had opportunities in Lagos that his relatives in South Carolina could no longer enjoy.

When Church Vaughan and his family arrived in Lagos in early 1868, exhausted and nearly destitute, they knew only a handful of people there. One was Sarah Harden, a Sierra Leonean repatriate who had married the African American missionary Joseph Harden. It had been Joseph Harden who welcomed Vaughan to Lagos when he first set foot there in 1855, and until Harden's death nine years later, the two men had gotten together from time to time on mission business. Now the Vaughans sought shelter in the mission house Harden had built, where the widow Sarah was living with her two young sons and some female pupils, barely making ends meet as a teacher of Baptist children. Without regular maintenance, the small bamboo structure had become a run-down shack, but housing was scarce in Lagos, and the Vaughans had to be grateful for what they could get.[6]

Back when Vaughan had first arrived in Yorubaland, Joseph Harden had shown him a Lagos that seemed brash and ungodly. Now however, even with uncomfortable living conditions and no job or property to his name, Vaughan had reason to think that his future in Lagos would be bright. Much more than in the other parts of Yorubaland where he had lived, Lagos operated largely under rules that he understood. Whatever he may have thought about British colonialism in principle, Vaughan shared the values it placed upon property rights, Christianity, and the abolition of slavery. In the 1860s and into the 1870s, in fact, many Lagosians, especially those unconnected to the indigenous royalty, saw the cession of Lagos to the British as "a great blessing."[7] It had ushered in a commercial boom that offered new wealth to entrepreneurial Lagosians. It created institutions that protected private property and personal safety. And because colonialism in those years did not bring many Europeans, professional opportunities abounded for local people with western education or familiarity with western ways. The up-and-comers tended to be Yoruba speakers who were outsiders to Lagos: Sierra Leoneans, Brazilians, and also some immigrants from the interior. Unlike these other recent arrivals, Vaughan did not have kin or many countrymen in Lagos. Like them, however, Vaughan could draw on skills he had learned elsewhere to help him succeed in this new environment. In many respects, in fact, Lagos was a better place to start over than to start out.

The Vaughans did not have to impose on Sarah Harden very long. They had arrived in Lagos along with some seven hundred other refugees who left Abeokuta after the attack on missionaries there in October 1867. Seeing these Christians as promising residents, colonial administrator John Glover obtained land at Ebute Metta, the mainland across the lagoon from Lagos Island, and had it organized into equal-sized plots for allocation to each refugee family. To make their rights to the land clear, the government issued documents subsequently known as "Glover tickets" to each household head. Although disputes ensued decades later over who owned this land and how they acquired it — especially because an official destroyed the government's copies of the Glover tickets — his plot constituted Vaughan's first real estate since he left behind the lots allocated to him in Liberia.[8]

Three times since he had come to Yorubaland, Church Vaughan had lost all of his possessions, twice during violent attacks. The ticket granting him title to land at Ebute Metta, however, suggested that his property rights would be secure under British colonial administration. Moreover, a number of courts had been organized by early British administrators to deal with disputes involving debt, property, and other civil as well as criminal matters, presided over by European merchants or educated Africans. A police force, drawn largely from slaves of northern origin or run away from neighboring territories, was on hand to enforce the law.[9] Thus, Vaughan could make contracts for labor and expect that they would be honored; he also could guardedly expect not to have his property plundered and his house destroyed without consequence.

Fortuitously for Vaughan, the Ebute Metta settlement was plotted out by an old acquaintance: Robert Campbell, the Afro-Jamaican who earlier in the decade had accompanied Martin Delany in a bid to establish a settlement in Abeokuta. In 1863 Campbell had returned to Lagos with his family and embarked on a varied career as a businessman and government official. By the time Vaughan arrived in the city, Campbell had, among other pursuits, joined the colonial government as its acting official surveyor.[10] In this capacity he may have helped position Vaughan on one of the better-located plots in the new Ebute Metta layout.

Vaughan's "Glover ticket" had more symbolic than practical value, however. Ebute Metta may have reminded him of the parcel of land he had been allocated along the St. Paul's River in Liberia. While Lagos, like Monrovia, was unsuited for farming both in the quality of its soil and the temperament of its inhabitants, Ebute Metta was already providing food crops to the city nearby.[11] As in Liberia, however, Vaughan had no interest in making his living from the land. Instead, he must have spent nearly every day working as a builder, either for his fellow settlers at Ebute Metta or on Lagos Island, a hired canoe ride away.

Though Vaughan continued to identify with the Baptist Church, its American missionaries were no longer his source of material or spiritual support. Andrew Phillips's constant illness and then his departure for the United States left Richard Stone in charge of the Baptist mission, a position he seemed to relish in spite of his dissatisfaction with the resources at his disposal. Several months after he arrived in Lagos, Stone turned Sarah Harden out of the mission house where she had lived since her marriage ten years earlier—with reluctance not only for the inconvenience caused to her, but especially because he found the house Joseph Harden had built to be "a miserable structure with leaky roof and only two habitable rooms."[12] Though Reverend Stone hoped to rebuild the house and construct a new Baptist chapel, he had no funding from the U.S.-based Mission Board, whose treasury was empty after the American Civil War. As he complained in March 1868, "After exercising the most rigid (almost niggardly) economy, I have only a few pounds on hand, and will have to go to *cooking* and *washing* unless a remittance comes very soon."[13] Under the circumstances—of both finance and personality—Church Vaughan did not reprise his earlier role as mission carpenter for hire and instead found other clients. This was not difficult.

In spite of recurrent warfare along interior trade routes and conflicts between British and local authorities, Lagos was booming when Vaughan arrived there. As the foreign slave trade wound down in the second quarter of the nineteenth century, coastal entrepreneurs had increased their exports of other commodities, including cotton, ivory, and especially oil and kernels from the oil palm trees that grew abundantly in nearby forests. Used as an industrial lubricant and also in the manufacture of soap, candles, and margarine, palm products were increasingly demanded in Europe, and trading firms began to locate warehouses on the West African coast, especially in Lagos. Under British colonial administration, the trade in palm products was encouraged even further, in part because it was seen as a counter to the slave trade, but also because it provided a steady stream of customs revenue. In the early 1860s, Lagos's total exports were valued, on average, at £166,763 per year; by the second half of that decade they were up to £499,214; and they reached £632,439 per year by the late 1870s. In other words, exports increased almost 200 percent over the course of the 1860s, and just over 25 percent from the latter 1860s to the end of the 1870s, a period of much slower growth. Already in 1857, a group of Lagos chiefs had told Rev. Samuel Crowther that they had never before seen so much wealth flowing into their country; when Vaughan arrived ten years later the economy was running in high gear.[14]

Economic opportunities generated by the export trade, along with continuing insecurity in the interior, attracted a stream of new settlers to Lagos. Shortly before Church and Sarah Vaughan walked there from Abeokuta, Lagos's population was estimated at 25,000. Fifteen years later, in 1881, it had grown to 38,000, which included only 111 Europeans. The numbers kept increasing, so that by 1911 Lagos's population numbered three times what it had been in 1866. People came for many reasons, including to escape interior warfare or slavery, or as part of another migrant's retinue of dependents. But it was the lure of wealth through trade that called many of them to the city, even though few new migrants ultimately became rich. "The real Lagosian loves above everything else to be a trader," a resident missionary wrote in 1881. By that year, at least half of the town's population made their living from commerce.[15]

Many of the most visible and prosperous traders were returnees from the Atlantic slave trade. Though Sierra Leoneans and Brazilians had begun to arrive in Yorubaland from the late 1830s, there were few guarantees of their security in Lagos until the British Consulate was established in 1851. By the mid-1860s, probably around a thousand Sierra Leoneans and equal numbers of Brazilians (counted together with the small numbers of Cuban returnees who joined their community) had settled in Lagos, and their numbers tripled over the next two decades.[16] Their prior commercial experience, initial capital, contacts with Europeans, and Western education enabled some Sierra Leoneans to move quickly into the import-export trade and rise to the top of the local elite. In fact, it was mostly Saro whom Martin Delany was describing when he noticed, passing through Lagos in 1859, that "the merchants and business men of Lagos [are] principally native black gentlemen, there being but ten white houses in the place . . . and all of the clerks are native blacks."[17] In contrast, Brazilian immigrants arrived with very little capital, limited facility in English, and no connections to European merchants. As a group, they did not occupy the same position in the trading economy as the Saro did, although a few Brazilian merchants organized extensive ventures with partners in Brazil.[18] Both groups of repatriates, however, literally made their mark on the city's landscape. When in 1853 Lagos's King Dosunmu issued seventy-six written land grants, they went mostly to Brazilians and Sierra Leoneans, who continued to acquire landed property.[19] To this day, central Lagos's streets bear the names of early returnees, including Savage, Cole, Doherty, and Davies in the Olowogbowo area settled by Sierra Leoneans and Bamgbose, Pedro, Martins, and Tokunboh in the Brazilian quarter (*Tokunboh* meaning a person who has returned from abroad).[20]

Lagos's bustling trade economy, the in-migration of thousands of newcomers, and the accumulation of wealth by some entrepreneurs all generated a building boom, as merchants, government officials, and missionaries erected houses, offices, churches, warehouses, and other structures more substantial than the mud and thatch dwellings of ordinary Lagosians. With his twelve years of experience building in Yorubaland, plus his carpentry background in South Carolina and Liberia, Vaughan became one of the most sought-after builders in the city. Many years later, the editor of one of Lagos's newspapers recalled, probably of Vaughan, that "we have never known but one competent mechanic in Lagos, and he has long since retired from practice."[21] Though there was no work for him at the Baptist mission, Vaughan found enough well-paying contracts in Lagos to move relatively quickly into the ranks of the city's upwardly mobile.

Within two years of coming to Lagos, Vaughan was able to save enough from his carpentry business not only to send gold to his South Carolina relatives, but also to begin investing in real estate. In 1869, he bought land in central Lagos from Robert Campbell, who had received it years earlier through a grant from the Lagos king.[22] The purchase represented a good investment, as buildable land on the swampy island was limited and in great demand. Moreover, the property could provide collateral for loans, should Vaughan decide (as he later did) to expand into trade.[23] Fittingly, Vaughan's new plot was located at the corner of Campbell Street, named for Robert Campbell, and Joseph Street, named after Joseph Harden. Vaughan built a house for his family there, leaving his Ebute Metta property to accommodate his apprentices or eventually earn rent. From this central location, Vaughan was nearer than before to his clients and building projects. He was also now living on the same street as the Baptist mission; though perhaps it was not a coincidence that Vaughan bought his plot just as Richard Stone was closing operations for lack of funds and departing for the United States.[24]

On Joseph Street, Vaughan was based right outside Lagos's Brazilian quarter, or *Popo Aguda*. While many of the Sierra Leonean immigrants to

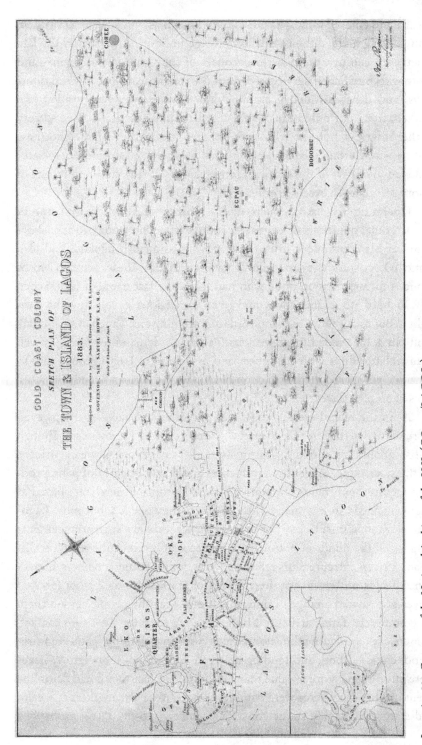

Lagos in 1883. Courtesy of the National Archives of the U.K. (CO700/LAGOS5).

Yorubaland entered trade, Brazilians were known as builders and craftsmen, many having learned their skills in bondage in South America. By the late nineteenth century, the two-story houses of the wealthiest of them—and those who hired their services—featured wrought ironwork, arched doorways, and other distinctive architectural features. Vaughan resided and worked, then, not only near people who had, like him, left a slave society of the Americas, but also who were engaged in the same kind of business that he was. Certainly later in his life, his most trusted business associates included members of the Brazilian (and related Cuban) community, one of whom served as an executor of his will.[25]

Operating a construction business confronted Vaughan with one of the perennial questions of Lagos's economic life: who would do the labor? Some of his apprentices from the Baptist mission in Abeokuta had also come to Lagos, and they continued to work with him. These included Moses Stone, a former mission pupil who had taken the last name of his teacher, Rev. Richard Stone, and who would go on to religious leadership in his own right.[26] But as apprentices completed their training and Vaughan's contracts multiplied, he needed more workers. Vaughan's demand for labor, as well as his relationships with customers and associates in Lagos, forced him to consider, yet again, whether this son of an enslaved African American would himself employ slaves.

As in the inland areas, slavery was pervasive in Lagos—perhaps even more so than in the interior, given the colony's economic dynamism. Though British abolitionists touted "legitimate trade" as a means to wean Africans off the slave trade, in fact the production and transportation of palm products required enormous amounts of labor. European merchants based at Lagos managed to hire many of the workers they needed, but most Lagosians wanted neither to pay nor to work for wages, since such arrangements minimized the bonds of patronage between employers and employees. Instead, African entrepreneurs relied on wives, junior family members, dependents, pawns, and slaves acquired at interior markets for their labor forces.[27] Slaves also served a range of other functions. Wealthy people settled them on commercial farms at Ebute Metta, growing food for the Lagos market. Some slaves worked within households, washing clothing, gathering firewood, cooking food, and tending children. For would-be investors, slaves were often a safer store of value than buildings, because they could flee in the event of a fire—and fires were common. Slaves were also markers of wealth and status in a highly status-conscious society.[28] In the 1850s, probably a majority of Lagos's population were slaves, and this percentage diminished only slowly over time.[29]

Lagosians of all stripes held slaves, including the recently free themselves. As a group of "Native Traders and residents at Lagos" wrote to a British commissioner in 1864, "We who are the originators of this communication, were born slaves, and our parents before us, and we have risen by our energies at this time, we have become the possessors of slaves, but we only use them as laborer, or any other capacity that demands assistance." Even many Sierra Leoneans and Brazilians who had returned to Lagos and the interior—people who had themselves been captured in the slave trade, or whose parents had been captured—bought, employed, and sometimes sold slaves, as did Christians. For this reason, missionaries tended to adopt a tolerant attitude toward local slavery, for fear of offending indigenous allies or turning fledgling converts away.[30]

As Kristin Mann has detailed, similar considerations quickly undermined colonial opposition to slavery in Lagos. Though British intervention there had been motivated by the goal of ending the overseas slave trade, as the traders' memorial from 1864 suggested, a distinction was made between trafficking in slaves and holding them. Slavery itself had been abolished throughout the British Empire in 1833, and the law deemed the practice illegal in all British possessions abroad. In 1866, after five years of equivocation, metropolitan officials ruled that Empire-wide antislavery laws did apply in Lagos, since it was a Crown colony. Yet this put Lagos's local administrators in a delicate position. Though they were mindful of Britain's antislavery reputation and they did not want to seem hypocritical, their highest priorities were to maintain political stability and increase colonial revenue, which they believed would be threatened by aggressive abolition measures. Moreover, British officials and missionaries viewed local slavery as a benign institution very different from forced labor in foreign countries. They also believed that the palm oil trade would improve the conditions of local slaves and gradually end slavery by providing income that might be used for self-purchase. For these reasons, and in spite of their opposition to the slave *trade*, officials felt no great urgency to oppose domestic slavery, and they only selectively intervened in the relationship between Lagosians and their slaves. Administrators ended the legal status of slavery and allowed bondspeople to sue their owners for freedom, but they did little to encourage wage labor or transform the social position of ex-slaves. By the time Vaughan arrived in Lagos six years after its annexation, British officials maintained the fiction that Lagos's slaves were in fact free, and if they remained with their "employers," it was of their own choosing. It was therefore up to slaves themselves to redefine their relationships with current and former owners.[31]

Only gradually did enslaved people take advantage of the fact that the courts and the police would generally not return runaways. Part of the ideology of local slavery was that faithful service would be rewarded with improved conditions, free time for the slave to work for herself/himself, prospects for marriage, permission to accumulate property, or help in starting a trade. The ultimate reward was to move out of slavery and into the master's kin group. Though such social mobility was more often the ideal than the reality, its prospect kept many slaves tied to masters even as they became increasingly autonomous under the changing conditions of colonial rule. Moreover, as a practical matter, slaves and ex-slaves needed housing and, if they wanted to enter a trade, capital or credit. To obtain these, they generally either had to stay with old masters or find new ones, who might offer improved conditions but still would expect deference and labor.[32]

This was the context in which Vaughan sought to recruit laborers. Like other employers, his main prospects for workers—other than purchasing slaves himself—included fugitive slaves who took refuge in Lagos, free immigrants arriving from elsewhere, and enslaved people from Lagos who wanted to leave their owners.[33] Members of all three groups needed to be provided with room and board; and like slave masters attempting to retain their workers or recruit others, Vaughan made housing and credit available to his workmen. But in a context in which owners/employers used their control over land, tools, and credit to keep their subordinates firmly tied to their households, Vaughan stood out for his generosity in helping his workers assert their own autonomy. He established a workshop for training carpenters and draughtsmen. While other traders charged five to fifteen percent interest on loans and lorded over their debtors, Vaughan made loans without interest so that his apprentices could begin their own businesses in various occupations. Some of them took his last name, creating other lineages of Nigerian Vaughans that persist to the present.[34] Christopher Beyioku Vaughan was a mechanic turned trader who lived in the Brazilian quarter and ultimately served as one of the three executors of Church Vaughan's will.[35] Mr. J. A. Vaughan worked as a teacher at an industrial institution in the 1880s before becoming a trader in the early 1890s.[36] Someone named Joseph Vaughan worked as a butcher.[37]

Although Vaughan may have earned the loyalty of his workers, this did not make him the kind of Big Man that many Lagosians aspired to be. Already he had no visible extended family to assist and call upon for services, as most of the wealthy did. He seems not to have been interested in generating an entourage or enlarging his reputation as a patron, which required not only extending loans and providing jobs and housing but also living opulently, hosting events, and dispensing gifts. "He was a practical and exemplary artisan," an admirer later wrote, "and though he had wealth in abundance, yet he led a very simple but useful life."[38] His business model was to keep relatively few workers, and to accumulate capital—rather than people—to enhance the lives of himself and his immediate family.

Moreover, Vaughan continued to be as independent of Yoruba politics as he had been before coming to Lagos. Many of the Sierra Leonean, Brazilian, and Cuban immigrants to the city were not only of Yoruba heritage but had been born in one or another of the Yoruba kingdoms. They and other Lagosians identified with warring groups in the interior and formed bitterly hostile factions in the city. Since neither he nor his wife was of Yoruba background, however, Vaughan could remain apart from these destructive alliances, doing business with all comers, avoiding politically motivated reprisals, and focusing his energies on business and his family. He also could avoid losing favor with officials or missionaries as their loyalties to different Yoruba communities shifted in the late 1860s and 1870s.[39]

Surrounded in the Brazilian quarter by people whose skills in the building trades rivaled his own, Vaughan began to turn from carpentry to a related occupation: supplying the iron and hardware necessary for construction. Joseph Harden and Robert Campbell had had a similar idea several years earlier, when they went into business making and selling bricks.[40] Trade offered greater earning potential and prestige than mechanical work, especially since iron roofs were in great demand in fire-prone Lagos.[41] In addition, the hardware business could be conducted with relatively few workers, reducing Vaughan's need to cultivate a labor force. Lacking patrons who might help him get a loan, however, Vaughan had to come up with the capital for his initial inventory himself, "by dint of hard work and thrift."[42] Five years after his arrival in Lagos, in 1873, he finally was able to open his hardware store.[43] At that point he was forty years old, probably relieved to put aside the physical demands of construction work.

Vaughan's foreign background had given him the skills to become a successful carpenter in Yorubaland; now it also shaped his career as a trader. Lagosians involved in commerce were principally connected to its export trade, selling palm oil and palm kernels to agents of European commercial firms. The most successful of them were able to draw on a network of connections to inland suppliers, first relatively near the coast and then by the 1870s in Ibadan and eastern Yorubaland.[44] Vaughan's weak links to the interior, however, made the export trade unrealistic for him. In contrast, retailing imported hardware was a logical choice, given his experience as a builder and his proximity to Brazilians in related occupations. Though the import trade became more popular later in the nineteenth century, Vaughan was one of its pioneers. In this he joined the ever-enterprising Robert Campbell, who had sold books and office supplies in the 1860s, and the Saro Richard Beale Blaize, who made a fortune in the 1870s and '80s retailing foreign manufactures in his Marina Warehouse and Showroom. In place of exporters' ties to the hinterland, these businessmen from the Americas relied on connections to suppliers abroad as well as local customers and merchants who could arrange bills of exchange.[45] But they all suffered financially in the 1870s and into the next decade, a period of economic recession in which the profit margins of most merchants narrowed after the boom years of the 1860s.[46] That Vaughan started his hardware business and kept it alive during these more difficult times reveals his careful planning and deliberate avoidance of risk.

Vaughan's store may have begun at his Joseph Street house, but before long he had purchased a plot at 35 Kakawa Street, still relatively near the Brazilian quarter but closer to the marina and customs house where his imports entered the island. There, Vaughan built a two-story frame house like the ones he had first seen in Monrovia, with his store on the lower floor and a residence for his growing family above.[47] Now he could rent out two properties—his first one at Ebute Metta and the house he had built on Joseph Street—as well as earn income from the hardware business, "in which he became very successful."[48] Within less than a decade of moving to Lagos, then, Vaughan had created a secure life for himself and his family—materially comfortable, without fear of political violence, confident in economic and social autonomy.

His self-reliance during this period is clear from the one surviving letter written by Church Vaughan himself. In 1872, after Reverends Phillips and Stone had left Lagos for good, Vaughan wrote to the Foreign Mission Board of the Southern Baptist Convention. The letter was subsequently published in the Convention's *Home and Foreign Journal* as part of an appeal for funds to send a missionary to Yorubaland, because in it Vaughan did convey the request of Lagos Baptists that a missionary be sent to minister to them. "A good number of our fellow members [of the Baptist congregation] came to me on Sunday evening last, and expressly desired that a letter should be written to you in the first part of this week" to describe the present condition of the church and the "earnest desire" for a missionary, he reported. But Vaughan was decidedly unenthusiastic about this prospect, insisting that the congregation was doing just fine, and in fact that one of their own, his former apprentice Moses Ladejo Stone, was proving to be a very able preacher. Vaughan set himself apart from the other Baptists both by background and by intellectual self-assertion: "Excepting myself, who am a native of Camden, South Carolina, United States, the members of our church are all heathen born natives of Africa, and, as a matter of course, they are very dependent, as they think, on missionary labor to keep them together." Though Vaughan too had been baptized by a missionary, he saw the others (but not himself) as "truly uncultivated Christians, and such as have not moral courage enough to stand hard by the Cross, and look up to Christ, 'the Good Shepherd,' nor have their faith to believe effectually that the Holy Ghost . . . is able, and will keep the vineyard of Christ in perfect good order." Sixteen years later, Vaughan would lead a revolt against the Baptist missionary sent to Lagos, putting into practice his belief that African Christians could lead their own churches. In 1872, though, he was more circumspect, wondering only who might be authorized to lead the little church and conduct baptisms in the absence of an ordained minister. "Therefore, if it is practicable," he wrote, "do send us a missionary, and if not, do write encouraging letters to the church, with such instructions or advice as you may think best." The letter was signed, "Your brother in Christ, James C. Vaughan."[49]

A year before Vaughan wrote this letter, his old Baptist comrade Andrew Phillips had paid a visit to Lagos on his way back to the United States from a brief missionary recruitment tour in Liberia.[50] No account survives of the encounter that probably occurred, in which the two caught up after three years of separation, and Phillips reported news of Vaughan's family, the delivery of the gold coins, and events in the American South. But in hearing about life during Reconstruction in his home country, Vaughan could not have avoided comparing it with his own in Lagos.

During the first two decades of British administration in Lagos, Vaughan and other newcomers could count on the security of their persons and possessions, and many became prosperous. This was in part because the colonial government promoted trade and guaranteed property rights, and also because few Europeans were present to dominate positions in the economy or administration.[51] But the economic opportunities open to Vaughan and other expatriates from the diaspora were less available to Lagos's slaves. For them, food and shelter came at the price of hard labor and personal submission. British antislavery may have initiated important changes in Lagos's politics and economy, but it affected the lives of the island's bondspeople slowly and inconsistently. Though Vaughan personally distanced himself from slavery, he could observe slaveholders' determination to maintain power over their subordinates, and slaves' and ex-slaves' efforts to improve their situations. Similar processes, he knew, were at work back in South Carolina, where his relatives and others were living through the second great revolution in American history.

Vaughan's 1872 letter to the Foreign Mission Board arrived in a land torn apart by violent conflict over largely the same issue that it addressed: black self-determination. The Civil War and subsequent Thirteenth Amendment to the U.S. Constitution had ended slavery. Now, Reconstruction offered freedpeople the promise of real citizenship—for once, making clear that people of African descent could have a legitimate place in the United States. Supporters of radical change had come into power at national and state levels, opening the way for black political participation like none seen before or for a long time since. In alliance with the federal government, activist officeholders—black and white—sought to remake the South. Yet most whites wanted little or no change. From planters down to former Confederate foot soldiers, they were determined to close every opportunity black people opened up, through whatever legal or illegal means they could. South Carolina, and particularly its upland counties, sat at the center of the battles over the South's future. There, the most progressive and regressive thrusts of the Reconstruction era clashed, as formidable black political power met determined, violent resistance. As Vaughan learned of these developments from a safe distance across the Atlantic, his relatives and others in his home state struggled for their livelihoods, the education of their children, and their rights and dignity as American citizens—with grounds for optimism as well as apprehension.

At the end of the Civil War and in the face of general slave emancipation, former slaveholders and their allies had attempted to reclaim political and economic power, as if the Confederacy had not been defeated. South Carolina's first postwar government, like that of other former Confederate states, was shaped by President Andrew Johnson's lenient policy toward former rebels. In December 1865, a state legislature composed of the prewar elite passed what became known as "Black Codes," a series of restrictions on the labor, mobility, and legal status of people of color—both the newly emancipated and formerly free, like the Vaughans. Though the commander of the federal jurisdiction to which South Carolina was assigned declared the Black Codes invalid within ten days of their passage, white supremacists remained defiant. At the local level, they used many of the tools of antebellum slavery—pass systems enforced by patrols, beatings, whippings, and even murder—to keep freedpeople working under planters' terms and to enforce the general subordination of black to white.[52]

But southern politics changed dramatically after Republicans, members of the party of emancipation, swept nationwide elections for U.S. Congress in 1866 and then passed measures designed to ensure African American citizenship. The Reconstruction Acts of 1867 enfranchised all males twenty-one years of age or older, including black people, and called for new conventions to rewrite state constitutions. Prospects for black political power in South Carolina were especially strong, as people of color comprised almost 60 percent of the state's population. The new state constitution, written in an 1868 convention with a black majority, was designed to create a new order in South Carolina based on equal opportunity before the law. Both voting rights and education were to be available to all South Carolinians "without regard to race and color." While white elites raged against what they saw as "a negro constitution," elections in the wake of its ratification brought Republicans into nearly all state and local offices and sent six black men to the U.S. Congress. More than three hundred Carolinians of color held public office at the state or federal level between 1868 and 1876, far more than in any other southern state. South Carolina's House of Representatives had sizable black majorities from 1868 to 1876, and African Americans were a significant presence in the state senate. They used their political power to ratify the Fourteenth and Fifteenth Amendments to the U.S. Constitution—guaranteeing equal citizenship and voting rights regardless of race or previous servitude—as well as fund public schools and open public accommodations to all South Carolinians regardless of race.[53]

South Carolina was now in the forefront of freedom struggles in the Atlantic world—which is why it attracted the attention of the former Yorubaland explorer and would-be colonizationist Martin Delany. After returning from West Africa, Delany had thrown himself into the fight for emancipation in the United States. He helped recruit troops for the all-black Fifty-Fourth Massachusetts Regiment of the U.S. Army, in which his son Toussaint served along with two of Frederick Douglass's sons. President Lincoln commissioned Delany as a major in the Union army in early 1865, making him the first African American to hold field rank in United States history. After the war ended, Delany worked in the South Carolina lowcountry for the federal Bureau of Refugees, Freedmen, and Abandoned Lands, helping to negotiate land transfers to assist the newly freed. In 1868 he participated in the convention that drafted the new South Carolina state constitution. Though ten years earlier he had seen emigration as the most promising of African Americans' stark choices, Delany now committed himself to an American future, with South Carolina as his base.[54]

Yet Delany and other activists faced enormous challenges. The great potential of black politics in South Carolina set off a white backlash more intense than anywhere else in the South. Whites claimed that the state's black majority was creating what the editors of a Columbia newspaper called "an African dominion" in the United States, "a new Liberia" in the South. (One wonders what Vaughan, who actually knew Liberia and African dominions, made of such analogies if they were reprinted in the newspapers he read in Lagos.) White South Carolinians never accepted the new state government as legitimate, and they were unrelenting in their efforts to silence black men's new political voice.[55]

White supremacists made their strongest stand in South Carolina's upcountry, the part of the state where Vaughan's relatives lived, and where sizeable black populations were politically viable but not the insurmountable majorities of the coast. In 1868, local dens of the Ku Klux Klan, a white supremacist confederation founded two years previously in Tennessee, began to spread throughout the upcountry. In part a continuation of the old system of local, vigilante slave patrols, the KKK appealed to longstanding beliefs about white honor and black danger. Its immediate goal was to thwart black political participation and thereby neutralize Republican lawmakers, effectively making the KKK, as one historian put it, "the terrorist arm of the Democratic party." Yet it also sought to restore labor discipline on white-owned farms and plantations, undermine black churches and schools, and intimidate those African Americans who achieved even a modicum of economic success. The organization's leaders were planters and professionals, many of them former Confederate officers, but members were drawn from every class of white society, including poor whites determined not to occupy the lowest rung of the social and economic ladder. Their weapons were propaganda, economic retaliation, harassment, intimidation, assault, and murder.[56]

Terrorist attacks began almost immediately. A month after the state constitution was ratified, the Vaughans could hear rumors circulating in Camden about an impending Ku Klux Klan raid. The Camden *Journal* reported that the town's black "citizens" (derisively placed in quotation marks in the article) prepared to give the nightriders a "warm" reception; but "they did not appear, to the disappointment of some and the gratification of others."

Three days later, however, one of Kershaw County's two newly elected delegates to the state legislature, a white Republican "scalawag" from Charleston named S. G. W. Dill, was shot to death outside his house, along with a black man serving as bodyguard. None of the arrested suspects would divulge any information, and no one was ever charged for the crime. Over the next few months, a General Assembly representative from Abbeville and a state senator from Orangeburg County, both in the upcountry, were also assassinated. There were rumors of plots to kill the governor, the state attorney general, and other prominent Republicans.[57]

In an attempt to ensure public safety, the Republican-controlled South Carolina government authorized a new state militia in 1869. Since local whites refused to join, it became virtually all black, with Martin Delany as its commander in chief. By late 1870 there were nearly one hundred thousand militiamen in South Carolina, about 11 percent of them armed. Black self-defense seemed to work, and for about eighteen months the Klan kept quiet. Then, shortly after elections in 1870, violence like no one had seen before exploded. In the upcountry town of Laurensville, more than two thousand armed whites murdered nine Republicans, including a state legislator, the probate judge, and a constable. In northwestern York County, where some 80 percent of white males joined the Klan, eleven African Americans were murdered, approximately six hundred assaulted and whipped, and black churches and schools were burned. The failure of state and local officials to crack down against the violence only encouraged the insurgents. Hundreds of people slept in the woods for safety, as nighttime raids occurred regularly for nearly eight months.[58]

As eyewitnesses later testified, there was a pattern to the typical Klan attack. Repeatedly, hooded nightriders forced their way into freedpeople's homes and demanded to talk to the man of the house — generally someone allied with the Republican Party. If the man was not there, they threatened, beat, whipped, and in some instances raped the woman (or girl) at home, demanding to know his whereabouts. When the terrorists found the man they sought, they would interrogate him about his political activities, demand any weapon he might have, order him to renounce the Republican Party, drag him outside, bind him, and whip him as slaves had been whipped in antebellum times. The most politically active were targeted for the worst violence: in York County, for instance, Jim Williams, the outspoken captain of a militia company, was forced to climb a tree with a rope tied around his neck, the other end lashed to a perpendicular limb. When Williams refused to jump and thus hang himself, a Klansman climbed up and pushed him, then hacked his clinging fingers with a knife until he was forced to drop. His body was later found with a note pinned to his breast: "Jim Williams on his big muster." Preacher and educator Elias Hill, whose shrunken legs had been crippled since his youth, was pulled from bed and cut repeatedly with a horsewhip, leaving him still aching three months later.[59]

York County, roughly sixty miles northwest of Camden on the North Carolina border, saw the most Klan activity in the entire American South, its determined den leader later forming the model for the main character of the racist 1915 film *Birth of a Nation*.[60] Yet racial violence came even closer to the Vaughans' Kershaw County home. In February 1871, a battle in nearby Chester County between white vigilantes and the local militia "should have been called rather a massacre of the blacks," according to a correspondent from the New York *Tribune*. As the militiamen fled the Klan's assault, "the whites pursu[ed] them and kill[ed] all they could catch." The journalist concluded, "It is impossible to doubt the existence and constant activity of Ku Klux bands in all the Northern counties of South Carolina." Two months later in Clarendon, where Church's brother Burrell Vaughan had lived, the body of Peter J. Lemon, the black county commissioner, was found in the road alongside his carriage, riddled with more than twenty gunshot wounds. Enraged mourners at his funeral formed a protest march to demand justice but disbanded in the face of hundreds of armed whites and the threat of even more to come from bordering Sumter County.[61]

In Camden, freedmen, but not former Confederates, observed national Independence Day on the Fourth of July 1871 (not incidentally, the anniversary of the planned slave uprising of more than a half-century earlier). Church Vaughan's nieces and nephew probably joined the public celebrations, and perhaps his sister Sarah did as well. As two militia companies paraded the streets in celebration, a white Camden police marshal named John Smyrl arrested an allegedly unruly marcher. When other militiamen threatened the officer with their bayonets, a formerly enslaved Baptist preacher and a former Confederate soldier stood side by side to shield Smyrl. A one-legged former Confederate officer who arrived in his buggy also helped diffuse the situation.[62] Though it might have heralded this act of interracial cooperation, the Camden *Journal* instead editorialized (ungrammatically) that "the negro mob, which, on any provocation, undertakes to set the laws aside and avenge its own wrongs, *real* or *fancied*, prove to the world their own unfitness for self-government or citizenship, and not only renders all concerned liable to punishment by the laws of their own choosing, but disgraces their race, and endangers the continuance of their liberty." Assuming the worst about

African government (which again would have raised eyebrows among the better informed), the editors warned that Americans would never tolerate "a condition of beastly anarchy, paralleled only in the wilds of Dahomey or the degraded, corrupt and abominable communities of San Domingo, the half way house to Dahomey." African Americans, the article admonished, should realize that "they can never trample upon the rights of the white man but to their own ruin." A week after the July 4 incident, militiamen were ordered to surrender their state-issued weapons (which few did), and officials called for the arrest of Frank Carter, one of the militia leaders, for helping to distribute "the very means to bring on bloodshed."[63]

The scale and intensity of Klan activities throughout the upcountry prompted Governor Robert K. Scott, under pressure from black legislators, to repeatedly request military assistance from Washington. In March 1871, the federal government sent additional troops, still far fewer than the number of armed militants, to South Carolina. The next month, the U.S. Congress passed the Ku Klux Klan Act, which made "the deprivation of any rights, privileges, and immunities secured by the Constitution" a federal violation and empowered the president to suspend the writ of habeas corpus in a finite area, thereby permitting the arrest of suspects not formally charged or indicted for a crime. Congress also created the Joint Select Committee to Inquire into the Conditions of Affairs in the Late Insurrectionary States, whose members began hearing testimony in Washington then launched a tour of the South in South Carolina. In July 1871, a subcommittee traveled upcountry, where they heard testimony in Yorkville. Three months later, as a result of those and other hearings, President Grant suspended the writ of habeas corpus in nine inland counties — which did not include Kershaw but did include bordering Chesterfield, Chester, Fairfield, and Lancaster, as well as nearby York County. By early 1872, federal troops had arrested 472 South Carolina whites on charges of violating the constitutional rights of freedpeople.[64]

In the congressional hearings in the summer of 1871 and the federal trials that followed, the tide seemed to be turning against the Klan. Fifty-three black witnesses came forward when the subcommittee of the Joint Select Committee met in South Carolina. African Americans testified, served on the juries, and observed the federal trials, in spite of credible threats of reprisals from white supremacists. Though less than fifteen years previously the Supreme Court had ruled that descendants of black slaves could never be citizens of the United States, they now acted as witnesses and jurors to find white defendants guilty of infringing upon their civil rights. By the end of

1872, more than a hundred defendants had been convicted, while some two thousand upcountry whites fled from the state to escape federal prosecution, some — in an ironic echo of the route African Americans had previously taken in search of freedom — traveling as far as Canada.[65]

Yet ultimately the trials accomplished little. In the U.S. circuit court in which they were heard, judges dismissed many of the indictments as unconstitutional and construed the proceedings on narrow legal grounds. Moreover, the scale of the trials simply overwhelmed the federal court system. By mid-1872 some thirteen hundred people had been indicted but only 158 cases had been processed and twenty-three defendants convicted; more than a thousand cases remained pending. Over the next two years the prosecutions collapsed altogether. With a new U.S. attorney general lacking the will to continue the proceedings, President Grant extended clemency to those Klan defendants not yet tried and pardoned those who had been convicted and were still serving sentences.[66] Even as he took part in the hearings, York County teacher, preacher, and assault survivor Elias Hill doubted they would succeed and organized a group of 167 freedpeople wishing to flee to Liberia. As one prospective emigrant explained, "We are down here & cant [sic] rise up."[67]

There would have been little motivation for white supremacists to mobilize as they did, however, were African Americans not realizing real political and economic gains. Though they confronted measures to control their labor and restrict their advancement, black people experienced rising standards of living during Reconstruction as they negotiated labor contracts, earned wages, and sold their own crops. As an English observer reported in 1871, "That the Negroes are improving, and many of them rising under freedom into a very comfortable and civilized condition is not only admitted in all the upper circles of society, but would strike even a transient wayfarer like myself in the great number of decent coloured men of the laboring class and of happy coloured families one meets."[68] Though this seems perhaps overly sanguine in the face of crop failures, low cotton prices, scarcity of credit, and general economic hardship, dramatic new possibilities were opening up for African Americans, not only for civic participation but also in education and land ownership. Through these crucial avenues, reformers and ordinary African Americans hoped that black achievement could be safeguarded and passed down through generations.

In its largest and most far-reaching initiative, the Republican-controlled South Carolina state government established free public schools for all of the state's children. Slave illiteracy had been nearly ubiquitous, and for over three decades schools even for free people of color had been illegal.[69] Seeing black people as inherently intellectually limited, white supremacists were in favor of education for African Americans only at a rudimentary level; and they vehemently opposed racial integration in schools. Republican lawmakers did not press the issue of school segregation as long as educational opportunities for blacks and whites were not blatantly unequal, but they did institute a broad scheme of universal primary education, compulsory for at least two years. Results were tempered but impressive: between 1869 and 1876 the number of African American children in public schools rose from 8,200 to 70,800, representing an increase from 9 to 44 percent of the black school-age population. Though most teachers were white, the percentage of black teachers rose from a quarter in 1873 to a third just three years later, most of them southern born. Concentrating on primary education, lawmakers left the operation of secondary schools to agents of northern benevolent societies. However, in what white conservatives regarded as one of its most heinous acts, the state legislature reopened South Carolina College, which had been closed during the war, as the University of South Carolina, without racial restrictions. It was the only southern state university to admit black students. Now shunned by whites, its student body became 90 percent black by 1875, and there were African Americans among the faculty and trustees.[70]

If he were able to observe the expansion of education in his hometown, Church Vaughan would have noticed at least one familiar face. The Kershaw County commission in charge of organizing schools and hiring teachers comprised three local Republicans, including Vaughan's former employer with whom he had lived in the early 1850s — the probate judge J. F. Sutherland. Further, the county commissioner of education was Frank Carter, the former militia leader, whose younger relative would soon marry Vaughan's niece Harriet Josephine McLaughlin (the daughter of his youngest sister, Mary).[71] Yet Vaughan would find only some of his siblings' school-age grandchildren in classrooms. Many of those born in the 1860s — grandchildren of Church's brother Burrell Vaughan or his sister Elizabeth Hall — never learned to read or write. By their twenties, these grand-nieces and -nephews of Church Vaughan were working as field hands or day laborers. It was only the children of Vaughan's nieces Maria Sophronia (daughter of Church's sister Sarah and informal wife of J. F. Sutherland) and Harriet Josephine Carter who were well educated, largely in the 1880s and 1890s in private schools like Camden's Mather Academy and the Howard School in Columbia.[72]

In order to fund its massive expansion of public education, South Carolina's legislature raised taxes, especially property taxes but also a generalized poll tax. "Heavy taxation," as historian Joel Williamson put it, "was the core of the Republican program in Reconstruction South Carolina." This was because property taxes, and particularly a levy on unused agricultural land, could accomplish multiple goals at once: fund education and other state public services, as well as force landowners either to expand cultivation and thus employ more laborers or renters, or else sell unused land at prices that the landless could afford to pay. In addition, counties and municipalities levied their own taxes, elevating overall tax burdens even though state rates were relatively low. In Kershaw County, for instance, total yearly taxes amounted to about 2 percent of the total value of taxable property. Readers of the Camden *Journal* and other South Carolina newspapers saw numerous advertisements for tax-driven land sales in every issue. In 1873, 270,000 acres of South Carolina land were seized for taxes; the next year the state total was 500,000 acres.[73]

Some black Carolinians were able to take advantage of these conditions and purchase land, realizing one of the great ambitions of African Americans before and after emancipation. Yet the perhaps nine thousand individuals who acquired land through private market transactions fell far short of the multitudes who had hoped for and expected far-reaching land redistribution after the Civil War. Under Union occupation, some parts of coastal South Carolina had come under federal schemes for breaking up plantations and making land available to former slaves. These programs were soon halted and then reversed, however, leaving only about two thousand with secure titles to lands on the Sea Islands.[74] Then in 1869, South Carolina's lawmakers created a land commission, which purchased tracts of land and resold them to small farmers under liberal conditions. Though the commission was notorious for corruption in its early years, by 1876 approximately fourteen thousand black families (about one seventh of the state's black population) had been settled on commission lands, including 6,360 acres in Kershaw County.[75] By 1890, approximately 20 percent of black agriculturalists owned at least some land, which left the vast majority in some kind of tenancy or sharecropping arrangement.[76]

Those who did manage to acquire land learned that tax levies fell on white and black, planters and smallholders alike. In 1872, the same year that the propertied Church Vaughan wrote his letter to the Foreign Mission Board, one of the three town lots in Camden acquired by his nephew William Hammond just two years earlier came up for sale. Tragically, Hammond had recently died at the age of only thirty-one, and his widow Henrietta was evidently unable to pay Kershaw County's property taxes. The lot and the house on it were forfeited and sold by the county treasurer. Three years later, Henrietta Hammond sold another of the properties on Market Street for eighty dollars, and the third seems to have passed back to the family from which William Hammond purchased it.[77] In fact, the Vaughans' distant cousins the Dibble family, proprietors of a Broad Street grocery store that lasted some forty years, cast their lot with the conservative Democratic Party, presumably because radical reforms that came with high taxes were not in their interest.[78]

If some black property owners objected to Republican tax policies, white resistance was vehement. "This is a TAXATION which is tantamount to CONFISCATION," cried a Charleston newspaper headline, in what became a common refrain.[79] Members of the state's prewar aristocracy organized tax-payers' conventions in 1871 and 1874 to rail against the Reconstruction legis-lature, its tax policies, and the allegedly wasteful ways it spent "their" money. A delegation from the latter convention traveled to Washington, D.C. to pre-sent their grievances about what they called "schemes of public plunder" to President Grant and the U.S. House of Representatives.[80] Though the visit brought no immediate reaction, widespread opinion was nonetheless turn-ing against interventionist government in the South.

In 1873 the national economy entered an economic depression. Under pressure to constrain finances, national and state leaders began to lose their enthusiasm for Reconstruction. Even Martin Delany came to doubt that black votes and aggressive government would radically transform the South. Increasingly convinced that white economic power would always thwart black advancement, he began to call for cooperation between employers and workers and compromise between Republicans and Democrats. "Save what you can while you have a chance," he repeatedly counseled African Ameri-cans, predicting that because of their poverty and landlessness, their political influence would be fleeting.[81] In 1874, Delany ran for lieutenant governor of South Carolina on a "reform" ticket, warning as he accepted his party's nomi-nation that "my race . . . has all and everything to lose in a contest such as might be brought about by antagonism of the races."[82] Though the election was won by the Republican candidate, Daniel H. Chamberlain, the party's old activism was no longer on the state political agenda. Elected on a re-form platform himself, Chamberlain immediately began to reorganize state programs and investigate fraud (which had been rampant under his prede-cessors). To the approval of the state's white elite, his administration cut taxes, reduced the size of the state militia, and removed many black trial jus-tices and local school officials, often replacing them with white Democrats.

Chamberlain became further estranged from black Republicans when in late 1875 he blocked the appointment of two African American judges elected by the legislature. Meanwhile, as the state Republican Party fractured, Democrats were organizing both politically and militarily for a takeover.[83]

Already the collapse of the federal KKK trials after 1872 and subsequent drawdown of federal troops had removed any real threat to white insurrectionists in South Carolina. Civil War hero Wade Hampton famously declared that it was time for white southerners to "dedicate themselves to the redemption of the South."[84] Though they no longer used the name Ku Klux Klan, white supremacists organized rifle, saber, and gun clubs, through which they continued to terrorize their political opponents. The violence became especially intense in the run-up to the gubernatorial election of 1876, in which Hampton challenged Chamberlain, now considered by black Republicans as their best hope. Hampton called for members of the white military clubs to exercise "force without violence," a message they received only by half. In Hamburg, a predominantly black town in inland Aiken County, two hundred armed whites confronted the black militia after a testy July 4 exchange between militia members and two white travelers. After the militia was forced to surrender, five of its members were shot in cold blood. In the same county two months later, white terrorists murdered between thirty and fifty African Americans they had captured in a standoff, including state representative Simon P. Coker of neighboring Barnwell County. Though the governor declared rifle clubs illegal and President Grant sent eleven hundred federal troops to South Carolina, violence and intimidation continued. Hampton's campaign stop in Camden in early October brought out an estimated five thousand mounted Red Shirts, Democratic Party supporters known for wearing their hunting attire and brandishing their weapons. The Red Shirts came out for Governor Chamberlain's visit to town as well, riding in their "endless columns" among the "throngs of negroes," perhaps including the Vaughans, who "packed the sidewalks." According to Camden historians who remembered the event, "Perfect bedlam reigned for hours."[85]

Even a Democratic observer described the tense, fraud-ridden state election of 1876 as "one of the grandest farces ever seen." Violence, intimidation, and Democratic Party vote-rigging resulted in two claimants for the governorship, along with two parallel state Houses of Representatives. The rival state governments operated for four months, while a similar stalemate at the federal level delayed the election of a new United States president. In South Carolina, white taxpayers—joined by small numbers of black property holders—refused to pay their state levies, though they voluntarily contributed 10 percent of their previous year's tax liability to Hampton's parallel government. While Chamberlain's treasury dwindled, Hampton's administration funded the operation of state agencies. Meanwhile, the disputed presidential election was resolved through a compromise by which the Republican candidate, Rutherford B. Hayes, received the backing of southern legislators in exchange for a pledge to remove the remaining federal troops from former Confederate states. In April 1877, the last U.S. military units began to withdraw from South Carolina, and an embittered Daniel Chamberlain and his staff vacated their offices in the state house. Reconstruction was over.[86]

Although African Americans had begun over the previous decade to claim their rights as free citizens, that process halted and reversed in the last quarter of the nineteenth century. South Carolina's new government was determined to squelch political participation by the state's black majority. By barring African Americans from membership in state and local Democratic Party organizations, and through a host of new restrictions on voting, white lawmakers disfranchised tens of thousands in South Carolina and across the South. More than ninety-one thousand black South Carolinians voted in the 1876 election, but by 1888 less than fourteen thousand did so. In 1872, ninety-six black legislators occupied positions in the state house; by 1890 there were only seven.[87] Though some money still went to black schools, between 1880 and 1895 the state's per capita expenditure for black pupils declined by more than half, while that for whites increased slightly.[88] Segregation of public facilities became the law. And threats to white supremacy were met with violence. Lynching was less pervasive in South Carolina than in some other southern states; however, more than one hundred African Americans were murdered through mob violence between the late 1880s and 1905, or approximately six per year, concentrated in the upcountry.[89] In Camden on July 4, 1882 (exactly eleven years since the standoff there between black militamen and Klansmen, and sixty-six years since the abortive slave uprising), L. W. R. Blair, an outspoken political independent who had run for governor two years previously, was fatally shot while addressing a crowd of black supporters. The Vaughans must have heard the rumors that a group of the town's leading white men determined that Blair's death would be in the interest of the state and drew lots to choose who would kill him. Blair's assailant James L. Haile did not deny the murder charge, but was acquitted at trial on spurious claims of self-defense.[90]

As Reconstruction collapsed, black southerners again began to see emigration as their best option. In 1877, several Charleston entrepreneurs formed the Liberian Exodus Joint Steam Ship Company, intending to finance emigrants' transportation to Africa through sales of company stock. Martin Delany served on the board of directors, partially reprising his role in Abeokuta by negotiating with the Liberian government for land grants for settlers. By the end of the year, sixty-five thousand of the state's four hundred thousand black residents had registered their desire to emigrate with the company, though it ultimately managed to send only one contingent to Africa.[91] Meanwhile, the rejuvenated American Colonization Society dispatched five ships carrying emigrants to Liberia in the two years following the final withdrawal of federal troops from the South. In 1879 the society leaders estimated that a half-million blacks from the South were willing to move to Liberia.[92] The actual numbers proved to be much smaller: 3,880 new colonists ventured to Liberia between the end of the Civil War and 1900.[93] Yet they represented only a portion of the latter nineteenth century's upsurge in what historian Steven Hahn termed "grassroots emigrationism." Like the thousands of African Americans who removed to Kansas or Indiana, or indeed the multitudes who moved north in the twentieth century, these settlers were voting with their feet for a vision of freedom that included physical security, political agency, and access to land and livelihoods for themselves and their children.[94]

If he heard about the new Liberian settlers, as he likely did, Vaughan could identify with their plight. He too had fled white supremacy in South Carolina. But Vaughan had not been at home in Liberia either—and neither were some of the post–Civil War emigrants. Elias Hill died of malaria shortly after he landed at Monrovia, along with many in his party. The Liberian government of the 1870s was roiled by scandal, and labor conditions for native Africans continued to deteriorate. Many of the surviving new settlers returned to the United States, or tried to do so—an impulse that Vaughan surely could understand as well.[95] If American white supremacy was intolerable, it was only one version of the slavery-like conditions that snaked through the Atlantic world.

In Lagos, too, slaves and former slaves struggled to make a decent living, to exercise choices over where and with whom they would live, and to be treated with respect. As in "redeemed" South Carolina, black people in colonial Lagos—regardless of their former status as slave or free—had little formal political influence. Yet there, Vaughan was able not only to enjoy a comfortable standard of living, but also to pass along wealth and opportunity to the generations who followed him.

As his relatives in South Carolina struggled for their rights and livelihoods, Church Vaughan faced his own devastating setbacks in Lagos. For the fourth time, he lost his home and possessions. Death stalked his family, snatching away babies and children. Through these tragedies, however, Vaughan continued his upward trajectory. Not only did he continue to build a prosperous, comfortable life for himself and his family, but he positioned his surviving children to build upon his successes themselves. Determined to provide advantages he did not grow up with and his South Carolina relatives could not enjoy, Vaughan invested in business, landed property, and a first-rate education for his offspring. Through these means, and in spite of his heartbreaks, he laid the foundation for a Vaughan dynasty in Africa.

On January 17, 1875, fire swept through Vaughan's neighborhood. Conflagrations occurred frequently in Lagos, where countless structures of bamboo and thatch made the island the "veritable *fire-place*" of the West Coast, according to a local journalist. In fact there had been nearly a dozen substantial fires since Vaughan had moved there. Five years earlier, flames fanned by high, hot winds had consumed nearly a third of the city and killed four people. This time the fire engulfed Kakawa and nearby Odulanmi Streets, burning at least one hundred houses, one of them Vaughan's. Before the blaze died out, it reduced the Vaughan family's house to ashes and consumed all of their belongings.[96]

His real estate holdings were probably what enabled Vaughan to rebuild yet again, providing some rental income and a place to stay while he reestablished his business and residence. Devastating as the fire had been, it also did create more demand for his hardware and metal products as Lagosians rebuilt. Everyone who could afford it wanted iron roofs for their houses—especially as fires recurred just about every dry season. In fact, in January 1877, more than a third of Lagos's buildings, including over a thousand houses, burned in a great fire spread by harmattan winds. Vaughan reestablished his store on Kakawa Street and later purchased a plot on nearby Igbosere Road, where he moved his family into a new house. This section of the Brazilian quarter was one of the "sophisticated and expanding parts of town," where prosperous merchants built ornate, two-story house/business compounds featuring arched doorways, wrought ironwork, dormer windows, and of course metal roofs.[97] Over the next decade, Vaughan purchased at least four other plots of land in Lagos and Ebute Metta, including a fourteen acre tract on the mainland from Robert Campbell, part of what had formerly been known as "Campbell's Farm."[98]

Yet more tragedy struck the Vaughan family. Church and Sarah Vaughan's second child, Ebenezer, had been given a name from the Old Testament that commemorated God's help to the Israelites in defeating the Philistines.[99] Though they had suffered tribulations, Church and Sarah Vaughan must have been thankful for their good fortune in establishing a new home for their little family in Lagos. Yet the child died in infancy. Two years later, in September 1870, Burrell Carter Vaughan was born, named after Church's late brother; a daughter followed him in May 1873. She was named Emily, perhaps after Emily Hooper, Church's dear friend from his voyage to Liberia, whom he might have known had recently returned to North Carolina. In January 1876, almost exactly a year after the fire, Sarah Vaughan gave birth to another daughter, named Sarah Ann after her father's sister (and perhaps her mother). Shortly after the mother's convalescence, however, little Emily began to "suffer greatly" from dysentery. "The case is almost hopeless," wrote a newly arrived Baptist missionary after paying her a visit. "She is one of our S.S. [Sunday school] children—although very low, she never fails to extend her hand to me when she sees me coming. We commended her into the care of Him who said, 'Suffer little children to come unto me.'" The next day, after the clergyman had administered some medicine, Emily's condition seemed to improve. Her mother gave her a bath and tucked her into a cozy room, with doors and windows shut. There, however, the temperature rose, and Emily began vomiting. The next afternoon she was dead. Her family and two Baptist missionaries held a funeral in the nearby cemetery the following day.[100] As if they had not already suffered enough grief, Church and Sarah Vaughan soon lost their infant daughter, Sarah Ann, too.

In eleven years of marriage, Church and Sarah Vaughan had welcomed five children into the world, only two of whom survived. They would lose another child as well, Mary Sillah (fittingly named from the Hebrew for *shadow*), who died before her fourth birthday in 1883.[101] Yoruba people had (and have) a name for the spirit of a child who repeatedly is born and then dies: *àbíku*. Families who lost young children in succession believed that it was the same spirit who kept coming and going, repeatedly causing anguish for their parents. Mothers and fathers of suspected *àbíku* took special precautions with their young ones, putting charms around their ankles or cutting their hair in order to make them unattractive to the hidden spirits who might like to take them back from the world of the living. With his steadfast

Christianity, Vaughan would have denied that an *àbíkú* was responsible for his children's deaths. But in a town where much day to day activity took place on verandahs and courtyards and gossip was practically the municipal pastime, others must have suggested it, and maybe his wife believed it too.[102] Their last child, a daughter born in 1882, was the only one to bear a Yoruba name along with her English ones: Ibiremi, short for Ibiremilekun. The name is often rendered in English as "comfort," although in a more complete translation it means "the birth assuaged my tears."[103]

The little girl's English middle name, Arabella, derived from the Latin word *orabilis*, which means "prayerful" or an "answered prayer." But its meaning only partially explains the choice of this name. Thirty years earlier on his voyage to Liberia, Vaughan had passed some of his time in the company of young Arabella Jacobs, also from South Carolina. He had already named his son James Wilson and daughter Emily after memorable shipmates from that life-changing journey. With the use of the name Arabella he created a third living reminder.

But if the new baby's middle name invoked Vaughan's past, her first name was thoroughly contemporary: it was Aida, the central character of a Verdi opera that had taken the world by storm in the 1870s. In the story, Aida was a beautiful Ethiopian princess held in Egypt as a slave and involved in a tragic love affair with an Egyptian military commander. That the Vaughans named their daughter after a character in a Verdi opera first performed in Cairo illustrates the circulation of world news and culture in late nineteenth-century Lagos. The 1870s saw the efflorescence of "Victorian Lagos," a time remembered later as one of social ease and openness, when well-to-do Africans built a cosmopolitan milieu combining their western education, diasporic sensibilities, and local alliances. Merchants, educators, and professionals, most of them Sierra Leonean or Brazilian in origin, sought to uplift themselves and their society by sharing what they saw as the best elements of foreign cultures. They formed social and literary clubs to debate societal, philosophical, and political questions of the day. They were conversant with events in Europe and America. They had high hopes for themselves and for Africa, and they believed that British administration was justified, at least temporarily, because of its civilizing influence. Elite Lagosians desired high-quality education for their children, whom they hoped would become professionals themselves. They wanted to associate with sophisticated, European-style recreations, so they organized and attended music concerts, dramatic performances, fancy dress balls, horse races, and cricket matches, and they held *soirées* and "at homes" in their residences. "I never knew what real, black aristocracy was until I was in Lagos," wrote an African American after her 1886 visit. "In Lagos I have seen as fine a turnout as I have seen on Fifth Avenue, New York; coachman and footman dressed in English costume; black ladies and gentlemen riding on horseback, and driving in buggies. Their houses are furnished in tiptop English style." When their children got married, the celebrations were costly, elaborate, and well publicized. Robert Campbell, among others, participated actively in the island's social and intellectual life, serving as a leader of the Freemasons Lodge, the Lagos Scientific Society, the Lagos Mutual Improvement Society, and the Lagos Gymnastics Club, as well as attending countless events and meetings.[104]

Lagos newspapers of the 1880s did not mention Church Vaughan in connection with the many educational and recreational events that they reported—though as his children grew up, they regularly appeared in such accounts. Whether it was his hardscrabble background, his tutelage as a young man by rather severe Baptist missionaries, or his own determined work ethic, Church Vaughan seemed to keep his distance from the social life of Victorian Lagos. He was an avid reader, however, who "kept himself in touch with contemporary thought, and his information of matters and things generally was very wide," as an observer put it.[105] How else could he have come up with Aida as the name of his infant daughter?

Though Church and Sarah Vaughan may not have participated in many elite social activities, they joined their wealthy contemporaries in their children's education. Growing up under the shadow of black slavery and white oppression in South Carolina, Church Vaughan had gained his literacy informally and secretly. His wife, if she could read and write at all, had been taught in a mission station as a refugee. Many of Vaughan's nieces and nephews and their children in South Carolina remained illiterate. Church Vaughan's children, however, received the best education Lagos had to offer. Since there were no government or Baptist schools until later, the Vaughans sent their sons to those established by the British missionary societies. For the equivalent of today's high school, James Wilson and Burrell attended the CMS Grammar School, an institution founded in 1859 which produced nearly all of Lagos's early African clergy and civil servants and many of the city's top merchants.[106] The school had been established by Thomas Babington Macaulay, an educated Saro and the son-in-law of the clergyman Samuel Ajayi Crowther. By the time the Vaughan boys attended, Macaulay was assisted by Nathaniel Johnson, whose father, Henry Johnson—formerly the assistant to CMS missionaries in Ibadan—had likely helped Church Vaughan escape from captivity at the outbreak of the Ijaye war two decades earlier.

The curriculum included grammar, composition, literature, arithmetic, history, geography, bookkeeping, sciences, and Latin and Greek.[107] Later in his life, James Wilson Vaughan published poetry in English and Yoruba; Burrell Vaughan was urged by his parents to become a doctor, though ill health later interrupted his education.[108] Thus the boys received a top-notch liberal education, largely from African educators. When Aida Arabella was old enough, after her father had died, her brothers sent her to England to complete her schooling.

As he and his sons got older, Church Vaughan also provided them with a sound economic foundation. At the age of sixteen, James Wilson Vaughan finished high school and began to assist his father in the hardware and iron trades. He handled the work so capably that soon he was doing most of the family's business. It may have been his idea to call the operation "Sheffield Store," after the English town known for its iron products and knives, probably where the Vaughans ordered their supplies. Later, he was joined by his younger brother Burrell.[109] By training them in the family business, Church Vaughan was helping to ensure his sons' future prosperity. He also bought land in Lagos for each of his surviving children—three plots purchased within a week of each other in 1884, the year James Wilson turned eighteen. One, with a house already on it, was situated right next door to the family homestead on Igbosere Road. James Wilson may have moved there after his 1889 marriage to the daughter of an elite merchant who served as Lagos's police chief (though she and her father both died within months of the wedding, presumably of contagious illness). The second plot, at Massey and Agarawu Streets toward the densely inhabited indigenous quarter of the town, ultimately became the site of the family's second store ("Excelsior," meaning "higher," but also a brand name of wood shavings for packing), which Burrell oversaw. The third parcel of land, near Massey Square, may have been envisioned for little Aida Arabella, who was only two years old at the time.[110]

Later, in their own adulthoods, Church Vaughan's children built upon the foundation he had provided for them. James Wilson and Burrell Vaughan maintained and grew the family hardware, iron, and tool stores, becoming, according to a business guide published in 1920, "the only native trader[s] who, apparently, can compete with the European firms in the hardware trade."[111] They augmented the properties their father had purchased with many others, and they built grand residences for their own families. After his second marriage in 1891, James Wilson Vaughan built a large compound farther down Igbosere Road from his parents' place, which he christened

Camden House after his father's hometown. Later, at the site of the family store on Kakawa Street, he erected a Brazilian-style mansion with commercial space on the bottom and housing on the top; it remains one of the few architectural gems in an otherwise greatly changed urban area. Burrell Vaughan's official residence was a large house attached to his Excelsior Store, but he maintained several other homes in Lagos as well as land and houses on the island, the mainland, and at Ibadan. In her middle age, Aida Arabella Vaughan erected on one of her several properties a home called Conway House, after her American great-grandfather Bonds Conway.[112] In their turn, Church and Sarah Vaughan's grandchildren, all of them educated, built upon their own inheritances. Through personal ups and downs and the general trauma of recent Nigerian history, the Vaughan family has remained one of Lagos's most venerable. Thus, in spite of the heartbreaking loss of his young children and the devastating damage of fire, Church Vaughan was able to build a life of security and prosperity for his family, and to pass resources and opportunity to his descendants. In this way, he was considerably more fortunate than his relatives back in South Carolina.

Decades after the fact, descendants of Vaughan's relatives in South Carolina remembered not only that he had sent gifts, but that he had come back to America himself. In 1975, Bessie Boykin Rayford, a ninety-one-year-old great-grandchild of Vaughan's half-aunt Harriet Conway, told an interviewer that when she was a small girl in Camden, her African relative returned for a visit. "He wore a jacket of several different colors with a top hat to match," she said of Vaughan, suggesting that he arrived with great fanfare in thoroughly African attire. "The whole town, both black and white, turned out to see him, and there was a parade for him down the main street of Camden."[113] In this account, Vaughan seems like the biblical Joseph with his many-hued coat, reunited with his family after having been separated by distance and slavery. Not for the first or last time, Vaughan's story seems almost too poetic to be true.

In fact, no other evidence—in Camden newspapers, immigration and travel records, departure notices in the Lagos press, or anywhere else—suggests that Church Vaughan ever returned to South Carolina. Instead, a well-educated Yoruba man by the name of Orishetuka Faduma came to the United States in 1891 to attend divinity school at Yale. Four years later, he made a tour of the American South, including a two-week stop in Columbia, South Carolina. Whether he traveled to nearby Camden and appeared in public in the colorful Yoruba *agbada* outfit of his homeland is unclear. But it

J. W. Vaughan House,
29 Kakawa Street,
Lagos, 2006. Photo
by the author.

B. C. Vaughan house, 91 Apapa Road, Ebute Metta. From O. A. Akinyeye, *Eko, Landmarks of Lagos, Nigeria.*

certainly is possible that this was the African visit that Mrs. Rayford, then a child of eleven, remembered many years later.[114]

It is hard to imagine that Church Vaughan would have gone back to Camden for a visit in his later life. Certainly he *could* have done it: he had enough money to cover the costs of travel, and his sons could have run the family business in his absence. But what would have motivated him to make such an arduous, expensive journey? Whom would he have gone to see? His last remaining sibling, his older sister Sarah, died sometime in the 1880s.

James F. Sutherland, the white cabinetmaker and judge from New York with whom Church had lived in the early 1850s, had died before that, after fathering two children with Church's niece Maria Sophronia, whom Church had last seen when she was three years old. She too may have died in the 1880s, though it is possible that she merely left no written records after that. The only other close relative whom Church Vaughan had known in South Carolina was his brother's daughter Maria, who had been thirteen but living outside of Camden at the time Vaughan left. A divorced mother of four in 1880, she was scratching out a living, like so many of woman of color, washing and ironing; her own daughter worked as a farm laborer. The best off of all of Vaughan's relatives was his sister Mary's daughter Harriet, born four years after his departure for Africa, who received some of the gold that he had sent in 1869. In 1874, Harriet had married William W. Carter, the son of a grocer and housewife whose census designations as "mulatto" suggest they may have been free before the Civil War.[115] Carter was educated, and though he worked as a farmer and then a barber, he later became a teacher, and Harriet was able to forgo paid employment in order to care for their twelve children. One of these, a daughter born in 1891, was given the same unusual name as her African-born, nine-year-old cousin, Aida Arabella.[116] Even if Church Vaughan did not pay a visit to South Carolina, then, he did continue to communicate important news to his family members there.

Vaughan's most ambitious and successful relatives did not stay in Camden.[117] Harriet Carter's husband William was probably related to Republican activist Frank Carter, a teacher, superintendent of Camden schools, and briefly a delegate to the General Assembly during Reconstruction. After Reconstruction ended, William occasionally participated in Radical Republican political meetings, and it may have been this, or perhaps his relative's activities, that prompted Ku Klux Klan terrorists to set fire to the family's home. In the first decade of the twentieth century, the Carters relocated to Hudson, New Jersey.[118] Around the same time, their cousin William Sutherland—Maria Sophronia's son—who had attended the Avery Normal Institute and Howard College of Dentistry, also moved with his new wife to New Jersey, where he established a dental practice.[119] Like so many other black southerners, and a half-century after Church Vaughan had done the same thing, these Vaughan descendants concluded that their best course of action was to leave.

In Lagos, Vaughan may well have shared the sentiments of the Yoruba traveler Orishetuka Faduma. In an interview with an American journalist during his 1895 stop in South Carolina, Faduma suggested that intelligent and ambitious African Americans should move to Africa. "The majority of the members of the tribe to which I belong are in a better condition than the mass of the negroes in this country," he asserted. "Though they are not surrounded by the high civilization that the negroes here enjoy, yet they have one thing that the negroes here do not have—the consciousness of their own manhood—and when my people are civilized they make strong men in every sense of the word. They do not have a low idea of themselves and are not conscious of any inferiority to others."[120]

This was the crux of the difference between Lagos and the American South. In Lagos, colonial rule imposed limits upon Africans' political autonomy and shaped the economy in ways favorable to European commerce. Nevertheless, black Lagosians, especially those from the African diaspora, could and did achieve considerable wealth and social recognition. During Vaughan's lifetime, colonial officials in fact *wanted* Africans to succeed, not only to vindicate their rule but also to provide tax revenue for the official treasury. Despite its economic illogic, white elites in the American South instead wanted African Americans to fail, in order to validate and perpetuate their subordination.

The American Church Vaughan found his place in Lagos. There, under British colonial rule, he had experienced freedom like never before. He and other newcomers were largely free from extractive patronage relationships, and they were certainly free from vulnerability to kidnapping and slave raids. The ablest and luckiest among them were free to make a good living. Vaughan knew that these freedoms were less available to Lagos's slaves and other subordinate people. Yet he picked his battles. He did not rage against slavery in Lagos—nor had he done so in Ijaye or Liberia. But Lagos was becoming infected by a new strain of white supremacy, carried not least within the Baptist church he knew well. It was against this that Vaughan ultimately decided to make his stand.

six

VAUGHAN'S REBELLION

In March 1888, Church Vaughan, his sons, longtime fellow Baptists Sarah Harden and Moses Ladejo Stone, and several others convened a meeting to discuss their relationship to the Southern Baptist Church. For years they had endured slights and insults from its missionary William David; now he was insisting that he could treat one of their number, a popular preacher, practically as one of his servants. Yet one of the principles of Baptist organization was that ministers served their congregations, not the other way around. Vaughan had been a Baptist for more than thirty years, and Baptist missionaries from the American South had brought him to Yorubaland and given him his start there. He still believed in the denomination's key tenets: salvation through faith, Jesus Christ as Lord and Savior, and the Bible as the word of God and final written authority. But Vaughan and the others were fed up with missionary racism and convinced they could better lead the Lagos Baptists themselves. Since it was clear that Reverend David would never share church authority, they determined to do something West African Christians had never done before: secede. Together they formed the Native Baptist Church (later known as the Ebenezer Baptist Church), which became the first nonmissionary Christian congregation in West Africa and one of the earliest on the African continent. Soon nearly all of the Lagos Baptists joined it, eviscerating the white-run mission.[1]

Vaughan's bid for religious autonomy heralded a movement that became widespread in Lagos and well beyond. In the late nineteenth and early twentieth centuries, independent African Christian churches proliferated in Yorubaland and all over colonial Africa. The phenomenon became known as "Ethiopianism," from the biblical passage "Ethiopia shall stretch forth her hands to God" (Psalm 68:31) — Ethiopia standing in the Bible for Africa in general. Through the medium of Christianity, Ethiopianism expressed African self-assertion and, some scholars have argued, early anticolonial nationalism.[2] Religious protests in Lagos, however, rarely targeted the colonial government. The town's king and chiefs had felt the weight of British intervention from its beginnings in 1851, of course; and in their general reluctance to intervene in local slavery, British administrators had offered little hope for Lagos's most downtrodden. However, African Christians appreciated the colonial government's guarantee of law and order, which made their prosperity possible. Rather than oppose the administration, they struggled within and against the mission bodies, institutions that more closely affected their lives and identities.[3]

Vaughan's personal conflict between loyalty to the Baptist church and frustration with missionary racism mirrored that of other Lagosian Christians. Nether Vaughan nor any other leader of the independent church movement ever repudiated Christianity itself, nor did they aim to alter its basic theology or organizational structure. They were not only committed Christians, but they owed their very identities as educated elites to the mission churches. The Church Missionary Society, or the Wesleyans, or even the Baptists, had helped make them what they were, whether traders or teachers, clerks or catechists. For nearly two generations, missionaries in Yorubaland had described their project as spreading Christianity and educating Africans; and by the 1880s some Lagosians and others were declaring that work a success. Already "civilized" themselves, they were ready — eager, in fact — to take on the leadership of the churches and continue that vital project.

The trouble was that the ground was shifting under their feet, as the European "scramble for Africa" got under way in a new ideological climate. Even before European representatives met at the Berlin Conference of 1884–85 to stake their African claims, the character of British involvement in what is now Nigeria had begun to change, a process that continued through the end of the century. A new, more open racism brought condescension and European attempts to separate themselves from the Africans among whom they lived. Increasing numbers of European personnel pushed Africans out of their posts in the civil service and foreign-owned commercial firms. Though elite Africans continued to prosper, their opportunities became more circumscribed than before; moreover, they were offended by the new attitudes. These they felt most keenly in the mission churches, whose white leaders sought to reverse decades-old policies and monopolize control over African congregations. Increasingly, missionaries asserted that African capacities were inherently limited, and thus intensive European oversight was necessary.[4]

The new missionary attitudes struck especially hard at diasporic Lagosians. Immigrants from Sierra Leone, Brazil, and elsewhere, as well as their children, had formerly seen foreign missionaries as their liberators and advocates.[5] Now, however, they felt abandoned, as the antislavery ideologies and policies that had benefited them were replaced by a general disparagement of Africans and their capacities. They responded in two overlapping ways, both with important effects for Nigerian history. On the one hand, educated Yorubas, especially those with diasporic connections, began to highlight and celebrate some of their cultural differences from Europeans, even as they struggled to maintain and extend their roles within the mission churches. On the other, diasporic Africans also spearheaded the movement for Christian independence, beginning with Baptists connected to the United States and including Saro in the Anglican and Methodist churches. Understanding the new racism as a phenomenon of the wider Atlantic world, Vaughan and the other Christian rebels drew on a strategy of separation from white establishments, which African Americans had been pursuing both at home and abroad. As the independent church movement progressed, it was fed both by Yoruba cultural nationalism and links reaching well beyond Yorubaland.

Vaughan celebrated his sixtieth birthday during the upheaval within the Lagos Baptist Church. Though he led the opposition to missionary racism, he left the new church's further development to younger men. Throughout his adult life, what he most valued was autonomy. From his days in Ijaye and Abeokuta, he had tried to separate himself from the Baptist mission, only to find danger when he did. During his early years in Lagos, he not only worked to establish his own business, but he engaged in religious worship without missionaries. In his profitable self-employment, in his family life unconnected to any local kin group, in his limited participation in the social life of Victorian Lagos, and now in his separation from the mission church, Vaughan revealed how important it was to him to be his own man, not part of any given collectivity. Perhaps it is somewhat ironic, then, that in asserting his independence Vaughan placed himself at the helm of an increasingly widespread movement. More characteristic may have been his subsequent distance even from the church he helped to create.

In 1872 when the Lagos Baptists had prevailed upon Church Vaughan to request a missionary from the Southern Baptist Convention, he had done so with little enthusiasm. Since the departure of Richard Stone in 1869, the congregation had largely looked after itself. Initially, a resident Methodist missionary had performed some services for the Baptists, but after he left for England, the little church was in local African hands. Moses Ladejo Stone, trained as a carpenter by Vaughan and as a Baptist by the missionary Richard Stone, was emerging as a first-class preacher; Sarah Harden, the Sierra Leone-born widow of the African American missionary Joseph Harden, gave him advice and encouragement; and Vaughan provided some financial support. As the Foreign Mission Board back in Richmond struggled to raise funds in the postwar American South, Vaughan and his fellow Baptists experienced by default what they—and members of every other denomination in Lagos—would struggle for in the racially charged era to come: African autonomy.

Yet this religious independence was fleeting. Not one but two new Baptist missionaries arrived in 1875, each named William, each objectionable in his own way, and each displaying a different characteristic of the nineteenth-century Atlantic world. Twenty-five-year-old William ("Willie") David had grown up in white privilege outside of Meridian, Mississippi, his wealthy, slaveholding grandfather urging him to take up a more gentlemanly profession than the ministry. In school he had distinguished himself by his piety, zeal, and family connections rather than his intellectual accomplishments.[6] William Colley, a year his senior, was a new graduate of the Richmond Institute, a training school for freedmen originally located in a former slave mart. Born and raised in rural Prince Edward County, Virginia, he and his mother had likely been enslaved before emancipation, though Colley's "light brown" complexion may have come from a white father, listed on an application for a Freedman's Bank account simply as "Mr. W."[7] Willie David was an obnoxious racist, imbued with a deep sense of white supremacy even if he did want to help save black souls. His colleague William Colley chafed under David's condescension but also lorded himself over Lagos Christians. Ultimately it was to him rather than David that local Baptists most objected, at least in print. Colley's dual conflicts—with David and with local Africans—would prompt his formation of a separate, African American missionary society, drawing from a long black American tradition of autonomous institutions and also serving as an example for Lagos Baptists.

Neither Church Vaughan, Sarah Harden, nor Moses Stone were part of the reception when the two new missionaries arrived in Lagos, so David and Colley had to communicate with the spectators through a local interpreter. This did not, however, diminish their sense of self-importance as saviors for Lagos Baptists. "I do not think I ever saw people so rejoiced," David wrote of his initial welcome in the city. "Immediately they had a meeting in their bamboo chapel to thank God, who had answered their prayers. It was a mutual thanksgiving."[8]

If Vaughan was keeping his distance until he knew more about the newly arrived Americans, he did not have to wait long for news to travel through town about what kind of men they were. Though David rented seemingly suitable accommodations from a wealthy African merchant, "The workmen who have been engaged in repairing and whitewashing the house have progressed so slowly that I have not been able to get in my room yet," as the missionary wrote in his diary. "So this afternoon I stood by and derided them." Verbal abuse did not improve the workers' pace, however, so David tried the next strategy a Mississippi planter might use to exert his will: "Before I could have my way I had to use a club upon one of them, which settled the matter. They worked splendidly and were quite obedient." A few days later, David reported that "the usual number of men have been working around the house with their characteristic laziness." This time he asked Colley to supervise them, with no better results: "Pretty soon we heard him flogging one of them, who the first opportunity afterwards, ran from the room into the street, where he met his employer who asked why he left, and after telling that he had been flogged, was ordered back. After that there was no more trouble with the men." It is hard to fathom how a recently arrived African American, who may well have felt the lash on his own back at one time, so readily beat an African workman, except as some grisly enactment of the relationship between owner and slave driver, or perhaps as a performance of equality with his white associate. It is even harder to imagine that this new graduate of a training institute for freedman would have shared David's patronizing view of African education. "Some persons might think this a poor way to Christianize them," the white missionary wrote in his diary, "but these *claim* to be civilized. One (the one I clubbed) told me today he had studied Greek and Latin. I suppose they also belong to the Church Mission Society."[9]

In Lagos's stratified society, raging against a hired worker was not so unusual. But David's sense of superiority extended to Lagosians more broadly, including Christians of other denominations, stalwart Baptists, and even the top of the city's African elite. After David and Colley undertook their first public baptisms in a river in January 1876, rumors spread that òyinbós (whites) were drowning people, and several Lagosians connected with the Church Missionary Society came to confront them. David related the incident as a battle of wills in which he emerged victorious over the doubters.

"After a short discussion," he wrote, "they were made to confess their error before a large crowd of heathen who had gathered to listen; and a little later they left, vanquished, amid the jeers of the populace."[10] His attitude was similar within his own congregation, where David insulted the venerable Sarah Harden by breaking a long-held pattern of calling her name first on the Sunday roster. Challenged on the point, he defiantly asserted his authority as leader of the church.[11]

Even more publicly, David entered into an ill-tempered dispute with his landlord James Pinson Labulo Davies, at one time the wealthiest and most influential African in the city. Captured in Yorubaland then rescued from a slave ship and taken to Sierra Leone, "Captain" Davies had been trained there in navigation and employed on one of the vessels in the British Navy's anti-slavery squadron, from which he witnessed the 1851 bombardment of Lagos. After his navy service, Davies captained merchant vessels owned by liberated Africans from Sierra Leone, trading on their and his own behalf along the West African coast. He settled permanently in Lagos in 1856 and soon became the most successful of the immigrant merchants, shipping cotton and palm oil in his own boats (condemned slavers he had purchased at auction) and employing dozens of workers. In London in 1862, Davies married Sarah Forbes Bonetta in a service led by Henry Venn, honorary secretary of the Church Missionary Society. Davies's new wife had as a child been virtually adopted by the British naval captain who liberated her from a slave ship. She became a protégée of Queen Victoria, who later served as godmother to the Davies's first child. In fact, Sarah Davies and Rev. Samuel Crowther were the only Africans whom the Royal Navy had orders to evacuate in the event of an uprising at Lagos. In 1872, Lagos's governor chose J. P. L. Davies as the first African (unofficial) member of the legislative council; he was also the first African Justice of the Peace. Though Davies's businesses were affected by economic recession by the time he rented a house to the Baptist missionary Willie David, he nonetheless represented the top of the city's African elite—wealthy, politically influential, and closely connected to the Church Missionary Society.[12]

Reverend David was aware of Davies's position—he referred to his former landlord, perhaps with sarcasm, as the "adopted son-in-law of the Queen of England"—but treated Davies as brusquely as he did all other Lagosians. Three months after his arrival, the missionary broke his lease with Davies in order to move into lodgings he considered more comfortable, "as there are not any natives around as to be quarreling and fighting, nor are there so many nuisances, etc." When Davies insisted on three months' notice, David "caught some of his spirit, threw the keys down in front of him and walked away." Davies sued the missionary in court for the money due and, not surprisingly, won. A show of sympathy from some of the women in his congregation consoled David, who reassured himself that some Africans did appreciate his work in Lagos and that black Lagosians were essentially the same as the African American slaves he had known in his youth. "I *have* heard Africans charged with ingratitude, which is true in certain cases as may be found among my race," he wrote, "but as a general thing they have a great deal of gratitude, which I have noticed in American slavery and African freedom."[13]

By the time of the lawsuit, Church Vaughan was becoming personally acquainted with Reverend David, who not only made purchases at Vaughan's Kakawa Street hardware store as he began to build a new chapel, but essentially turned Vaughan into his personal banker. In order to provide the Baptist mission with local currency, its parent organization in Richmond arranged to send money to the Bank of England, credited to Vaughan's account and used by him, presumably, to pay his British hardware suppliers. In turn, Vaughan advanced the equivalent in local currency and store credit to David. It was a measure of Vaughan's economic status as well as his American identity that he was the only merchant in Lagos willing and able to make this arrangement.[14] His relationship with the mission was not entirely business, though: in early 1876, it was Reverend David who visited little Emily Vaughan when she was ill, and both he and Reverend Colley conducted her funeral. Further, two young men in whom Vaughan had taken a fatherly interest — Moses Stone and Sarah Harden's son Samuel — became closely associated with the mission: Stone as a preacher later sent to reopen the old Baptist station at Ogbomosho and Harden as a Lagos-based assistant and private pupil. Yet David referred to Vaughan as an "ex-member of our church," and Vaughan showed no signs of rejoining.[15]

Church Vaughan could well remember a different kind of missionary attitude than the Reverend David's. A generation earlier, Thomas Jefferson Bowen and William Clarke had worked assiduously to understand Yorubaland and its people, on their own terms, as part of their evangelical mission. They respected African ways and views even when they disagreed with them; and they were convinced that everyone was capable of spiritual and intellectual development. When Vaughan accepted baptism from Clarke, it was an induction into a religion that offered him salvation on equal terms with other believers. God is no respecter of persons, Baptists insisted; each individual is competent to communicate with God through Jesus Christ and responsible for his own faith and actions. But now, Willie David's brand of missionary work was steeped in condescension for black people, who, he believed, should be spiritually saved, but whose prospects for civilization were otherwise limited.

David was not alone in these views, which reflected not only new forms of white supremacy in the United States South, but also changing ideas about race in the wider Euro-American world. Already, physical anthropologists, some of the skull-measuring variety, endeavored to differentiate and rank the "races" of humanity, producing titles such as Charles Hamilton Smith's *The Natural History of the Human Species* (1848), Robert Knox's *The Races of Man* (1850), and Joseph Arthur de Gobineau's four-volume *Essay on the Inequality of Human Races* (1854). Though Charles Darwin intended no such interpretation, his *Origin of the Species by Natural Selection*, published in 1859, was taken to confirm racial hierarchies that could not be eliminated by cultural change. A massive mutiny within the British-controlled army in India in 1857 and an uprising among Jamaican freedpeople in 1865 dramatically suggested to intellectuals and policymakers in the empire that perhaps people of color could not be "civilized" in a European image after all—a conclusion shared by many white Americans after the Civil War.[16] When David wrote to the Foreign Mission Board requesting additional *white* missionaries, he argued that the other denominations, particularly the Church Missionary Society, as well as the British colonial government all reserved their leadership posts for whites.[17] "The European missionaries were beginning to see themselves as rulers," a Nigerian historian wrote of Lagos in the late 1870s, "and the word 'native' was acquiring a new and sinister meaning."[18]

Though the missionaries David and Colley had arrived together and shared an evangelical project, they were divided not only by race and background, but by David's refusal to treat a black colleague as anything other than subordinate. David blamed his difficulties in working with black Americans on "that sensitiveness so characteristic of the African race, and especially so of the Negro of the South." In other words, it was not that African Americans had legitimate grievances, but simply that they refused to accept their presumptive inferiority. "What would be taken by one of us [white men] from the other as brotherly suggestions for the good of the work," David continued, "would be regarded by a colored colaborer as an assertion of authority or superiority." Of course David *did* assert authority and superiority: in the same breath, he suggested to the Foreign Mission Board that "if you are going to the expense of sending out and supporting men from America, let us have the best. Let us have white men."[19] Meanwhile, Colley sent out his own call, writing in 1876 that "I hope the colored brethren will begin their work in Africa this year, either by sending a man or supporting one. This is *their* field of labor. I ask when will they obey their Saviour's commission?"[20]

If David was animated by racist self-importance, the Baptist congregation also found William Colley objectionable. Colley took charge of the Lagos station while David, determined to reestablish the Baptist mission in the Yoruba interior, based himself in Abeokuta, which had again opened to foreign missionaries. Soon thereafter, David's health deteriorated and he embarked on eight months' leave abroad, returning only briefly before beginning a two-year stint in the United States. While David was away, Colley patched up relations with Sarah Harden by arranging to send her eighteen-year-old son Samuel to the United States, where in 1877 he enrolled at Colley's alma mater, the Richmond Institute.[21] Yet like his white co-missionary, Colley also considered himself superior to local people and at times treated them with contempt. In this respect, the African American may have reminded Church Vaughan of settlers he had known in Liberia—and in fact, Colley would later end up in Liberia. Over two years in the late 1870s, as Colley penned letters to the Foreign Mission Board complaining about the privations he endured in Lagos, his African parishioners repeatedly denounced Colley through the same channels, charging him with unjust conduct, immorality, and violence.[22]

Their complaints largely centered on Colley's dismissal in June 1878 of Lewis Murray, a popular local Baptist who had been hired to teach at the small mission school. Murray had done nothing to merit the loss of his job, his defenders insisted, and was being punished for having earlier complained to the board about Reverend Colley's conduct. Moreover, "since the time that Colley came here there was a woman brought with them and until now the woman is still living with the said Colley." Actually, it seems that there were two women, a Mrs. Parmer hired as a housekeeper for the mission and residing in a room adjoining Colley's, and her young adult daughter Sallie, who slept in a different bedroom on the other side of her mother's. The parishioners insinuated that the unmarried Colley enjoyed an improper relationship with one of them, though it is not clear from surviving correspondence which one. Finally, the Lagos Baptists asked, "Is it right for a minister of God to be beating and horsewhipping any of his converts?" Colley had inflicted such treatment on a woman named Mary, "who is trying to give her soul to Christ," and who had come to clean the church. Altogether, at least twelve letters of complaint about Colley reached the Foreign Mission Board in Richmond. Some of them were composed on behalf of other parishioners by emergent Baptist leaders Levi Green and Samson L. Milton, both of whom would, a decade later, work with Church Vaughan to build their own Christian institution, independent of foreign missionaries.[23]

Colley's own words on the matter have not survived, but he clearly interpreted the conflict in light of the racial slights he had been enduring from David and the Southern Baptist mission board. After all, he was even better positioned than the Lagos parishioners were to observe David's behavior and attitudes. (Indeed, local Baptists did not write letters of complaint about David, only about Colley.) In late 1879 Colley either resigned or was fired, depending on the account, and he returned to Richmond.[24] Soon he began to canvass the American South promoting the formation of a national black Baptist foreign mission organization. Black churches in several states had already formed missionary societies in reaction to white racism as well as a conviction that African Americans had a special role to play in evangelizing their distant African relatives. Now Colley worked to unite and expand their efforts. In November 1880, 151 ministers and active laypeople from eleven states met in Montgomery, Alabama, to found the (African American) Baptist Foreign Mission Convention, with William Colley as the first corresponding secretary.[25] It began sending missionaries to Liberia, including Colley and his new wife, in 1883.[26]

In the United States, the formation of such separate institutions as churches and schools had begun among small groups of free black people after the American Revolution. By the Reconstruction era, they pervaded the South. Though black churches were the most obvious of the independent bodies, thousands of fraternal, benevolent, educational, and mutual-aid societies sprang into existence. By creating their own organizations, black Americans were responding both to the refusal of whites to offer them equality and to their own quest for self-determination. As W. E. B. DuBois later wrote, the black church was "the first social institution fully controlled by black men in America."[27] In Lagos, Africans had of course long formed and led organizations of various kinds. However, within the Christian churches—institutions vital for African economic mobility and social identity—African leadership was now limited and increasingly under threat. As new forms of white supremacy similar to those in the American South became more and more evident in Lagos, there too, Africans began to consider separation. To do so, however, meant risking the value so clearly attached to missionary institutions.

By and large, Lagos Christians remained committed to the mission churches out of longtime loyalty, because the missions connected educated Africans to a global religious community, and, most of all, because thus far the missions had offered ample scope for African advancement through education and leadership. They were, in fact, the institutions most responsible for creating a Western-educated elite in Yorubaland, able to profit from new commercial opportunities and reproduce generations of literate professionals.[28] Over time, however, new developments within and outside of the European-led churches undermined the status and prospects of African Christians. They were appalled, for instance, when the Church Missionary Society reversed its decades-old policy of support for African clergy, spectacularly humiliating its most venerable African leader. Other Africans were pushed out of European trading firms or the civil service. As colonialism tightened its grip on Lagos and its hinterland beginning in the 1880s, elite Africans protested against racial discrimination, in part by celebrating elements of local culture. They also continued to press for authority within established institutions, including the Christian churches. Only a few voices began to call for an end to missionary domination altogether, Vaughan's — tentatively at first — among them.

The most obvious indication of the changes afoot was the treatment of Samuel Ajayi Crowther, Africa's Anglican bishop. Crowther represented the highest aspirations of Yoruba Christians for personal development and church leadership: he was a brilliant linguist and published author as well as a devoted Christian evangelical. He had been one of the two pioneers of the Church Missionary Society in Abeokuta, shaping and benefiting from its explicit policy of training Africans who would one day take over its work. He accompanied the first British Niger expedition in 1841–42 and subsequent expeditions along the river in the 1850s. On behalf of the CMS, Crowther founded the Niger Mission in 1857 with an all-African staff. Seven years later, the Sierra Leonean repatriate became the most powerful African Christian in the world when he was appointed bishop of "the countries of Western Africa beyond the limits of our dominions," according to the royal license authorizing his consecration. Though in practical terms his focus was the lower Niger River, Crowther made his home much of the time in Lagos, a location central to his broad purview. Because of the dispersed nature of his diocese as well as personal temperament, he supervised the African clergymen under him fairly lightly, and this became the rationale for CMS authorities to strip him of his authority. His residence in Lagos also made his treatment one of the city's most closely followed issues.[29]

Although in 1875 the CMS had created a "native pastorate" in Lagos, bringing in the Yoruba-descended Sierra Leonean clergyman James Johnson as its head, it also began around that time to undertake a new policy regarding African church leadership, particularly targeting Crowther. In 1879, a newly formed finance committee, composed largely of white missionaries based at Lagos, removed the financial oversight of the Niger Mission from Bishop Crowther's hands. A year later, the bishop was summoned to defend his management of the mission before a commission of inquiry convened in Madeira. Though Crowther acquitted himself to the satisfaction of the society's London leadership, the incident was widely regarded as a grave insult to the revered churchman and to African Christians more generally. Then in 1882, in a move that no European bishop would have ever faced, a white general secretary was appointed to supervise Crowther. Though the aged clergyman labored on, his real and symbolic authority within the Anglican Church was nearly extinguished — and was not again exercised by an African church leader to a similar degree for another fifty years.[30]

In Crowther's travails, elite Lagosians saw worrisome portents of other new developments. Several newly formed, African-owned Lagos newspapers reported incidents of racial discrimination, for example the 1885 removal from Christ Church of a memorial plaque in honor of the Saro doctor and CMS stalwart Nathanial T. King while one honoring a European clergyman was allowed to remain.[31] Recently arrived European personnel, many with inferior qualifications but all at higher pay grades, displaced local people from the civil service.[32] European-owned commercial firms began to extend their reach into the interior, attempting to bypass coastal African middlemen while importing new white staff members. In fact Crowther's son Josiah, after marketing cotton from Abeokuta in the 1850s, had entered the Niger Delta palm oil business. There, by the early 1870s, he served as agent-general of the West Africa Company; but he was dismissed, along with all African staff, when the four British companies on the Niger amalgamated into the United African Company in 1879.[33]

Immigrants from Sierra Leone, Brazil, and elsewhere, as well as their children, had formerly seen the British as their protectors and advocates. Now, as the antislavery ideologies and policies that had benefited them were replaced by a general view that African capacities were limited and even educated Africans required white leadership, their protests became more frequent and insistent. Their outrage is best expressed in an 1881 letter to the secretary of the Church Missionary Society written by Henry Johnson, archdeacon of the Upper Niger (and thus one of Crowther's lieutenants), who had been educated in Sierra Leone, England, and even Palestine (to learn Arabic). "You in England cannot fancy how some of those who come here inflated with the idea that they are the 'dominant race,' do treat with something like contempt the natives of the country," he began. "The truth is that they regard us this day in pretty much the same light as our forefathers were, who were rescued from the ironpangs of slavery by the philanthropists of a former generation." Yet "Eloquent Johnson," as he was called by Lagosians, made clear that his generation did not need saving, and he resented the implication. "We are not oversensitive," he continued, "but at the same time we are not unduly pachydermatous. . . . But does anyone think we have no feelings at all, or no rights which are to be respected?" And then the real issue, expressed in the gendered language of the day: "Having educated us, you will not allow us to think and speak and act like men."[34]

In the face of mounting affronts, Lagosians began to emphasize and celebrate some of their differences from Europeans. Yoruba culture, they asserted, was as rich and as capable of spurring great advancement as European ways, which local people perhaps had adopted too uncritically in the past. Beginning in 1881, James Johnson, the African head of Lagos's largest Anglican congregation (known as "Holy Johnson" for his religious enthusiasm and to distinguish him from "Eloquent" Henry Johnson), campaigned against the use of English names in baptisms. Notices began to appear in newspapers of names changed from European to African. Though English still predominated in the public life of the Lagos elite, they introduced Yoruba songs in compositions and entertainments.[35] In 1885, two African leaders within the Baptist mission, S. A. Allen and David Brown Vincent, published Ìwé Òwe (Book of Proverbs) and Ìwé Àló (Book of Riddles) to great popular acclaim.[36] By the end of the century, cultural nationalism would flourish into a robust movement in which many educated Africans not only cast off their European names in favor of Yoruba ones but replaced their shirts and trousers with Yoruba dress, investigated and disseminated Yoruba history and culture, and worked to give Christianity a more African basis.[37] In the early 1880s, however, Lagosians asserted the value of their African heritage primarily when they perceived it to be under attack, such as when the government proposed a new education ordinance in 1882.

Because the Christian missions were the only institutions offering Western education, the colonial government had for the previous decade been making modest grants to their schools. According to the new proposal, mission schools receiving grants would be required to teach exclusively in English rather than the current mix of English and Yoruba. Reading and writing the English language, arithmetic, and needlework (for girls) would also be compulsory, while the teaching of English grammar, English history, and British Empire geography were especially encouraged. Though at least one local newspaper editor reminded readers of the utility of an English education, other Lagosians were furious. The wealthy Saro merchant and publisher Richard Beale Blaize referred to the contemporary European encroachment in Africa when he asked, "Is the ulterior object of the Education Bill to promote the conquest of West Africa by England morally through the English language, and secure that morally which African fevers perhaps prevent it acquiring physically?"[38]

Like Henry Johnson, Blaize referenced the slave past of the town's repatriate community, while insisting that current initiatives went too far. "Is there a purpose to throw around our souls chains heavier than those which had, before emancipation, bound our bodies?" he asked. "Surely the way to elevate a people is not first to teach them to entertain the lowest idea of themselves and make them servile imitators of others." Though the Lagos elite in many ways owed their current positions to British antislavery, they now were in a better position to question British policies toward them: "We are British subjects, and are grateful for England's protection and all its beneficial work for Africa. We respect and reverence the country of Wilberforce and Buxton [leaders in the British antislavery movement] and most of our Missionaries," Blaize explained, "but we are not Englishmen. We are Africans, and have no wish to be any other than Africans, and in Lagos, Yoruba Africans. We shall not sit tamely to witness the murder, death and burial of one of those important distinguishing national and racial marks that God has given to us in common with other tribes, nations and races, and not protest against it with all the energy that we can command."[39]

Vaughan had entered the public discussion himself the previous year, albeit anonymously, with his involvement in the publication of a pamphlet directed to African Christians called *The Hamite's General Economy*. Widely circulated in Lagos and summarized in a letter by the leading African Anglican there, the unsigned publication—which unfortunately does not survive—"invites African clergy and Christian Laity together to establish a church for themselves on their own national and racial line in which both polygamy and slavery should be fully tolerated." Intervening in theological issues that had been contested among Anglo-American Protestants for decades, the pamphlet also was said to deny the divinity of Christ, question the necessity for clergy as mediators between believers and the divine, and disparage the right of church leaders to discipline members. The pamphlet was addressed to Christians in the interior Yoruba towns, but it also resonated with a portion of the Christian, largely Saro, community of Lagos who were beginning to assert the value of African culture. "The growing idea," as James Johnson summarized the pamphlet, "is that practical Christianity is not inconsistent with either polygamy or slave holding; that these are among the social customs, the national and racial habitudes that Christianity is not expected to disturb wherever it finds them to exist; that men are free, left free by God and the Controlling force of circumstances to elect between polygamy and monogamy as it suits their tastes dispositions and conveniences; that Europeans have of their own accord elected monogamy; that Africans have found polygamy and slave making and slave keeping indispensable to social life in their own country; and that these states and conditions of social life are not to be considered sinful or treated as social evils but rather as permissible and lawful states and conditions."[40]

Because, according to Johnson's summary, "Its authorship is credited to an African or Negro born in America but who has been now many years resident in the country," at least one historian has attributed the publication to Church Vaughan.[41] Yet a number of clues suggest that it was not in fact him but a close associate who wrote the pamphlet. The author, according to Johnson, "had long lived at Abeokuta and been employed as a missionary mechanic in the service of the S. American Baptist Missionary Society. There, it is said he had lived in Polygamy, no doubt after he had left the mission service, [and] had bought slaves and made wives of them. He resides now at Lagos and professes to live in monogamy." Though the lack of evidence that Vaughan purchased slave wives in Abeokuta is not necessarily conclusive (and his wife Sarah Omotayo may have once been enslaved), it is doubtful that his couple of years' residence there could be interpreted by a contemporary as a "long" time. Moreover, Vaughan was sufficiently well known in Lagos that if Johnson were referring to him, the clergyman would probably have used his name. Finally, Johnson heard "that the author of Hamite's Economy had the help of some person in setting up his work." Vaughan's letter to the Foreign Mission Board, written a decade earlier, certainly does not indicate a lack of literary skills that would necessitate such assistance.

Rather, *The Hamite's General Economy* may well have been written by Vaughan's old friend from as early as their Liberia days, Henry Sewell Pettiford. The historical record had last placed Pettiford in Abeokuta defending the city from attack in 1864 and then joining Egba forces against the Ibadans near Ijebu territory. Pettiford apparently did not leave Abeokuta for Lagos when the missionaries were expelled in 1867. But at some point he did move there, because in the early twentieth century his descendants lived near the Vaughans on Igbosere Road and were considered practically as relatives.[42] Given that someone with his distinctive last name was listed as a member of the Lagos Baptist church in 1881, Pettiford must have moved to the city by then, perhaps driven by the interior warfare that erupted again in 1877.[43] Church Vaughan probably took him in or helped him find a place to live. And when unknown circumstances—perhaps the news of Colley's new African American mission society—compelled Pettiford to pen his public address calling for an independent, culturally sensitive church, the more literate Vaughan offered assistance. Even if they were not alone in their views, however, neither of them was willing to risk the personal attention and potential controversy that might come with affixing their name to the work.[44]

Although the pamphlet irritated "Holy Johnson," it did not have much of an impact otherwise. As early as 1872, Edward Blyden—now Liberia's foremost intellectual, with a wide following on the West African coast—had written in favor of an independent African church and a West African university. But most Lagosian Christians were deeply loyal to the parent churches, in spite of the growing white supremacist attitudes of European missionaries through the 1870s and '80s.[45] Even as Europeans undertook their voracious "scramble" for Africa, in fact, elite Lagosians debated whether this would ultimately be of benefit or detriment to the continent. One month after the conclusion of the Berlin Conference, in which European delegates drew lines on maps to divide Africa among themselves, David Vincent objected to further colonization at a public meeting sponsored by the Lagos YMCA, but he was careful to distinguish the laudable aims of missionaries from the avaricious schemes of "murders and whoremongers, thieves, and robbers." "It was *commercial* Europe that invented slave labour and discovered the victims of slavery," he specified in February 1885, "but it was *evangelical* Europe that promulgated the edict of universal emancipation. It was adventurous Europe, under the title of the 'Anthropological Society,' that placed us, the inhabitants of this good land, in the category of the brute creation; but it was *Missionary* Europe that proved us *men*."[46] A year later, CMS members calling themselves "Paul, Silas and others" railed in the pages of the Lagos *Observer* against "*haughtiness, absolutism, stubborn persistencies and dictatorial proclivities*" within the mission church, ending their call for a breakaway

African Anglican congregation with the cry, "Secession! Secession!! Secession!!!"[47] But it was not until the end of the decade that a small group of rebels finally made a bid for congregational independence, and it was not the well-established, though frustrated, Anglicans who did so. Instead, the American Baptist mission suffered the first defection, with Church Vaughan and his comrades leading the way.

Notwithstanding his possible involvement in Pettiford's pamphlet, Church Vaughan generally tolerated the Baptist missionaries and the changing climate of the early 1880s. After all, he was doing much better than his relatives in South Carolina. His business was growing, at least partly because of contracts from the Baptist mission as it undertook several building projects in the first half of the decade. And for some time it was possible to imagine that not all missionaries shared the same sense of superiority as Reverend David or his CMS counterparts. In fact, Vaughan formed a friendship with one of the three white recruits who joined David's mission in 1884. But when that man, apparently the only sympathetic white missionary he knew, was fired, Vaughan's tolerance began to give out. And by 1888, when David undermined the Baptists' own version of Bishop Crowther, Vaughan's longtime protégé Moses Stone, and defended his actions in terms of white supremacy, Vaughan declared his independence.

Vaughan's relationship with David and the Baptist mission remained relatively cordial through the first half of the 1880s. He supplied building materials and banking services as David built a new Baptist school building beginning in 1883 and a substantial new brick church three years later.[48] It may be no coincidence, in fact, that Vaughan was able to purchase three new properties in 1884, as the new schoolhouse was completed. Vaughan's fourteen-year-old son Burrell enrolled as a pupil.[49] Given these connections to the missionary, Vaughan may have kept his disapproval to himself that year when David embarked on a trip to the United States, bringing a ten-year-old boy, Manly Ogunlana Oshodi, with him. Oshodi was to serve as the exotic centerpiece of a fund-raising campaign through the American South, reciting from the Bible in English and Yoruba while wearing the outlandish costumes of traditional Yoruba masquerades.[50]

However much he did business with the mission, made financial contributions to its building fund, and even attended services, however, Vaughan could not have been impressed with most of the American personnel who arrived in the 1880s. In 1882, twenty-five-year-old Peyton Eubank and his new wife became Reverend David's first white reinforcements, fulfilling requests he had made for years. Eubank was as condescending about Africans as David was, soon writing back to the Foreign Mission Board attributing the difficulty of spreading Baptist Christianity in Yorubaland to insurmountable African shortcomings. In Eubank's view, these included: "1. The African's satisfaction with his condition. 2. His lack of veracity and the consequent distrust of him. 3. His ignorance and superstition. 4. The adverse power of family influence. 5. Native slavery to base passions. 6. The low moral and spiritual life among professed Christians." On the other hand, the young missionary was encouraged by the fact that "Christianity [was] attracting the attention of the more thoughtful"; and in general, he thought that "the Yoruban's confidence in the white man" offered possibilities for evangelization.[51] Three more white missionaries—Wiley W. Harvey, Charles Edwin Smith, and Strother Moses Cook—were recruited during David's American tour with the young African on display and arrived in 1884.[52] Harvey soon reported from Abeokuta, "It is not from the goodness of their [Africans'] hearts that we are permitted to go among many of them, but [from] their cowardice, superstition and their notions of the whiteman's strength." Later he produced a brief book about working in Africa entitled, predictably, "The Dark Continent."[53]

Strother Moses Cook, however, was a man Vaughan could appreciate. The two got to know each other when Cook rotated to the Lagos mission from the interior along with Moses Ladejo Stone, whom Vaughan had known since the Yoruba preacher's youth. The best educated of the Baptist missionaries, Cook had attended the National Normal University in Lebanon, Ohio, and worked as a teacher before entering the Southern Baptist Theological Seminary in Louisville, Kentucky. Unlike his colleagues, Cook mixed freely in local society and took the time to get to know Africans, forming an enduring friendship with Moses Stone. "The only way to know a country and its people," he wrote, "is to become interested in it sufficiently to make an effort to find out some facts, and know a few things that are true." Before coming to Lagos, Cook and his comrades had been told "strange stories about the people and the dangerous climate," but he later realized that he had been misled. "If you ever come to Africa," Cook recounted, "you will find that about one half of the strange and hideous stories you hear are untrue." Rather than trafficking in stereotypes, he exchanged courtesies with local chiefs and listened sympathetically to the complaints of African teachers and mission agents about their low rates of pay. As an approving Lagosian later wrote of Cook, "He was without affectation and without prejudice."[54]

Cook's fellow missionaries, however, were appalled by his liberal attitudes, and they complained both to him and to mission superiors back in Richmond. Charles Smith alleged that Cook suffered from "weakness and childishness of mind," the only possible explanation for his breaking ranks with other missionaries. "One day Bro Eubank was very justly punishing a mission boy," Smith charged, "when bro Cook rushed into the room and said 'I want this stopped.'" Cook sympathized with "native" complaints about other missionaries "and sometimes was very outspoken in his approval." In what must have been both galling and scandalous to his white comrades, Cook proudly proclaimed "that he was raised by a Negro woman, and reared up to human consciousness on a Negro's breast." For the other missionaries, Cook's disavowal of white supremacist discipline was unacceptable. At their request, Cook was fired from the mission and recalled to the United States in mid-1886. There, after unsuccessfully pleading his case before the Foreign Mission Board, he maintained his interest in Yorubaland from his home in Kentucky. The next year, Cook returned to Lagos on his own initiative, staying some six months and vowing to remain in touch with the African Baptists there after his return to America.[55]

For Vaughan, the dismissal of its only white man who treated Africans with respect was the beginning of the end of his relationship with the Baptist mission. Because their spacious new church building was reaching completion, the missionaries no longer placed frequent orders at Vaughan's hardware store. And in mid-1887, he terminated his role as their banker. Several months earlier, Vaughan's English purchasing agents had declined to take any more bills of exchange forwarded from the missionaries, complaining about the five weeks' time it took to receive payment on them. Vaughan agreed to continue exchanging the bills himself, but only on condition that the missionaries pay a 1 percent surcharge to protect him against the risk that he might not be able to redeem them. No longer as inclined as he may have been earlier to extend credit to the missionaries, Vaughan now acted the hard-nosed businessman. David looked elsewhere for financial services, arranging by the end of the year to exchange bills with the American shipping company Yates and Porterfield, which occasionally sent a vessel to Lagos.[56]

By this time, David was not only financially estranged from Vaughan, but he was becoming increasingly alienated from Vaughan's longtime fellow Baptists. After the new Baptist Academy opened, for instance, Sarah Harden's little school for girls had to close for lack of pupils, and she asked that as a missionary widow she be paid a pension to replace her previous salary. Such payments were standard practice; and furthermore, as even Reverend Eubank had written earlier, "she is certainly deserving." David rebuffed her request, however, leaving her so "much displeased and grieved" that she considered appealing directly to the Foreign Mission Board. "I think the Board should take no notice of such letters from native agents," David wrote back to Richmond. "Let us manage them."[57]

It was precisely in "managing" local personnel that David most antagonized Vaughan and other leading Baptists. Just as newly arrived Britons with the Church Missionary Society connived further to sideline Bishop Crowther and other African agents—who, in David's view, caused "much *trouble* and *grief*"—so did David undermine the leading African in his own church, Moses Ladejo Stone.[58] Vaughan's onetime apprentice, Stone had been a dedicated Baptist since the 1860s. He, along with Sarah Harden and Church Vaughan, had kept the congregation together after the departure of the last missionaries in 1869. Shortly after David's initial arrival in Lagos in 1876, he had sent Stone as an interpreter to Abeokuta and then to Ogbomosho. Stone remained for seven years as pastor of the Ogbomosho church, enduring personal attack as war again engulfed the region beginning in 1877. In 1880, at the behest of his African parishioners, David ordained Stone as a Baptist minister. When Reverend David left on furlough to America in 1884, Stone served as pastor of the Lagos church, which he managed on his own. But David's views were clear that black people should be supervised by whites. By late 1885, he designated Stone as "assistant pastor," under the supervision first of Strother Moses Cook and then, after Cook's forced departure, David himself. Though both men were thirty-eight years old, married fathers, and respected preachers, David viewed Stone as a perpetual subordinate, and treated him accordingly.[59]

In spite of Stone's crucial role as the only African minister in the Baptist church, the "assistant pastor" hardly earned a living wage and his attempts at educational advancement received no encouragement. His salary of sixty pounds per year was less than two-thirds of what "native" Methodist and Anglican preachers in Lagos were paid, in spite of his repeated requests to Reverend David for a raise. From the time he and his family arrived there from Ogbomosho, Stone relied on money borrowed from Vaughan to make ends meet, and Cook advanced money to him as well. Further, though Stone was the least educated of the eleven "native" preachers in Lagos—seven of whom held university degrees—David also refused his requests for higher education. Stone captivated audiences with his eloquent Yoruba sermons, heavily peppered with parables and proverbs from the language's deep reservoir, yet his English was extremely weak. His Western education had been spotty and informal, beginning with the missionary Richard Stone and

Vaughan when he was a child, continuing when David and Colley arrived in Lagos, pausing during the years he was in Ogbomosho, and resuming briefly when he and Cook shared the Lagos mission station. During that time, he gave Cook lessons in the Yoruba language in exchange for tutoring from the missionary. But this fell far short of Stone's educational ambitions.[60]

Even within the Baptist mission, other Africans were better educated than Reverend Stone. David Brown Vincent, the headmaster of the Baptist elementary school, was the son of a CMS catechist of Yoruba origin from Sierra Leone, and he had attended CMS schools in Ibadan and Lagos before becoming a Baptist in the early 1880s.[61] And in 1886, Samuel Harden became principal of the newly opened Baptist Academy upon his return from nine years in the United States.[62] The son of Sarah Harden and her long-deceased African American missionary husband Joseph Harden, Samuel had studied at the Richmond Institute in Virginia and the Worcester Institute in Massachusetts through the efforts of Baptists in Africa and America. For his part, Stone wondered aloud why he might not be given similar opportunities, given his long service to the mission.

Although David continued to refuse Stone's requests for American education or better pay, he may have agreed that the mission would build a house in Lagos for the assistant pastor and his family. With a £150 mortgage financed by Church Vaughan, Stone purchased a plot of land on Wesley Street and began to construct a comfortable house on it. Yet either David reneged on their deal or it had never been made in the first place, because Stone was left entirely responsible for the cost of the house. Anxious about his finances, he took up trading to earn extra money. When David objected on the grounds that a preacher ought to devote all his time to the ministry, Stone yet again asked David for a pay raise. David again refused.[63]

One Sunday in February 1888, Church Vaughan became suspicious when he did not see Stone at morning services. Together with other elders of the congregation, Vaughan sought out Reverend David to ask what had happened. Stone had resigned, they were told, and David had accepted his resignation on behalf of the congregation. Vaughan and the others were appalled: shouldn't they be involved in decisions about Stone's salary, they wanted to know, since in fact contributions from the congregation financed part of it? And more importantly, according to Baptist principles of congregational decision-making, shouldn't they have been consulted before David accepted Stone's resignation? The priesthood of all believers, a central tenet of Baptist faith, implied that the affairs of the church were the concern of all members.

David answered that since he was in charge of the mission, he could dismiss Stone "as he would any of his servants."[64]

David's sense of entitlement to run the mission as his own private estate stemmed at least in part from the fact that he was funding it with his own resources. After his first wife died of fever, David had married a second time in 1886 to Justa Greer, a wealthy widow from Shugualak, Mississippi. When they were ready to return to Africa from America, the Foreign Mission Board was short of the funds for their fare. Drawing on the estate of Mrs. David's first husband, the missionary couple loaned fifteen hundred dollars to the board, more than enough to cover their travel costs. Then when the new Lagos church was being built, Reverend David drew again on the funds he and his wife had loaned the board: five hundred dollars toward the construction of the building. In his view, any money spent to augment Stone's salary would in essence come out of the missionary's own (or rather, his wife's) pocket.[65]

David may also have chosen his words deliberately when he referred to mission personnel as his "servants," knowing that his listeners would take "servants" to mean "slaves." Nearly all of those who came to see David that day had seen captivity or forced servitude up-close, either in their own lives or through the memories of their parents. Levi Green Agbelusi, who in 1876 had been ordained as the first African Baptist deacon in Nigeria and had been one of the chief complainants against William Colley, had originally come to Lagos as a slave and had been baptized by Rev. Joseph Hardin, the Baptist missionary who himself was the son of freed American slaves. Agbelusi's nephew and former ward David Vincent, later known as Mojola Agbebi, was the son of Yoruba returnees from Sierra Leone. Others present, including Moses Stone, John Ajala Stone, W. L. Mills, and J. B. Clay, were onetime Ijaye refugees who had evaded capture themselves.[66] Was David reminding the Baptist delegation of his own background as a member of a white master class and their own personal familiarity with slavery? Was he in essence telling the black Baptists, *"I could own you"*? Certainly Vaughan and the others took it this way. If your church is intended to be a *barracoon*, they told David at the next meeting—using the word for a slave pen in the Atlantic trade—then they wanted no part of it.[67]

Within days, sixty of the Baptist church's eighty members met at Stone's house on Wesley Street to form a separate congregation. Though they considered severing all denominational ties, Vaughan convinced them to remain Baptist—especially since the denomination's structure was based on independent, self-governing congregations. Instead, they fired off a report of their actions and the precipitating circumstances to the Southern Baptist Foreign Mission Board. At Sarah Harden's suggestion, they called their new organization the Native Baptist Church, a name they considered more inclusive than something with "Yoruba" in the title. Stone was their pastor, paid by contributions from the members (though they amounted only to three pounds per month, leaving him even more impoverished than before). Soon the rebels were joined by Samuel Harden and David Vincent, whom Reverend David fired from the Baptist Academy when they refused to make a public statement in support of the missionary. A committee of elders was elected, including Levi Green Agbelusi as foreman, James Wilson Vaughan as treasurer, and Samuel Harden as financial secretary. A few weeks later, the separatists appointed David Vincent and Church Vaughan as deacons. Vaughan had a temporary shed constructed in the backyard of Stone's house, where the congregation began holding its services.[68]

At this point, as Samuel Harden later recalled, the separatists were willing to return to the missionary church if he, Stone, and Vincent were reinstated to their former positions.[69] But animosity increased on both sides, fueled by long-simmering resentments as well as a new war of words. Cryptically reporting the dispute, the Lagos press declined to offer particulars, "as representations have been made to us which, from their conflicting nature, we would consider it most prudent not to meddle with."[70] Rumors—which the missionaries attributed to Moses Stone—circulated that David had referred to church members as goats and beasts, and that it had been David, not Colley, who had the improper relationship some years earlier with the mission housekeeper Mrs. Parmer. Attempting to regain the initiative, Reverend David along with his fellow missionaries Eubank and Smith drew up and signed a leaflet, which they then circulated by hand throughout the town. It proclaimed that the Baptist mission had withdrawn fellowship from Stone because he was unqualified for the ministry, having been repeatedly untruthful. The same day—April 30, 1888—the missionaries met with remaining members of the mission church and passed a resolution excluding Stone from the pulpit. They also reported their actions to Richmond, complaining in particular about the "ungrateful, unkind, unjust and untrue utterances" of the separatists. Stone defended himself over the next month, writing both to the Foreign Mission Board and circulating in Lagos a printed document titled "A Protest Against and Denouncement of Statements Made in a Paper Which Had Been Privately Circulated in Lagos to Injure the Reputation of Rev. M. L. Stone."[71]

After associating with Baptist missionaries nearly all of his adult life, Vaughan now stood as the senior member of the rebellion against them. He signed as "chairman" at least two letters to the Foreign Mission Board expressing support for Stone and complaints about David, with Harden as vice chairman and Sarah Harden a member of the committee.[72] When renewed negotiations over returning to the parent church broke down and the secessionists determined to form a new institution of their own, Vaughan provided money for the construction of a more permanent building in Stone's compound. The former carpenter personally supervised the building project, which was completed in November. Though Vaughan had become the "big man" of the Lagos Baptists, however, his patronage still had its limits. The money for the new church building was specified as a loan, just as Vaughan's assistance to Stone had been. As treasurer of the new church, his son and business partner James Wilson Vaughan was to see to it that the funds would be repaid once the congregation got on its feet.[73]

Nevertheless, Vaughan's influence was so great that David identified him as the principal obstacle to reconciliation with the breakaway members. In July 1888 he opined to the Foreign Mission Board—without further explanation—that many of the secessionists would "gladly return, but I doubt whether any will be able to break away from Vaughan and the other leaders for some time yet." Alluding to past debates within the church about whether to accept polygamists, he continued that "Vaughan has the kind of church he has long wanted—one of tares, adulterers etc., and will not let any come away, as he holds them responsible for the money he spent in building the church for them."[74] Three months later, David reiterated—seemingly protesting too much—that the majority of those who had left his church were undesirable Christians anyway, but then complained again of Vaughan's alleged financial hold over the Native Baptists. "Stone is in debt personally to Vaughan," he wrote, "and the members with him are also in debt to V for the chapel he built for them. The members are tired of their new Master. V is dissatisfied with his unruly church and is demanding his money from them."[75]

It was not only Vaughan but other diasporic Africans whom the Baptist missionaries blamed for their troubles, ignoring their own role in offending local Christians. "I regret to say," David wrote during the dispute, "that in Lagos racial prejudice against all white men—Government, missionaries is strong, and growing rapidly. It has been engendered by Sierra Leone emigrants to this place."[76] In this he agreed with agents of the Church Missionary Society, who were particularly annoyed by the educated Saro: the missionary Graham Wilmot Brooke referred to them in 1889 as "swarms of ragamuffins."[77] But David's colleague Charles Smith complained that African Americans in Africa were also a problem, because they "introduce American (Negro) notions and prejudices." As evidence, he asserted, "Our trouble in Lagos has been made much worse by an American Negro (Vaughan) and one educated in America (Harden). . . . In the present trouble in Lagos, I have already expressed my views. Except for Vaughan the American Negro and Harden educated in America, the trouble would have been settled at first."[78]

Whether or not Vaughan's and Harden's enthusiasm for church separatism was stronger than that of other leaders of the Native Baptist Church—or of Saro within the CMS—both of them certainly were familiar with African American self-run institutions, and both had experienced better treatment from white colleagues than they were currently getting. At the Richmond Institute, Harden had studied theology among some seventy Virginia freedmen who would later staff the state's black churches and schools. By the time he had arrived there in 1877, the institute no longer held classes in the former slave barracoon known as "Lumpkin's Jail"; still, Harden was surrounded by African Americans with strong memories of slavery, opposition to white supremacy, and commitment to black uplift through their own institutions. After two years in Virginia, he moved north to continue his studies in Massachusetts. At the Worcester Academy boarding school, Harden lived with his three teachers and nine fellow students, nearly all of them white New Englanders. He taught school in Massachusetts for several years after his graduation, again living largely among white people who had not been raised in a slave society.[79] Returning to Lagos in 1886, Harden must have found in his near-uncle Church Vaughan the only other person with a sense of what he had observed and experienced. Both men owed their educations to the Southern Baptist Church, but now they chafed at the racism of its white missionaries and could well imagine a congregation without them.

If the missionaries thought that diasporic Africans were its only supporters and that the Native Baptist Church might not last, though, they were mistaken. Reverend David left Lagos permanently in November 1888 ostensibly because of illness, but likely because he had had enough of struggling with the rebels. The Lagos newspapers implied that he had been recalled by his mission board.[80] His successor C. C. Newton spent the next several years trying to effect a reconciliation between the mission and breakaway church. Native Baptists told him, again linking the missionary church with slavery, that they would "not go back into bondage."[81] In 1892, four years after the split, Newton did convince Moses Stone to return to the parent church

Ebenezer Baptist Church, Lagos. Constructed in 1893 and replaced in 1974. Reproduction of a photograph hanging in the current church building.

as preacher (in part by paying off his debt to Vaughan and thus following through on the promise David may have made to fund Stone's mortgage). The native Baptists appointed David Vincent as their new minister, and in 1893, now calling themselves the Ebenezer Baptist Church, they moved into a brand-new brick building financed by James W. and Burrell Vaughan, Church Vaughan's sons, in honor of their father and located on the site of his first house in Lagos. "The Native Baptist Church has exhibited such a spirit of determination and power of energy and enterprise as has evoked the admiration of the whole community," reported a Lagos newspaper. "And now, possessing a beautiful Chapel and a Native minister of their own, it is to be hoped that their continued progress will be assured being unfettered with foreign money and mandates."[82] That building at the corner of Joseph and Campbell Streets was demolished and replaced beginning in 1974, and the Ebenezer Baptist Church endures today, with a Vaughan descendant still serving as a deacon.[83]

Like the missionary church from which it broke away, the Native Baptist Church never attracted as many members as the CMS or the Methodists, mission societies connected to Britain. Yet its foundation is considered a watershed in the history of Nigerian nationalism. The native Baptists opened the door for Christians to escape from missionary oversight, offering a local model of institutional separation in response to the new colonial and missionary racism of the late nineteenth century. Other breakaway churches followed in 1891, 1901, 1906, and 1917. As a historian of Nigerian missions put it, the continuing struggles within the mission churches as well as the new independent bodies reflected "the desire of Nigerian converts to manage their own affairs in the institution to which they had become most closely associated and thereby demonstrate their ability to rule, to evangelize and to administer."[84]

By the time the Native Baptist Church celebrated its third anniversary in 1891, the trends it encapsulated—separation as a response to white supremacy, influenced by the African diaspora—were on full display in Lagos. The Church Missionary Society's white-majority finance committee replaced nine African missionaries on the Niger with Europeans, so antagonizing Bishop Crowther that the long-suffering octogenarian finally resigned. According to the Baptist missionary C. C. Newton, "When those who were dismissed from the Niger Mission arrived in Lagos and filled the air with the talk of the wrongs which they had endured at the hands of the white missionaries there were many sympathizers here, among them Stone's people." Within the Lagos CMS church, its African leader James "Holy" Johnson organized financial support from wealthy Lagosians in order to make the Niger Delta mission independent, with Crowther at its head. Though Crowther agreed to the plan, he suffered a stroke and died in late 1891, leaving the autonomous Delta pastorate to live on without him until a reconciliation with the CMS in 1897. Meanwhile, as Newton put it, "a wave of bitter race feeling has swept over Lagos this year."[85]

British imperial expansion only worsened the antagonism. As the controversy within the CMS unfolded in 1891, colonial forces seized Ilaro, part of the Egba kingdom near Lagos. British officials publicly made plans for an expedition the next year against the kingdom of Ijebu-Ode, which had thus far resisted missionaries and European traders. Missionaries strongly supported what they saw as the military prelude to religious expansion, and this pushed some Lagosian Christians even further away from them than before. The Baptist Reverend Newton, for example, finally given a chance to preach at the Native Baptist Church, was hissed and scoffed at when his sermon included support for the British expeditions.[86]

As the tension built in Lagos, Edmund Wilmot Blyden—the pan-African intellectual with whom Vaughan had crossed paths in Liberia three decades earlier—visited the city to offer moral support in connection with the Niger Mission dispute. This "most distinguished negro philosopher," as even the American missionary Newton acknowledged, was well known in West Africa and its diaspora for his two decades of publications celebrating the character and potential of Africans and their descendants. Now his appearance in Lagos helped to solidify incipient desires there for religious autonomy and cultural assertion. His first public appearance, in December 1890, was a speech at the Hope School, which David Vincent had founded in part to train teachers and preachers for the Native Baptist Church.[87] Just over a year earlier, at a sermon marking the church's first anniversary, Vincent had insisted that local Christianity must be clearly African. "To render Christianity indigenous to Africa, it must be watered by native hands, pruned with the native hatchet, and tended with native earth," he had exhorted. After the sermon's text was published, Blyden endorsed Vincent's views in a letter to the *Lagos Weekly Times*. Blyden made a similar case in his January 1891 public lecture in Lagos, entitled "The Return of the Exiles and the West African Church." Before a large and enthusiastic audience, Blyden called for the establishment of a nondenominational African church purged of the foreign cultural influences he believed had sullied the pure Christianity of the Bible. Blyden insisted that "the Christ we worship must be an African . . . the Christ revealed in the Bible is far more African than anything else."[88] Several months later, frustrated Lagosians from the CMS, Wesleyan, and Baptist churches formed the United Native African Church, an ecumenical congregation "founded for the evangelization and amelioration of our race, to be governed by Africans."[89] David Vincent became their minister, a post he held until he took up the pulpit of the Native Baptist Church in 1894.

Church separatism was one way that Lagosians responded to late nineteenth-century colonialism and racism; Yoruba cultural nationalism was another, though the two movements overlapped in practice and personnel. On an 1894 trip to Liberia for religious ordination, for instance, David Vincent changed his name to Mojola Agbebi and replaced his European ministerial costume for native dress, which he wore even when he toured Britain and the United States in the early 1900s. Agbebi more than nearly any other Lagos-based clergyman worked to reconcile Christianity and African institutions. As he put it on the first anniversary of the Native Baptist Church in 1889, "To be successful we have to study the names, designs, and influences of the stone and wooden gods of our fathers. . . .The lives and doings of our heathen sages, the origin of the several gods of whom our brethren worship will be useful instruments in the hands of the aggressive missionary."[90] Soon, a number of works of Yoruba history were in production, including Otonba Payne's *Table of Principal Events in Yoruba History* (1893), J. O. George's *Historical Notes on the Yoruba Country and its Tribes* (1895), and Samuel Johnson's monumental *History of the Yorubas* (completed in 1897). In response to the persistent denigration of African culture by European missionaries and officials, these efforts — all by active Christians — showcased the richness, vitality, and legitimacy of Yoruba traditions. Perhaps ironically, this "minor cultural renaissance" was spearheaded in large measure by Saro and Brazilians with origins both in Yorubaland and the African diaspora.[91]

Church Vaughan's own diasporic affiliations tended to reach back to the

Americas rather than to an African past. He never pretended to be a Yoruba man, and he left the celebration of local culture to others. Instead, he reconnected with an old friend from the United States who shared his Baptist faith and independent spirit. Around the time that Blyden came to Lagos in 1890, so did Strother Moses Cook, the white Baptist who had earlier been hounded out of the mission for too closely fraternizing with Africans. Cook had remained in contact with Moses Stone and had recently left the Baptist Church himself. Now a minister of the Harrodsburg, Kentucky, Church of Christ (a so-called Cambellite church), Cook had come back to support the Native Baptists — and perhaps, as a rueful missionary charged, "widen the breach between them and the mission" — taking up residence in Vaughan's house on Igbosere Road.[92] Lodging with Vaughan, his wife Sarah, their son Burrell, little daughter Aida, and the family servants (James W. Vaughan lived in his own house nearby), Cook could witness the comings and goings of Vaughan's business associates and keep in close touch with the African Baptists. He attended services at the Native Baptist Church and assisted Stone as he could, though the congregation's members insisted that no white missionary would lead them. After several months, however, Cook established his own small Cambellite ("Disciples of Christ") congregation, which met for devotionals in Vaughan's backyard. Though Vaughan himself remained a Native Baptist, he saw no harm in providing a space for Cook and his dozen or so followers, especially since the Disciples of Christ shared many Baptist beliefs. Indeed, his association with Cook, who continued "talking matters that affect the character of some of the missionaries who were here with him when he was a Baptist," represented Vaughan's past links to the Baptist mission as well as his repudiation of white supremacy within it and his autonomy even within his own congregation.[93]

Now an old man, Vaughan had been connected with Baptist missionaries for more than half his lifetime. They had given him his real start in life, bringing him to Yorubaland, offering him protection, opening his mind and spirit, and developing the skills that enabled him to make a living. At the time, Lagos had been a weak outpost of British colonialism surrounded by independent African polities. The missionaries of the 1850s and '60s — Anglican, Methodist, and Baptist — had seen their role as spreading "civilization" to Africans, who would then take it up themselves. They concentrated in particular on African refugees from slavery and the slave trade, who generally came to share their reverence for Christianity and education. For Vaughan, working and learning with the missionaries had been a crucial step in attaining the autonomy that in his view formed the essence of freedom.

But now a new generation of white missionaries and British officials was convinced not that Africans should be educated for leadership and autonomy, but that all black people were permanently inferior to whites. Moreover, instead of an isolated colony with few Europeans, Lagos was now the beachhead from which the British were moving to annex all of Yorubaland and beyond, a process they would complete in the 1914 amalgamation of "Nigeria." Vaughan had achieved considerable material success, but along with other African elites he resented the burgeoning new colonialism and its accompanying white supremacy. Though Vaughan remained steadfast as a Baptist and refused to dismiss the intentions of all white missionaries, he also took his stand against them — not by embracing a somewhat imagined Yoruba cultural identity, but by asserting the independence and capabilities of people of color, as his contemporaries in the United States were also doing.

In mid-1893, Church Vaughan was nearing the end of his life. He had prepared for it with his characteristic prudence. Four years earlier he had made a will, naming as executors his eldest son James Wilson Vaughan, the merchant Juan A. Campos, and his longtime associate and former apprentice Christopher B. Vaughan. Because he had already transferred considerable assets to James Wilson by that time, Church identified his other children, Burrell and Aida Vaughan, as the primary recipients of land, houses, and cash. As was customary, his wife Sarah was bequeathed the use of one of his houses (next door to the family house on Igbosere Road) for the rest of her life, when it would pass to their son Burrell. Vaughan must have been imagining his legacy, for he stipulated that his residence on Igbosere Road should be inherited by his daughter Aida when she married or turned twenty-one, but that neither she nor her heirs could sell or dispose of it until the third generation.[94]

More recently, in January 1893, Vaughan had added a codicil to his will. At that point he anticipated becoming a grandfather, for James Wilson and his wife Clara were expecting their first child. The addendum to the will granted "a specific legacy" of a thousand pounds to James Wilson, a huge sum to be taken out of the portion of the estate that would otherwise be divided among the three Vaughan siblings. It also directed that Burrell Vaughan should inherit a piece of property that Church had recently purchased (for fifteen pounds) on the waterfront of Ebute Metta.[95] The codicil did not state Church's reasoning behind these new bequests, though they seem intended to solidify James Wilson's place as the new head of the Vaughan dynasty. Church surely approved of his eldest son's comportment as a husband, soon-

James Wilson Vaughan (seated) and Burrell Carter Vaughan (standing), probably early 1920s. Photo in possession of the author.

James Churchwill Vaughan. Courtesy of Rotimi Vaughan.

to-be father, head of the family business, and church leader. Burrell Vaughan, at twenty-three, may have been harder for Church to relate to. Though he too was active in the Ebenezer Baptist Church, and he eventually made a fortune in business and land speculation, he enjoyed sports, music, and parties. In addition to his "church wife," he ultimately had children with two additional "outside wives," a common practice among Yoruba "big men."[96]

It may have been around the time he revised his will that Church Vaughan hired one of Lagos's commercial photographers to produce his portrait.[97] An impressive new building for the Ebenezer Baptist Church, financed by the Vaughan brothers specifically in honor of their father, was nearing completion; perhaps he intended for his image to hang on one of its walls.[98] More than a century later, the resulting large print was preserved in a gilded frame, possessed by Vaughan's grandson Oladenji Vaughan and reproduced in the homes of other Vaughan family members as well. It shows Vaughan as a prosperous, Western-oriented elder, seated in a cushioned armchair and wearing a dark woolen suit, starched white shirt, waistcoat, and bow tie. His thickset frame suggests past physical strength as well as a plentiful diet. Vaughan wears round spectacles, and his hairline is receding. His beard is nearly all gray, though his hair still has some brown in it. Vaughan sits straight, neither looking directly at the camera nor smiling. In his hand rests a folded piece of paper or placard, facing the viewer so that its lettering may be read:

No. 1 MANUSKRIPT OV
The Humathist Bul.
Ritten bi J. C. Von
ov
Lagos West Afrika
1881

Clearly an intentional message for viewers of the portrait, this short text presents a mystery now. Why would the literate J. C. Vaughan use phonetic spelling and render his name differently than he did elsewhere? Perhaps the writing was added to the photographer's glass plate negative by a less educated person such as the photographer or his assistant after the portrait was taken.[99] But even more tantalizing is the question of the "No. 1 MANUSKRIPT" of "The Hamathist Bul.," surely an abbreviation of "Bulletin," written by J. C. Vaughan of Lagos in 1881. Did Vaughan produce a publication, or even a series of publications, that has not survived? In the Old Testament, the Hamathites were a Hamitic family, included among the descendants of Canaan.[100] "Hamathist," then, could be used here as a stand-in for African or black. It also brings to mind the title of *The Hamite's Economy*, the pamphlet circulated in 1881 presumably by Vaughan's friend Sewell Pettiford. The photograph itself is unlikely to have been taken then, when Vaughan at fifty-three was younger than he appears in the portrait, and when photography studios were rare in West Africa.[101] If instead it dates from the early 1890s, then the sign Vaughan held was a deliberate reminder of an earlier time. By invoking his "Hamathist" publication from 1881, in fact, Vaughan may

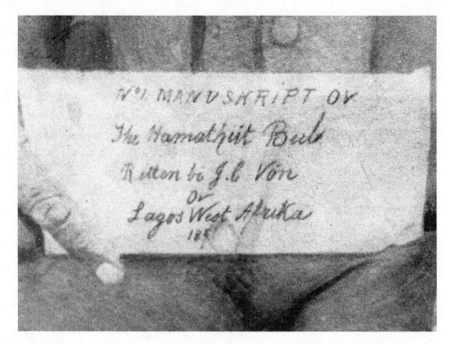

Close-up of placard, James Churchwill Vaughan portrait.

well have been reminding viewers of his early support for a separatist Christian church and, along with it, his venerable role among the Native Baptists. Regardless of his hospitality to Strother Cook's "Cambellites," or his strict accounting of the Church's debts to him, or any other difference of outlook, Vaughan wanted to be remembered as a Baptist who dared to promote independence.[102]

James Churchwill Vaughan died at his home on Igbosere Road in Lagos on September 13, 1893, at the age of sixty-five. He had lived long enough to meet his grandson, James Churchwill Omosanya Vaughan, born three months earlier. (*Omosanya* means "the child compensates for my suffering"—seemingly a reference to the premature death of James Wilson Vaughan's first wife.) By the time he breathed his last, the elder Church Vaughan had outlived by far all of his eight siblings in America, and he left his widow and three children in material comfort. Vaughan's passing was announced in Lagos newspapers, and he was buried under an imposing monument in the town cemetery.[103]

If in his last moments Church Vaughan thought back on his life, he surely must have been satisfied with his successes. He had survived South Carolina, Liberia, Ijaye, and Abeokuta, and he had thrived in Lagos. A stranger to

Yorubaland, he had built a solid business, a respected family, and a venerable reputation. He had led a renewal of the church that had helped to make him who he was. Vaughan would be remembered with affection and pride, and not only in Nigeria. In the United States too, younger generations of his family would keep his name alive for more than a century—a prospect he probably never anticipated. What would surprise him even more, if he were able to look out from the land of the ancestors, was what his descendants remembered about him: that Church Vaughan was a Yoruba man who had finally found his African roots.

seven

AFTERLIVES

"The Vaughan Family: A Tale of Two Continents," featured in *Ebony* magazine in 1975, was conceived, researched, and written by Era Bell Thompson, the magazine's longtime international editor and a veteran writer about Africa. "While other black families delve into genealogy in search of identity," she wrote, "the descendants of Scipio [Vaughan] know who they were, where they are and enjoy each other's company."[1] As the introduction to this book discussed, the *Ebony* story was a dramatic tale of African roots lost, found, and maintained—and one that was not entirely accurate. It centered on J. C. Vaughan, who returned to his ancestral African homeland and found people bearing his father's "tribal marks." After making a life for himself in Nigeria, the article continued, Vaughan returned to South Carolina to visit relatives, creating links between his Nigerian and American families that persist to the present.

It is easy to imagine why the story of Church Vaughan as a Yoruba man who connected his African and American families appealed to *Ebony*'s publishers in the mid-1970s. Thompson's story, in fact, seems to comprise the magazine's answer to Alex Haley's *Roots*, whose publication the next year was eagerly anticipated (and which had already been sold as a television miniseries).[2] *Roots* highlighted the centuries-long struggles of the author's ancestors, beginning with the African captive Kunta Kinte. Part of its enormous appeal was that it traced Haley's family tree to a specific African progenitor, something impossible for most African Americans. As Thompson's article pointed out, however, Scipio Vaughan's American descendants were not only aware of their African ancestors, but they had remained in touch with African relatives for over a century. Aida Arabella Stradford, Church

Era Bell Thompson with James Olabode Vaughan in Ikoyi Cemetery, 1974.
Photo by Moneta Sleet Jr. Courtesy of Johnson Publishing Company, LLC.

Vaughan's American grand-niece named after his own daughter, served as one of Thompson's primary informants, sharing a short family history that she had composed in the 1960s. "I have related some of the facts concerning my family tree," Stradford wrote then, "not only because I regard it as interesting and somewhat inspiring, but also for the purpose of proving that while genealogical trees do not flourish among us, nevertheless, there are some of which we may be justly proud."[3] Indeed, the Vaughan story had the potential to be even more satisfying than *Roots* to readers interested in African American family connections with Africa, since the Vaughans' kinship ties were not only historical but maintained in the present. "We were two steps ahead of Alex Haley," a twenty-six-year-old American Vaughan relative told a reporter in 1982. "When I was in college and everyone was talking about 'Roots,' I showed people an article about our family in *Ebony* magazine. They were all so impressed."[4]

The *Ebony* story is essentially one of cultural nationalism: it rests on the assumption that ancestry, and with it culture, determined who the Vaughans were and where they belonged. In real life, however, Church Vaughan kept his distance from the Yoruba cultural nationalism that was beginning to swirl around him in the late nineteenth century. In every place he lived, in fact, he demonstrated that ancestry and culture did *not* dictate where, how, or with whom he should make his way. Vaughan's life story directly contradicts the country marks version told by his descendants: his bonds to Africa were based far less on genealogy than on the opportunities he found and the work he did there.

Just as the best stories are meaningful ones, the best ancestors are those who appeal to our current interests and desires. Church Vaughan's remarkable biography hardly needs embellishment. Yet Vaughans on both sides of the Atlantic have been repeating for many years that Scipio Vaughan had been born and captured in Africa, and that Church Vaughan recognized his father's facial markings on people he encountered when he reached Yorubaland. Why and how did the story of Church Vaughan as a Yoruba man returned to his roots come to define his legacy? What did it mean to Vaughan descendants when they remembered it? And given that the country marks story is not in fact true, what meaning should we take from the "real" Vaughan story, the one recounted in this book, today?

Certainly Church Vaughan was not thought of as a returned Yoruba descendant at the time of his death. Nor, in fact, did his widow and sons even highlight his connection to the Ebenezer Baptist Church when they composed his memorials. Instead, they largely pointed to his impressive economic and personal achievements, which seemed even more noteworthy because Vaughan was an outsider to Yorubaland. Independence, persistence, and prosperity: these were the legacies that outlived Vaughan in Lagos.

Church Vaughan's obituary appeared in the *Lagos Weekly Record* in mid-September 1893, ten days after he took his last breath.[5] Perhaps unsurprisingly, some of the biographical details it contained were a little off: his birthplace was listed as Charleston rather than Camden, South Carolina; his birth in April 1827 instead of 1828; and his years in Liberia do not hew to the exact chronology either. Two themes ring clearly through this account of Vaughan's life, however: his dogged independence, and his perseverance in overcoming misfortune. Although, as recounted in the obituary, Vaughan "was employed for some time as a carpenter for the American Baptist Mission," he "subsequently established himself at Ijaye where he began farming on his own account." No mention was made of his capture in the Ijaye-Ibadan War; rather, "On that country being broken up by the Ibadans he went to Abeokuta and established himself near Atadi, where he renewed his farming operations, supplementing them with sugar-making, board-sawing and other pursuits." Again, it is Vaughan's independence that emerges, followed by his triumph over adversity. "In the outbreak against the missionaries in 1867," the obituary—and Vaughan's survivors—told readers, "he was included with them, and despoiled of everything he possessed, was driven from the country with only the things he wore, and he arrived in this colony with only five pounds which he happened to have in money, and which he managed to save from his despoilers." Notably here, Vaughan was "included with" the missionaries, the precise nature of his affiliation left undefined. Yet he was clearly an American, and somewhat of a stereotypical one: "Being, however, a first-class workman and possessed of that push and energy imbibed from America, Mr. Vaughan started life as it were anew, and by dint of hard work and thrift he, in a few years, secured a competence and eventually abandoned carpentry and embarked in business in which he became very successful." Vaughan, in short, was a self-made man, and not only in commerce but in his own intellectual development. "Mr. Vaughan never had the advantage of any school education, and what book-learning he possessed was entirely self-acquired," yet he was "a keen observer and a profound thinker, [who] by constant reading kept himself in touch with contemporary thought, and his information of matters and things generally was very wide." Moreover, Vaughan enabled others to follow his example by teaching them "the means wherewith to obtain a livelihood, and through which they, in some instances, have also acquired a competence, and it is in this respect that the deceased's usefulness becomes conspicuous." It was on the issue of "usefulness" that the encomium pivoted to its somewhat defensive conclusion: "Mr. Vaughan fulfilled, in his life, the highest duty of man — to perform with all diligence and faithfulness the sphere of labour in which his lot was cast."[6]

After the obituary was published and Vaughan was buried, his widow and sons got another chance to craft a lasting memorial to his achievements, this time in stone. Ikoyi cemetery had opened two miles from central Lagos in 1879. There, above-ground crypts, elaborate carved cherubs, sculpted angels, and mammoth crosses continue to mark the graves of well-known Nigerians, including businessmen, educational leaders, and pillars of the Church Missionary Society.[7] Near the front, Vaughan's sons erected a columned, white marble tower bearing an inscription that wrapped around its four sides:

> Sacred to the memory of James Churchwill Vaughan, native of
> Camden, South Carolina, born April 1, 1828. He migrated to Africa in
> the year 1853, leaving behind a large family, owing to the oppressive
> laws then in force against colored men in the Southern States. His
> life in Africa was characterized by many vicissitudes in all of which
> he proved himself equal to the attendant difficulties. He died on the
> 13th of September, 1893. And though after my skin, worms destroy
> this body, yet in my flesh shall I see God. Job XIX.26.

If they had been frustrated with sloppy reporting in their father's newspaper obituary, James Wilson and Burrell Vaughan got the details right in this short, permanently rendered, biography of their father. And given the constraints of space and perhaps even expense in inscribing his tombstone, the brothers boiled down Church Vaughan's legacy to its essentials: a birth; a journey, with its motivation and its cost; a life of overcoming challenges; and a death.

Raised both in the Baptist Church and the wider Yoruba community, though, the Vaughans knew the value of a well-chosen allusion. Church Vaughan may have been particularly attracted to the story of Job and perhaps even recounted it from time to time, comparing himself to the pious man who nevertheless suffered many tribulations. The Old Testament figure Job had been prosperous before God tested him with the loss of his possessions, his children, and then his health. Yet Job's steadfast refusal to reproach God ultimately resulted in his restored body, a new family, and twice his original prosperity. The one-sentence inscription from the book of Job on Vaughan's imposing grave marker, then, was meant to invoke his whole story — at least

Views of James Churchwill Vaughan's grave marker, Ikoyi Cemetery, Lagos.
Photos by the author, 2003.

the way he or his survivors wanted it told. Like Job, Vaughan achieved great wealth only after repeated tests of his perseverance and faith.

In the years after Vaughan's death, he continued to be remembered as an American, a hard worker, a prosperous businessman, and a person of faith. In spite of his association with the Ebenezer Baptist Church, Vaughan was not lauded in print as a leader of the independent church movement—even when a minister from the United Native African Church recounted his life story in a 1905 newspaper article. Nor was he linked to the Yoruba cultural nationalism promoted by some of his independent Christian contemporaries. The same newspaper tribute praised Vaughan as an important figure in local history, but reminded readers that he was from elsewhere: "As a foreigner he has exerted a potent influence in the whole Yorubaland."[8] Almost twenty years later, his name still appeared publicly in connection with the hardware business he had founded. Under the headline "Ogbeni [Mr.] J. C. Vaughan," a 1923 advertisement in a new Yoruba-language newspaper touted the building materials as well as motor cars available at reasonable prices at the two Vaughan stores. "Mr. Vaughan has been trading in various tools for the last fifty years," the Yoruba text asserted, as if he were still alive. "The man is a giant [literally, an elephant] in the tools/hardware trade."[9]

By this time, as the Yoruba-language advertisement suggests, Vaughan's children and grandchildren were both wealthier and more Nigerian than he had been. The family had gone from well-off to rich, and from limited to deep involvement in local issues. Because of their success in the hardware business, Vaughan's sons James Wilson and Burrell Vaughan were by 1920

Portrait of Kofo Ademola, from Gbemi Rosiji, *Lady Ademola*. Rights courtesy of Kunle Ademola.

listed in the *Red Book of West Africa*, a guide to the most prominent coastal merchants.[10] The Vaughan brothers remained active in the Ebenezer Baptist Church, which James served as a deacon and Burrell as the church organist. They sent their much younger sister Aida Arabella to England for finishing school, where she met members of a prominent Saro Nigerian family named Moore. Later she married Eric Moore, a barrister and the second unofficial member of the Lagos Legislative Council. Their daughter Kofoworola Moore (later Lady Kofo Ademola) became the first African woman to earn a degree from Oxford University. She rose to prominence as an advocate for women's education and social reforms, and as the wife of Nigeria's first African chief justice, Sir Adetokunbo Ademola, son of the *alake* (ruler) of Abeokuta. In 1923, Dr. James C. Vaughan, grandson and namesake of the family patriarch, returned from medical school in Scotland and with others formed the Union of Young Nigerians, which stood for "the interests of the youths of the country and for the general welfare of all."[11] Ten years later he helped to found one of Nigeria's earliest political parties, the Nigerian Youth

Dr. James C.
Vaughan.
Courtesy of
Rotimi Vaughan.

Movement. Thus, two generations after Church Vaughan came to Yorubaland, his descendants were in the forefront of Nigerian society and politics.

By then, the Vaughans had become so important that ceremonial poems,
called *oriki*, were composed in their honor. *Oriki* is a long-standing genre of
Yoruba-language praise poetry, full of metaphors and historical allusions, reminding listeners of the lineage and accomplishments of their subjects.[12] At
weddings, funerals, and other public gatherings, Church Vaughan's daughter
Aida Moore came to be greeted with a verse that translates roughly as, "Thou
precious child of the lord of the land / Heiress to boundless wealth and
property / Heiress who jiggles and plays with precious beads!" According
to her daughter's biographer, the first line is a reference to Moore's mother
Sarah Omotayo, a native of the kingdom of Benin, which once held authority
over Lagos. The second phrase, mentioning her inherited wealth, seems
to be a nod to her father, while the third points out Moore's own accomplishments as a trader in jewelry and imported chinaware.[13] Additionally,
Church's grandson James Richard Oladeinde Vaughan, the wealthy younger

son of James Wilson Vaughan and his wife Clara Zenobia Allen, became the subject of a long, complicated *oriki*. Though it is now associated with the Vaughan family in general, the set of verses alludes to his mother's heritage in Ibadan and her family's historic connection to the king of Oyo.[14] Neither of the two *oriki* say anything about the family patriarch's origins — probably because there was no glory in descent from an American slave. Nor did Church Vaughan's twenty-one-year-old granddaughter Kofo Moore mention them when she penned a short autobiography as a student at Oxford in 1936. "The paternal branch of my mother's line originated from America," she wrote simply. "We are still in touch with these relations."[15]

At the time of Church Vaughan's death and decades later, Lagosians recalled him as a refugee from American racial oppression, who through determination and pluck survived his ordeals, built a successful business, and founded a family of public-minded high achievers. Though his American origins were unusual, and slave descent was not something to bring up, nineteenth-century Lagos was full of slaves, ex-slaves, and descendants of freedpeople trying to make a new start. Vaughan was understood to belong there, his children and grandchildren even more so. How, then, did his legacy later come to be about an alleged return to his ancestral roots?

If the version of the Vaughan story recounted in *Ebony* was not entirely true, and it was not told by Vaughan's survivors in Lagos, then the challenge is to find out where it came from. At what point did someone in the family begin describing Church Vaughan as a Yoruba man returned to his origins, and under what circumstances? What can the emergence of this story reveal not only about its tellers, but about the relationship between Africa and America in the century after Vaughan's life?

Reconstructing the history of the country marks story requires some deduction, and two clues offer a start. In the years before the *Ebony* magazine article was published, two American Vaughan descendants each penned their own versions of their family's story. Though the accounts differ, they both hinge on Church Vaughan's return to his ancestral homeland, as signified by the country marks that he recognized from his father. Vaughan's grand-niece Aida Arabella Stradford's version, written sometime between 1965 and 1968 and used as a source for the *Ebony* article, begins with the African Scipio, captured in Abeokuta around 1805 (before the town was founded, in fact) and attempting suicide during the Middle Passage to America. It continues through his marriage to a Cherokee "Indian maiden" to the return of his sons Burrell and James Churchill Vaughan to Africa. In Abeokuta, Burrell (who in this account seems switched with his brother) "knew by the tribal marks on his father's face that he was among his ancestors."[16] So much of this rendition of the Vaughan story is unsubstantiated that it must have been based either on long (mis-)remembered snatches of conversation or on assumption. The other written version was less ambitious. In 1969, Mabel Murphy Smythe, an economist and diplomat descended from Church Vaughan's half-aunt Harriet Conway, wrote a short family history to send to a friend. "Mother had told us the story of how one African arrived in the United States, married a woman of our family, then urged his children — at least one of them — to return to his father's people," she wrote. "Eventually one son, whose last name was Vaughn, returned to Nigeria, found his father's family (which he recognized through the ritual facial scars like those of his father), and settled there, marrying a local woman."[17]

Though they were cousins several times removed and lived hundreds of miles apart, Aida Stradford and Mabel Smythe were well acquainted, Stradford having grown up with Smythe's mother Josephine Dibble Murphy in Camden, South Carolina, before moving North.[18] It is therefore not surprising that their family histories were similar. But where did the idea about Scipio Vaughan's country marks originate? Most likely, both versions of the story had a common source: the 1925 American visit of Church Vaughan's daughter Aida Arabella Vaughan Moore, who met Smythe's mother and grandfather in Camden and who probably also met Stradford in Chicago. She seems to have been the source of the poignant story of her father's "return" to Africa that has been preserved and repeated for nearly a century. Emerging from Mrs. Moore's remarkable encounters with relatives in the United States, the country marks story reflected both the transatlantic relationships among the Vaughans and wider currents of the Jazz Age.

We can only speculate about what brought American and Nigerian Vaughans together in the 1920s. Church Vaughan had certainly written to his American relatives from time to time; otherwise his niece would not have named her daughter, born in Camden in 1891, after Aida Arabella Vaughan, born in Lagos nine years earlier. Aida Vaughan continued the transcontinental correspondence herself.[19] Her letters have not been located, but they must have become increasingly significant to her American cousins in the second decade of the twentieth century, when massive transformations in African American life prompted new attention to Africa.

These developments began, as did African American history itself, with migration. Legions of black Americans, including some of the Vaughans, left the Jim Crow South for new opportunities in the urban North. Five hundred thousand black southerners moved north between 1915 and 1920; over a million and a half followed them over the next decade. They headed to Chicago, Pittsburgh, Cleveland, and elsewhere, but their primary destination was Harlem, a section of northern Manhattan where, due to a real-estate slump, developers sold housing built for whites to African Americans. By the end of the 1920s, this roughly three-square mile urban area contained nearly a quarter of a million inhabitants, making it the largest settlement of black people that had ever existed anywhere in the world. Harlem attracted migrants from every corner of the African diaspora, including the West Indian Marcus Garvey, whose Universal Negro Improvement Association, founded shortly after he arrived in 1915, linked black economic empowerment with an ambitious—and fruitless, as it turned out—scheme to settle African Americans in Liberia. Harlem also spawned a renaissance in American arts, from jazz to painting to literature—much of it reflecting a post–world war search for cultural authenticity and spiritual renewal, and some of it inspired by Africa. With new currents in anthropology explaining human difference in terms of culture rather than biology—that is, beginning to repudiate "scientific" racism—Africans seemed not so much "backward" as exotic, their presumptively more "authentic" culture (usually singular, not plural) offering inspiration and fascination for disillusioned postwar westerners.[20]

Aida Arabella Stradford was one of them. In 1921 or '22, presumably after some earlier correspondence, the Nigerian cousin after whom she was named, Aida Arabella Vaughan Moore, suggested that she visit the family in Lagos. Stradford, pregnant with her third child, was unable to make the trip, but her sister Sarah Carter Thompson went in her stead, her passage paid by the Vaughan brothers in Nigeria. Born in South Carolina, thirty-six-year-old Thompson lived in Harlem with her husband, an employee in a medical clinic, along with a boarder, and had formerly worked as a hairdresser. The previous year she had spent two months in Cuba, where she surely saw black people engaged in various kinds of work and occupying a range of social positions, as they did in Harlem. Nevertheless, Thompson could not escape the prevailing images of Africa as exotic and largely primitive. She must have been dumbstruck when she entered the gracious central Lagos home of Aida Moore or visited the newly constructed Kakawa Street mansion of James Wilson Vaughan.[21]

The Vaughans and the Moores were established members of the Lagos elite: wealthy, cultured, and engaged in the social and political life of the town. The Moores were fluent in Yoruba, but they had been educated abroad and spoke the King's English, which they honed in their children by insisting that only English be spoken in their house on Sundays.[22] At the time of Thompson's visit, the colonial government had just opened up three seats on the Lagos Legislative Council for elected African representatives; her cousin Aida's husband Eric Moore, vice president of the newly formed Nigerian National Democratic Party, won one of them.[23] In addition to supporting his activities, Aida Moore was a redoubtable businesswoman in her own right, while overseeing a large household of children, foster children, servants, and frequent guests. She remained close to her brothers and their families, sometimes taking her children and others to join excursions in the Vaughans' motor cars for picnics at Ebute Metta (the mainland opposite Lagos Island), where her brother Burrell had just built an enormous "villa" on his farmland.[24] During her time in Lagos, Sarah Thompson surely heard about the injustices of colonialism: Eric Moore's political party promoted local self-government and the Africanization of the civil service, among other goals; the previous year, James Wilson and Burrell Vaughan had financed a legal case brought by the royal family of Lagos against a land grab by the colonial government.[25] But she could not miss that even under colonialism, her African relatives were thriving in ways that seemed much more difficult back home.

Three years after hosting Thompson in Lagos, Aida Vaughan Moore returned the visit, bringing her daughter Gladys Motunde to attend Vassar College.[26] While in the United States, Moore took the opportunity to see relatives in New York and probably Chicago as well as make a pilgrimage to her father's hometown of Camden, South Carolina. By this time, many of her American relatives, especially those who had undertaken the Great Migration north, were relatively well-off professionals. Sarah Thompson, perhaps deeming her apartment not grand enough for an elite visitor, installed Mrs. Moore in the home of her cousin William Sutherland, a dentist from Camden who had recently moved with his family to a "magnificent estate" in the otherwise all-white suburb of Glen Ridge, New Jersey.[27] Moore may have also visited the Harlem homes of two of Thompson's brothers, both of them physicians, one of whom had recently purchased a house in an area that came to be known as Striver's Row.[28] Though direct evidence is lacking, she surely would have gone to see the cousin who had been named after her, Aida Arabella Stradford, who lived with her family in Chicago's vibrant African American neighborhood Bronzeville.[29] Like Moore, Stradford was married to a politically active lawyer: C. Francis Stradford was a founder of the National Bar Association and years later would argue against restrictive housing covenants before the U.S. Supreme Court.[30] In Camden, however, the class differences between Moore and her American relatives became more obvious. Hosted by distant cousin Eugene Dibble and his daughter Josephine Murphy, who came from Atlanta for the occasion, the Nigerian guest "created something of a stir by refusing to set foot in the kitchen (on the grounds that kitchens were for servants, not for lady visitors)." Charming as Mrs. Moore may have otherwise been, the granddaughter of her host "presumed that Africans . . . were neither very democratic nor practical."[31]

Even though Aida Vaughan Moore knew her father's reasons for leaving Camden, she still must have found the visit disheartening. Her cousin showed her the "old homestead," which must have been her great-grandfather Bonds Conway's house, as there was no existing Vaughan property to see. Moore was so impressed that when she built a new Lagos residence some years later as a wealthy widow, she had "Conway House" emblazoned in glass over the front door.[32] Nevertheless, white supremacy was on full display in 1920s Camden, where every aspect of social and economic life—businesses, schools, hospitals, churches, and more—was segregated by race. A tourism industry had developed in the early twentieth century, offering white northerners escaping harsh winters a facsimile of Old South "gentility" in resort hotels replete with obsequious black servants. African Americans were expected to defer to whites wherever they met, regardless of the circumstances. Some years before Moore's visit, a black worker at her host Eugene Dibble's grocery store was lynched by a gang that included a white employee from the same store, presumably over some workplace disagreement.[33]

It was not only in the South that Mrs. Moore learned about white supremacy in America. Everywhere she went, people remembered the Red Summer of 1919, when more than thirty "race riots"—that is, mass white attacks on black people—erupted across the United States, and at least forty-three African Americans were lynched. One of the most violent outbreaks had been in Chicago, where twenty-three blacks and fifteen whites were killed and more than five hundred were injured in nearly two weeks of street fighting after a black swimmer accidentally wandered into an area of the lakefront claimed by whites.[34]

In Chicago or elsewhere, Moore surely learned about her cousin Aida Stradford's father-in-law John B. Stradford, who took refuge in the city shortly after the 1921 race riot in Tulsa, Oklahoma, the deadliest in U.S. history. The senior Stradford, an attorney and successful businessman, had owned a sixty-five-room hotel in Tulsa's Greenwood District, the wealthiest black community in the United States, known as the "Black Wall Street." It was burned down, along with thirty-five city blocks, in a white rampage set off by the questionable arrest of a black teenager for allegedly touching a young white woman. During a sixteen-hour mob assault, perhaps as many as three hundred African Americans were killed, more than eight hundred were injured, and some ten thousand lost their homes to arson. Stradford and sixty-nine other black men were indicted on spurious charges of inciting the riot. Fearing he would be lynched, Stradford fled the state, but he was apprehended in Kansas and jailed pending extradition back to Oklahoma. Urgently, he wired his son in Chicago. When C. Francis Stradford arrived, he filed a writ of habeas corpus to have his father released on bail. Once the five-hundred-dollar fee was paid, the Stradfords hurried to Chicago, where there was little chance that a judge would intervene in the case. The senior Stradford credited his son with saving him from being murdered back in Oklahoma. He never returned to the state, and the charges hung over him until his death in 1935.[35]

It was out of these 1925 encounters between Aida Moore and her American relatives that the Vaughan family story as later recounted in print (and by nearly every living family member to this day) likely emerged. If Aida Moore suggested that her American-born father was a Yoruba descendant who found his father's people in Africa, as we must assume she did, the tale can be seen as a gracious gesture from a guest to her hosts, a parable that highlighted and celebrated the connections between this elite Nigerian and her embattled American cousins. "It is only when you are stranded in a hostile country that you need a romance of origins," Saidiya Hartman has written; and Aida Moore must have sensed this too.[36] The meaning of her story was primarily familial—which may account for its transmission almost exclusively through women. And coming as it did from an elegant, wealthy Nigerian, in a period when the exotic African was in high style, the story brought glamour to those associated with it. "Mother was always talking about our African relatives," Aida Stradford's daughter recalled decades later. "As a small child I knew that Africa was not a jungle, and I was proud of my African cousins."[37]

How, though, did the story come to Aida Moore's mind? In Yorubaland such tales of family members lost by slavery and found again were not, in fact, far-fetched. Her father had known at least one person who had returned from the exile of slavery and had been famously reunited with long-lost relatives: none other than Bishop Samuel Ajayi Crowther, who was captured in Yorubaland as a young teenager. After the ship in which Crowther was carried away was intercepted by the British Navy, he was resettled at Sierra Leone and educated by missionaries. Decades later, in the 1840s, he returned to Yorubaland on behalf of the Church Missionary Society. Soon after his arrival in Abeokuta, he was reunited with his mother and two sisters, whom he had not seen in twenty-five years. "We [he and his mother] grasped one another," Crowther wrote in a well-publicized account, "looking at each other with great silence and astonishment; big tears rolled down her emaciated cheeks."[38] Church Vaughan knew Crowther in the 1850s and '60s through the networks of Christians in and around Abeokuta. Surely he had heard of Crowther's reunion with his long-lost family, as well as many other stories of Brazilian and Sierra Leonean returnees who had reconnected with loved ones in Yorubaland.[39] These may have inspired Vaughan or one of his children to tell a similar family reunion story of their own.

A narrative bestowing Yoruba roots upon the Vaughans would also have been useful to Aida Moore in Lagos. During the 1920s, Lagosian political activists (many of them descendants of Atlantic immigrants) were forging common cause with the indigenous population to bolster their claims to be legitimate representatives of the people. For some time, the colonial government had denied members of the educated elite greater political voice on the grounds that they were out of touch with traditional rulers and their subjects and could not represent them. Thus when the Nigerian National Democratic Party (NNDP) was founded in 1923, its president Herbert Macaulay (Samuel Crowther's grandson) involved it in issues relevant to Lagos's royal lineage, local chiefs, and market women. As the wife of the NNDP's vice president, Aida Moore had a strong incentive to assert that her father was a Yoruba man, and that she, her family, and members of her social class had ties to the indigenous population.[40]

Although the Vaughan tale was most likely planted when Aida Moore visited the United States in the 1920s, it took root in the 1950s, as multiple connections between American and Nigerian family members moved it back and forth across the Atlantic. In 1956, Aida Moore's grand-niece Ayo Vaughan-Richards, then a graduate student in nursing at the University of Edinburgh, spent two months in Chicago with the Stradfords, from whom she undoubtedly heard that her American ancestor was also a returned Yoruba descendant. The American cousin Mabel Smythe (Eugene Dibble's granddaughter) may have told the same story when she met Vaughan-Richards and Aida Moore's daughter Kofo Ademola on a visit to Nigeria with Operation Crossroads (a precursor to the Peace Corps) in 1958. The following year, Kofo Ademola traveled to the United States as part of an official tour with her husband, then chief justice of the Federation of Nigeria. In Chicago, she visited her cousins the Stradfords, whom her mother probably met thirty years previously. As Mrs. Ademola's friend and biographer later recounted, "This brought home to the Admolas how unusual it was for African Americans to be able to discover their original roots in Africa, and to maintain contact with the relatives they found."[41] Kofo Ademola, Ayo Vaughan-Richards, and Jewel Stradford Lafontant, who had been a small child when Aida Moore came to the United States, maintained the Vaughan connections for more than forty years. The friendship between Lafontant and Vaughan-Richards, two successful, charismatic women linked through family history across thousands of miles, was celebrated in Nigerian and American newspapers in 1973 and the feature in *Ebony* two years later.[42]

For Vaughan-Richards and other Nigerian Vaughans, the country marks story was as welcome as it was in America and as useful as it may have been half a century earlier in Lagos. As she conducted her own research into her family's history in the 1980s, in fact, Ayo Vaughan-Richards sought to attribute specific facial scars, linked to a particular Yoruba polity, to her ancestor Scipio. She concluded that his country marks must have been those of Owu, once an independent kingdom and, after its destruction in warfare, a quarter within Abeokuta. According to her cousin Olabode Vaughan, now the family's unofficial historian, in spite of their elite status, the Vaughans were still sometimes considered outsiders in Lagos because of their relatively shallow Yoruba roots. "You are a Vaughan?" people might ask, "*Níbo ni ìwọ ti wá?* [Where are you from?]"[43] The story of the tribal marks, as interpreted by Vaughan-Richards, provided an answer: Abeokuta, the home of a long line of eminent Nigerians, some of them connected through marriage to the Vaughans, and specifically its illustrious Owu district.

The story the *Ebony* article told, of Church Vaughan's return to his ancestral home and his descendants' enduring transcontinental connections, was of course only partly true. It reflected an intense interest in African American heritage in the 1970s, spurred by assertions of black pride in the wake of the civil rights movement. But it also dated to an earlier moment of African American fascination with Africa, the 1920s. The visit of Church Vaughan's daughter to the United States at that time reinforced to her American relatives that they were exceptional. It also highlighted the impediments that they and all other African Americans faced—results of a structure of white supremacy different from what Aida Moore and her family experienced in Nigeria. If the story of Scipio Vaughan's country marks is fundamentally about connections, the genealogy of how it emerged also illustrates how far apart the branches of the family had grown between the mid-nineteenth and mid-twentieth centuries.

Every act of remembering is also an act of forgetting. The myth-like story of Church Vaughan as a Yoruba man lost and found makes genealogy, and presumed cultural authenticity along with it, a solution to problems of racism, oppression, and exclusion. But Church Vaughan's primary strategy for survival and success was not to make assertions about his heritage; it was to build wealth. He achieved his goals through hard work, acumen, and getting himself to the right place at the right time. In fact, although the country marks story gives Vaughan African roots, it was his unrootedness—his mobility—that brought about the prosperity and security he was able to bequeath to his descendants.

"Exit" and "voice," in the well-known formulation of economist Albert O. Hirschman, comprise two options for those ill served by their institutions or communities. Depending on their degree of loyalty to the system, the dissatisfied can try to leave, or they may exert pressure for reform.[44] Church Vaughan's mobility was an attempt to find a safe haven in a perilous world. His exit from the United States and his exercise of his "voice" in Nigeria tell us something about his different levels of attachment in each place. More broadly, though, they also point to the different opportunities for black people on two sides of the Atlantic in the mid-nineteenth century. Though it might seem surprising to Americans today, Vaughan's brightest future turned out to be in Africa. In spite of the attraction of a story about shared ancestry and, implicitly, culture, it is important to remember just how much political and economic structures—and their differences over time and space—mattered.

This was the viewpoint of the family member whose life journey most closely resembled Vaughan's. Bill Sutherland was a child when Aida Moore visited his home in Glen Ridge, New Jersey, in 1925. His remarkable adult life was deeply connected to Africa, beginning with opposition to South African *apartheid* in the early 1950s, continuing as an advisor to the leaders of newly independent Ghana later in the decade, and through forty years' subsequent residence in Tanzania.[45] Sutherland moved to Africa exactly a century after his great-grandmother's brother Church Vaughan did, prompted by similar pessimism about prospects in the United States. "I thought that America, in the height of the McCarthy period—I didn't foresee Martin Luther King, I didn't foresee the women's movement or all these other—I thought things were going to just go down, down, down in America," he recounted in 2003. Asked if it was his family connections that turned his attention to Africa, Sutherland replied, "I knew that we would see our African cousins every now and then, and one of them gave me a palm fan and all. But that wasn't what made me go to Africa." Instead, while in Paris and London speaking against the Korean War — a pacifist, Sutherland had been imprisoned for refusing induction during World War II — he met "African students who were so gungho about African liberation and the freedom of their countries." As a result of these encounters, Sutherland "decided that I wanted to put my lot in with the African liberation movement."[46] Beginning in Ghana, Sutherland served as a bridge between African American activists and Africans working to build their new nations in the aftermath of colonialism. It was he, for instance, who assembled the list of African American invitees, including Dr. Martin Luther King Jr., to Ghana's independence ceremony in 1957. Like Church Vaughan had done when he led the rebellion against Baptist missionaries in Lagos, Sutherland saw American racism and colonialism as shared features of a transcontinental system of inequality and oppression.

The Vaughan family saga illuminates aspects of that system in the nineteenth century, revealing an Atlantic world in which slavery, under that or a different name, was robust and freedom was fragile. We know about Church Vaughan's life because he was able to survive, prosper, and found a family. His achievements, however, should not obscure the painful, frustrating, and often dead-end struggles of his contemporaries, both in the United States and in Africa. By the accident of his birth and the vigilance of his parents, Vaughan entered a world of slavery in South Carolina without the yoke of bondage upon him. Still, racial oppression pushed him to leave his home and family for Liberia. By good fortune, he did not die there of malaria or yellow fever or poverty, but instead was able to make a living with his carpentry skills. These, along with sheer coincidence, brought him into contact with the missionaries who took him to Yorubaland. There, his talents and hard work began to pay off, but it was largely good luck and advantageous connections that kept him alive and out of a slave pen when he was captured by warring forces. Years later Vaughan arrived in Lagos at probably the most propitious historical moment, when refugees from the world of slavery were remaking the town as a place of commerce and sociability. Though he encountered racism — enough finally to incite his overt protest — he was able to create a family and the wealth that would undergird it for the next century. But the verse from the Book of Job on Vaughan's grave marker tells us that his rewards came only after persistent struggle and hardship. Satisfying as the story of James Churchwill Vaughan's alleged return to his origins may be, we should not let the romance of cultural nationalism obscure the hard road that he trod.

Church Vaughan's "return" to Africa was rare, but it also points to a wider phenomenon. Slavery and various forms of unfreedom were far more common for Africans and their diasporic descendants than were security and self-determination. Yet during his lifetime, some mobile refugees from the African diaspora successfully navigated the narrow opportunities open to them in the Atlantic world. In part this was because reformers of one kind or another had defined *slavery* as a particular evil and created places of refuge or opportunities for trade and education for some of its victims.[47] These were not available to the many Africans and people of African descent whose oppression was not defined strictly as *slavery*—the "apprentices" of Liberia, unwilling wives or "servants" in Lagos and elsewhere, and even sharecroppers of the postbellum American South. But Church Vaughan and his diasporic contemporaries also possessed an especially wide view of the world, which allowed them to compare their prospects across different locations and apply skills and insights acquired in one place to their endeavors in another. It should come as little surprise, then, that in some parts of West Africa, "repatriates" from Sierra Leone, Brazil, and even Camden, South Carolina were innovators and agitators in business, religion, and politics.

It is striking, in fact, how many Vaughan descendants on both sides of the Atlantic have been prominent activists and public servants. In 1935, Dr. James C. Omosanya Vaughan, a physician trained in Scotland, became the first president of the Nigerian Youth Movement, a nationalist political party whose program included universal suffrage, increased self-government, an end to racial discrimination, and mass education. His cousin Kofo Moore Ademola advocated girls' education, famously arguing that "brains have no gender." In the United States, Bill Sutherland's sister Muriel and her husband Otto Snowden founded Freedom House Community Center in the heart of Boston's African American community in 1949; decades later the MacArthur Foundation awarded her a "genius" grant. Aida Stradford's daughter Jewel Lafontant, an attorney and lifelong Republican like her father and grandfather, was appointed deputy solicitor general of the United States by President Nixon in 1973, later serving as U.S. ambassador-at-large. Mabel Smythe also served as U.S. ambassador, to Cameroon, beginning in 1977. Jewel Lafontant's son John Rogers Jr., founder and CEO of the largest minority-owned mutual fund firm in the United States, was part of the inner circle of President Obama's 2008 campaign.[48] Their motivations and strategies may well have been shaped by the Vaughan family's diasporic consciousness and networks.

As the popular Nigerian slogan says, however, "no condition is permanent." Though Church Vaughan found his refuge in West Africa, and Lagos still seemed to promise more for black people than did American cities in the 1920s, by the late twentieth century the relationship had reversed. A century of colonialism not only created "Nigeria," but turned it into a country fractured by politicized ethnicity, dependent on a single export (oil), and governed through patronage. These trends have only been exacerbated in recent decades by self-serving political leaders sustained through their connections to international companies. While African Americans achieved unprecedented (if still limited) economic mobility and political inclusion, ordinary Nigerians have found their prospects for success increasingly circumscribed since the heady days of early nationhood in the 1960s. Economic restructuring programs foisted on Nigeria by global lenders in the mid-1980s brought sharp declines in living standards for all but the wealthiest, followed a decade later by the military dictator Sani Abacha's all-out assault on the Nigerian middle class, from which it has only recently recovered. The strength of the local currency, the *naira*, against the U.S. dollar gives a sense of Nigeria's economic fortunes as a whole, as well as the ability of Nigerians to purchase imports or, for some, travel abroad: from parity with the U.S. dollar in the 1970s, the naira fell to ten to one in the early 1990s and to more than two hundred to one in 2016.

Buoyed by their inherited resources, Church Vaughan's descendants in Nigeria have largely weathered these storms. Most are neither government officials nor large-scale businesspeople, and so their fortunes have not risen with Nigeria's tiny, oil-soaked elite. But Vaughan's grandchildren and great-grandchildren continued to invest in property and education, and if the family members are no longer among Nigeria's wealthiest, they remain comfortably well-off. Ayo Vaughan-Richards and Kofo Ademola were able to visit the United States through the 1980s, for instance, though they faced new difficulties in doing so.[49] Their own children and grandchildren still maintain bonds to Nigeria, even if many of them now base themselves at least partially abroad.

Over the past two decades, other Nigerians have left their country for the United States, Europe, the Middle East, or South Africa in droves. Their streams are part of a huge global wave, as millions of people around the world undertake migration and arduous labor to deal with oppression, violence, and lack of opportunity. As Church Vaughan's life has shown, an outlook that transcends national borders and fixed identities can be a resource in a harsh, unfair world. Some assiduous and savvy migrants have been fortunate, as he was, in navigating the currents of racism and global inequality. Most, however, face their own rocky shoals.

Seen historically, there is something poignantly ironic in contemporary African migration to the United States. The same forces that drove Vaughan out of his homeland, namely slavery and racial oppression, fueled the nineteenth-century economic expansion that helped create America's current prosperity. That is to say, slavery built up the United States just before colonialism—itself a successor to international slaving—began to underdevelop Africa.[50] Just because these days many thousands of Nigerians seek entry into the United States, we should not read history backward and assume that America always offered hope to the downtrodden. Today (some) African Americans may have found their civic voice, but the Vaughan family saga reminds us of a time when many determined their best chance to be exit, and their best destination was Africa.

Such an exit is reflected in the story in which Church Vaughan recognized his father's country marks in Africa. At first glance, the family legend seems to offer hope that the devastating cultural and familial ruptures caused by the Atlantic slave trade could in some way be mended. The fact that the tale was invented dashes those hopes, bringing home yet again the magnitude of the slave trade's human tragedy. What the story does instead, though, is bring family together after a different, more individual rupture: Church Vaughan's own departure from the United States. Rather than reflect his search for kinsmen in Africa, the tale of the country marks helped sustain the bond between his African descendants and their African American cousins. *He migrated to Africa in the year 1853, leaving behind a large family, owing to the oppressive laws then in force against colored men in the Southern States.* Vaughan's story, the real one cryptically described on his tombstone as well as the myth, reminds us how much the African diaspora was conceived and experienced through family relations. Though slavery separated his ancestors from kin and community in Africa, Church Vaughan was enmeshed in family in South Carolina, and he created new ties in Nigeria. The Vaughan family's Atlantic bonds emerged not only from the painful history of the slave trade, but also from the way some diasporic migrants took risks on unlikely journeys—and sometimes even succeeded.

ACKNOWLEDGMENTS

Writing a book about journeys and connections caused me to make many of my own. I began working on it as a fellow of the National Humanities Center, to whose donors and staff I give my earnest thanks and offer this belated evidence that I did in fact get something accomplished. Over successive years, I benefited from the American Council of Learned Societies' Ryskamp Fellowship, the University of North Carolina's Spray-Randleigh Fellowship, UNC's Institute for the Arts and Humanities, the National Endowment for the Humanities, and the John Simon Guggenheim Foundation. These fellowships, along with grants from UNC's African Studies Center, Center for Global Initiatives, and College of Arts and Sciences, enabled research in four countries as well as periods of intensive writing, without which this book would not exist.

I began research in South Carolina as a trained Africanist—which is to say, I didn't know much. Laura Edwards has my sincere thanks for pointing me toward essential readings and important archives, and for brainstorming with me about the world of Scipio Vaughan. Theda Purdue gave insight on South Carolina's Catawbas. Thanks to Carol McNaughton, Sarah Murray, and other helpful staff at the Camden Archives and Museum; Billie McLeod at the Kershaw County Registry of Deeds; the professionals at the South Carolina State Archives and the University of South Carolina Library; Eric Plaag for research assistance; and especially Elsie Taylor-Goins, whose impressive genealogical research transformed my project, whether she knew it or not.

Before I even contemplated going to Liberia, I was introduced to its history by Verlon Stone and Sarah Keil of Indiana University's Liberia collection. Claude Clegg shared his wisdom about the American colonization project there; I hope he won't mind that I picked up and expanded his story of Marshall Hooper (and I'm so pleased that now he's my UNC colleague). Brandi Hughes gave extensive advice on doing research in Liberia, not least that I should contact Professor Bill Allen. To him I owe great thanks for going out of his way to introduce me to his country and help me trace Vaughan's path to Millsburg.

Church Vaughan's early days in Yorubaland first came alive for me in the archives of the Southern Baptist Convention, both at the International Mission Board (IMB) headquarters in Nashville, Tennessee, and especially in the archives of the IMB in Richmond, Virginia. My heartfelt gratitude goes to Edie Jeater, Jim Berwick, Scott Peterson, Kyndal Owens, and the rest of the talented staff there, as well as to Bill Sumners and Taffey Hall in Nashville. More scholars should use those terrific archives! At the Nigerian Baptist Theological Seminary's library in Ogbomoso, Nigeria, I thank Elizabeth Adetutu for her help with my research and her tolerance when I was reluctant to attend mandatory chapel services. I remain appreciative of the work of the staff at the Ibadan branch of the Nigerian National Archives and the special collections of the University of Ibadan Library, including Mrs. V. O. Aribusola and the capable Mr. Mike. Ẹṣẹ́ púpọ̀ to my academic hosts and friends in Ibadan and Lagos, beginning with LaRay Denzer and the late Folayegbe M. Akintunde-Ighodalo, who first put me on the trail of the Nigerian Vaughans, and including the late Professor and Mrs. Jacob Ade Ajayi, Professor Ayodeji Olukoju, and Dr. Funke Adeboye. Dr. Duro Adeleke painstakingly translated and interpreted the Vaughan family oriki. Professor Olutayo Adesina deserves special thanks for his repeated hospitality, academic inspiration, good company, and willingness to explore Ijaye on a hazy harmattan day. Chris Bankole's warmth and good humor make her house a special oasis in Ibadan; big, grateful hugs to her, and kind regards to Aunty Gladys as well.

The Vaughans of Lagos and their diaspora, after some initial worry about a foreigner writing "their" story, have graciously shared memories, materials, and hospitality. Deacon Olabode Vaughan, the family's senior member, took an interest in this project from the beginning and showed me his own well-archived files. I'm especially grateful for the family reunion that he and his lovely wife, Yinka Edwards, hosted on my behalf in 2011, and which included, among others, Dr. Femi Vaughan, Taiwo Vaughan, Idowu Vaughan, Dorcas Vaughan, Gboyega and Christine Ademola, and Olabopo Odiachi. Rotimi Vaughan is the source of many of the family portraits in this book, including the portrait of Church Vaughan; I'm grateful not only for access to those but for his hospitality and collaboration over many years. Kunle Ademola was an early and consistent source of support, and I also thank him for kindly sharing the photographs of his mother. Remi Vaughan-Richards valiantly carries on the legacy of her formidable parents, Ayo and Alan Vaughan-Richards, who conducted their own research into the Vaughan story in the 1980s. She is not only a creative whirlwind herself but great fun to boot. Along with Remi, her cousin Funke Adeniji helped to make my most recent stay in Lagos very enjoyable. I shared a previous trip, in 2011, with another of their cousins, Funmi Pearce. I'm deeply saddened that Funmi did not live to see the publication of this book. From our first meeting in London in 2007, Funmi was an excellent sounding board and sometime research partner, traveling with me more than once and locating Lagos land records even after I had returned to the United States. Quirky, energetic, and committed to sharing her family's story, she is gone far too soon.

Over the years many people have offered comments, suggestions, and specific help on parts or all of this project. In particular, I thank my fellow campers at the National Humanities Center, especially Cara Robertson, Deborah Harkness, Pete Sigal, Robin Moore, Piotr Sommer, Ed Curtis, and Tim Tyson; "classmates" at UNC's Institute for Arts and Humanities, especially our inspirational leader Laurie Maffley-Kipp; and my African history writing group and dear friends, Lynn Thomas, Stephan Miescher, and Laura Fair. Kristin Mann generously shared her wisdom and materials on Lagos history before offering brilliant comments on the entire manuscript. I thank Bronwen Everill, Betsy Schmidt, and Mary Rolinson for sharing materials, the late John Peel for his wise counsel, and Sylvia Hoffert for discussing with me the Malletts of North Carolina. Josiah Olubowale patiently assisted with Yoruba translations, and Olubukola Gbadegesin helped me interpret Church Vaughan's portrait. Seminar participants and lecture audiences at the University of North Carolina, Louisiana State University, University of Wisconsin, University of Florida, University of York (U.K.), King's College London, North Carolina Central University, Guilford College, Emory University, East Carolina University, Virginia Tech, Michigan State, University of Ibadan, and University of Lagos have improved this project from earlier versions. I also thank Luise White, Pamela Scully, Clifton Crais, James T. Campbell, Frederick Cooper, Joseph Miller, Steven Pierce, Vince Brown, and Caryl Phillips for their encouragement and ideas. Sharla Fett, Laura Premack, and Randy Browne read and commented on early chapter versions. Laura and Wendell Lindsay heroically read a draft of the whole manuscript. My UNC colleagues

Sarah Shields, Kathryn Burns, and others have listened to me talk about this project for far too long. Cecelia Cancellaro and Chuck Grench stepped in to bring the book across the finish line.

If a book is a bit like its author's child, then John Wood Sweet is this one's uncle and godfather. Brilliant historian, talented writer, unofficial editor, travel buddy, and beloved friend, John brainstormed ideas, puzzled over mysteries, considered strategies, and read multiple drafts of every piece of every chapter. Anything good in this book has his traces on it; the flaws are probably where I disregarded his advice. I can't thank him enough for his generosity, insight, and patience. And I look forward to the birth of his own new historical baby.

A couple of years ago, when I was well into this project, my son Julian suggested that I should write a book. I took it as a healthy sign that he was so unaware of my labors. So instead of acknowledging my family for making sacrifices so that I could get this project done, I thank them for other things: Dianne Lindsay, for being my greatest cheerleader; Wendell and Laura Lindsay for their consistent support and interest; Amelia, Julian, and Ellie for their creativity and humor, and for reminding me of what's important. And most of all, I thank Matt Andrews for his warmth, wisdom, and wit, and for sharing my intellectual life and everything else. This book is dedicated to him, with love.

NOTES

Abbreviations

AR	*African Repository*
BNA	British National Archives
BP	Bowen Papers, Cecil Roberson Collection
CAM	Camden Archives and Museum
CMS	Church Missionary Society Papers
CG	*Camden Gazette*
CJ	*Camden Journal*
FMJ	*Foreign Mission Journal*
HFJ	*Home and Foreign Journal*
IMB	International Mission Board, Southern Baptist Convention
LH	*Liberia Herald*
LS	*Lagos Standard*
LWR	*Lagos Weekly Record*
NYCJ	*New York Colonization Journal*
NYT	*New York Times*
RACS	Records of the American Colonization Society
RC	Roberson Collection
SCDAH	South Carolina Department of Archives and History
SCL	South Caroliniana Library

Introduction

1. LaRay Denzer, "Emancipation and the Modern Woman in Lagos (Nigeria)," prepared for a conference on "Youth Policy and the Policies of Youth in Africa," Program of African Studies, Northwestern University, May 10–11, 2002, quotation on p. 11. The reference was to the grandparents of Kofo Ademola, a mid-twentieth-century advocate for women's education and the wife of Nigeria's first chief justice. Mrs. Ademola was the late sister of the woman I was visiting that day in 2002, Lande Ejiwunmi.

2. Interviews with Mrs. Lande Ejiwunmi, June 15, 2002, Ibadan; Mrs. Ayoka

Thompson, June 19, 2002, Ibadan; Mrs. Apinke Coker, June, 22, 2002, Lagos. I'm grateful to LaRay Denzer and the late Mrs. Folayegbe Akintunde-Ighodalo for their help in arranging these.

3. Thompson, "The Vaughan Family."

4. It should be emphasized that this was the story as told in the *Ebony* article. Current scholarship reveals that some returned Africans and their descendants did, in fact, reconnect with their relatives and country people in Africa—though these returnees came from Brazil and Cuba rather than the United States. In some cases, they were able to find their people in Africa on the basis of information they had received in the Americas. See Mann, "The Illegal Slave Trade" and Castillo, "Mapping."

5. Johnson, *History of the Yorubas*, 104–9.

6. Duval, *Baptist Missions*, 26.

7. Gomez, *Exchanging Our Country Marks.*

8. Scipio Vaughan's daughter Sarah (J. C. Vaughan's sister) reported her father's birthplace as Virginia in the *1880 United States Federal Census*, entry for S. A. Thomas in Camden, South Carolina (accessed through ancestry.com).

9. For an overview, see Lindsay and Sweet, *Biography and the Black Atlantic*. Recent and impressive examples include Crais and Scully, *Sara Baartman*; Pybus, *Epic Journeys*; Scott and Hébrard, *Freedom Papers*; Sensbach, *Rebecca's Revival*; and Sweet, *Domingos Álvarez*.

10. The field of Atlantic history has blossomed over the last decade. For overviews and critiques, see Bailyn, *Atlantic History*; Games, "Atlantic History"; Coclanis, "Atlantic World"; Canizares-Esguerra and Seeman, *Atlantic in Global History*; Benjamin, *Atlantic World*; Morgan and Greene, *Atlantic History*; Bailyn and Denault, *Soundings in Atlantic History*; and Miller, *Princeton Companion to Atlantic History*.

11. Curtin, *Rise and Fall*; Rodney, *How Europe Underdeveloped Africa*; Gilroy, *The Black Atlantic*.

12. Lovejoy, *Transformations in Slavery*.

13. Lindsay, "Boundaries of Slavery."

14. Miller, *The Problem of Slavery as History*; Lovejoy, *Transformations in Slavery*. For the same point illustrated in the United States, see Berlin, *Many Thousands Gone*.

15. Cooper, Holt, and Scott, *Beyond Slavery*.

16. Mann, *Slavery and the Birth of an African City*. More broadly, see Miers and Roberts, *The End of Slavery in Africa*.

17. Vaughan is buried in Ikoyi cemetery in central Lagos. The grave marker and its inscription are described further in chapter 7.

18. Berlin, *Generations of Captivity*; Hahn, *A Nation under Our Feet*; Painter, *Exodusters*; Wilkerson, *The Warmth of Other Suns*.

19. Campbell, *Middle Passages*; Hartman, *Lose Your Mother*; Phillips, *The Atlantic Sound*.

20. Ayo Vaughan-Richards, "The Vaughan Saga," annotated "Lagos–September 1986," in Jewel Lafontant-Mankarious papers, 30/310 IV ss.2. Box 2.

21. On the unevenness of diaspora, see Edwards, *The Practice of Diaspora* as well as Patterson and Kelley, "Unfinished Migrations."

22. Mann and Bay, *Rethinking the African Diaspora*; Matory, "The English Professors of Brazil" and *Black Atlantic Religion*. Pier Larson argues that the African diaspora must also be considered *within* Africa, as a product of dislocations associated with slaving within the continent. Larson, "Horrid Journeying." A similar point is in Palmer, "Defining and Studying the Modern African Diaspora."

23. Ajayi and Smith, *Yoruba Warfare*; Kopytoff, *A Preface to Modern Nigeria*; Lindsay, "'To Return to the Bosom of their Fatherland'"; Law, "Yoruba Liberated Slaves Who Returned to West Africa"; Castillo, "Mapping."

24. Shick, *Behold the Promised Land*; Clegg, *The Price of Liberty*; Tyler-McGraw, *An African Republic*.

25. Sweet makes a similar point in *Domingos Álvares*, 6.

26. "Diasporic consciousness," albeit in a rather rigid form, is explained in Safran, "Diasporas in Modern Societies."

27. Scott and Hébrard, *Freedom Papers*, 4.

28. The historical tradition of seeing Africa as "primitive" or even outside of history is a long one and includes Georg Hegel, Karl Marx, and Sigmund Freud. For overviews, see Curtin, *The Image of Africa*; Gates, *"Race," Writing, and Difference*; Mudimbe, *The Invention of Africa*; and more recently, Thomas, "Modernity's Failings."

29. Holt, "Slavery and Freedom in the Atlantic World"; Safran, "Diasporas in Modern Societies." Even Gilroy, in spite of his insistence on the modernity of the black Atlantic, barely addresses Africa in real, contemporary time. Piot, "Atlantic Aporias."

30. The critique, however, does not apply to recent works on African practices and beliefs in the Americas such as those by Sweet in *Recreating Africa* or *Domingos Álvares*; Brown, *The Reaper's Garden*; or Barcia Paz, *West African Warfare in Bahia and Cuba*.

31. Cooper, "Modernizing Bureaucrats, Backward Africans, and the Development Concept."

Chapter 1

1. South Carolina Budget and Control Board, Community Profiles, Camden Profile, http://www.sccommunityprofiles.org/place.php?PLACEID=40 (September 4, 2012).

2. Family Bible recorded by Maria Sophronia Lauly, December 5, 1869, in possession of Elsie Taylor-Goins.

3. Vaughan's name appears as Wylie, Wilie, and Willy in historical records. For his brief biography, see Kirkland and Kennedy, *Historic Camden*, vol. 1, 365. Some 250,000 white Virginians left the state between 1790 and 1820. Kulikoff, *Tobacco and Slaves*, 77.

4. Inabinet and Inabinet, *History of Kershaw County*, 23 and 35.

5. Berlin, *Generations of Captivity*, 130.

6. Ernst and Merrens, "'Camden's Turrets Pierce the Skies!'"; Edwards, *The People and Their Peace*, 22. According to the 1800 U.S. Census, Kershaw District contained 4,706 (free) white people; 2,530 slaves; and 104 free people of color. University of Virginia, Geospatial and Statistical Data Center, Historical Census Browser (2004), http://mapserver.lib.virginia.edu/collections/ (September 7, 2012).

7. "Excerpts from Robert Gilmor's Journal, 1806–1807," in *Five Visitors to Kershaw District, 1806–1832*, Harvey S. Teal; also available as Robert Gilmor, "Notes taken in a

tour through the states of Virginia, North Carolina, and South Carolina in the year 1806," South Caroliniana Library Manuscripts Collections, http://library.sc.edu/socar/uscs /1998/gilmor98.html (September 18, 2012).

8. Kirkland and Kennedy, *Historic Camden*, vol. 1, 362–65; Inabinet and Inabinet, *History of Kershaw County*, 105–6; Rawlins, *An American Journal*, 10–14.

9. State Land Grants, South Carolina Department of Archives and History, series number S213192, volume 0041, http://www.archivesindex.sc.gov/ (May 23, 2003).

10. Merrell, *The Indians' New World*, especially 135–37 (for the crises of the mid-eighteenth century), 195 (for 1759 smallpox deaths), 197–200 (for 1760 treaty), and 210 (for renting reservation land); Kirkland and Kennedy, *Historic Camden*, vol. 1, 48; Inabinet and Inabinet, *History of Kershaw County*, 40–47; Perdue and Green, *Columbia Guide*, 133–34 and 174.

11. Merrell, *Indians' New World*, 181; Gilmor, "Notes taken in a tour through the states of Virginia, North Carolina, and South Carolina in the year 1806."

12. Kulikoff, *Tobacco and Slaves*, especially chapter 2 and afterword.

13. McMillin, *The Final Victims*, 52, for colonial slave imports to South Carolina; other estimates are from "Voyages: The Transatlantic Slave Trade Database," www.slave voyages.org (September 4, 2012).

14. McMillin, *Final Victims*, 110–12; Gilmor, "Notes."

15. Berlin, *Generations*, 133. Wylie Vaughan placed a runaway ad for Tom, a 25-year-old "African born," in the *Camden Gazette* of July 7, 1817 (vol. 2, issue 65, 3).

16. Berlin, *Generations*, 113, 131; Kulikoff, *Tobacco and Slaves*, 77, 429–30; Johnson, *Soul by Soul*.

17. "Ten Dollars Reward," *CJ* (August 20, 1831): 3.

18. Ball, *Fifty Years in Chains*.

19. Claiborne & Wiley Vaughan by Brashergen@aol.com, March 25, 2001, http://www .rootsweb.ancestry.com/ (March 26, 2011).

20. For the dry goods store and the newspaper, see Kirkland and Kennedy, *Historic Camden*, vol. 2, 23. Wylie Vaughan apparently hired an editor to run the paper. Fisher Moses is listed in the November 26, 1818 issue; John Cambridge seems to have taken over as of June 1819. For the congressional bid, see *Camden Gazette*, vol. 1, no. 27 (October 3, 1816): 3. Vaughan's property is listed in Wilie Vaughan estate papers, Kershaw County Courthouse, probate office, apartment 70, package 2506, 3 (April 15, 1819). For slaveholding, see the 1810 census, Kershaw District, in which 63.9 percent of household heads owned slaves, and the average number of slaves per owner was 13.3. The largest slaveholder was John Chesnut, with 234 slaves; Richard L. Champion, Wylie Vaughan's brother-in-law, claimed thirty-five slaves.

21. Wilie Vaughan, "Land Transfer Agreement, with release of dower from Sarah Vaughan on reverse, 1812. Bonds Conway Papers, SCL. I'm grateful to Eric Plaag for copying and helping to interpret this record.

22. Kershaw County census compilation, 1810, ii; Edwards, *People and Their Peace*; Inabinet and Inabinet, *History of Kershaw County*, 622 fn 5. I thank Laura Edwards for sharing information with me about Conway and his context.

23. University of Virginia Library, Historical Census Browser (September 21, 2012).

24. Berlin, *Generations*, 136–40; Berlin, *Slaves without Masters*; Wikramanayake, *A World in Shadow*; Johnson and Roark, *Black Masters*.

25. Willy Vaughan is listed as paymaster of McWylie's 2nd Regiment S.C. Militia, serving with fellow Camden businessman Captain Chapman Levy. Index to Compiled Service Records of Volunteer Soldiers Who Served during the War of 1812 in Organizations From the State of South Carolina, Microfilm ID M652, Record Group 94, National Archives and Records Administration, http://freepages.military.rootsweb .ancestry.com/~york/1812/McWylies.html (August 15, 2012). However, in *Historic Camden*, Wilie Vaughan is listed as a member of Captain Francis Blair's company, a unit not listed in the NARA record. Kirkland and Kennedy, vol. 2, 63. Thanks to Glen Inabinet for his help with these records.

26. Wilie Vaughan's will signed June 23, 1814, and recorded November 12, 1820, CAM, Wills vol. 2, sect. I, 10.

27. 1810 federal census.

28. Ada Arabella Stradford, "Memoirs of the Vaughan Family," n.d. [late 1960s] in Lafontant-Mankarious Papers. This story is repeated in Thompson, "The Vaughan Family."

29. Kirkland and Kennedy, *Historic Camden*, vol. 1, 55–60.

30. I'm grateful to Theda Purdue for first suggesting to me that Maria Conway was Catawba rather than Cherokee.

31. Family Bible recorded by Maria Sophronia Lauly, December 5, 1869, in possession of Elsie Taylor-Goins. The exact entry about Nancy Carter is difficult to make out. It seems to say, "Nancy Carter was born 1770 May the 11 [two unclear words] Dst Bettys Neck." For the plantation called Bettie's Neck, see Inabinet and Inabinet, *A History of Kershaw County*, 105.

32. Merrell, *Indians' New World*, 181–82, 211.

33. Kirkland and Kennedy, *Historic Camden*, vol. 1, 359–60.

34. Merrell, *Indians' New World*, 126.

35. Merrell, "Racial Education."

36. Conway's third wife was named Dorcas (1785–1826), and together they produced nine children, all born free. In 1814, a trial witness named Noel Vaughan attested that Dorcas Conway's grandmother was Mary Hathcock, a woman from "an Indian family of people." Recorded in Kershaw County Deeds, vol. 1, 162 (February 9, 1820).

37. Merrell, "Racial Education."

38. Churchill or Churchwel Carter appears in the census for Chester, South Carolina, in 1790, 1800, 1810, 1820, 1830, and 1840, and in 1850 in Kemper, Mississippi, as a sixty-year-old born in South Carolina (which suggests that the Churchill Carter in the 1790 census was his father). Burrell Carter appears in the 1810 and 1820 censuses in Sumter County, South Carolina, and in 1830 in Kershaw County. United States *Censuses*, accessed through ancestry.com (September 5, 2012).

39. *1830 United States Federal Census* (Kershaw County, South Carolina), accessed through ancestry.com.

40. Inabinet and Inabinet, *A History of Kershaw County*; Merrell, *Indians' New World*, 225 (quoted). The original Hagler weathervane is now on display in the Camden

Archives and Museum with a replica atop the Camden Opera House. Images of him continue to decorate public spaces in Camden.

41. Kershaw County Censuses and Historical Census Browser. The 1820 Kershaw County census listed 5,625 whites and 6,692 slaves, along with 112 free people of color.

42. Ball, *Fifty Years in Chains*, 47–49 and 88–89. On slaves' malnutrition, see Johnson, *River of Dark Dreams*, chapter 7.

43. General Thomas Brown to William Hawkins, July 14, 1812, quoted in Altoff, *Amongst My Best Men*, 117 and 130; Taylor, *The Internal Enemy*, 155–59.

44. Taylor, *Internal Enemy*.

45. Inabinet, "'The July Fourth Incident' of 1816"; Kirkland and Kennedy, *Historic Camden*, vol. 2, 61–62.

46. "Legislature of South Carolina: Governor's Message," *CG* (December 5, 1816): 1–2; Aptheker, "Maroon Communities."

47. "State v. Abraham," Kershaw County Magistrates and Freeholders Court, July 23, 1816, Trial Papers 1802–1861, box 1, file 21, SCDAH. John Fox is listed in the 1810 census as residing in Edgefield, South Carolina, and owning seventy slaves.

48. R. [Mrs. Wm] Blanding to Hannah Lewis, July 4, 1816, in William Blanding Papers, SCL.

49. Proceedings of the Town Council: Insurrection Contemplated by the Negroes, July 2, 1816, in Kershaw County Magistrates and Freeholders' Court trial papers, box 1, SCDAH.

50. R. Blanding to Hannah Lewis, July 4, 1816, in William Blanding Papers, SCL.

51. Francis A. Deliesseline, quoted in Holland, *A Refutation of the Calumnies Circulated against the Southern and Western States*, 75; and also in Gordon, *Sketches*, 42–44.

52. *CG* (July 11, 1816). A week later, the paper clarified that "those who were professors of religion did not belong exclusively to one church." Inabinet, "'The July Fourth Incident' of 1816"; Kirkland and Kennedy, *Historic Camden*, vol. 2, 188.

53. R. Blanding to Hannah Lewis, July 25, 1816, in William Blanding Papers, SCL.

54. Henry William DeSaussure to Timothy Ford, July 9, 1816, Timothy Ford Papers, South Carolina Historical Society.

55. Deliesseline quoted in Holland, *Refutation* and Gordon, *Sketches*.

56. Ball, *Fifty Years in Chains*, 46–47.

57. Trial Record of Slaves Charged with an Attempted Insurrection, July 3–17, 1816, Kershaw County Justices and Freeholders Court, SCL.

58. Schweninger et al., *Race, Slavery, and Free Blacks*, reel 9, nos. 0353 and 0356; Inabinet, "'The July Fourth Incident' of 1816." But Sip Chesnut is listed as living alone with a black woman about his own age in the 1840 Kershaw County census.

59. *Miscellaneous Kershaw County Papers*, cited in Inabinet, "'The July Fourth Incident' of 1816."

60. *The Statutes at Large of South Carolina*, VI, act no. 2129, 54 (1839); act no. 2132, 58; act no. 2173, 82–87; act no. 2193, 98, all cited in Inabinet, "'The July Fourth Incident' of 1816." For Vaughan and McWylie as managers of the arsenal, see *CG*, vol. 3, no. 131 (October 17, 1818): 1.

61. Schweninger et al., *Race, Slavery, and Free Blacks*, reel 9, no. 0591.

62. Kirkland and Kennedy, *Historic Camden*, vol. 2, 190.

63. Ibid., 187.

64. Edwards, *The People and Their Peace*, 114–16.

65. R. Blanding to Hannah Lewis, July 25, 1816, in William Blanding Papers, SCL.

66. Runaway ad in the *CG* (July 7, 1817): 3.

67. Wilie Vaughan, estate papers, Kershaw County Probate Office, apartment 70, package 2506.

68. Transfer dated April 12, 1819, Wilie Vaughan estate papers, apartment 70, package 2506, Kershaw County Probate Office; also registered April 15, 1819, with Kershaw County Deeds, vol. I, KR 4, "Wylie Vaughan," 57–61.

69. 1820 federal census; Kirkland and Kennedy, *Historic Camden*, vol. 2, 103.

70. Kershaw County Deeds, vol. 1, 428, March 23, 1821, SCDAH.

71. McCalls and Brown to estate of Wilie Vaughan, June 22, 1822, in Wilie Vaughan estate papers, apartment 70, package 2506, Kershaw County Probate Office.

72. Edgar, *South Carolina: A History*, 328–29. Vesey went to the gallows protesting his innocence, and historian Michael Johnson has argued that there was in fact no slave conspiracy at all. Johnson, "Denmark Vesey and His Co-Conspirators" and "Reading Evidence." For a rebuttal to Johnson's allegations, see Edgerton, "Forgetting Denmark Vesey."

73. University of Virginia, Geospatial and Statistical Data Center, Historical Census Browser (2004), http://mapserver.lib.virginia.edu/collections/ (September 7, 2012).

74. McCord, *The Statutes at Large of South Carolina*, 459–61; Wikramanayake, *World in Shadow*, 19–20, 58, 151; Johnson and Roark, *Black Masters*, 42–45; Rucker, *The River Flows On*, 177.

75. Petition of Free Negroes of Camden District, 1792, quoted in Wikramanayake, *World in Shadow*, 67.

76. Kirkland and Kennedy, *Historic Camden*, vol. 2, 192–93; Wikramanayake, *World in Shadow*, 62–63.

77. Wikramanayake, *World in Shadow*, 54–63; Johnson and Roark, *Black Masters*, 44–49.

78. John Workman, William B. Parker, Hugh McCall, John D. Winn (assessors), "Assessment of the intrinsic value of the occupied and unoccupied tenements in the town of Camden, March 9th, 1826 viz: —," *CJ* (March 29, 1826); 1832 tax list for the town of Camden, published in *The South Carolina Magazine of Ancestral Research* 8, 1 (1980): 27–28.

79. 1830 Kershaw County census, ancestry.com (September 6, 2012). If Sarah Vaughan still had the slaves listed by her husband in 1819, then no other male slave but Scipio would have fallen in the thirty-six to fifty-five age range.

80. *State v. John B. Mathews, John Blair, Scipio*, December 26, 1834, Court of General Sessions, Indictments, Kershaw District, SCDAH. I thank Laura Edwards for sharing her notes on this case with me. A search of the houses of the three accused turned up no evidence of the stolen cotton.

81. Johnson and Roark, *Black Masters*, especially p. 45.

82. "Sip Vaughan" entry, *1840 United States Federal Census*, through ancestry.com (September 6, 2012).

83. Wikramanayake, *World in Shadow*, 65; Berlin, *Slaves without Masters*.

84. Guardianship registered May 30, 1823, in Petitions for Guardianship of Free Persons of Color, 1816–1861, Kershaw County, Court of Common Pleas, SCDAH.

85. Wikramanayake, *World in Shadow*, 56–64, quotation on 56.

86. Edwards, *People and Their Peace*.

87. *State v. Jesse Harris* (1821) and *State v. James Roberts* (1826), Court of General Sessions, Indictments, Kershaw District, SCDAH. Thanks to Laura Edwards for sharing her notes on these cases with me.

88. Guardianships registered March 30, 1823, and March 23, 1832, in Petitions for Guardianship of Free Persons of Color, 1816–1861, Kershaw County, Court of Common Pleas, SCDAH. On John Boykin, see Kirkland and Kennedy, *Historic Camden*, vol. 1, 351.

89. Schweninger et al., *Race, Slavery, and Free Blacks*, petitions nos. 0584 and 0588, reel 10; "20 Dollars Reward," *CJ* (April 25, 1829): 1. On Mickle and phrenology, see Kirkland and Kennedy, *Historic Camden*, vol. 1, 391.

90. The land transaction is in "Conveyance: John M. DeSaussure to H. R. Cook in trust for Scipio Vaughan," March 26, 1838, Kershaw County Deeds, SCDAH, and also in the Kershaw County Register of Deeds, Camden, book O, 232, recorded May 28, 1838. In November 1837, John Vaughan authorized John DeSaussure to sell his land in Camden for him; town lot number 1224 was sold to Joseph Cunningham on August 2, 1838, with Henry R. Cook as one of the witnesses. Kershaw County Register of Deeds, book O, 255–56.

91. *1840 United States Federal Census*, through ancestry.com (September 6, 2012).

92. For restrictions on literacy and assembly, see Witt, *Patriots and Cosmopolitans*, chapter 2; Johnson and Roark, *Black Masters*, 50; and Hager, *Word by Word*. On church members, see Records of the First Baptist Church, Kershaw County, Camden, 1810–1838, Manuscript Collection, SCL. In 1851, Camden merchant J. K. Douglas reported to the American Colonization Society's secretary William McLain that Church Vaughan was not a member of any congregation. Douglas to McLain, July 24, 1851, reel 65, RACS.

93. Scipio Vaughan owned lots 1052, 1053, and 1054 on the corner of Market and Rutledge Streets. Bonds Conway's largest concentration of town property entailed fourteen plots on Market, York, King, and Lyttleton Streets (Kershaw County Deeds, vol. I, 195–197, SCDAH). Harriet Conway and Morreau Naudin's lots were numbered 1144, 1145, and 1146, on Church Street between Rutledge and York (Dibble Family vertical file, CAM). A 1925 map of Camden, based on one from 1906 and showing numbered plots, is in Kirkland and Kennedy, *Historic Camden*, vol. 1.

94. "In the shadow" comes from Wikramanayake, *World in Shadow*. Also see Berlin, *Slaves without Masters*. Information on the Vaughan siblings is compiled from Thompson, "The Vaughan Family," genealogical information from Elsie Taylor-Goins, and the 1840 census.

95. Thomson, "The Vaughan Family"; Mabel Murphy Smythe (Haith) interview with Ann Miller Morin, May 2, 1986, 10.

Chapter 2

1. "Local Matters," *Baltimore Sun* (November 10, 1852).

2. "List of Emigrants by the Barque Joseph Maxwell," *AR* 29 (January 1853): 23–26.

3. J. W. Lugenbeel to Rev. William McLain, November 2, 1852, and Lugenbeel to McLain, November 7, 1852, reel 68, RACS.

4. Lugenbeel to Colonel A. Reese, November 25, 1852, reel 194, RACS.

5. Staudenraus, *The African Colonization Movement*, chapter 3; Shick, *Behold the Promised Land*, chapter 1.

6. Pybus, *Epic Journeys of Freedom*; Schama, *Rough Crossings*.

7. Kramer, *Nationalism in Europe and America*; Anderson, *Imagined Communities*.

8. Jefferson, *Notes on the State of Virginia*, 147 and 154 quoted; also see Staudenraus, *African Colonization Movement*, chapter 1; Berlin, *Slaves without Masters*, 103–7; and Burin, *Slavery and the Peculiar Solution*, 10–11.

9. Miller, *The Search for a Black Nationality*, chapter 1.

10. Sidbury, *Becoming African in America*, chapter 5.

11. Miller, *Search*, chapter 3; Campbell, *Middle Passages*, 30–39; Sidbury, *Becoming African*, chapters 5–6; Harris, *Paul Cuffe*; Thomas, *Rise to Be a People*.

12. Quoted in Campbell, *Middle Passages*, 44.

13. "A Voice from Philadelphia," January 1817, in Garrison, *Thoughts on African Colonization*, part 2, 9. For African American opposition to the American Colonization Society in general, see Power-Greene, *Against Wind and Tide*.

14. Sidbury, *Becoming African*, chapter 7.

15. Kopytoff, *A Preface to Modern Nigeria*, 25 for the first statistic; for the second, *Voyages: The Transatlantic Slave Trade Database* http://slavevoyages.org/tast/database/search.faces?yearFrom=1808&yearTo=1866&mjslptimp=60200 (March 28, 2013).

16. Shick, *Behold*, 29; Miller, *Search*, 55–57.

17. Of the many descriptions of the founding of Liberia, the most engaging is chapter 1 of Campbell's *Middle Passages*. A classic account is Staudenraus, *African Colonization Movement*, chapter 6; also see Shick, *Behold*.

18. "Table of Emigrants," *AR* (May 1851): 149.

19. Burin, *Slavery*, 16–17.

20. Burin, *Slavery*, 17; Shick, *Behold*, 28; also see Clegg, *The Price of Liberty*.

21. Fanning, *Caribbean Crossing*; Dixon, *African America and Haiti*, chapter 1; Miller, *Search*, 74–82; Power-Greene, *Against Wind and Tide*, chapter 1; also see Clegg, *Price of Liberty*, 44–51.

22. Everill, "'Destiny Seems to Point Me to That Country'"; Campbell, *Middle Passages*, 60.

23. Staudenraus, *African Colonization Movement*, 179–84 and 232–33; Clegg, *Price of Liberty*, 129–35; Burin, *Slavery*, 19–20; Berlin, *Slaves without Masters*, 203–4. The figures are from Burin as well as the "Table of Emigrants" in the 1851 *African Repository*.

24. Clegg, *Price of Liberty*, 141; Staudenraus, *African Colonization Movement*, chapter 17; Burin, *Slavery*, 18.

25. Walker, *Walker's Appeal*, 62; see also Power-Greene, 48–50.

26. Zinn, *A People's History of the United States*, 175.

27. Burin, *Slavery*, 26; Miller, *Search*, 89–90; "A Voice from Baltimore," March 21, 1831, in Garrison, *Thoughts on African Colonization*, part 2, 21–22; Berlin, *Slaves without Masters*, 205–6.

28. American Colonization Society, *Eighteenth Annual Report* (1835): 15–17.

29. Garrison, *Thoughts on African Colonization*.

30. Thirty-four emigrants from South Carolina went to Liberia in May 1832; 146 left in December 1832; and two emigrated in November 1833. "Table of Emigrants," *AR* (May 1851): 149.

31. Berlin, *Slaves without Masters*, 195, 214–15; Wikramanayake, *A World in Shadow*, 166–68.

32. Death dates are from the family Bible. Information on yellow fever is from Humphreys, *Yellow Fever and the South*, 5–6.

33. Bonds Conway's will dated August 10, 1843, recorded in Will Book A, 49, February 14, 1843, apartment 17, package 556, CAM; Family Bible. On the Conways buried in the Cedar Cemetery for free African Americans, see Taylor-Goins and Taylor-McConnell, *Naudin-Dibble Family*, 7.

34. Perdue and Green, *Columbia Guide*, 133–34; Inabinet and Inabinet, *A History of Kershaw County*, 125; Merrell, *The Indians' New World*, 248–57, 254 quoted.

35. J. K. Douglas to W. McLain, July 24, 1851, reel 65, RACS.

36. Berlin, *Slaves without Masters*, 229; Wikramanayake, *World in Shadow*, 100–101.

37. Edwards, *The People and Their Peace*, 174–75. Jacob Hammond's age is surmised from his listing in the 1840 census as between the ages of twenty-four and thirty-five.

38. Lists of free people of color who registered guardians in Kershaw County between 1840 and 1865 are in "Kershaw County Miscellaneous Indexes: Index to Declarations of Intent to Become a Citizen, Citizenship Petitions, Guardianships of Free Persons of Color," and Kershaw Court of Common Pleas, "Petitions for Guardianship of Free Persons of Color, 1816–1861," SCDAH. Jacob Hammond is not listed, although all other male adults connected to the Vaughan family are. I'm grateful to Laura Edwards for helping me to place this case in its historical context.

39. Jacob Hammond Estate Papers, Kershaw County Probate Judge, apartment 30 package 1064, SCDAH. Joy is listed in the 1840 U.S. census as living with seven slaves, six other white family members, and forty-five students. His connections to the Kirkland and Blanding families (elite planters) are suggested by his children's names and the fact that he lived in their Kirkwood neighborhood. Information on Joy (1806–1858) is in the Joy Family vertical file, CAM. Doby's occupation is listed in the census and in the 1848 Kershaw County Tax Roll in Draine, *Kershaw District, South Carolina Tax List 1848 and 1849*. William Hammond had a living stepmother, Harriet Vaughan Hammond, but she was not considered legally to be his guardian.

40. The inconsistencies in the record are especially pronounced when the probate record, ibid., is compared to the conveyance record in the Kershaw County Register of Deeds, book R, 573–74, dated December 21, 1850.

41. Petition, William Hammond, through attorneys Loeitner and Dunlap, to James F. Sutherland, judge of the probate court, July 21, 1869. William P. Hammond Estate Papers, Kershaw County, Probate Judge, apartment 30, package 1070, SCDAH.

42. Family Bible in possession of Elsie Taylor-Goins.

43. Draine, *Kershaw District, South Carolina Tax List 1848 and 1849*, 11 and 25.

44. 1850 U.S. census; family Bible.

45. Kershaw County Miscellaneous Indexes: Index to Declarations of Intent to

Become a Citizen, Citizenship Petitions, Guardianships of Free Persons of Color, 1832–1865, SCDAH; 1850 U.S. census. Basken Coleman does not appear in the 1840 census or in the list of applicants for guardians. He may have been one of the nine slaves listed in the 1840 census in the household of J. B. Coleman, who lived in Fairfield, South Carolina. Burrell Vaughan does not appear at all in the 1850 U.S. census; in the 1860 census he is listed in nearby Clarendon County.

46. Merrell, *Indians' New World*, 253–54. Burrell Vaughan is not, however, listed in the rough Catawba census taken in 1849. *Correspondence relative to the Catawba Indians*.

47. In addition to the 1850 U.S. census, Sutherland is listed in an 1845 business directory reprinted in Kirkland and Kennedy, *Historic Camden*, vol. 2, 30. Sutherland's children with Maria Sophronia Vaughan are named in the family Bible, which she annotated herself.

48. Rawlins, *An American Journal*, 69–70; *CJ* (March 7, 1829, and May 7, 1831).

49. "25 Dollars Reward," *CJ* (May 14, 1831); "1832 Tax List for the Town of Camden"; Kirkland and Kennedy, *Historic Camden*, vol. 2, 139. There is no official record of John Vaughan emancipating his slaves; if he did, as his cousin Richard Rawlins claimed, it was an informal process. Rawlins, *American Journal*.

50. Kirkland and Kennedy, *Historic Camden*, vol. 2, 404.

51. Kershaw County's slave population increased from 6,692 in 1820 to 8,333 in 1830 and 9,578 by 1850. University of Virginia, Geospatial and Statistical Data Center, *Historical Census Browser*; Inabinet and Inabinet, *History of Kershaw County*, 146–47; Edgar, *South Carolina: A History*, 276–77, including the quote from the *Camden Journal*. On the "Second Middle Passage" more generally, see Berlin, *Generations of Captivity*, chapter 4; and Johnson, *Soul by Soul*.

52. Inabinet and Inabinet, *History of Kershaw County*, 146–47; Kershaw and Kennedy, *Historic Camden*, 103.

53. Tallant, *Evil Necessity*, 125–28; Rawlins, *American Journal*, 197; Lavery, "Reexamining the *Examiner*."

54. *Examiner*, June 19 and July 3, 1847.

55. *Examiner*, October 2, 1847, October 23, 1847, November 13, 1847, November 20, 1847; "Republic of Liberia," February 5, 1848; "The Young Republic," February 19, 1848.

56. Rawlins, *American Journal*, 197; Lavery, "Reexamining"; Harold D. Tallant, *Evil Necessity*, 124–29.

57. Kirkland and Kennedy, *Historic Camden*, vol. 1, 23; Rebecca Bonney to Lucy Carpenter, March 19, 1850, William Blanding Papers, SCL; *Lloyd's Steamboat Directory*, 207–9.

58. The site of the Episcopal cemetery was later taken over as a public space, with circuses held on the spot by about 1880. At that point, the bodies buried there were transferred to Camden's Quaker Cemetery, where they still lie. During the removal, Virginia Vaughan's remains were found to be petrified, her hair having grown almost to her feet. Kirkland and Kennedy, *Historic Camden*, 282.

59. Clegg, *Price of Liberty*, 171–72.

60. State v. Burwell Vaughan a colored free man, January 23, 1843, and State v. Peter Conway a free colored man, February 7, 1843, both in Kershaw County Court of Magistrates and Freeholders, Dockets, SCDAH.

61. Burin, *Slavery*, 28 and table 2; Berlin, *Slaves without Masters*, 355–57; Clegg, *Price of Liberty*, 174.

62. J. K. Douglas to William Blanding, February 3, 1849, William Blanding Papers, SCL.

63. Lugenbeel to Douglas, August 1, 1851, reel 192, RACS.

64. Lugenbeel, *Sketches of Liberia*, 1 and 42 quoted.

65. Lugenbeel, *Sketches*, 9–10.

66. J. K. Douglas to William McLain, January 30, 1852, reel 66B, RACS. On economic motivations for emigration in this period, see Everill, *Abolition and Empire*, 74.

67. J. K. Douglas to McLain, January 30, 1852, reel 66B, RACS; *1850 U.S. Federal Census—Slave Schedules*; Rachel Blanding to Lucy Carpenter, November 6, 1849, and R.A. Bonny to William Blanding, February 2, 1850, William Blanding Papers, SCL.

68. McLain to Douglass, February 4, 1852, reel 192, RACS. A blank application form for emigrants is in reel 314. For Church Vaughan's answers, see the table of Applicants for Emigration, reel 314 and the "List of Emigrants by the Barque Joseph Maxwell," *AR* 29 (January 1853): 26.

69. Douglas to McLain, January 30, 1852, reel 66B, RACS.

70. Family genealogist Elsie Taylor-Goins deposited a typed copy of this document with the Camden Archives, having obtained it in the 1980s from Josephine Dibble Murphy's papers at Atlanta University. This suggests that Vaughan's half-aunt Harriet Conway Naudin or her daughter Ellie Dibble kept a copy. Interview with Elsie Taylor-Goins, October 20, 2005. The document was also available to the granddaughter of Church Vaughan's youngest sister, Mary, who mentioned it in the brief family history she wrote in 1965. Aida Arabella Stradford, "Memoirs of the Vaughan Family," n.d. [1965], in Jewel Lafantant-Mankarious Papers. I have found neither Church Vaughan's original completed application nor this appendix in the RACS.

71. Family Bible, in possession of Elsie Taylor-Goins.

72. Douglas to McLain, March 16, 1852, reel 67, RACS; McLain to Douglas, March 22, 1852, reel 192, RACS.

73. "Information about Going to Liberia" n.d., reel 306, RACS.

74. Douglas to McLain, April 26, 1852, reel 67, RACS.

75. On the initial settlement, see Staudenraus, *African Colonization Movement*, 234–36; Clegg, *Price of Liberty*, 145; Burin, *Slavery*, 82–89. For the 1851–52 events, see J. J. Roberts, "Letter from President Roberts," *AR* 28, 5 (1852): 139 and Shick, *Behold*, 106–7.

76. Frederick Douglass speech, January 26, 1851, Rochester, New York, reprinted in *The Frederick Douglass Papers*, 2: 300; Delany, *The Condition, Elevation, Emigration and Destiny*, 169–70.

77. *Frederick Douglass Papers*, April 29, 1852, quoted in Miller, *Search*, 129.

78. D. M. Ussery to McLain, October 11, 1852, references Douglas, and also another local supporter named John Roper [Roger?], reel 68, RACS. For Ussery, see the 1850 federal census for Lancaster, South Carolina, listing him as a farmer with four children and one hired black servant.

79. McLain to Ussery, September 28, 1852, reel 193, RACS. The information was also reiterated to them by Rev. A. J. Witherspoon, also of Lancaster, South Carolina. McLain to Witherspoon, September 28, 1852, reel 193, RACS.

80. Lugenbeel to Peter Jacobs, August 3, 1852, reel 193; Ussery to McLain, August 9, 1852, reel 68; Lugenbeel to Ussery, September 23, 1852, reel 193; McLain to Rev. A. J. Witherspoon, September 28, 1852, reel 193; Ussery to McLain, October 11, 1852, reel 68; Lugenbeel to McLain, October 22, 1852, reel 68, RACS.

81. McLain to Ussery, September 28, 1852, and McLain to Ussery, October 14, 1852, reel 193, RACS.

82. Ussery to Lugenbeel, October 5, 1852, and Lugenbeel to McLain, October 22, 1852, reel 68, RACS; "Immigration," *CJ* (October 26, 1852).

83. Tombstone in Ikoyi Cemetery, Lagos, Nigeria. Vaughan arrived in Africa in 1853, although he left the United States in 1852.

84. Harriet Vaughan Hammond disappeared from historical records after the 1850 census. Though her birth is noted in the family Bible, her date of death is not.

85. Lugenbeel to McLain, November 2, 1852, reel 68, RACS.

86. J. W. Lugenbeel to William McLain, October 15, 1852, October 18, 1852, November 2, 1852, reel 68, RACS. Marshall Hooper's story is in Clegg, *Price of Liberty*, 176–79.

87. Hooper to McLain, November 14, 1849, and April 10, 1850, reel 154, RACS; Sion Harris to William McLain, May 20, 1849, in Wiley, *Slaves No More*, 227; J. Rambo to McLain, April 10, 1851, reprinted in the *AR* 27 (1851): 227–28. The Hoopers left the United States on the *Liberia Packet* in February 1849. Brown, *Immigrants to Liberia*, 33.

88. Marshall Hooper to Rev. William MacLaine [*sic*], July 26, 1852, and Hooper to McLain, August 1, 1852; Lugenbeel to McLain, October 12, 1852; all in reel 68, RACS. Information on the Hooper and Mallett families is with their personal papers in the Southern Historical Collection at UNC-Chapel Hill. Mallett Street and Hooper Lane are located near campus in downtown Chapel Hill. I thank Sylvia Hoffert for sharing with me her insights on this family.

89. McLain to Hooper, July 29, 1852, and August 5, 1852, reel 193; Hooper to McLean, August 1, 1852, reel 68, RACS. There is no mention in these 1852 documents of Hooper's house in Wilmington.

90. McLain to Hooper, August 5, 1852, reel 193; R. E. Troy to McLain, October 4, 1852, reel 68; Hooper to McLean, September 20, 1852, reel 68; Lugenbeel to Hooper, September 24, 1852, reel 193, RACS.

91. Lugenbeel to McLain, October 8, 1852, October 12, 1852, and October 14, 1852, reel 68, RACS.

92. Lugenbeel to McLain, October 12, 1852 and October 15, 1852, reel 68, RACS.

93. McLean to Lugenbeel, October 21, 1852, reel 193, RACS.

94. Lugenbeel to McLain, October 28, 1852, reel 68, RACS.

95. Lugenbeel to McLain, November 2, 1852 and November 7, 1852, reel 68, RACS.

96. Lugenbeel to McLain, November 7, 1852, reel 68, RACS.

97. Lugenbeel to McLain, November 2, 1852, November 7, 1852, and November 11, 1852, reel 68, RACS.

98. Hooper to McLain, October 15, 1855, reel 77 and November 10, 1855, reel 78, RACS.

99. Hooper to Lugenbeel, March 15, 1853, reel 155, RACS.

100. "Information about Going to Liberia," *AR* 28 (April 1852): 102–107.

101. James Hall, "Voyage to Liberia: Getting Under Way," *AR* 33, 9 (September 1857):

270–75. Features of the ship are from a diagram of the similar *Liberia Packet* in Everill, *Abolition and Empire*, 134.

102. James Hall, "Voyage to Liberia: The Emigrants. Every-day Life on Shipboard. The Voyage and the Ship," *AR* 33, 10 (October 1857): 296–303; J. W. Lugenbeel to Col. A. Reese, November 25, 1852, reel 194; H.W. Dennis to McLain, March 16, 1853, reel 156, RACS; "List of Emigrants by the Barque Joseph Maxwell," *AR* 29, 1 (January 1853): 23–26.

103. Hooper to Lugenbeel, March 15, 1853 and HW Dennis to Rev. W. McLain, January 25, 1853, reel 155, RACS.

104. Marshall H. Hooper to Lugenbeel, March 15, 1853, reel 155, RACS.

105. John Moore to [William McLain], June 14, 1853, RACS, quoted in Berlin, *Slaves without Masters*, 169.

Chapter 3

1. *Constitution of Liberia* (1847), available at http://www.onliberia.org/con_1847.htm (accessed June 11, 2015).

2. Observer, "Grand Demonstration — Roberts and Benson," reprinted from the *Liberia Herald* in the *AR* 29 (October 1853): 306–9.

3. Edward Blyden, "American Colonization," *NYCJ* (August 1851), also quoted in Holden, *Blyden of Liberia*, 29.

4. See Osborne, "A Note on the Liberian Archives."

5. McKay, *Report of Rev. John McKay*, 5.

6. Bowen, *Central Africa*, 29.

7. Ibid., 30.

8. Ibid., 32; Foote, *Africa and the American Flag*, 193; William Nesbit, "Four Months in Liberia, or, African Colonization Exposed," in Moses, ed., *Liberian Dreams*, 89 (quoted).

9. "Emigrants for Liberia," *Weekly Commercial* (Wilmington, NC), November 24, 1852.

10. Augustus Washington, "Liberia as It Is, 1854," in Moses, ed., *Liberian Dreams*, 207 quoted. For Dennis's biography, see Dunn et al., *Historical Dictionary of Liberia*, 106.

11. H. W. Dennis to Rev. W. McLain, September 28, 1853, reel 155, RACS. On Lewis, see Nesbit, "Four Months in Liberia," 98.

12. Shick, *Behold the Promised Land*, 74–5; Clegg, *The Price of Liberty*, 89–92 and 211; Cowan, *Liberia, as I Found It*, 86–90; J. Rambo (quoted) to Rev. Wm. McLain, April 10, 1851, reprinted in the *AR* 27 (1851): 227–28 . For more on African "half towns" surrounding settler farms, see Allen, "Liberia and the Atlantic World," 34 and 40.

13. Dr. Henry I. Roberts to Dr. Lugenbeel, April 15, 1853, reel 156, RACS; H. W. Dennis to McLain, April 21, 1853, reel 156, RACS; Washington, "Liberia as It Is, 1854," 206.

14. H. W. Dennis to Rev. W. McLain, March 16, 1853 and Ralph Moore to McLain, March 15, 1853, reel 156, RACS.

15. Hooper to Lugenbeel, March 15, 1853, reel 155, RACS.

16. J. S. Smith to Lugenbeel, April 13, 1853, reel 155, RACS; "Late Intelligence from Liberia," *AR* 29 (June 1853): 182.

17. Dennis to McLain, April 20 and April 21, 1853, reel 156; Smith to Lugenbeel, June 25, 1853, reel 155; Dr. Henry I. Roberts to Lugenbeel, April 15, 1853, reel 156, RACS.

18. Shick, *Behold*, 27–28; "Table of Emigrants," *AR* 29, 3 (January 1853): 86; "Sketch

of the History of Liberia," *AR* 28, 5 (1852): 129; Lugenbeel, *Sketches of Liberia*, 9; Foote, *Africa and the American Flag*, 198. For diseases among North Carolina emigrants to Liberia, see Clegg, *Price of Liberty*, 227–37.

19. "List of Emigrants by the Barque Linda Stewart," *AR* (January 1853): 29; Lugenbeel to McLain, October 12, 1852, reel 68; Wm. H. Starr to McLain, November 16, 1852, reel 69, RACS.

20. R. E. Henry to McLain, February 22, 1853; Dennis to McLain, January 25, 1853; and J. S. Smith to Lugenbeel, April 13, 1853; H. W. Dennis to Rev. W. McLain, September 28, 1853, reel 155, RACS.

21. J. M. Moore, letter to the editor, *Liberia Herald* (July 19, 1854); Nesbit, "Four Months in Liberia," 90; Washington, "Liberia As It Is, 1854," 206 (quoted). Also see H. W. Dennis's defensive reply to Moore's letter in the *LH* (August 2, 1854).

22. Dennis to McLain, April 21, 1853, and Dennis to McLain, n.d. [missing first page, but probably April 1853], reel 156, RACS, emphasis in the original.

23. Dennis to McLain, n.d. [probably April 1853], reel 156, RACS.

24. Matilda Skipwith Richardson to Sally Cocke, June 20, 1854, in Wiley, *Slaves No More*, 81; and Miller, *Dear Master*, 114–15. I thank Sara Keil for finding information on Lomax and Richardson in the Indiana University Library's Liberia collection.

25. Johnson, *History of the Yorubas*, 353.

26. Holsoe, "A Study of Relations"; Staudenraus, *African Colonization Movement*, 88–89; Shick, *Behold*, 91. The Matilda Newport story (which has no written corroboration) was in circulation by 1853, when an African American visitor named Daniel H. Peterson heard it. See his "The Looking-Glass: Being a True Report and Narrative of the Life, Travels, and Labors of the Rev. Daniel H. Peterson (1854)," in Moses, *Liberian Dreams*, 51–52. For a personal account of some of the last celebrations of Matilda Newport Day, until the postcoup government discontinued them in 1980, see Cooper, *The House at Sugar Beach*.

27. Holsoe, "Study of Relations"; Everill, *Abolition and Empire*, 103; Clegg, *Price of Liberty*, 101. According to the *Voyages* database, estimated numbers of slaves exported from the Windward Coast were 2,369 in 1820; 678 in 1821; 956 in 1822; 0 in 1823; 2,023 in 1824; and 1,234 in 1825. ("Windward Coast" estimates by year, www.slavevoyages.org [September 29, 2011].) Clegg's estimates are higher.

28. On Blanco and Gallinas, see Rediker, *The Amistad Rebellion*, 43–52 and Johnston, *Liberia* vol. 1, 164–66; on Conneau, see Theodore Canot (his pen name), *A Slaver's Log Book*, as well as Mouser, "Théophilus Conneau" and Jones, "Theophile Conneau."

29. In this way they were different from other freed people who moved to Africa from the Americas. A considerable number of the Brazilians who "repatriated" to the Bight of Benin worked in the slave trade, and it was not uncommon for them as well as Sierra Leonean re-captives to own slaves locally. See chapter 5.

30. Holsoe, "Study of Relations"; Staudenraus, *African Colonization Movement*, 155.

31. Holsoe, "Study of Relations"; Clegg, *Price of Liberty*, 105–11; Johnson, *Bitter Canaan*, 65–67; Peyton Skipwith to John H. Cocke, November 11, 1839, in Wiley, *Slaves No More*, 51–52; Thomas Buchanan, "Letter 1—No Title," *AR* 15 (1839): 276.

32. Sanneh, *Abolitionists Abroad*, 112; Lloyd, *The Navy and the Slave Trade*, 275–76. By 1814 there were ten thousand recaptives in Sierra Leone, mostly in Freetown. Over the

next half-century, about three thousand new recaptives were landed at Sierra Leone per year, eventually numbering more than 150,000. See Peterson, *Province of Freedom* and Fyfe, *A History of Sierra Leone*.

33. Payton Skipwith to John H. Cocke, December 29, 1840, in Wiley, *Slaves No More*, 55.

34. Canney, *Africa Squadron*, chapters 1–2; DuBois, *The Suppression of the African Slave-Trade*, 98, 110–11; Foote, *Africa and the American Flag*, 152–54; "Case of the Captured Slave Ships," *AR* 15, 17 (1839): 273, quoted.

35. Peyton Skipwith to John H. Cocke, May 20, 1839, in Wiley, *Slaves No More*, 49.

36. Canney, *Africa Squadron*, 203; van Sickle, "Reluctant Imperialists." Total numbers of captured slavers come from Canney, *Africa Squadron*, 222, and Lloyd, *The Navy and the Slave Trade*, 275–81.

37. van Sickle, "Reluctant Imperialists"; Staudenraus, *African Colonization Movement*, 241; Shick, *Behold*, 105; "The Liberian Cutter 'Lark,'" *LH* (June 25, 1849).

38. Shick, *Behold*, 61; Joseph Jenkins Roberts, "Appeal to the Government and People of the United States," in *American Colonization Society Papers*, Library of Congress, May 19, 1849, http://www.loc.gov/exhibits/african/afam003.html (September 26, 2011).

39. "Slave Canoes Captured," *LH* (September 30, 1848); *LH* (June 30, 1848); John Day to Rev. James B. Taylor, April 3, 1849, IMB.

40. Day to Taylor, April 23, 1849, IMB; Solomon S. Page to Charles W. Andrews, April 22, 1849, in Wiley, *Slaves No More*, 106–7.

41. James C. Minor, adjutant of the First Regiment, wrote a detailed account of the operation that was published in three installments in the *Liberia Herald* of June 25, July 27, and September 28, 1849. Also see Wiley, *Slaves No More*, 322–23 and Foote, *Africa and the American Flag*, 183. There is no indication that the two thousand slaves were ever released to colonists.

42. Solomon S. Page to Charles W. Andrews, n.d. [1849], in Wiley, *Slaves No More*, 107–8; Sion Harris to William McLain, May 20, 1849, in Wiley, *Slaves No More*, 227; Day to Taylor, April 3, 1849, IMB; *LH* (May 18, 1849).

43. "Slave Barracoon Destroyed," *LH* (January 5, 1853); see statistics in slavevoyages. org.

44. J. J. Roberts, "Letter from President Roberts," *AR* 28, 5 (1852): 139. Also see Wiley, *Slaves No More*, 107 and Shick, *Behold*, 106–7.

45. Blyden to Rev. J. P. Knox, February 1852, in Holden, *Blyden of Liberia*, 34. For an account of the expedition, see B. V. R. James, "Campaign in Bassa," reprinted in the *NYCJ* (July 1852).

46. "News from Liberia," *NYCJ* (May 1853).

47. Matilda R. Lomax to Mr. J. H. Cokes, April 20, 1853, in Wiley, *Slaves No More*, 77.

48. *LH* (March 16, 1853), reprinted in Holden, *Blyden of Liberia*, 38; J. J. Roberts, "Letter from President Roberts," *AR* 29, 8 (1853): 227; "Annual Message of President Roberts," December 6, 1853 in McKay, *Report of Rev. John McKay*.

49. J. J. Roberts, "Letter from President Roberts," *AR* 29, 8 (1853): 227.

50. "Immigrants," *LH* (March 14, 1853): 2.

51. "African Emigration," *Anti-Slavery Reporter* 1, 9 (1853): 209; J. J. Roberts, "From Liberia," *AR* 30, 4 (1854): 111; "Apprentices from Africa," *NYCJ* (July 1853).

52. Edward Blyden in the *Liberia Herald* (March 16, 1853 and April 6, 1853), reprinted in Holden, *Blyden of Liberia*, 38–44.

53. Williams, *History of the Negro Race*, vol. 1, 106–7; J. J. Roberts, *Annual Message of President Roberts* (December 6, 1853), 22–24, printed in *Report of Rev. John McKay*; J. J. Roberts, "From Liberia," *AR* 30 (Apr 1854): 111–2.

54. J. J. Roberts, March 14, 1853, printed as "Further from Liberia," *AR* 29 (June 1853): 173. Also see "Boombo of Little Cape Mount," *AR* 29 (June 1853): 184 and "Trial and Sentence of Boombo," *AR* 29 (August 1853): 245.

55. *LH* (April 6, 1853), reprinted as "Trial and Sentence of Boombo," *AR* 29, 8 (August 1853): 245.

56. Blyden in the *Liberia Herald* (March 16, 1853), printed in Holden, *Blyden of Liberia*, 40.

57. Dennis to McLain, April 21, 1853, reel 156; Roberts to McLain, April 10, 1853, reel 155, RACS.

58. "Information about Going to Liberia," n.d. [1853?], reel 306, RACS.

59. See Allen, "Rethinking" and "Historical Methodology." For a description of trying to start a farm along the St. Paul's, see William C. Burke to Robert E. and Mary C. Lee, August 20, 1854, in Wiley, *Slaves No More*, 191.

60. "Notice," *LH* (May 24, 1853); A.F. Russell, "For the Liberia Herald," *LH* (August 16, 1854); Dennis to McLain, June 11, 1853, reel 156, RACS.

61. Sion Harris to William McLain and J. W. Lugenbeel, March 3, 1853, in Wiley, *Slaves No More*, 240; *LH* (March 3, 1852). Also see the report of Harris's death by lightning strike in the *AR* (August 1854).

62. John McKay, *Report*.

63. *LH* (March 3, 1852); Cowen, *Liberia, as I Found It*, 71. For successful cash-crop farmers, also see Shick, *Behold*, 112.

64. J. S. Smith to Lugenbeel, April 13, 1853, reel 155, RACS. For more on similarities between Americo-Liberian and Southern American architecture, see Belcher et al., *A Land and Life Remembered*. Few of the buildings Belcher photographed in the 1970s have survived.

65. Armistead Miller, "Letter from Liberia," June 18, 1852, printed in the *NYCJ* (March 1853).

66. "Who Wants Bricks?" was the title of an advertisement placed in the *Camden Journal* of May 24, 1850, by J. F. Sutherland, with whom Church Vaughan was then living and working. In this and other advertisements over the next five years, Sutherland announced that he had hard bricks ready for delivery.

67. A. B. Hooper to Samuel Tillinghast, September 27, 1853, in Wiley, *Slaves No More*, 264–65. Also see the letter from Deserline T. Harriss to Rev. J. B. Pinney, printed in the *NYCJ* (April 1853).

68. *LH* (March 3, 1852); Williams, *Four Years in Liberia*, 146.

69. Shick, *Behold*, 66. No more recaptives were settled in Liberia until 1860, when the American squadron captured nine slave ships and landed 4,701 Africans there. See Sharla Fett, *Recaptured Africans*.

70. See Lovejoy and Richardson, "Trust, Pawnship, and Atlantic History" and "The Business of Slaving."

71. See Shick, *Behold*, 65–66, for a benign portrait of this institution. Such assimilation did in fact occur, so much so that the term "Congo," originally describing the receptive Africans (since most came from Central Africa), became synonymous with "Americo-Liberian." The apprenticeship system persisted to very recent times, and is still described as a route to class mobility and education for "country" (that is, indigenous) Liberians.

72. Cowan, *Liberia, as I Found It*, 82.

73. Clegg, *Price of Liberty*, 101–2; Johnson, *Bitter Canaan*, 72.

74. Massachusetts Colonization Society, *Tenth Annual Report*; Johnson, *Bitter Caanan*, 81.

75. Day to Rev. James B. Taylor, Bexley, April 23, 1849, IMB.

76. Forbes, *Dahomey and the Dahomans*, 148.

77. "Liberia and Its Slavery," *AR* 27, 6 (1851): 179 (emphasis in the original); "Liberia and its Slavery—the Pawn System," *Anti-Slavery Reporter* 6, 65 (1851): 82.

78. "Liberia and Its Slavery."

79. J. J. Roberts, "The President of Liberia and Lieutenant Forbes," *AR* 28, 1 (1852): 11; "Commander Forbes and Liberian Slave Trade," *LH*, reprinted in the *NYCJ* (December 1851).

80. Nesbit, *Four Months in Liberia*, 90, 102, and 104.

81. Williams, *Four Years in Liberia*, 172.

82. Interview with Dr. Othello Brandy, chairman of the Liberian Lands Commission (Monrovia, July 25, 2013).

83. Peyton Skipwith to John H. Cocke, February 10, 1834, in Wiley, *Slaves No More*, 36; Foote, *Africa and the American Flag*, 196–97; Matilda Skipwith Lomax to John H. Cocke, May 19, 1852, and September 26, 1853, in Wiley, *Slaves No More*, 75 and 60; Miller, *"Dear Master*," 120; "Five Letters on Liberian Colonization," 212.

84. Susan Capart to John Kimberly, March 1, 1857, in Wiley, *Slaves No More*, 270; Henry and Milly Franklin to Dr. James Hunter Minor, January 27, 1858, quoted in Tyler-McGraw, *An African Republic*, 139; unnamed colonist reportedly quoted by the brother of President Roberts, in "Colonization Meeting in New York," *AR* 28, 11 (November 1852): 334.

85. For example, James C. Minor to Mary B. Blackford, February 12, 1846, in Wiley, *Slaves No More*, 23.

86. William McLain to Marshall Hooper, December 28, 1854, reel 239, RACS; Marshall Hooper [mistranscribed as Hober] on the schooner *Fason* from Monrovia to New York, arrived September 13, 1855, *New York Passenger Lists, 1820–1957*, microfilm M237 roll 156, list number 879, via ancestry.com.

87. Clegg, *Price of Liberty*, 187; S. S. Mallett to McLain, September 30, 1858, reel 84, RACS; *Public Laws of the State of North-Carolina, Passed by the General Assembly at its Session of 1858-'59*, 370; "Returning to Slavery," *Western Democrat* (Charlotte, North Carolina), January 11, 1859 (question mark in the original); Record of the ship *Thomas Pope*, July 18, 1871, microfilm M237_345, line 17, list number 688 in *Passenger Lists of Vessels Arriving at New York, New York, 1820–1897* (National Archives Microfilm Publication M237, 675 rolls), via ancestry.com. Sarah Mallett died February 3, 1871, according to ancestry.com.

88. Evidently on the basis of conversations with Vaughan's sons, the missionary Louis Duval wrote that Church's parents had been Methodist. There is no evidence from Camden or elsewhere to corroborate this. Duval, *Baptist Missions in Nigeria*, 70.

89. Stepp, "Interpreting a Forgotten Mission," 39–46; Carter, "John Day," chapter 1; Dunn et al., *Historical Dictionary of Liberia*, 99; Shick, *Emigrants to Liberia*, 27. John Day's brother Thomas Day was a well-known, free black cabinetmaker in North Carolina. Among his constructions was shelving for the UNC library.

90. "Africa," *HFJ* (September 1853): 11.

91. Harden to Brother Taylor, March 2, 1857, IMB.

92. See Maffly-Kipp, *Setting Down the Sacred Past*, chapter 4 and Sylvia M. Jacobs, "The Historical Role of Afro-Americans," in Jacobs, *Black Americans and the Missionary Movement*, 16. For black Southern Baptist missionaries in particular, see Stepp, "Interpreting," 209.

93. Joseph M. Harden, "New Virginia," *HFJ* (September 1855): 11.

94. Foreign Mission Board, Southern Baptist Convention, *Ninth Annual Report* (1854).

95. W. H. Clarke, "Africa," *HFJ* (January 1855): 27.

96. Tupper, *Foreign Missions*, 392.

97. Clarke quoted in Tupper, *Foreign Missions*, 389; Clarke to Rev. A. M. Poindexter, April 14, 1855, IMB.

98. John Day, "Liberian Mission," *HFJ* (July 1855): 3; Bowen to Taylor, April 11, 1855, BP; Brown, *Immigrants to Liberia*, 36; Day to Rev. A. M. Poindexter, May 28, 1855, IMB.

99. Bowen's diary, September 10, 1855 and n.d. [probably March or April] 1856, BP.

100. British missionary Adolphus Christian Mann recorded in his journal for November 2, 1855, that "I engaged with permission of Rev. Mr. Clark (American Baptist Mission) his carpenter, who is an emigrant from America to Monrovia to which place he intends to return at the end of the terms under which he is engaged." CMS, Nigeria—Yoruba Mission 1844–1880, CA 2/O66/89.

Chapter 4

1. Vaughan's arrival is reconstructed from others' accounts from around the same time: Bowen, *Central Africa*, 209 on the steamship; Stone, *In Afric's Forest and Jungle*, 14, and Clarke, *Travels and Explorations in Yorubaland*, 1 on the sharks; Delany quoted in Miller, *The Search for a Black Nationality*, 205. On Lagos's commerce more generally, see Hopkins, "An Economic History of Lagos" (the introduction for the period before 1880 and p. 169 on currency) and Mann, *Slavery and the Birth of an African City*, chapter 4.

2. Mann, *Slavery*, 122 ("Liverpool"); Brown, "A History of the People of Lagos," 10 (four square miles); Mabogunje, *Urbanization in Nigeria*; Peil, *Lagos: The City Is the People*; Kopytoff, *A Preface to Modern Nigeria*.

3. "Letter from Rev. Jos. H. Hardin," *HFJ* 5, 7 (January 1856): 28.

4. On clothing in Lagos, see Brown, "A History," 26–28.

5. Slave export numbers are from Mann, *Slavery*, 38, along with estimates in *Voyages: the Transatlantic Slave Trade Database* (accessed September 30, 2013). On the "age of confusion," see Peel, *Religious Encounter* as well as Ajayi and Smith, *Yoruba Warfare*.

6. Clarke, *Travels*, 3.

7. Ibid., 5–6; A. D. Phillips, "The Yoruba Kingdom," *The Commission* (February 1859): 241–42; Stone, *In Afric's Forest*, 17; Townsend (comp.), *Memoir of the Rev. Henry Townsend*, 159–60, reprinting the report of Dr. Irving (1853). Irving estimated Abeokuta's population as a hundred thousand.

8. Ajayi and Smith, *Yoruba Warfare*; Law, *The Oyo Empire*; Biobaku, *The Egba and Their Neighbours*; Johnson, *History of the Yorubas*.

9. Townsend, *Memoir*, chapter 8 (quotation on 79); Bowen, *Central Africa*, 119–22; Biobaku, *The Egba*, chapter 4; Ajaye and Smith, *Yoruba Warfare*, chapter 6; Tucker, *Abbeokuta*.

10. Ajayi and Smith, *Yoruba Warfare*, 29; Johnson, *History*, 282; Charles Phillips, November 12, 1857, CA 2/077/22, CMS.

11. Stone, *In Afric's Forest*, 50, 60–61; W. H. Clarke, "Yoruba Mission. Africa. Description of Ijaye," *HFJ* 5, 4 (October 1855): 16 (quoted); Peel, *Religious Encounter*, 37. Bowen estimated the Ijaye population as thirty-five thousand (*Central Africa*, 221), while Stone thought it was more like a hundred thousand (*In Afric's Forest*, 49).

12. Stone, *In Afric's Forest*, 53; Bowen's diary, January 6, 1854, and February 24, 1855, BP.

13. See Original Papers of Adolphus Mann and Charles Phillips, Nigeria—Yoruba Mission (CMS), including Mann's journal entry for May 9, 1854 (CA 2/O66/83) and Phillips's for November 3, 1853 (CA2/078/7). "This day an action of shocking cruelty was performed by Are," wrote Phillips. After killing one of his wives for the crime of adultery, he split the woman's belly and took out the heart and liver and ate it raw in the open street before a very large assembly of his townspeople. . . . Such actions of the heathen cruelties is very common in Are's character." Also see Peel, *Religious Encounter*, 82–83.

14. Biographical information on Bowen is in Duval, *Baptist Missions in Nigeria*; Roberson, *A History of the Baptists of Lagos*; and Okedara and Ajayi, *Thomas Jefferson Bowen*.

15. Bowen, *Central Africa* and *Grammar and Dictionary*.

16. Bowen to Rev. Jas. B. Taylor, December 11, 1860, IMB. For a fictitious account based on the Bowens' experience in Nigeria, see Orr, *A Different Sun*.

17. "Letter from T. J. Bowen," December 15, 1853, AR 30 (October 1854): 291.

18. Bowen to Taylor, October 1, 1855, IMB; Bowen, *Central Africa*, 96–97.

19. Lurana Bowen letter to her father's slaves, July 16, 1855, BP.

20. Bowen letter, n.d. [late March/early April, 1856], BP.

21. J. A. Atanda, introduction to Clarke, *Travels and Explorations*, xxiii.

22. David Hinderer to Rev. H. Venn, October 26, 1855, CA2/049/24, CMS. Clarke and Vaughan were joined by a new missionary, A. D. Phillips, in January 1856.

23. Bowen to Taylor, October 27, 1853, BP; Ajayi, *Christian Missions in Nigeria*, 112; Burton, *Abeokuta and the Cameroons Mountains*, 162. The CMS missionary Adolphus Mann, whose station was located half a mile from the Baptists in Ijaye, hired Vaughan a couple of months after the carpenter arrived to help him finish windows and doors in his own buildings. Mann's diary, October 24, 1854, CA 2/O66/84, CMS.

24. Bowen's hand-drawn map accompanied his letter to J. B. Taylor, April 11, 1855, BP.

25. "Letter from W. H. Clarke" dated January 23, 1856, in *HFJ* 5, 11 (May 1856): 44.

26. Stone, *In Afric's Forest*, 28 (quoted), 64–66; Roberson, *A History of Baptists in Nigeria*, 50.

27. Adolphus Mann, Annual Letter, February 22, 1856, CA2/O66/101, CMS; Law, *From Slave Trade to "Legitimate" Commerce*; Mann, *Slavery*; Peel, *Religious Encounter*, 63–71.

28. Diary, December 13, 1853, BP. For Henry Townsend's analogous experience in Abeokuta, see Ajayi, *Christian Missions*, 112.

29. Letter from Lurana Bowen to her relatives, published in the *Christian Index* (April 13, 1854): 58.

30. Diary entry, March 25, 1855, BP; Adolphus Mann, Annual Letter, February 22, 1856, CA2/O66/101, CMS.

31. Adolphus Mann journal, October 22, 1856, CA 2/O66/92 (on self-redemption); Henry Townsend to Rev. H. Venn, December 31, 1856, CA2/O85/32, CMS; R. W. Priest to Taylor, December 29, 1857, IMB.

32. This Baptist institution was founded in 2002. Okedara and Ajayi, *Thomas Jefferson Bowen*, 54.

33. Clarke, *Travels*, 93.

34. Ibid.; Johnson, *History*, 269–73.

35. Clarke, *Travels*, 98–99; Lurena Bowen to her parents, October 2, 1855, BP; Bowen, *Central Africa*, 177; Stone, *In Afric's Forest*, 23; Burton, *Abeokuta*, 59.

36. Information about Jeremiah Clarke at ancestry.com. Also see Mary Adeline Biscoe Hillyer, "J. Clarke" (December 1845, Eatonton, Georgia) http://trees.ancestry.com/tree /12717186/person/-197506377/storyx/b8f389f5–78a0–414e-95de-114612ff8930?src=search (January 20, 2011).

37. Tupper, *Foreign Missions*, 392.

38. Clarke, *Travels*, 23, 34.

39. Ajayi, *Christian Missions*, 121–22.

40. Clarke to Taylor, October 19, 1854, IMB; Lurana Bowen to her mother, June 18, 1855, BP.

41. "The Late James Churchwill Vaughan," *LWR* (September 23, 1893).

42. Bowen to Taylor, February 13, 1856, BP; Tupper, *Foreign Missions*, 416.

43. Hinderer to Rev. H. Venn, October 26, 1855, CA2/049/24, CMS. "Mr. and Mrs. Bowen have left that town [Ijaye] for good, leaving Mr. Clark with a few carpenters and a school master I believe from Liberia in charge of the station."

44. Clarke, *Travels*, 102.

45. Tupper, *Foreign Missions*, 392–404.

46. Strobel, *European Women*; Stoler, *Carnal Knowledge*.

47. Stone, *In Afric's Forest*, 129.

48. Clarke traveled to Oyo with the Trimbles in February 1857, Ilorin with Phillips and the Trimbles in April 1857, and Oyo with Phillips and Cason in May 1857. Clarke, *Travels*, 103–5.

49. W. H. Clarke, "Letter from Rev. W. H. Clarke," *The Commission* (November 1856): 149–150.

50. Clark to Taylor, October 19, 1857, IMB.

51. Harden to Taylor, December 23, 1857; Priest to Poindexter, August 30, 1857; Harden

to Taylor, June 30, 1858; Harden to Taylor, January 4, 1859, all IMB. For missionaries' salaries, see the annual minutes of the Foreign Mission Board, http://archives.imb.org/solomon.asp.

52. Brown, *Immigrants to Liberia*, 47 and 52; Cecil Roberson, "Richard Russell: Carpenter and Benefactor," *Historical Pamphlets of Nigerian Baptists*, RC; Harden to Taylor, June 30, 1858, and January 4, 1859, IMB; Reid to Taylor, April 10, 1860, IMB; Trimble to Taylor, January 12, 1858, IMB; W. H. Clarke, "Letter from Rev. W. H. Clarke," *The Commission* (July 1858); Stone, *In Afric's Forest*, 67, 111, 165, chapters 15–16.

53. See Atanda's introduction to Clarke's *Travels and Explorations*. Atanda surmises that the rift between Clarke and the board, together with Clarke's unusually open-minded views of Africans, explains why his memoir was never published by the Southern Baptist Publication Society.

54. Tupper, *Foreign Missions*, 397.

55. Reid to Harden, January 19, 1859, IMB.

56. Stone, *In Afric's Forest*, 67, 72–73.

57. Ibid., 129. By "the country," Stone may have meant West Africa, since Russell arrived in Yorubaland only shortly before Stone himself did. He had, however, spent several years in Liberia before that.

58. Stone, *In Afric's Forest*, 130; Ajayi and Smith, *Yoruba Warfare*, 83.

59. M. R. Delany, "Official Report of the Niger Valley Exploring Party," in Bell, *Search for a Place*, 121 and 77.

60. Peel, *Religious Encounter*, 34–39; Johnson, *History*.

61. Phillips to Taylor, August 3, 1859, and March 1, 1860, IMB.

62. Hinderer to Venn, March 19, 1860, CA2/049/40, CMS.

63. Johnson, *History*, 332.

64. Peel, *Religious Encounter*, 39; Ajayi and Smith, *Yoruba Warfare*, part 2, chapter 3; Biobaku, *The Egba*, 64; Johnson, *History*, chapter 18; Stone, *In Afric's Forest*, 128–29.

65. Hinderer, *Seventeen Years*, 211–12; Johnson, *History*, 334; Peel, *Religious Encounter*, 64–65; Stone, *In Afric's Forest*, 130.

66. Robert Campbell, "A Pilgrimage to My Motherland: An Account of a Journey among the Egbas and Yorubas of Central Africa in 1859–60," in Bell, *Search for a Place*, 227.

67. Stone's account of his adventure is in *Afric's Forest*, chapters 15–16. Campbell, "Pilgrimage," in Bell, *Search*, 224–27, recounts the story as told to Campbell by Stone and Richard Russell.

68. Campbell, "Pilgrimage," 225–26; Stone, *In Afric's Forest*, 132–36; R. H. Stone to Taylor, February 22, 1860, IMB.

69. Campbell, "Pilgrimage," in Bell, *Search*, 244.

70. Stone to Taylor, February 22, 1860, IMB.

71. Stone, *In Afric's Forest*, 143.

72. Ibid., 152.

73. Miller, *Search*, 115–33, 144. This discussion of Delany is based on Miller's book, chapter 6; Blackett, "Martin R. Delany and Robert Campbell"; and Campbell, *Middle Passages*, chapter 2.

74. See chapter 2.

75. Matory, "The English Professors of Brazil" argues that Bowen's propagandizing helped to create an image in the Americas that Yoruba people were superior among Africans.

76. "Letter from T. J. Bowen, Esq., to provide for the exploration of the River Niger, in Africa," U.S. Senate, 34th Congress, 3d Session, Mis. Doc. No. 46 to accompany bill S. 607 (February 18, 1857); Bowen to Lippincott and Co., November 21, 1868, BP.

77. Delany, *Official Report*, in Bell, *Search*, 36.

78. Blackett, *Beating against the Barriers*, chapter 3.

79. Illustrious twentieth-century Abeokuta natives include the music star Fela Anikulapo Kuti and his cousin Wole Soyinka, who won the Nobel Prize in Literature in 1985. On cotton in Abeokuta, see Peel, *Religious Encounter*, 129 and Ajayi, *Christian Missions*, 167–68.

80. Martin R. Delany, *Official Report*, in Bell, *Search*, 77.

81. Reid to Taylor, December 1, 1859, IMB.

82. The text of the treaty is in Campbell, *A Few Facts*, 16–17 and in both Campbell, *A Pilgrimage* and Delany, *Official Report*.

83. Townsend to Venn, February 6, 1860, CA2/O85/74, CMS.

84. Gollmer to Venn, May 4, 1861, CA2/O43/67, CMS; Ajayi, *Christian Missions*, 191–92; Miller, *Search*, 254.

85. Campbell, *Pilgrimage*, 224.

86. T. A. Reid to Taylor, March 20, 1860, IMB; also Stone's account in a letter fragment, n.d., in his correspondence file.

87. Campbell, *Pilgrimage*, in Bell, *Search*, 236.

88. Blackett, *Beating*, 171–82.

89. Johnson, *History*, 353.

90. Stone, *In Afric's Forest*, 242.

91. Completed in the 1890s but not published by the CMS until 1921. On Henry Johnson and Samuel Johnson's education with the Hinderers, see Ajayi, *Christian Missions*, 164 and Toyin Falola, introduction, in Falola, *Pioneer, Patriot, and Patriarch*.

92. Johnson, *History*, 334–35.

93. R. H. Stone to Taylor, June 21, 1860, IMB.

94. Sanneh, *Abolitionists Abroad*.

95. Campbell, *Pilgrimage*, 227–28.

96. Stone, *In Afric's Forest*, 165, 158.

97. Reid to Poindexter, May 14, 1860, IMB; Ajayi and Smith, *Yoruba Warfare*, 83; Philips to Poindexter, January 6, 1861, IMB.

98. The military history is in part II of Ajayi and Smith, *Yoruba Warfare*, chapter 3 and also Johnson, *History*, chapter 18.

99. Johnson, *History*, 336.

100. Ajayi and Smith, *Yoruba Warfare*, 89; Stone, *In Afric's Forest*, 175; Mann to Rev. W. Knight, Annual Letter for 1860, February 1861, CA2/O66/105, CMS.

101. Johnson, *History*, 353.

102. Stone, *In Afric's Forest*, 182; Johnson, *History*, 344.

103. Ajayi and Smith, *Yoruba Warfare*, 98–99; Mann to Rev. H. Venn and Major H. Straith, September 19, 1860, CA 2/O66/13, CMS; "The Late Town of Ijaye," *African Times* (London), September 23, 1862; Stone, *In Afric's Forest*, 183.

104. Ibadan's commander Ogunmola, for instance, kept track of how many of his slave soldiers died by ordering that their caps be kept in a huge, six-foot-high basket: eighteen hundred were counted within two years of the start of the fighting. Johnson, *History*, 354.

105. From estimates in *Voyages: the Transatlantic Slave Trade Database* (accessed April 8, 2011). One shipload became the last African slaves to enter the United States— brought to Mobile, Alabama, in 1860 on a bet that this could be done in spite of its illegality. After emancipation, the Baptist missionary A. D. Phillips tracked them down in hopes of returning them to their homeland as emissaries of Christianity. They lived and died, however, in Alabama. Diouf, *Dreams of Africa in Alabama*; Phillips to Taylor, August 16, 1870, IMB.

106. Johnson, *History*, 345; Stone, *In Afric's Forest*, 185–86; Phillips to Taylor, November 6, 1860, IMB; Mann to Venn and Straith, September 19, 1860, CA 2/O66/13, CMS.

107. Phillips to Poindexter, January 6, 1861, IMB; Mann to Knight, Annual Letter for 1860, February 1861, CA 2/O66/105, CMS.

108. Stone, *In Afric's Forest*, 186; Phillips to Poindexter, January 6, 1861, Phillips to Taylor, November 6, 1860, and Phillips to Taylor, December 4, 1860, IMB.

109. Stone to Taylor, April 1, 1861, IMB.

110. Gottlieb Buhler, Half-yearly report, January to July 1861, CA2/O24/44, CMS; Stone, *In Afric's Forest*, 215; Duval, *Baptist Missions*, 93.

111. Gollmer, Finance Letter No. 10, November 4, 1861, Manuscript Collection, Kenneth Dike Library, University of Ibadan; Stone to Poindexter, March 2, 1861, and April 29, 1861, IMB.

112. Phillips to Taylor, November 6, 1860, and December 4, 1860, IMB.

113. Cecil Roberson, "Richard Russell: Carpenter and Benefactor," and "The Ifole," *Historical Pamphlets of Nigerian Baptists* (Richmond: IMB, n.d.), RC.

114. Stone to Poindexter, April 29, 1861, IMB; Buhler, Half-Yearly Report January to July 1862, CA2/O24/46, CMS; Stone, *In Afric's Forest*, chapter 23; Johnson, *History*, 352; *The African Times* I, 12 (June 23, 1862).

115. The rebuilding began in 1895. Interview in Ijaye with Tijani Sakini, said to be Kurunmi's modern successor, and Adeyemi Eesuola, December 7, 2015.

116. Stone, *In Afric's Forest*, 218; "The Late James Churchwill Vaughan," *LWR* (September 23, 1893); "from 'A General History of the Yoruba Country': James Churchwill Vaughan," *LS* (December 6, 1905); Roberson, *History of Baptists in Nigeria*, 304; *Iwe Irohin* (Appendix), January 1864, in file marked "Newspapers: Excerpts of Baptist Work, 1907–1920," RC, IMB.

117. Johnson, *History*, 361–62; Buhler to Venn, March 30, 1864, CA2/O24/31 and Maser to [illegible], April 6, 1864, CA2/O68/52b, CMS; *African Times*, May 23, 1864.

118. Johnson, *History*, 357; Townsend to Venn, June 30, 1864, CA2/O85/117 and Maser to Revd and Dear Sir, July 6, 1864, CA2/O68/54, CMS.

119. Phillips to Taylor, October 22, 1857, IMB; Stone, *In Afric's Forest*, 141; Ryder, *Benin and the Europeans*, 258.

120. C. A. Gollmer, journal entry for August 11, 1860, CA2/O43/134, CMS.

121. Stone, *In Afric's Forest*, 218–19. Stone returned to the United States at the end of 1862, however, so he is unlikely to have arranged Vaughan's marriage in 1865.

122. On Yoruba marriage, see Johnson, *History*, 113–17; on slave wives, see Hopkins, "A Report on the Yoruba, 1910," 82.

123. Johnson, *History*, 358–59, 363; Ajayi and Smith, *Yoruba Warfare*, 120.

124. For Ephraim Wilson, see chapter 2. For Wilsons in Camden, see Kirkland and Kennedy, *Historic Camden*, vol. 2, 357.

125. Phillips to Taylor, January 1, 1867, IMB; "Correspondence with Church Missionary Society, November 21, 1867 re The Late Disturbances at Abeokuta," CO 147/13, BNA; Peel, *Religious Encounter*, 132–36; Ajayi, *Christian Missions*, 201.

126. Phillips to Taylor, November 4, 1867, IMB; Cecil Roberson, "The Ifole," in *Historical Pamphlets of Nigerian Baptists*, RC.

127. Unsigned letter to "My dear Sir," October 16, 1867, CA2/O11/35, CMS and also in CO 147/13, BNA; Grimmer to Methodist Secretaries, November 4, 1867, Methodist Missionary Society London; Phillips to Taylor, November 4, 1867, IMB; Ajayi, *Christian Missions*, 201.

128. Phillips to Taylor, November 4, 1867, IMB.

129. Allen to Venn, January 28, 1868, CA2/O18/6, CMS; Kopytoff, *Preface*, 154–55; Peel, *Religious Encounter*, 135–36.

130. "The Late James Churchwill Vaughan," *LWR* (September 23, 1893); Thompson, "The Vaughan Family."

Chapter 5

1. This itinerary has been pieced together from a number of sources, starting with Thompson, "The Vaughan Family." For Phillips's movements, see his letters to Taylor of July 9, 16, and 29, 1869, in his correspondence file, IMB; other trips in the American South are mentioned in the *Home and Foreign Journal* of February 1869, December 1869, February 1870, August 1870, and November 1870. On Reid in South Carolina, see Foreign Mission Board, Southern Baptist Convention, "Twenty-Fourth Annual Report," May 6, 1869, http://archives.imb.org/solomon.asp. The railway link between Greenville and Camden was touted in advertisements for the Southern Baptist Theological Seminary, which ran in the *Camden Journal*. See, for example, the issue of June 29, 1871. Information on the Vaughan relatives comes from the family Bible inscribed by Maria Sephronia Vaughan Lauly beginning in 1868, now in the possession of Elsie Taylor-Goins, Columbia, South Carolina.

2. On Sherman's forces in Camden, see Kirkland and Kennedy, *Historic Camden*, vol. 1, 164 and Inabinet and Inabinet, *History of Kershaw County*, 184–86. For taxes, see Kirkland and Kennedy, *Historic Camden*, 159–61 and Inabinet and Inabinet, *History of Kershaw County*, 180.

3. Births and deaths are from the family Bible. Areas of residence and occupations of various family members have been reconstructed from censuses accessed at ancestry. com. Curiously, the 1870 census contains no records for Church Vaughan's most immediate surviving family members—his sister Sarah Vaughan Thomas and her daughter Maria Sophronia Lauly, his brother Burrell's adult children Burrell Jr. and

Maria, and his sister Mary's teenaged daughter Harriet Josephine MacLaughlin—
though they were enumerated in 1860 and 1880.

4. William Hammond, through attorneys Loeitner and Dunlap, to James F.
Sutherland, July 21, 1869 and William Hammond's will dated November 13, 1871, both
in William P. Hammond Estate Papers, Kershaw County Probate Judge, apartment
30, package 1070, SCDAH; conveyance from estate of John Workman to William
Hammond, January 8, 1870, Kershaw Country Register of Deeds, book Y, 205–7.

5. Family Bible.

6. For Sarah Harden in the mission house, see Phillips to Taylor, December 4, 1867,
and Stone to Taylor, January 28, 1868, IMB.

7. Echeruo, *Victorian Lagos*, 17.

8. Mann, *Slavery*, 253–54; Kopytoff, *Preface*, 232; Meek, *Land Tenure*, 59–60.

9. Hopkins, "Property Rights and Empire Building"; Mann, *Slavery*, 105, 110.

10. Blackett, Beating against the Barriers, 180.

11. Brown, "A History of the People of Lagos," 50.

12. Stone to Taylor, January 28, 1868, IMB. Also see Stone, *In Afric's Forest and Jungle*,
275–78.

13. Stone to Taylor, March 18, 1868, IMB.

14. Mann, *Slavery*, 118–29 (statistics on 127–28); Lynn, *Commerce and Economic
Change*; Law, *From Slave Trade to "Legitimate" Commerce*; Journal of the Rev. Samuel
Crowther, quarter ending March 31, 1857, CA2/O32, CMS, quoted in Mann, *Slavery*, 130.

15. Baker, *Urbanization and Political Change*, 33; Echeruo, *Victorian Lagos*, 30; J. Buckley
Wood, "On the Inhabitants of Lagos: Their Character, Pursuits, and Language," *Church
Missionary Intelligencer* (1881): 683–91, 687 quoted; Mann, *Slavery*, 143.

16. "Report from the Select Committee on Africa (Western Coast); Together with
the Proceedings of the Committee, Minutes of Evidence, and Appendix," *Parliamentary
Papers* 1865 (c. 412), vol. 5, 68. See also Lindsay, "'To Return to the Bosom of Their
Fatherland'"; Kopytoff, *Preface*, 171; Castillo, "Mapping"; Brown, "History," 37 and
57, where he estimates the populations of Sierra Leoneans and Brazilians in Lagos in
the early 1860s as closer to twenty-five hundred; and Zachernuk, *Colonial Subjects*, 24,
who estimates the population of "native foreigners" in Lagos in 1861 as between three
thousand and five thousand.

17. M. R. Delany, "Official Report of the Niger Valley Exploring Party," in Bell, *Search
for a Place*, 113–14.

18. Mann, *Slavery*, 124–26; Kopytoff, *Preface*, chapter 5.

19. Mann, *Slavery*, 248.

20. Akere, "Linguistic Assimilation," 187 as well as Brown, "A History," 45.

21. Lagos *Observer* (September 14, 1882), quoted in Brown, "A History," 119 (though
mistakenly suggesting that the builder was Robert Campbell).

22. Conveyance between Robert Campbell and James Churchill Vaughan, July 12,
1869, Lagos Land Registry, Ikeja. I remain grateful to the late Funmi Pearce for helping
to track down this record.

23. Mann, *Slavery*, 263.

24. Southern Baptist Convention Foreign Mission Board, *Twenty-Fifth Annual Report*,
May 5, 1870, http://archives.imb.org/solomon.asp.

25. On the Brazilian quarter, see Akinsemoyin and Vaughan-Richards, *Building Lagos*. Juan A. Campos was listed as one of the three executors of J. C. Vaughan's will, dated January 20, 1893 and located in the Probate Registry, Lagos, vol. 1, 259–262. I thank Kristin Mann for sharing this with me.

26. Moses Ladejo Stone's obituary, *LWR* (May 10, 1913).

27. Mann, *Slavery*, 16, 151–54.

28. Brown, "History," chapter 4, though the most extensive source on slavery in Lagos is Mann's book.

29. Mann, *Slavery*, 73.

30. "Memorial addressed by Native Traders and residents at Lagos to His Excellency H. St. George Ord, R.E., Her Britanic Majesty's Commissioner," December 27, 1864, CA2/O9/16, CMS; Mann, *Slavery*, 19 and 164; Castillo, "Mapping."

31. Mann, *Slavery*, chapter 5. For slavery emancipation in colonial Africa more generally, see Miers and Roberts, *The End of Slavery*, and Cooper, "Conditions Analogous to Slavery."

32. Mann, *Slavery*, 220–26.

33. Ibid., 231.

34. Ibid., 146–47, 311–12; A Yoruba historian, "from 'A General History of the Yoruba Country': James Churchwill Vaughan," *LS* (December 6, 1905); Adeoye Deniga, "James Churchwill Vaughan," in *African Leaders*, 2nd ed. (1919), RC, IMB.

35. See Jury Lists in Payne, *Payne's Lagos and West African Almanack and Diary* for 1882, 1887, 1893, and 1894; the Jury List for 1889 is in the Colony of Lagos, *Government Gazette* for that year.

36. *Payne's Lagos and West African Almanack and Diary*, 1882 and 1888; "Petition from the principal merchants of the colony praying for annexation of Porto Novo," December 8, 1877, CO 147/33, BNA; Sawada, "The Educated Elite and Associational Life," 182.

37. Colony of Lagos, *Government Gazette*, January 30, 1886, and September 30, 1893; Jury List in *Payne's Lagos and West African Almanack and Diary*, 1894.

38. Deniga, "James Churchwill Vaughan." On Yoruba self-aggrandizement and "Big Men," see Barber, *I Could Speak*.

39. I'm grateful to Kristin Mann for this point. See Mann, *Slavery*, 114–15; Zachernuk, *Colonial Subjects*, 29–30; and, for an example of the links between repatriate Lagosians and hinterland polities, Peel, *Ijeshas and Nigerians*, 90.

40. Harden to Poindexter, April 8, 1862, IMB; "Lagos," *The African Times* II, 19 (January 23, 1863); Blackett, *Beating*, 178; Brown, "History," 141–42.

41. Brown, "History," 147, 155.

42. "The Late James Churchwill Vaughan," *LWR* (September 23, 1893). On trade and credit, see Mann, *Slavery*, 144–49.

43. Macmillan, *The Red Book of West Africa*, 108.

44. Mann, *Slavery*, 136–39.

45. Brown, "A History," 147 and 158; Hopkins, "Richard Beale Blaize" and "An Economic History of Lagos," 64–67; Mann, *Slavery*, 156–57.

46. Mann, *Slavery*, 155–59; Hopkins, *Economic History*, 132–34.

47. Deniga, "James Churchwill Vaughan."

48. "The Late James Churchwill Vaughan."

49. Letter from James C. Vaughan, October 7, 1872, *HFJ* (January 1873): 26.

50. A. D. Phillips, "Missionary Exploration of Liberia," *AR* 47 (1871): 262–65.

51. Mann, *Slavery*, 104. There were, however, some racist incidents between European personnel and Africans, especially Saro, which increased by the 1880s. See Brown, "History," 215.

52. Foner, *Reconstruction*, chapter 5, especially 200; Williamson, *After Slavery*, 73–74; Zuczek, *State of Rebellion*, 18; Edgar, *South Carolina: A History*, 383–85; Berlin, *Slaves without Masters*.

53. Edgar, *South Carolina*, 388–93; Witt, *Patriots and Cosmopolitans*, 114.

54. Ullman, *Martin R. Delany*; Campbell, *Middle Passages*, 94–95.

55. Witt, *Patriots*, 114; Edgar, *South Carolina*, 388.

56. Trelease, *White Terror*, xlvi–xlvii quoted; Zuczek, *State of Rebellion*, 56–58; Williams, *The Great South Carolina Ku Klux Klan Trials*, 27–28; Edgar, *South Carolina*, 397–98; Witt, *Patriots*, 116; Foner, *Reconstruction*, 425–33.

57. Kirkland and Kennedy, *Historic Camden*, vol. 2, 201–2; Edgar, *South Carolina*, 398; Zuczek, *State of Rebellion*, 54.

58. Williams, *Trials*, 26; Edgar, *South Carolina*, 398–400; Witt, *Patriots*, 116.

59. Williams, *Trials*, 29–36; Witt, *Patriots*, 118, 124–25; Foner, *Reconstruction*, 431.

60. Witt, *Patriots*, 115.

61. "The South — The Tribune's Correspondents" and "The Clarendon Trouble," *CJ* (May 4, 1871).

62. Kirkland and Kennedy, *Historic Camden*, vol. 2, 209; Inabinet and Inabinet, *History of Kershaw County*, 209–210.

63. "A Few Words about the Riot of the 4th Instant," and "The Riot and its Consequences," *CJ* (July 13, 1871).

64. Williams, *Trials*.

65. Witt, *Patriots*, 120–28.

66. Edgar, *History*, 401, Witt, *Patriots*, 141.

67. Witt, *Patriots*, chapter 2; John Wallace to William Coppinger, December 25, 1871, reel 109, RACS, quoted in Witt, 135.

68. Robert Somers, *The Southern States since the War, 1870–1871* (New York, 1871) 54, quoted in Williamson, *After Slavery*, 177–78. On economic changes for African Americans, see Foner, *Reconstruction*, 392–411.

69. But see Hager, *Word By Word*.

70. Williamson, *After Slavery*, 215–29; Edgar, *South Carolina*, 391–92.

71. "Commissioners of Education," *CJ* (August 22, 1872). Brief biographical information on Frank Carter is in Foner, *Freedom's Lawmakers*, 41–42, but it does not mention his family. A cryptic reference to him as "Ned's son," suggests that he might be related to Harriet Josephine McLaughlin's husband William Carter, whose father was a Camden grocer named Edward Carter. Census information on Edward Carter does not confirm this, but his age in relation to Frank Carter's leaves the possibility open. Mrs. E. W. Bonney to her son, November 29, 1869, E. W. Bonney Papers, quoted in Williamson, *After Slavery*, 381. Frank Carter is mentioned as a teacher at Kershaw

County's Jackson School, operated by the Freedman's Bureau, in Teal, *Public Schools, 1868–1870*, 12.

72. Information derived from the 1870 and 1880 censuses for Chaney and Willis Pool, children of Burrell Carter Vaughan's daughter Maria Vaughan; Margaret, Milly, and William Hall, children of Elizabeth Hall's son Henry James Hall; and James Chesnut, the son of Elizabeth Hall's daughter Rebecca Hall.

73. Williamson, *After Slavery*, 149 (quoted) and 152; Inabinet and Inabinet, *History of Kershaw County*, 216–17; Edgar, *South Carolina*, 394.

74. Williamson, *After Slavery*, 142.

75. Bleser, *The Promised Land*, 157 and 167.

76. Williamson, *After Slavery*, 155.

77. "List of Delinquent Lands in Kershaw County," *CJ* (February 22, 1872); Conveyance from Henrietta Hammond, Executrix, to Lucy Middleton, September 13, 1875, Kershaw County Register of Deeds, letter book DD, 117. The conveyance mentions that the plot next to the one being sold was occupied by Mariah (Maria) Workman. She seems to have been the sister of John Workman, from whose estate William Hammond purchased the three plots on Market Street. 1850 Kershaw, South Carolina, census, accessed at ancestry.com.

78. The family of Andrew Henry Dibble was related to the Vaughans through Dibble's wife Ellie Naomi Naudin, the daughter of Harriet Conway and Moreau Naudin. Harriet Conway was half-sister to Church Vaughan's mother Maria Conway. Three of their sons (out of twelve children) operated grocery stores in downtown Camden through the latter 1890s and into the early twentieth century. One is now listed as a historic site by the Kershaw County Historical Society. See Taylor-Goins and Taylor-McConnell, *Naudin-Dibble Family* and Teal, *Kershaw County District Business Directory*, 9, 13, 15, 17, 20. In 1872, Andrew Henry Dibble was elected as a Camden town warden on the Democratic ticket. "Municipal Ticket," *CJ* (March 28, 1872) and "Election Notice," *CJ* (April 4, 1872). On black property holders supporting Democrats, see Williamson, *After Slavery*, 156.

79. Charleston *Daily News* (March 24, 1871), quoted in Williamson, *After Slavery*, 157.

80. Williamson, *After Slavery*, 157–58; Edgar, *South Carolina*, 402.

81. Ullman, *Martin R. Delany*, 443; Foner, *Reconstruction*, 546–47.

82. Ullman, *Martin R. Delany*, 454.

83. Foner, *Reconstruction*, 543–44.

84. Edgar, *South Carolina*, 401.

85. Ibid., 403; Zuczek, *State of Rebellion*, chapter 8; Kirkland and Kennedy, *Historic Camden*, vol. 2, 222.

86. Foner, *Reconstruction*, chapter 12, 574 (quoted); Edgar, *South Carolina*, 404–6.

87. Edgar, *South Carolina*, 413–15.

88. Williamson, *After Slavery*, 228.

89. Finnegan, *A Deed So Accursed*, 6.

90. Kirkland and Kennedy, *Historic Camden*, vol. 1, 225–26; Inabinet and Inabinet, *History of Kershaw County*, 274.

91. Witt, *Patriots*, 146; Ullman, *Martin R. Delany*, 503.

92. "Table of Emigrants Settled in Liberia by the American Colonization Society," *AR* 54 (July 1878): 92; "Table of Emigrants Settled in Liberia by the American Colonization Society: Recapitulation," *AR* 59 (April 1883): 60; Report of the Board of Directors, *AR* 55 (April 1879): 49. Also see Campbell, *Middle Passages*, 103–13.

93. Staudenraus, *African Colonization Movement*, 251.

94. Hahn, *Nation under Our Feet*, chapter 7. Witt prefers "lawyering with their feet" in *Patriots and Cosmopolitans*, 152.

95. Witt, *Patriots*, 147–50. On Liberia, see Liebenow, *Liberia*, and Sundiata, *Brothers and Strangers*.

96. Echuero, *Victorian Lagos*, 19; Payne, *Table of Principal Events*, 8; Deniga, "James Churchwill Vaughan."

97. Echuero, *Victorian Lagos*, 18–19 (quoted); Payne, *Payne's Lagos Almanack and Diary for 1878*, 56; Akinsemoyin and Vaughan-Richards, *Building Lagos*.

98. Indenture between James Churchwill Vaughan and Robert Campbell, April 17, 1882, Herbert Macaulay Papers, box 75, file 4, Kenneth Dike Library, University of Ibadan; Conveyances in the Lands Registry, Lagos between Emmanuel James Scott and James Churchill Vaughan (October 13, 1884), Emmanuel Richman and Vaughan (October 20, 1884), Ajala and Vaughan (October 13, 1884), Samuel Macaulay and others and Vaughan (October 3, 1891).

99. Ayo Vaughan-Richards notes from the family Bible, in Jewel Lafontant-Mankarious Papers and Femi Vaughan's family Bible, Lagos; 1 Sam 7:12.

100. Diary of W. J. David, February 23–28, 1876, RC.

101. Ayo Vaughan-Richards's notes from the family Bible.

102. Indeed, Rev. William David mentioned the belief in *àbíku* in his diary shortly before recording that Emily Vaughan was ill. See entries for late February 1876, p. 34, in the Cecil Roberson transcription, RC.

103. I thank Josiah Olubowale for his help with Yoruba names.

104. Echeruo, *Victorian Lagos*; Mann, *Marrying Well*; Zachernuk, *Colonial Subjects*, chapter 2; Smith, *An Autobiography*, 463–64 (quoted). Club meetings and events are listed in Payne's *Almanack* for each year. For Campbell, see 1878 and 1881 in particular.

105. "The Late James Churchwill Vaughan," *LWR* (September 23, 1893).

106. "The Late Mr. J. W. Vaughan," *Nigerian Spectator* (December 1, 1923): 11. Burrell Vaughan also attended the Baptist elementary school. "The Baptist Elementary Treat," Lagos *Observer*, (April 10, 1884).

107. Kopytoff, *Preface*, 244–45; Ajayi, *Christian Missions*, 153–54.

108. "From Nigerian Who is Who," *Nigerian Advocate* (November 7, 1923); "African Biographies: James Churchwill and Burrell Carter Vaughan," RC.

109. "The Late Mr. J. W. Vaughan," *Nigerian Spectator* (December 1, 1923): 11.

110. Emmanuel James Scott to James Churchill Vaughan and Ajala to James Churchill Vaughan, both October 13, 1884, and Emmanuel Richman to James Churchill Vaughan, October 20, 1884, in Lagos Lands Registry, Ikeja. I am grateful to the late Funmi Pearce for locating these records. For the "Excelsior Store," see *LWR* (September 26, 1896): 8. For J. W. Vaughan's first marriage, see John A. Payne, "Memorable Occurrences in Lagos and the West Coast of Africa Generally, from September 1, 1887, to August 31, 1892," in

Payne's Lagos and West African Almanack and Diary for 1893. For his second marriage, to Clara Zeneobia Allen, see Ayo Vaughan-Richards's copies from the family Bible in Jewel Lafontant-Mankarious papers and Femi Vaughan's family Bible, Lagos.

111. Macmillan, *Red Book*, 108.

112. James Churchwill Vaughan Will, dated January 20, 1893, Lagos Probate Registry, vol. 1, 259–62; Burrell C. Vaughan Will, dated September 23, 1918, Lagos Probate Registry, vol. 7, 59–64; Michael Ayo Vaughan interview with Kristin Mann, Lagos 1974; Lindsay interview with James Olabode Vaughan, July 14, 2003, Lagos and with Olabode Vaughan and Kunle Ademola, June 27, 2006, Lagos. I thank Kristin Mann for sharing her materials with me.

113. Thompson, "The Vaughan Family," 57.

114. "'Gwing Back to Africa': Burden of the Advice an Educated African Gives To the Negroes Living in the United States," *The State* (Columbia, South Carolina), August 31, 1895, 2. I appreciate the help of Sarah Murray at the Camden Archives and Museum in verifying that there is no record of a Vaughan visit from Africa to Camden in the 1880s or 1890s. Faduma was born of Yoruba parents in Guyana and relocated with them to Sierra Leone, where until he changed it in 1887, his name was W. J. Davies. Lynch, *Edward Wilmot Blyden*, 219; Moore, *Orishatukeh Faduma*.

115. Marriage is in the family Bible; Carter's parents and education are in the 1870 census for Kershaw, South Carolina.

116. 1890 Kershaw Business Directory; 1870, 1880, and 1900 censuses; family Bible.

117. His distant cousins the Dibbles, noted above, did stay successfully in Camden, where several opened general stores, one of which is now marked as a historic site.

118. 1880 census, Flat Rock, Kershaw, South Carolina, accessed through ancestry.com (on farming); 1890 Camden Business Directory (barber); 1900 census (teacher, literate, twelve children, housewife); Inanibet and Inanibet, *History of Kershaw County*, 249 (on attending Radical Republican meetings); Thompson, "The Vaughan Family," 60 (on attack by nightriders); 1910 census, Weehawken ward 3, Hudson, New Jersey, accessed through ancestry.com (on relocation to New Jersey).

119. Taylor-Goins and Taylor-McConnell, *Naudin-Dibble Family*, 27; 1910 census.

120. "'Gwing Back to Africa,'" *The State* (August 31, 1895): 2.

Chapter 6

1. The foundation of the Native (Ebenezer) Baptist Church is described in many sources, including Emmanuel A. Ojo, "Historical Sketch of the Native Baptist Church now known as 'Ebenezer Baptist Church' and 'Araromi Baptist Church' (founded April, 1888)" (1938), RC; Webster, *The African Churches among the Yoruba*; Ajayi, *Christian Missions in Nigeria*, chapter 8; Ayandele, *The Missionary Impact on Modern Nigeria*, 197–201; Babalola, *A Short History of Ebenezer Baptist Church*, held at the IMB; Roberson, *A History of Baptists in Nigeria*, chapter 9; Roberson, *A History of the Baptists of Lagos*; Vaughan et al., *The Making of the First Indigenous Church in Nigeria*.

2. Shepperson and Price, *Independent African*. For Nigeria, Ayandele, *Missionary Impact*, chapters 6–8; Ajayi, "Nineteenth Century Origins"; Farias and Barber, *Self-Assertion and Brokerage*.

3. Peel, *Religious Encounter*, chapter 10.

4. Ajayi, "Nineteenth Century Origins"; Ayandele, *Missionary Impact*, chapter 8; Echeruo, *Victorian Lagos*, chapter 6.

5. Sanneh, *Abolitionists Abroad*.

6. Tupper, *Foreign Missions*, 427; J. B. Chamberlain to J. B. Taylor, September 8, 1871, in David's correspondence file, IMB. For David's grandfather Richard McLemore, see *1860 U.S. Federal Census - Slave Schedules*, accessed through ancestry.com, showing that he owned forty-five slaves.

7. Tupper, *Foreign Missions*, 427–28; William W. Colley application, November 8, 1870, *Registers of Signatures of Depositors in Branches of the Freedman's Savings and Trust Company, 1865–1874* (Washington, D.C.: National Archives and Records Administration), accessed through ancestry.com. A brief and somewhat inaccurate biography of Colley is in Anderson, *Biographical Dictionary*, 145.

8. Southern Baptist Convention Foreign Mission Board, *Thirty-First Annual Report* (May 11, 1876), http://archives.imb.org/solomon.asp; Tupper, *Foreign Missions*, 429.

9. Diary of W. J. David, October 30[?] and November 1, 1875, 16, RC.

10. Payne, *Table of Principal Events*; David diary, January 8, 1876, RC.

11. David diary, February 20, 1876, RC.

12. "Obituary: Captain James Pinson Labulo Davies," *LWR*; Kopytoff, *Preface*, 286–87; Mann, *Slavery and the Birth of an African City*, 124–25.

13. David diary, January 10, 17, and 20, 1876, RC.

14. David diary, February 3, 1876, RC; David to Tupper, July 16, 1887, IMB.

15. David diary, February 23, 1876, RC; Tupper, *Foreign Missions*, 429.

16. For example, Gould, *The Mismeasure of Man*; Holt, *The Problem of Freedom*.

17. Southern Baptist Convention Foreign Mission Board, *Thirty-Sixth Annual Report* (May 5, 1881), accessed at archives.imb.org.

18. Ajayi, *Christian Missions*, 260.

19. David and P. A. Eubank to Brethren of Board, October 2, 1883, IMB.

20. Annual Minutes, Foreign Mission Board, SBC, 1876, 36, quoted in Martin, *Black Baptists and African Missions*, 49.

21. "A Letter from Rev. W. W. Colley," *Foreign Mission Journal* (August 1877); Tupper to Colley, July 20, 1877, in Colley's correspondence file, IMB.

22. See correspondence in Colley's file, IMB. I thank Jim Berwick for his help with these records.

23. "Revd Dear Sir" from "Yours in Christ," Lagos, August 6, 1878, in Colley's correspondence file (quoted); David to Tupper, October 10, 1879, in David's correspondence file, IMB. In his *History of the Baptists of Lagos*, the missionary historian Cecil Roberson reports that Sallie Parmer was Reverend David's house girl and traveled to Abeokuta with him and Stone in 1876 (p. 30).

24. Colley's correspondence file, IMB; Tupper, *Foreign Missions*, 428.

25. Martin, *Black Baptists*, especially 56–65.

26. Colley was later investigated by his own mission board. In 1886, he shot and killed a Liberian man ("an African boy"), allegedly by accident, prompting an inquest by "twelve civilized men." Later, Colley met with two Liberian magistrates as well as the

governor, who determined, as had the inquest, that the killing was an accident. "The witnesses were all heathen," Colley reported. Martin, *Black Baptists*, 76 and 82–83.

27. Foner, *Reconstruction*, 89–102; DuBois, "Reconstruction and its Benefits," 782.

28. Ajayi, *Christian Missions* and "Nineteenth Century Origins"; Ayandele, *Missionary Impact*; Sanneh, *Abolitionists Abroad*.

29. Page, *The Black Bishop*; Ajayi, *Christian Missions*, chapter 7.

30. Ajaye, *Christian Missions*, chapter 8; Ayandele, *Missionary Impact*, chapter 7.

31. Brown, "A History of the People of Lagos," 220–21. Four African-owned newspapers operated in Lagos in the 1880s: the *Lagos Times*, launched by Saro businessman R. B. Blaize in 1876; the *Lagos Observer*, by another wealthy businessman, J. B. Benjamin, in 1878; the *Eagle and Lagos Critic*, by O. E. Macaulay, a member of the Crowther family, in 1883; and *The Mirror*, edited by P. Adolphus Marke beginning in 1887. Ayandele, *Missionary Impact*, 196–97.

32. For one complaint, see the *Lagos Observer*, March 20, 1886; also Ayandele, *Missionary Impact*, 247.

33. Kopytoff, *Preface*, 286; Ajayi, *Christian Missions*, 214, 233, and 242. The United African Company became the Royal Niger Company in 1886, chartered to rule northern Nigeria on behalf of the British government. Its corporate descendant is today's Unilever.

34. Henry Johnson to Hutchinson, March 31, 1881, G3/A2/01, CMS Papers, quoted in Ayandele, *Missionary Impact*, 184. Johnson was the older brother of Samuel Johnson, author of *A History of the Yorubas*. A biographical sketch of Henry Johnson is in Kopytoff, *Preface*, 289, and Ajayi, *Christian Missions*, 161.

35. Brown, "A History," 203. James Johnson was not related to Henry Johnson. See Kopytoff, *Preface*, 289, and, for a full biography, Ayandele, *Holy Johnson*.

36. "Notice," *Lagos Observer*, November 19, 1885.

37. Yoruba cultural nationalism, as the movement has come to be known, has been well studied, beginning with Coleman, *Nigeria: Background to Nationalism*, 327–28; Ajayi, "Nineteenth Century Origins," 207–8; Ayandele, *Missionary Impact*, chapter 8; Zachernuk, *Colonial Subjects*, chapter 3.

38. For the education bill and reaction to it, see Brown, "A History," 199–202; Ayandele, *Missionary Impact*, 256–57; and Law, "Local Amateur Scholarship," 62.

39. "The Education Ordinance," *Lagos Times*, July 12, 1882. An editorial in the *Lagos Observer* of July 20, 1882, was more sympathetic to the government's efforts.

40. James Johnson to F. E. Wigram, August 5, 1881, G3/A2/01, CMS.

41. Brown, "History," 282.

42. Interview with Olabode Vaughan and Dr. Femi Vaughan, Lagos, July 12, 2011; interview with Idowu Vaughan, Lagos, July 15, 2011.

43. A Mary Pettiford is listed under "Deaths in Parish" for 1881 in E. A. Alawode's unpublished "Historical Sketch of the First Baptist Church." I'm grateful to Kristin Mann for sharing her notes on this pamphlet with me.

44. Newell, *The Power to Name*.

45. Ajayi, *Christian Missions*, 267; Ayandele, *Missionary Impact*; Peel, *Religious Encounter*, especially chapter 10.

46. Vincent, *Africa and the Gospel*, 29–30. On educated Lagosian opinion about British imperialism in this period more generally, see Zachernuk, *Colonial Subjects*, 58–59.

47. Paul, Silas, and others, "Letter to the Editor," *Lagos Observer* (February 6, 1886).

48. W. J. David, "Baptism and Building," *FMJ* (February 1884): 3.

49. "Remeses," letter to the editor entitled "The Baptist Elementary Treat," *Lagos Observer*, April 10, 1884.

50. "Brother David's Visit," *FMJ* (July 1884): 2; Foreign Mission Board, "Fortieth Annual Report" (May 6, 1885); Duval, *Baptist Missions in Nigeria*, 109; Ajayi, *Christian Missions*, 268 fn 3. For "exotic" displays of African people during this period, see Rydell, *All the World's a Fair*.

51. Southern Baptist Convention Foreign Mission Board, *Thirty-Ninth Annual Report* (May 7, 1884). For Eubank's arrival and background, see *FMJ* (January 1882 and August 1884).

52. For their backgrounds, see *FMJ* of April 1884 and August 1884.

53. W. W. Harvey to Tupper, November 16, 1885; Harvey to Tupper, February 21, 1887, IMB. I appreciate Jim Berwick's help in obtaining materials from this file.

54. *FMJ* (August 1884); Strother Moses Cook, "My Story of the Yoruba Country, West Coast of Africa," handwritten (Louisville, Kentucky: 1892), 30 and 34; "Obituary: Rev. Strother Mosses [*sic*] Cook, A Devoted Missionary," *LWR* (June 8, 1907): 7. Also see "Memorial Service," *LS* (June 19, 1907).

55. FMB Minutes, September 6, 1886, and January 3, 1887, at archives.imb.org; Smith to Tupper, April 7, 1887, IMB; "Obituary: Rev. Strother Mosses Cook, A Devoted Missionary," *LWR* (June 8, 1907): 7. Cook arrived back in the United States in September 1887 via Antwerp on the ship *Belgenland* (*New York, Passenger Lists, 1820–1957*, accessed through ancestry.com).

56. David to Tupper, July 16, 1887 and December 15, 1887, IMB.

57. Eubank to Tupper, October 29, 1885; David to Tupper, February 24, 1887, IMB.

58. David to Tupper, February 24, 1887, IMB (emphasis in the original). On the new CMS missionaries, see Ayandele, *Missionary Impact*, 213–14 and Ajayi, *Christian Missions*, 250–51.

59. Webster, *African Churches*, 51–52; also see Stone's obituaries in the *LWR* (May 10, 1913) and *LS* (May 14, 1913).

60. Webster, *African Churches*, 53 and 55; Cook, "My Story."

61. David Brown Vincent later changed his name to Mojola Agbebi. There are many sources on his life, including Ayandele, *A Visionary of the African Church*.

62. Foreign Mission Board of the Southern Baptist Convention, "Forty-Second Annual Report" (May 6, 1887), at archives.imb.org.

63. Roberson, *History of the Baptists of Lagos*, 39–40; Webster, *African Churches*, 55.

64. Ojo, "Historical Sketch"; Babalola, "Short History"; Webster, *African Churches*, 55. On Baptist principles, I have found Stanley J. Grenz, *The Baptist Congregation* helpful.

65. Roberson, "History of the Baptists of Lagos," 39–40.

66. According to Ojo, "Historical Sketch," the "pioneers" of the NBC were: Daddy J. C. Vaughan, Deacon Levi Green Agbelusi, Dr. Mojola Agbebi (then David Brown Vincent), Rev. Lajide Tubi (then W. L. Mills) and Mrs. Tubi, Mr. and Mrs. S. O. Milton, Mr. J. B. Clay, Mr. and Mrs. John Ajala Stone, Mr. N. A. Williams, Sisters

Oniwande, Dorcas Ojo, Harriet Ojo, Mammy Fraser, Bros. J. W. and B. C. Vaughan, Bros E. Alao and J. Adejemi Ojo, Thomas Adams, Bada Ogunsawa, Sister Betsy Clay, Mrs. Allen, Benj. Laryonu[?], and W. Lajide Cole. Levi Green Agbelusi's background is mentioned in Roberson, "A History of the Baptists of Lagos, 33. Agbebi's Saro parents are mentioned in J. G. Campbell, "The Late Dr. Rev. Mojola Agbebi, M.S., Ph.D., D.D.," *Nigerian Pioneer* (June 22, 1917). The *Lagos Observer* of March 24, 1888 reported that the first members of the Native Baptist Church were "principally Ijayes."

67. The wording is attributed to "Daddy" Solomon Alawode. Ojo, "Historical Sketch."

68. "The Native Baptist Church," *LS* (March 4, 1893); "Report of the Celebration of the 19th Anniversary, Native Baptist Church," *LS* (April 17, 1907); Roberson, *History of the Baptists of Lagos*, 41–42; Roberson, *History of Baptists in Nigeria*, 181–83. The report to the board, evidently dated March 15, 1888, has not been located, but it is mentioned in Eubank to Tupper, April 30, 1888, IMB.

69. S. T. Ola. Akande, "The Founding of Ebenezer Baptist Church," *The Church Evangel* 2, 2 (February 1968): 5–9.

70. *Lagos Observer* (April 14, 1888): 4.

71. Smith to Tupper, May 2, 1888, IMB; "Report of the Celebration of the 19th Anniversary, Native Baptist Church," *LS* (April 17, 1907); Eubank to Tupper, April 30, 1888; Stone to Tupper, June 6, 1888, enclosing a printed copy of "A Protest Against and Denouncement of Statements Made in a Paper Which Had Been Privately Circulated in Lagos to Injure the Reputation of Rev. M. L. Stone," dated June 4, 1888, and signed by M. L. Stone, Pastor, Native Baptist Church, IMB.

72. J. C. Vaughan, Sam M. Harden, D. B. Vincent, and Sarah M. Harden to Tupper, November 14, 1888 in M. L. Stone's correspondence file, IMB. This letter refers to at least one other, probably from May 1888, by the same senders.

73. "The Native Baptist Church," *LS* (March 4, 1893); *LWR* (March 4, 1893): 2; Babalola, "Short History."

74. David to Tupper, July 25, 1888, IMB.

75. David to Tupper, October 18, 1888, IMB.

76. David to Tupper, July 25, 1888, IMB.

77. Quoted in Ayandele, *Missionary Impact*, 214.

78. Smith to Tupper, May 14, 1891, IMB.

79. *Annual Catalog of the Richmond Institute for 1879 and 1880*, including "Historical Sketch of the Richmond Institute" (Richmond: Wm. Ellis Jones, 1880); Worcester Massachusetts Census, 1880, accessed through ancestry.com; *Lagos Observer* (August 21, 1886).

80. *Lagos Observer* (November 10 and 17, 1888): 2; *FMJ* (December 1888): 1.

81. Ojo, "Historical Sketch."

82. *LWR* (September 22, 1894).

83. He is James Olabode Vaughan, whom I thank for his continued assistance.

84. Ayandele, *Missionary Impact*, 203 (quoted); also Webster, *African Churches*, 61–62.

85. Ajayi, *Christian Missions*, chapter 8; Ayandele, *Missionary Impact*, 215–32; Newton to Tupper, March 2, 1891, IMB; see also Webster, *African Churches*, 59.

86. Peel, *Religious Encounter*, 146–48; Webster, *African Churches*, 63; Newton to Tupper, April 21, 1892, IMB.

87. Lynch, *Edward Wilmot Blyden*, 221–23; Newton to Tupper, March 2, 1891, IMB.

88. Vincent, *Africa and the Gospel*, 9; Ayandele, *Missionary Impact*, 217–20 and 254 (Blyden quotation); Lynch, *Edward Wilmot Blyden*, 224–25. Also see Webster, *African Churches*, 65.

89. UNA Minutes, August 14, 1891, quoted in Webster, *African Churches*, 68.

90. Vincent, *Africa and the Gospel*, 15.

91. Ajayi, "Nineteenth Century Origins"; also see Matory, "The English Professors of Brazil" and Zachernuk, *Colonial Subjects*, chapter 3.

92. Newton to Tupper, March 2, 1891; also see Eubank to Tupper, February 5, 1889, and September 18, 1890, IMB. "Cambellites," sometimes known as Disciples of Christ, sought to restore Christianity to its early fundamentals, part of which entailed uniting the different denominations. The movement originated in the Second Great Awakening and was particularly concentrated in western Pennsylvania, West Virginia, and Kentucky. See Williams et al., *The Stone-Campbell Movement*.

93. Newton to Tupper, March 2 and May 22, 1891, IMB.

94. James Churchwill Vaughan's will dated 1889 with a codicil dated January 20, 1893, Lagos Probate Registry, vol. 1, pp. 259–262. I thank Kristin Mann for sharing with me her notes on this document. Though the residence at 24 Igbosere Road that Aida Vaughan inherited is now leased for office space, a reconstructed building and the land—prime urban real estate—is still owned by her descendants. Interview with James Olabode Vaughan, July 14, 2003, Lagos; Rosiji, *Lady Ademola*, 11.

95. Conveyance between Samuel Macaulay and others and James Churchill Vaughan, October 3, 1891, Lagos Land Registry.

96. "Burrell Carter Vaughan," in Adeoye Deniga, *African Leaders Past and Present*, RC; Michael Ayo Vaughan interview with Kristin Mann, March 1974, Lagos (with thanks to her for sharing this). On "outside marriages," see Mann, *Marrying Well*.

97. For photography studios in Lagos at this time, see Brown, "History," 149. The traveler Charles Smith reported that there were three commercial photographers in Lagos in 1894, "all natives." *Glimpses*, 160.

98. Vaughan, *The Making of the First Indigenous Church*, 21.

99. On retouching glass plate negatives in the nineteenth century Gold Coast, see Haney, "Lutterodt Family Studios," 76–78.

100. Genesis 10:18; 1 Chronicles 1:16.

101. On photography in West Africa, see Peffer and Cameron, *Portraiture and Photography*.

102. I thank John Wood Sweet, Jim Berwick, and Olubukola Gbadegesin for helping me puzzle through the possible meanings of this mysterious placard.

103. "The Late James Churchwill Vaughan," *LWR* (September 23, 1893).

Chapter 7

1. Thompson, "The Vaughan Family." On Thompson and her writing on Africa, see Campbell, *Middle Passages*, chapter 7.

2. Haley, *Roots*; Alex Haley, "My Furthest-Back Person—'the African,'" *NYT* (July 16, 1972).

3. Aida Arabella Stradford quoted in Thompson, "The Vaughan Family," 55. A copy

of her family history is in the Jewel Lafontant-Mankarious Papers. In her remark about family trees, Stradford was echoing Frederick Douglass's observation that "genealogical trees don't flourish among slaves." Douglass, *Life and Times*, 13.

4. Peter Kerr, "600 'Cousins' Meet to Celebrate Roots," *NYT* (June 28, 1982): B11.

5. The *Lagos Weekly Record*'s editor was John Payne Jackson, who like Vaughan had come to Nigeria from Liberia, where his parents had emigrated from the United States. Omu, "Journalism and the Rise of Nigerian Nationalism."

6. "The Late James Churchwill Vaughan," *LWR* (September 23, 1893).

7. Payne, *Table of Principal Events*, 14; CSO 26/26915, "Ikoyi Cemetery," NAI. I thank the late Mrs. Apinke Coker for showing me Vaughan's burial plot in June 2002 and Kunle Ademola for taking me there again in July 2003.

8. A Yoruba historian, "from 'A General History of the Yoruba Country': James Churchwill Vaughan," *LS* (December 6, 1905). According to Robin Law, the author of this article was Rev. Michael Thomas Euler Ajayi (1846–1913), a Sierra Leonean of Yoruba origin and a clergyman of the separatist United Native African Church, who revealed his identity in his own column in the *Lagos Standard*, February 28, 1906. Law, "Early Yoruba Historiography."

9. *Eko Akete: Iwe Irohin Ọsọsẹ* 11, 61 (September 8, 1923). I thank Josiah Olubowale for his translation help.

10. Macmillan, *The Red Book of West Africa*, 108.

11. Oyedokun, "The Young Nigerians," *Nigerian Spectator* (August 18, 1923): 8; Sklar, *Nigerian Political Parties*, 48.

12. Barber, *I Could Speak until Tomorrow*.

13. Rosiji, *Lady Ademola*, 11.

14. Copy of the *oriki* in possession of James Olabode Vaughan and also printed in Babalola, *Àwọn Oríkì Orílẹ̀ Mẹ́tàdínlógbọ̀n*, 125–28. I'm grateful to Dr. Duro Adeleke of the Department of Linguistics and African Languages, University of Ibadan for his painstaking translation and interpretation.

15. Moore, "The Story of Kofoworola Aina Moore," 324.

16. Aida Arabella Stradford, "Memoirs of the Vaughan Family," n.d., in Jewel Lafantant-Mankarious Papers. I estimate the date it was written from the text's reference to Ayo Vaughan-Richards as the mother of three children, which was only true between 1965, when her third child was born, and 1968, when she became the mother of a fourth.

17. Mabel M. Smythe, "One Black Family," unpublished autobiographical essay with a note saying "sent copies to JDM [her mother Josephine Dibble Murphy] & HM Bond 10/13/69," in Hugh H. and Mabel M. Smythe Papers, box 96, folder 3, Dibble Family Material.

18. Email communication from Elsie Taylor-Goins, April 16, 2013.

19. According to Mabel Smythe, Aida Moore had been corresponding with her grandmother in Camden, Sallie Lee Dibble, before the visits began in the 1920s. Smythe, "One Black Family"; Mabel Murphy Smythe (Haith) interview with Ann Miller Morin (May 2, 1986). I thank Mary Rolinson for sharing her copy of this interview with me.

20. There is a wealth of literature on these developments. I have drawn in particular on Wilkerson, *The Warmth of Other Suns* and Campbell, *Middle Passages*, 190–207.

21. Thompson, "The Vaughan Family"; *New York, State Census, 1925*, accessed through

ancestry.com; Sara Laughlin Thompson's passport applications, March 3, 1920, and May 29, 1922, *U.S. Passport Applications, 1795–1925,* accessed through ancestry.com; Akinyeye, *Eko, Landmarks of Lagos.*

22. Rosiji, *Lady Ademola,* 12–13.

23. Sklar, *Nigerian Political Parties,* 46; Coleman, *Nigeria: Background to Nationalism,* 196–98.

24. "BC Vaughan—New Villa," *LS* (March 26, 1913): 6.

25. For the land case, see Funso Afolayan, "Herbert Macaulay," in Shillington, *Encyclopedia of African History,* 871; Burrell Vaughan's role is mentioned in "Burrell Carter Vaughan," in Adeoye Deniga, *African Leaders Past and Present,* RC; Michael Ayo Vaughan interview with Kristin Mann, March 1974, Lagos (with thanks to her for sharing this).

26. Smythe, "One Black Family"; Rosiji, *Lady Ademola,* 15–18. Aida Arabella Moore arrived in New York on May 29, 1925, with her seventeen-year-old daughter Gladys Evelyn Moore. She then arrived back in South Hampton, U.K., traveling alone, on August 18, 1925. *Passenger and Crew Lists of Vessels Arriving at New York, New York, 1897–1957* and *Board of Trade: Commercial and Statistical Department and Successors: Inwards Passenger Lists,* both accessed through ancestry.com.

27. "Prejudice No Obstacle," *Newark Evening News* (June 6, 1934); I thank Elsie Taylor-Goins for sharing her clipping with me. Sutherland's then six-year-old son later remembered that Mrs. Moore gave him a palm fan from Africa; Thompson, "The Vaughan Family."

28. The brothers were William J. Carter and J. Emmett Carter, both podiatrists. William Carter's row house at 213 W. 138th Street, on "Striver's Row" in Harlem, is pictured in Thompson, "The Vaughan Family," 57.

29. They lived either at 3150 Vincennes Avenue or 3150 Vernon Avenue, as reported in "A Visitor from Cuba," *Afro-American* (Baltimore, October 24, 1925): 16 and "Society," *Chicago Defender* (June 26, 1926): 5.

30. C. F. Stradford and Truman K. Gibson, "Restrictive Covenants," *Chicago Defender* (May 18, 1940). A brief biography of Stradford is in Deton J. Brooks Jr., "Stradford Saved Father from Lynchers' Noose," *Chicago Defender* (June 5, 1943).

31. Smythe, "One Black Family."

32. Aerogram letter from A. Moore to Mr. H. H. Smythe, August 22, 1957, in file marked "Nigerian Field Trip—General," Hugh Smythe Papers, vol. 2, no. 20, microfilm reel 1; interview with Olabode Vaughan and Kunle Ademola, June 27, 2006, Lagos.

33. Crawford et al., "The Camden African-American Heritage Project," especially 38 and 42; Josephine H. Dibble Murphy interview (July 5, 1973), David Roberts Oral History Collection.

34. McWhirter, *Red Summer*; Tuttle, *Race Riot.*

35. Ellsworth, *Death in a Promised Land*; Monée Fields-White, "Greenwood, Okla.: The Legacy of the Tulsa Race Riot," *The Root* (February 24, 2011), http://www.theroot .com/articles/culture/2011/02/greenwood_oklahoma_from_the_black_wall_street _to_the_tulsa_race_riot.html (July 28, 2014). Stradford was posthumously cleared of all charges in 1996. See "Seventy-five years after the fact and six decades after his death, a black Tulsa businessman has been cleared of wrongdoing in connection with one of

the deadliest race riots in American history," *NYT* (October 26, 1996) and "Oklahoma Officials Clear Black Man in 1921 Riot and Apologize to Family," *Jet* (November 18, 1996): 8. Stradford's brief biography is in his obituary: "J. B. Stradford Dies in Chicago: Pioneer Business Man Amassed Fortune, *New York Amsterdam News* (January 4, 1936): 4.

36. Hartman, *Lose Your Mother*, 98.

37. Jewel Lafontant quoted in Thompson, "The Vaughan Family."

38. "Meeting of the Rev. Samuel Crowther with his Mother," *Church Missionary Gleaner* (June 1, 1847): 63; also see Page, *The Black Bishop*, 96.

39. The Baptist missionary Richard Stone, with whom Vaughan was connected, based a chapter in his memoir on his close acquaintance with Crowther. See Stone, *In Afric's Forest and Jungle*, chapter 4. On other family reunions, see Ajayi, *Christian Missions in Nigeria*, 27 and Kopytoff, *Preface*, 57. I have also benefited from conversations with Kristin Mann on this point.

40. I'm grateful to Kristin Mann for suggesting these possibilities. For the NNDP, see Coleman, *Nigeria*, 196–200. On processes of political incorporation in Lagos and Yorubaland, see Barnes, *Patrons and Power* and Peel, *Ijeshas and Nigerians*.

41. Rosiji, *Lady Ademola*, 81.

42. Kunle Akinshemoyin, "How America Strengthens Ties with Nigeria," *Sunday Times* (Lagos) (February 11, 1973): 14; Special to the *NYT*, "Return to West Africa Isn't New for Blacks from the Americas," *NYT* (September 2, 1973): 22; Thompson, "The Vaughan Family."

43. Interview with James Olabode Vaughan, Lagos, June 27, 2006. More on Vaughan-Richards's efforts is in Lindsay, "Remembering His Country Marks," although the interpretation in that essay is superseded by that in this book.

44. Hirschman, *Exit, Voice, and Loyalty*. For an application of this schema to African Americans in nineteenth-century America, see Witt, *Patriots and Cosmopolitans*. Interestingly, Hirschman's model was inspired by his observations in Nigeria.

45. Sutherland and Meyer, *Guns and Gandhi in Africa*; Campbell, *Middle Passages*, 329–34.

46. Transcript of Bill Sutherland interview with Prexy Nesbitt and Mimi Edmunds, July 19, 2003, in Brooklyn, New York, with an introduction by William Minter, from material for Minter et al., *No Easy Victories*. I thank Elizabeth Schmidt for sharing this with me.

47. Sanneh, *Abolitionists Abroad*; Cooper, Holt, and Scott, *Beyond Slavery*, 7–8.

48. Oladele, *A Life for Freedom and Service*; Rosiji, *Lady Ademola*; Sutherland and Meyer, *Guns and Ghandi*, 3; Eric Pace, "Jewel Lafontant-Mankarious, Lawyer and U.S. Official, Dies," *NYT* (June 3, 1997): D22; Patricia Sullivan, "Mabel Smythe-Haith; Envoy, State Department Official," *Washington Post* (February 25, 2006); M. P. McQueen, "Obama Pal Campaigns for Own Firm," *Wall Street Journal* (August 14, 2010).

49. Kofo Ademola to Jewel Lafontant (September 20, 1978), in Jewel Lafontant-Mankarious Papers, 30/310 VI. ss.2.

50. Baptist, *The Half Has Never Been Told*; Johnson, *River of Dark Dreams*. The second half of that formulation comes, of course, from Rodney, *How Europe Underdeveloped Africa*.

BIBLIOGRAPHY

ARCHIVAL SOURCES

The sources from Southern Baptist missionaries in Nigeria are located in three different repositories: the Southern Baptist Historical Library and Archives in Nashville, the International Mission Board Archives and Records Services in Richmond, and the Nigerian Baptist Theological Seminary in Ogbomosho, Nigeria. In many cases, the originals are held in Nashville or Ogbomosho with microfilm copies in Richmond. Here, I have listed the records that I consulted in each of the three locations and noted where they overlap. In the notes, I refer to the specific location where I found each particular document, notwithstanding its existence elsewhere. Since the research for this book was conducted, additional copies of some materials from the Cecil Roberson collection have been deposited in the David M. Rubenstein Rare Book and Manuscript Library at Duke University, but I have not listed them here.

Nigeria

Kenneth Dike Library, University of Ibadan
    Manuscript Collections
        Herbert Macaulay Papers
Land Registry, Lagos
    Conveyances
National Archives, Ibadan
    Church Missionary Society Papers, Yoruba Mission, CMS(Y)
    Colony of Lagos Government *Gazettes*
    Papers from the Chief Secretary's Office (CSO Series)
    Wesleyan Methodist Missionary Society Papers
Probate Registry, Lagos
    Wills
Nigerian Baptist Theological Seminary, Ogbomosho
    Cecil Roberson Collection

"The Bowen Papers," compiled by Cecil Roberson
  T. J. Bowen Missionary Correspondence
  T. J. Bowen Diary
  Lurana Bowen Diary
  W. J. David Diary (1875–1877)
  Adeoye Deniga, *African Leaders Past and Present*
  Historical Pamphlets of Nigerian Baptists
  A. Ojo, "Historical Sketch of the Native Baptist Church now known as 'Ebenezer
    Baptist Church' and 'Araromi Baptist Church' (founded April, 1888)" (1938)

United Kingdom

National Archives, Kew
  Colonial Office Files (CO 147, CO 700, CO 879)
  Foreign Office Files (FO 84, FO 881)
School of Oriental and African Studies Library, London
  Methodist Missionary Society-West Africa Correspondence

United States

James P. Boyce Centennial Library, Southern Baptist Theological Seminary, Louisville,
    Kentucky
  Strother Moses Cook, "My Story of the Yoruba Country, West Coast of Africa," 1892.
Camden Archives and Museum, Camden, South Carolina
  Wills
  Vertical Files
Vivian G. Harsh Research Collection of Afro-American History and Literature, Chicago
    Public Library
  Era Bell Thompson Papers
International Mission Board Archives and Records Services, Southern Baptist
    Convention, Richmond, Virginia
  Cecil Roberson Collection (on microfilm)
    "The Bowen Papers," compiled by Cecil Roberson
    W. J. David Diary (1875–1877)
    Historical Pamphlets of Nigerian Baptists
  Missionary Correspondence Files (microfilmed copies of those listed under Southern
    Baptist Historical Library and Archives, below)
Kershaw County Registrar of Deeds, Camden, South Carolina
  Conveyances
Library of Congress, Washington, D.C.
  American Colonization Society Papers
  Hugh H. and Mabel M. Smythe Papers
Oberlin College Archives, Oberlin, Ohio
  Jewel Lafontant-Mankarious Papers
Probate Office, Kershaw County Courthouse, Camden, South Carolina
  Jacob Hammond Estate Papers
  William P. Hammond Estate Papers

Wilie Vaughan Estate Papers

Schomburg Center for Research in Black Culture, Manuscripts, Archives and Rare
        Books Division, New York Public Library, New York, New York
    Hugh H. Smythe Papers

South Carolina Department of Archives and History, Columbia, South Carolina
    Court of Common Pleas, Kershaw County
    Court of General Sessions, Indictments, Kershaw District
    Deeds, Kershaw County
    Magistrates and Freeholders Court, Kershaw County, Trial Papers 1802–1861
    Miscellaneous Indexes, Kershaw County
    Probate Records, Kershaw County
    State Land Grants

South Carolina Historical Society, Charleston, South Carolina
    Timothy Ford Papers

South Caroliniana Library, University of South Carolina, Columbia, South Carolina
    William Blanding Papers
    Bonds Conway Papers
    Gilmor, Robert. "Notes taken in a tour through the states of Virginia, North Carolina,
        and South Carolina in the year 1806"
    Kershaw County Justices and Freeholders Court Records
    Records of the First Baptist Church, Kershaw County, Camden, 1810–1838

Southern Baptist Historical Library and Archives, Nashville, Tennessee
    Foreign Mission Board Historical Files, 1845–1986
    Missionary Correspondence Files (all also on microfilm at the International Mission
        Board Archives and Records Services in Richmond, Virginia)
        Thomas Jefferson Bowen, 1848–1867
        Jeremiah H. Cason, 1854–1869
        William H. Clarke, 1853–59
        W. W. Colley, 1874–79
        Strother M. Cook, 1884–91
        Solomon Cosby, 1880
        William Joshua David, 1871–1894
        John Day, 1846–1859
        P. A. Eubank, 1881–1911
        Joseph M. Harden, 1851–71
        Wiley Harvey, 1884–1890
        Christopher Newton, 1889–95
        A. D. Phillips, 1853–1879
        R. W. Priest, 1855–1890
        T. A. Reid, 1857–1911
        Charles E. Smith, 1884–1912
        Moses L. Stone, 1888–1912
        Richard H. Stone, 1858–88
        Seldon Y. Trimble, 1854–73
    Nigeria Mission Minutes and Materials

Robert W. Woodruff Library, Atlanta University Center, Atlanta, Georgia
    David Roberts Oral History Collection

INTERVIEWS

Liberia

Dr. Othello Brandy, July 25, 2013, Monrovia

Nigeria

Demi Ademola, July 22, 2003, Lagos
Gboyega Ademola, July 9, 2006, Lagos
Kunle Ademola, July 13, 2003; July 13, 2004, July 8, 2005, Lagos
Apinke Coker, June, 22, 2002, Lagos
Lande Ejiwunmi, June 15, 2002 and July 14, 2004, Ibadan
Michael Akiniyi Fadoyin, December 7, 2015, Ijaye
Tijani Sakuni and Adeyemi Eesuola, Dec. 7, 2015, Ijaye
Ayoka Thompson, June 19, 2002, Ibadan
Oladenji Vaughan, July 9, 2006, Lagos
Idowu Vaughan, July 15, 2011, Lagos
James Olabode Vaughan, July 14, 2003, July 12, 2004, July 9, 2006, Lagos
James Olabode Vaughan and Kunle Ademola, June 27, 2006, Lagos
James Olabode Vaughan and Akin George, July 12, 2004, Lagos
James Olabode Vaughan and Dr. Femi Vaughan, July 12, 2011, Lagos
James Olabode Vaughan and Rotimi Vaughan, July 9, 2006, Lagos
Michael Ayo Vaughan, interview by Kristin Mann, 1974, Lagos

United States

Mabel Murphy Smythe (Haith) interview with Ann Miller Morin, May 2, 1986, for
    the Association for Diplomatic Studies and Training. Foreign Affairs Oral History
    Project. Women Ambassadors Series. Online at http://www.adst.org/OH%20TOCs
    /Smith,%20Mabel%20-%201986.toc.pdf.
Elsie Taylor-Goins, Oct. 20, 2005, Columbia, South Carolina

PRIVATE COLLECTIONS

Elsie Taylor-Goins, Columbia, South Carolina
    Family Bible of Maria Sophronia Lauly
James Olabode Vaughan, Lagos, Nigeria
    Family papers
Dr. Femi Vaughan, Lagos, Nigeria
    Family Bible

NEWSPAPERS

African Repository	*Baltimore Sun*
African Times	*Christian Index*
Anti-Slavery Reporter	*Church Missionary Gleaner*

The Commission
Defender (Chicago)
Eko Akete: Iwe Irohin Ọṣọṣẹ (Lagos)
Examiner (Louisville, Kentucky)
Foreign Mission Journal
Gazette (Camden, South Carolina)
Home and Foreign Journal
Iwe Irohin (Abeokuta, Nigeria)
Journal (Camden, South Carolina)
Lagos Observer
Lagos Standard
Lagos Times
Lagos Weekly Record
Liberia Herald
New York Amsterdam News

New York Colonization Journal
New York Times
Newark Evening News
Nigerian Advocate
Nigerian Pioneer
Nigerian Spectator
The State (Columbia, South Carolina)
Sunday Times (Lagos)
Wall Street Journal
Washington Post
Weekly Commercial (Wilmington,
    North Carolina)
Western Democrat (Charlotte,
    North Carolina)

PUBLISHED PRIMARY SOURCES

American Colonization Society. *Records of the American Colonization Society.* Washington, D.C.: Library of Congress Photoduplication Service, 1971.

Annual Catalog of the Richmond Institute for 1879 and 1880. Richmond: Wm. Ellis Jones, 1880.

Babalola, Adeboye. *Àwọn Oríkì Orílẹ̀ Mẹ́tàdínlógbọ̀n.* Lagos: Longman, 2000.

Ball, Charles. *Fifty Years in Chains; or, the Life of an American Slave.* New York: H. Dayton, 1859.

Bowen, T. J. *Central Africa: Adventures and Missionary Labors in Several Countries in the Interior of Africa, from 1849 to 1856.* Charleston: Southern Baptist Publication Society, 1857.

———. *Grammar and Dictionary of the Yoruba Language, With an Introductory Description of the Country and People of Yoruba.* Washington, D.C.: Smithsonian Institution, 1858.

Burton, Richard F. *Abeokuta and the Cameroons Mountains: An Exploration.* London: Tinsley Brothers, 1863.

Campbell, Robert. *A Few Facts, Relating to Lagos, Abbeokuta, and Other Sections of Central Africa.* Philadelphia: King & Baird, 1860.

———. "A Pilgrimage to My Motherland: An Account of a Journey among the Egbas and Yorubas of Central Africa in 1859–60." In *Search for a Place: Black Separatism and Africa, 1860,* edited by Howard H. Bell. Ann Arbor: University of Michigan Press, 1860.

Canot, Theodore. *A Slaver's Log Book; or Twenty Years' Residence in Africa.* Englewood Cliffs, N.J.: Prentice Hall, 1976.

Church Missionary Society Archive. Section IV: Africa Missions. Part 4: Nigeria— Yoruba Mission 1844–1880. Original Papers. Marlborough, Wiltshire: Adam Matthew Publications, 1997.

Clarke, W. H. *Travels and Explorations in Yorubaland, 1854–1858.* Ibadan: Ibadan University Press, 1972.

Colony of Lagos. *Government Gazette*. Lagos: Government Printer, 1889–96.

Cooper, Helene. *The House at Sugar Beach: In Search of a Lost African Childhood*. New York: Simon & Schuster, 2009.

Correspondence Relative to the Catawba Indians: Embracing Gov. Seabrook's Letter to the Special Agent and Commissioners Appointed by Him. Columbia, S.C.: State Printer, 1849.

Cowan, Alexander M. *Liberia, as I Found It, in 1858*. Frankfort, Ky.: A. G. Hodges, 1858.

Delany, Martin Robison. *The Condition, Elevation, Emigration and Destiny of the Colored People of the United States*. Philadelphia: the author, 1852.

———. "Official Report of the Niger Valley Exploring Party." In *Search for a Place: Black Separatism and Africa, 1860*, edited by Howard H. Bell. Ann Arbor: University of Michigan Press, 1969.

Douglass, Frederick. *The Frederick Douglass Papers*. New Haven: Yale University Press, 1979.

———. *The Life and Times of Frederick Douglass, His Early Life as a Slave, His Escape from Bondage, and His Complete History to the Present Time*. Hartford, Conn.: Park Publishing Co., 1881.

Draine, Tony. *Kershaw District, South Carolina Tax List 1848 and 1849*. Columbia, S.C.: Congaree Publications, 1986.

Duval, Louis M. *Baptist Missions in Nigeria*. Richmond, Va.: Foreign Mission Board, Southern Baptist Convention, 1928.

1832 Tax List for the Town of Camden. *The South Carolina Magazine of Ancestral Research* 8, 1 (1980): 27–28.

Foote, Andrew H. *Africa and the American Flag*. New York: D. Appleton & Co., 1854.

Forbes, Frederick E. *Dahomey and the Dahomans*. London: Longman, 1851.

Garrison, William Lloyd. *Thoughts on African Colonization, or, an Impartial Exhibition of the Doctrines, Principles and Purposes of the American Colonization Society: Together with the Resolutions, Addresses and Remonstrances of the Free People of Color*. Boston: Garrison and Knapp, 1832.

Great Britain. House of Commons. *Parliamentary Papers*.

Hinderer, Anna. *Seventeen Years in the Yoruba Country*. 3rd. ed. London: Seeley, Jackson and Halliday, 1873.

Holden, Edith. *Blyden of Liberia: An Account of the Life and Labors of Edward Wilmot Blyden, LL.D. as Recorded in Letters and in Print*. New York: Vantage Press, 1966.

Holland, Edwin C. *A Refutation of the Calumnies Circulated against the Southern and Western States, Respecting the Institution and Existence of Slavery among Them*. Charleston: E. A. Miller, 1822.

Hopkins, A. G. "A Report on the Yoruba, 1910." *Journal of the Historical Society of Nigeria* 5 (1969): 67–100.

Jefferson, Thomas. *Notes on the State of Virginia*. Philadelphia: Prichard and Hall, 1788.

Lloyd's Steamboat Directory and Disasters on the Western Waters. Cincinnati: James T. Lloyd & Co., 1856.

Lugenbeel, James Washington. *Sketches of Liberia: Comprising a Brief Account of the Geography, Climate, Productions, and Diseases, of the Republic of Liberia*. 1st ed. Washington: C. Alexander, 1850.

Bibliography

Macmillan, Allister. *The Red Book of West Africa: Historical and Descriptive, Commercial and Industrial Facts, Figures, and Resources.* London: Frank Cass, 1920.

Massachusetts Colonization Society. *Tenth Annual Report of the Board of Managers of the Massachusetts Colonization Society.* Boston: T. R. Marvin & Son, 1851.

McCord, David J., ed. *The Statutes at Large of South Carolina.* Columbia, S.C.: A. S. Johnson, 1840.

McKay, John. *Report of Rev. John McKay, Colored Agent of the State Board of Colonization on Liberia.* Indianapolis: Austin H. Brown, State Printer, 1854.

Miller, Randall M., ed. *Dear Master: Letters of a Slave Family.* Athens: University of Georgia Press, 1990.

Moore, Kofoworola Aina. "The Story of Kofoworola Aina Moore, of the Yoruba Tribe, Nigeria." In *Ten Africans,* edited by Margery Perham, 323–43. London: Faber and Faber, 1963 [1936].

Moses, Wilson Jeremiah, ed. *Liberian Dreams: Back-to-Africa Narratives from the 1850s.* University Park, Pa.: Pennsylvania State University Press, 1998.

North Carolina Legislature. *Public Laws of the State of North-Carolina, Passed by the General Assembly at Its Session of 1858–'59.* Raleigh: Holden and Wilson, 1859.

Payne, John A. *Payne's Lagos and West African Almanack and Diary.* London: W. J. Johnson, 1882–1894.

———. *Table of Principal Events in Yoruba History.* Lagos: Andrew M. Thomas, 1893.

Rawlins, Richard Champion. *An American Journal, 1839–40.* Edited by John L. Tearle. Madison: Fairleigh Dickinson University Press, 2002.

Schweninger, Loren, Robert Shelton, Charles Edward Smith, and the Race and Slavery Petitions Project. *Race, Slavery, and Free Blacks: Series I, Petitions to Southern Legislatures, 1777–1867.* Bethesda, Md.: University Publications of America, 1999.

Smith, Amanda. *An Autobiography. The Story of the Lord's Dealings with Mrs. Amanda Smith the Colored Evangelist; Containing an Account of Her Life Work of Faith, and Her Travels in America, England, Ireland, Scotland, India, and Africa, as an Independent Missionary.* Chicago: Meyer & Brother, 1893.

Smith, C. S. *Glimpses of Africa, West and Southwest Coast.* Nashville, Tenn.: Publishing House A.M.E. Sunday School Union, 1895.

Southern Baptist Convention. Foreign Mission Board. *Annual Reports.* Online at http://archives.imb.org/solomon.asp.

———. *Minutes.* Online at http://archives.imb.org/solomon.asp.

Stone, R. H. *In Afric's Forest and Jungle; or, Six Years among the Yorubans.* New York, Chicago: Fleming H. Revell Company, 1899.

Teal, Harvey S., ed. *Five Visitors to Kershaw District, 1806–1832.* Pamphlet #7 in the Preserve series. Camden, S.C.: Kershaw County Historical Society, 1997.

———. *Kershaw County District Business Directory, 1854–1900.* Camden: Kershaw County Historical Society, 1999.

Townsend, George, comp. *Memoir of the Rev. Henry Townsend.* London: Marshall Brothers, 1887.

Tucker, Charlotte Maria. *Abbeokuta; or, Sunrise within the Tropics.* London: J. Nisbet and Co., 1854.

United States. *1790 United States Federal Census.*

———. *1800 United States Federal Census.*

———. *1810 United States Federal Census.*

———. *1820 United States Federal Census.*

———. *1830 United States Federal Census.*

———. *1840 United States Federal Census.*

———. *1850 United States Federal Census.*

———. *1860 United States Federal Census.*

———. *1880 United States Federal Census.*

Vincent, D. Brown. *Africa and the Gospel: Sermon, Debates, and Lecture.* Sierra Leone: Hon. T. J. Sawyerr and Lagos: Messrs T. A. King & Co., 1889.

Walker, David. *Walker's Appeal, in Four Articles; Together with a Preamble, to the Coloured Citizens of the World, but in Particular, and Very Expressly, to Those of the United States of America, Written in Boston, State of Massachusetts, September 28, 1829.* Boston: Revised and published by David Walker, 1830.

Wiley, Bell Irvin, ed. *Slaves No More: Letters from Liberia, 1833–1869.* Lexington: University Press of Kentucky, 1980.

Wood, J. Buckley. "On the Inhabitants of Lagos: Their Character, Pursuits, and Language." *Church Missionary Intelligencer* (1881): 683–91.

SECONDARY SOURCES

Ajayi, J. F. Ade. *Christian Missions in Nigeria: The Making of a New Elite.* Evanston: Northwestern University Press, 1965.

———. "Nineteenth Century Origins of Nigerian Nationalism." *Journal of the Historical Society of Nigeria* 2 (1961): 196–210.

Ajayi, J. F. Ade, and Robert Smith, *Yoruba Warfare in the Nineteenth Century.* 2nd. ed. Cambridge: Cambridge University Press, 1971.

Akande, S. T. Ola. "The Founding of Ebenezer Baptist Church." *The Church Evangel* 2, 2 (February 1968): 5–9.

Akere, Funso. "Linguistic Assimilation in Socio-Historical Dimensions in Urban and Sub-Urban Lagos." In *History of the Peoples of Lagos State.* Edited by Ade Adefuye, Babatunde Agiri, and Jide Osuntokun. Lagos: Lantern Books, 1987.

Akinsemoyin, Kunle and Alan Vaughan-Richards. *Building Lagos.* Lagos: F & A Services, 1976.

Akinyeye, O. A. *Eko, Landmarks of Lagos, Nigeria.* Lagos: Mandilas Group, 1999.

Allen, William E. "Historical Methodology and Writing the Liberian Past: The Case of Agriculture in the Nineteenth Century." *History in Africa* 32 (2005): 21–39.

———. "Liberia and the Atlantic World in the Nineteenth Century: Convergence and Effects." *History in Africa* 27 (2010): 7–49.

———. "Rethinking the History of Settler Agriculture in Nineteenth-Century Liberia." *International Journal of African Historical Studies* 37, 3 (2004): 435–62.

Atanda, J.A. *The New Oyo Empire.* London: Longman, 1973.

Altoff, Gerard T. *Amongst My Best Men: African-Americans and the War of 1812.* Put-in-Bay, Ohio: The Perry Group, 1996.

Anderson, Benedict R. *Imagined Communities: Reflections on the Origins and Spread of Nationalism*. New York: Verso, 2006.

Anderson, Gerald H., ed. *Biographical Dictionary of Christian Missions*. Grand Rapids, Mich.: Wm. B. Eerdmans Publishing, 1999.

Aptheker, Herbert. "Maroon Communities within the Present Limits of the United States." In *Maroon Societies: Rebel Slave Communities in the Americas*, edited by Richard Price. Baltimore: Johns Hopkins Press, 1996.

Ayandele, E. A. *Holy Johnson: Pioneer of African Nationalism, 1836–1917*. London: Frank Cass, 1970.

———. *The Missionary Impact on Modern Nigeria, 1842–1914: A Political and Social Analysis*. London: Longman, 1966.

———. *A Visionary of the African Church: Mojola Agbebi (1860–1917)*. Nairobi: East African Publishing House, 1971.

Babalola, Lagunju. *A Short History of Ebenezer Baptist Church*. Ibadan: Baptist Press, n.d. [1967].

Bailyn, Bernard. *Atlantic History: Concept and Contours*. Cambridge, Mass.: Harvard University Press, 2005.

Bailyn, Bernard and Patricia L. Denault, eds. *Soundings in Atlantic History: Latent Structures and Intellectual Currents, 1500–1830*. Cambridge, Mass.: Harvard University Press, 2009.

Baker, Pauline H. *Urbanization and Political Change: The Politics of Lagos, 1917–1967*. Berkeley: University of California Press, 1974.

Baptist, Edward E. *The Half Has Never Been Told: Slavery and the Making of American Capitalism*. New York: Basic Books, 2014.

Barber, Karin. *I Could Speak Until Tomorrow: Oriki, Women and the Past in a Yoruba Town*. Washington, D.C.: Smithsonian Institution Press, 1991.

Barcia Paz, Manuel. *West African Warfare in Bahia and Cuba: Soldier Slaves in the Atlantic World, 1807–1844*. Oxford: Oxford University Press, 2014.

Barnes, Sandra T. *Patrons and Power: Creating a Political Community in Metropolitan Lagos*. Bloomington: Indiana University Press, 1986.

Belcher, Max, Svend E. Holsoe, and Bernard L. Herman. *A Land and Life Remembered: Americo-Liberian Folk Architecture*. Athens, Ga.: University of Georgia Press, 1988.

Benjamin, Thomas. *The Atlantic World: Europeans, Africans, Indians and Their Shared History, 1400–1900*. Cambridge: Cambridge University Press, 2009.

Berlin, Ira. *Generations of Captivity: A History of African-American Slaves*. Cambridge, Mass.: Harvard University Press, 2003.

———. *Many Thousands Gone: The First Two Centuries of Slavery in North America*. Cambridge, Mass.: Harvard University Press, 1998.

———. *Slaves without Masters: The Free Negro in the Antebellum South*. New York: Oxford University Press, 1981.

Biobaku, Saburi O. *The Egba and their Neighbours, 1842–1872*. Oxford: Clarendon Press, 1957.

Blackett, Richard. *Beating against the Barriers: Biographical Essays in Nineteenth-Century Afro-American History*. Baton Rouge: Louisiana State University Press, 1986.

————. "Martin R. Delany and Robert Campbell: Black Americans in Search of an African Colony." *Journal of Negro History* 62 (1977): 1–25.

Bleser, Carol K. Rockroth. *The Promised Land: The History of the South Carolina Land Commission, 1869–89*. Columbia: University of South Carolina Press, 1969.

Brown, Robert T. *Immigrants to Liberia, 1843–1865: An Alphabetical Listing*. Philadelphia: Institute for Liberian Studies, 1980.

Brown, Spencer. "A History of the People of Lagos, 1852–1886." Ph.D. diss., Northwestern University, 1964.

Brown, Vincent. *The Reaper's Garden: Death and Power in the World of Atlantic Slavery*. Cambridge, Mass.: Harvard University Press, 2008.

Burin, Eric. *Slavery and the Peculiar Solution: A History of the American Colonization Society*. Gainesville: University Press of Florida, 2005.

Campbell, James T. *Middle Passages: African American Journeys to Africa, 1787–2005*. New York: Penguin, 2006.

Canizares-Esguerra, Jorge and Erik R. Seeman, eds. *The Atlantic in Global History, 1500–2000*. Upper Saddle River, N.J.: Prentice Hall, 2007.

Canney, D. L. *Africa Squadron: The U.S. Navy and the Slave Trade, 1842–1861*. Washington, D.C.: Potomac Books, 2006.

Carter, Janie Leigh. "John Day: A Founder of the Republic of Liberia and the Southern Baptist Liberian Missionary Movement in the Nineteenth Century." M.A. thesis, Wake Forest University, 1998.

Castillo, Lisa Earl. "Mapping the Nineteenth-Century Brazilian Returnee Movement: Demographics, Life Stories and the Question of Slavery." *Atlantic Studies* 13, 1 (2016): 25–52.

Clegg, Claude A., III. *The Price of Liberty: African Americans and the Making of Liberia*. Chapel Hill: University of North Carolina Press, 2004.

Coclanis, Peter A. "Atlantic World or Atlantic/World?" *William and Mary Quarterly* 63, 4 (2006): 725–42.

Coleman, James S. *Nigeria: Background to Nationalism*. Berkeley and Los Angeles: University of California Press, 1958.

Cooper, Frederick. "Conditions Analogous to Slavery: Imperialism and Free Labor Ideology in Africa." In Cooper, Holt, and Scott, *Beyond Slavery*, 107–49.

————. "Modernizing Bureaucrats, Backward Africans, and the Development Concept." In *International Development and the Social Sciences: Essays on the History and Politics of Knowledge*, edited by Frederick Cooper and Randall Packard, 64–92. Berkeley: University of California Press, 1997.

Cooper, Frederick, Thomas C. Holt and Rebecca J. Scott. *Beyond Slavery: Explorations of Race, Labor, and Citizenship in Postemancipation Societies*. Chapel Hill: University of North Carolina Press, 2000.

Crais, Clifton, and Pamela Scully. *Sara Baartman and the Hottentot Venus: A Ghost Story and a Biography*. Princeton: Princeton University Press, 2009.

Crawford, Lindsay, Ashley Guinn, McKenzie Kubly, Lindsay Maybin, Patricia Shandor, Santi Thompson, and Louis Venters. "The Camden African-American Heritage Project." Public History Program, University of South Carolina, 2006, at http://scholarcommons.sc.edu/pubhist_books/2.

Curtin, Philip D. *The Image of Africa; British Ideas and Action, 1780–1850*. Madison: University of Wisconsin Press, 1964.

———. *The Rise and Fall of the Plantation Complex: Essays in Atlantic History*. 2nd. ed. Cambridge: Cambridge University Press, 1998.

Denzer, LaRay. "Emancipation and the Modern Woman in Lagos (Nigeria)." Paper prepared for a conference on "Youth Policy and the Policies of Youth in Africa." Program of African Studies, Northwestern University, May 10–11, 2002.

Diouf, Sylviane A. *Dreams of Africa in Alabama: The Slave Ship Clotilda and the Story of the Last Africans Brought to America*. New York: Oxford University Press, 2007.

Dixon, Chris. *African America and Haiti: Emigration and Black Nationalism in the Nineteenth Century*. Westport, Conn.: Greenwood Press, 2000.

DuBois, W. E. Burghardt. "Reconstruction and its Benefits." *American Historical Review* 15, 4 (July 1910): 781–99.

———. *The Suppression of the African Slave-Trade to the United States of America, 1638–1870*. Oxford: Oxford University Press, 2007 [1896].

Dunn, D. Elwood, Amos J. Beyan, and Carl Patrick Burrowes. *Historical Dictionary of Liberia*. 2nd. ed. Lanham, Md.: The Scarecrow Press, 2001.

Echeruo, Michael J. C. *Victorian Lagos: Aspects of Nineteenth Century Lagos Life*. London: Macmillan, 1977.

Edgar, Walter. *South Carolina: A History*. Columbia: University of South Carolina Press, 1998.

Edwards, Brent Hayes. *Practice of Diaspora: Literature, Translation, and the Rise of Black Internationalism*. Cambridge, Mass.: Harvard University Press, 2003.

Edwards, Laura F. *The People and Their Peace: Legal Culture and the Transformation of Inequality in the Post-Revolutionary South*. Chapel Hill: University of North Carolina Press, 2009.

Edgerton, Douglas. "Forgetting Denmark Vesey; Or, Oliver Stone Meets Richard Wade." *William & Mary Quarterly*, 3rd ser., 59 (2002): 143–52.

Ellsworth, Scott. *Death in a Promised Land: The Tulsa Race Riot of 1921*. Baton Rouge: Louisiana State University Press, 1982.

Eltis, David. *Economic Growth and the Ending of the Transatlantic Slave Trade*. New York: Oxford University Press, 1987.

Eltis, David, et al. "Voyages: The Transatlantic Slave Trade Database." www.slavevoyages .org.

Ernst, Joseph A., and H. Roy Merrens. "'Camden's Turrets Pierce the Skies!': The Urban Process in the Southern Colonies during the Eighteenth Century." *William & Mary Quarterly*, 3rd ser., 30, 4 (Oct. 1973): 549–74.

Everill, Bronwen. *Abolition and Empire in Sierra Leone and Liberia*. Basingstoke, Hampshire: Palgrave Macmillan, 2013.

———. "'Destiny Seems to Point Me to That Country': Early Nineteenth-Century African American Migration, Emigration, and Expansion." *Journal of Global History* 7 (2012): 53–77.

Falola, Toyin, ed. *Pioneer, Patriot, and Patriarch: Samuel Johnson and the Yoruba People*. Madison, Wisc.: African Studies Program, University of Wisconsin, 1993.

Fanning, Sara. *Caribbean Crossing: African Americans and the Haitian Emigration Movement*. New York and London: New York University Press, 2015.

Farias, P. F. de Moraes, and Karin Barber, eds. *Self-Assertion and Brokerage: Early Cultural Nationalism in West Africa*. Birmingham, U.K.: Centre of West African Studies, University of Birmingham, 1990.

Fett, Sharla M. *Recaptured Africans: Surviving Slave Ships, Detention, and Dislocation in the Final Years of the Slave Trade*. Chapel Hill: University of North Carolina Press, 2016.

Finnegan, Terence. *A Deed So Accursed: Lynching in Mississippi and South Carolina, 1881–1940*. Charlottesville: University of Virginia Press, 2013.

Foner, Eric. *Freedom's Lawmakers: A Directory of Black Officeholders during Reconstruction*. Rev. ed. Baton Rouge: Louisiana State University Press, 1996.

———. *Reconstruction: America's Unfinished Revolution, 1863–1877*. New York: Harper and Row, 1988.

Fyfe, Christopher. *A History of Sierra Leone*. Oxford: Oxford University Press, 1962.

Games, Alison. "Atlantic History: Definitions, Challenges, and Opportunities." *American Historical Review* 111, 3 (2006): 741–57.

Gates, Henry Louis, Jr., ed. *"Race," Writing, and Difference*. Chicago: University of Chicago Press, 1985.

Gilroy, Paul. *The Black Atlantic: Modernity and Double Consciousness*. Cambridge, Mass.: Harvard University Press, 1993.

Gordon, Asa H. *Sketches of Negro Life and History in South Carolina*. Columbia, S.C.: W. B. Conkey, 1929.

Gomez, Michael Angelo. *Exchanging Our Country Marks: The Transformation of African Identities in the Colonial and Antebellum South*. Chapel Hill: University of North Carolina Press, 1998.

Gould, Stephen Jay. *The Mismeasure of Man*. New York: W. W. Norton, 1981.

Grenz, Stanley J. *The Baptist Congregation: A Guide to Baptist Belief and Practice*. Valley Forge, Pa.: Judson Press, 1985.

Hager, Christopher. *Word by Word: Emancipation and the Act of Writing*. Cambridge, Mass.: Harvard, 2013.

Hahn, Steven. *A Nation under Our Feet: Black Political Struggles in the Rural South from Slavery to the Great Migration*. Cambridge, Mass.: Harvard University Press, 2005.

Haley, Alex. *Roots: The Saga of an American Family*. Garden City, N.Y.: Doubleday, 1976.

Haney, Erin. "Lutterodt Family Studios and the Changing Face of Early Portrait Photographs from the Gold Coast." In *Portraiture and Photography in Africa*, edited by John Peffer and Elisabeth L. Cameron, 66–101. Bloomington: Indiana University Press, 2013.

Harris, Sheldon H. *Paul Cuffe: Black America and the African Return*. New York: Simon and Schuster, 1972.

Hartman, Saidiya. *Lose Your Mother: A Journey along the Atlantic Slave Route*. New York: Farrar, Straus and Giroux, 2007.

Hirschman, Albert O. *Exit, Voice, and Loyalty: Responses to Decline in Firms, Organizations, and States*. Cambridge, Mass.: Harvard University Press, 1970.

Holsoe, Svend E. "A Study of Relations between Settlers and Indigenous Peoples in Western Liberia, 1821–1847." *African Historical Studies* 4, 2 (1971): 331–62.

Holt, Thomas C. *The Problem of Freedom: Race, Labor, and Politics in Jamaica and Britain, 1832–1938*. Baltimore: Johns Hopkins Press, 1992.

———. "Slavery and Freedom in the Atlantic World: Reflections on the Diasporan Framework." In *Crossing Boundaries: Comparative History of Black People in Diaspora*, edited by Darlene Clark Hine and Jacqueline McLeod, 33–44. Bloomington: Indiana University Press, 1999.

Hopkins, A. G. "An Economic History of Lagos, 1880–1914." Ph.D. diss., University of London, 1964.

———. *An Economic History of West Africa*. London: Longman, 1973.

———. "Property Rights and Empire Building: Britain's Annexation of Lagos, 1861." *Journal of Economic History* 40 (1980): 777–98.

———. "Richard Beale Blaize, 1845–1904: Merchant Prince of West Africa." *Tarikh* 1 (1966): 70–79.

Humphreys, Margaret. *Yellow Fever and the South*. New Brunswick, N.J.: Rutgers University Press, 1992.

Inabinet, L. Glen. "'The July Fourth Incident' of 1816: An Insurrection Plotted by Slaves in Camden, South Carolina." *South Carolina Legal History*, Proceedings of the Reynolds Conference, 209–21. Columbia: University of South Carolina Press, 1980.

Inabinet, Joan A. and L. Glen Inabinet. *A History of Kershaw County South Carolina*. Columbia: University of South Carolina Press, 2011.

Jacobs, Sylvia M., ed. *Black Americans and the Missionary Movement in Africa*. Westport, Conn.: Greenwood Press, 1982.

Johnson, Charles S. *Bitter Canaan: The Story of the Negro Republic*. New Brunswick: Transaction Books, 1987.

Johnson, Michael P. "Denmark Vesey and His Co-Conspirators." *William & Mary Quarterly*, 3rd ser., 58 (2001): 915–76.

———. "Reading Evidence." *William & Mary Quarterly*, 3rd ser., 59 (2002): 202.

Johnson, Michael P. and James L. Roark. *Black Masters: A Free Family of Color in the Old South*. New York: W. W. Norton & Co., 1984.

Johnson, Walter. *River of Dark Dreams: Slavery and Empire in the Cotton Kingdom*. Cambridge, Mass.: Harvard University Press, 2013.

———. *Soul by Soul: Life Inside the Antebellum Slave Market*. Cambridge, Mass.: Harvard University Press, 1999.

Johnston, Harry Hamilton. *Liberia*. 2 vols. New York: Dodd, Mead and Co., 1906.

Johnson, Samuel. *The History of the Yorubas: from the Earliest Times to the Beginning of the British Protectorate*. Lagos: C.S.S. Bookshops, 1976 [1921].

Jones, Adam. "Theophile Conneau at Galinhas and New Sestos, 1836–1941: A Comparison of the Sources." *History in Africa* 8 (1981): 89–106.

Kirkland, Thomas J., and Robert M. Kennedy. *Historic Camden*. 2 vols. Columbia, S.C.: The State Company, 1905 and 1926.

Kopytoff, Jean Herskovits. *A Preface to Modern Nigeria: The "Sierra Leonians" in Yoruba, 1830–1890*. Madison: University of Wisconsin Press, 1965.

Kramer, Lloyd S. *Nationalism in Europe & America: Politics, Cultures, and Identities since 1775*. Chapel Hill: University of North Carolina Press, 2011.

Kulikoff, Allan. *Tobacco and Slaves: The Development of Southern Cultures in the Chesapeake, 1680–1800*. Chapel Hill: University of North Carolina Press, 1986.

Larson, Pier M. "Horrid Journeying: Narratives of Enslavement and the Global African Diaspora." *Journal of World History* 19, no. 4 (Dec. 2008): 431–64.

Lavery, Jennifer E. "Reexamining the *Examiner*: Louisville's Regional, Unitarian, Antislavery Newspaper, 1847–1850." Paper prepared for Collegium Annual Meeting, Ottawa, November 2009. http://www.uucollegium.org/Research%20papers/09paper _Lavery.pdf.

Law, Robin. "Early Yoruba Historiography." *History in Africa* 3 (1976): 69–89.

———, ed. *From Slave Trade to "Legitimate" Commerce: The Commercial Transition in Nineteenth-Century West Africa*. Cambridge: Cambridge University Press, 1995.

———. "Local Amateur Scholarship in the Construction of Yoruba Ethnicity, 1880– 1914." In *Ethnicity in Africa*, edited by Louise de la Gorgendière, Kenneth King, and Sarah Vaughan, 55–90. Edinburgh: Centre of African Studies, 1996.

———. *The Oyo Empire, c.1600–1836: A West African Imperialism in the Era of the Atlantic Slave Trade*. Oxford: Clarendon Press, 1977.

———. "Yoruba Liberated Slaves Who Returned to West Africa." In *The Yoruba Diaspora in the Atlantic World*, edited by Toyin Falola and Matt D. Childs, 349–65. Bloomington: Indiana University Press, 2004.

Liebenow, J. Gus. *Liberia: The Quest for Democracy*. Bloomington: Indiana University Press, 1987.

Lindsay, Lisa A. "Boundaries of Slavery in Mid-Nineteenth Century Liberia." In *Borderlands in World History, 1700–1914*, edited by Paul Readman, Cynthia Radding, and Chad Bryant, 258–75. New York: Palgrave Macmillan, 2014.

———. "Remembering His Country Marks: A Nigerian American Family and Its 'African' Ancestor." In *Biography and the Black Atlantic*, edited by Lisa A. Lindsay and John Wood Sweet. Philadelphia: University of Pennsylvania Press, 2014.

———. "'To Return to the Bosom of their Fatherland': Brazilian Immigrants in Nineteenth Century Lagos." *Slavery and Abolition* 15, 1 (1994): 22–50.

Lindsay, Lisa A., and John Wood Sweet, eds. *Biography and the Black Atlantic*. Philadelphia: University of Pennsylvania Press, 2014.

Lloyd, Christopher. *The Navy and the Slave Trade: The Suppression of the African Slave Trade in the Nineteenth Century*. London: Frank Cass & Co., 1968.

Lovejoy, Paul E. *Transformations in Slavery: A History of Slavery in Africa*. Cambridge: Cambridge University Press, 1983.

Lovejoy, Paul E., and David Richardson. "The Business of Slaving: Pawnship in Western Africa." *Journal of African History* 41 (2001): 67–89.

———. "Trust, Pawnship, and Atlantic History: The Institutional Foundations of the Old Calabar Slave Trade." *American Historical Review* 104 (1999): 332–55.

Lynch, Hollis R. *Edward Wilmot Blyden: Pan-Negro Patriot, 1832–1912*. London: Oxford University Press, 1970.

Lynn, Martin. *Commerce and Economic Change in West Africa: The Palm Oil Trade in the Nineteenth Century*. Cambridge: Cambridge University Press, 1997.

Mabogunje, Akin. *Urbanization in Nigeria*. London: University of London Press, 1968.

Maffly-Kipp, Laurie F. *Setting Down the Sacred Past: African-American Race Histories.* Cambridge, Mass: Harvard University Press, 2010.

Mann, Kristin. "The Illegal Slave Trade and One Yoruba Man's Transatlantic Passages from Slavery to Freedom." In *The Rise and Demise of Slavery and the Slave Trade in the Atlantic World*, edited by Philip Misevich and Kristin Mann. Rochester: University of Rochester Press, 2016.

———. *Marrying Well: Marriage, Status and Social Change among the Educated Elite in Colonial Lagos.* Cambridge: Cambridge University Press, 1985.

———. *Slavery and the Birth of an African City: Lagos, 1760–1900.* Bloomington: Indiana University Press, 2007.

Mann, Kristin, and Edna G. Bay, eds. *Rethinking the African Diaspora: The Making of a Black Atlantic World in the Bight of Benin and Brazil.* London: Frank Cass, 2001.

Martin, Sandy Dwayne. *Black Baptists and African Missions: The Origins of a Movement, 1880–1915.* Macon, Ga.: Mercer University Press, 1998.

Matory, J. Lorand. *Black Atlantic Religion: Tradition, Transnationalism and Matriarchy in the Afro-Brazilian Candomblé.* Princeton: Princeton University Press, 2005.

———. "The English Professors of Brazil: On the Diasporic Roots of the Yoruba Nation." *Comparative Studies in Society and History* (1999): 72–103.

McMillin, James A. *The Final Victims: Foreign Slave Trade to North America, 1783–1810.* Columbia: University of South Carolina Press, 2004.

McWhirter, Cameron. *Red Summer: The Summer of 1919 and the Awakening of Black America.* New York: Macmillan, 2011.

Meek, C. K. *Land Tenure and Land Administration in Nigeria and the Cameroons.* London: HMSO, 1957.

Merrell, James H. *The Indians' New World: Catawbas and Their Neighbors from European Contact through the Era of Removal.* Chapel Hill: University of North Carolina Press, 2009 [1989].

———. "The Racial Education of the Catawba Indians." *Journal of Southern History* 50 (1984): 363–84.

Miers, Suzanne, and Richard Roberts, eds. *The End of Slavery in Africa.* Madison: University of Wisconsin Press, 1988.

Miller, Floyd John. *The Search for a Black Nationality: Black Emigration and Colonization, 1787–1863.* Urbana: University of Illinois Press, 1975.

Miller, Joseph C. *The Problem of Slavery as History: A Global Approach.* New Haven: Yale University Press, 2012.

———, ed. *The Princeton Companion to Atlantic History.* Princeton: Princeton University Press, 2015.

Minter, William, Gail Hovey, and Charles Cobb Jr. *No Easy Victories: African Liberation and American Activists over a Half Century, 1950–2000.* Trenton, N.J.: Africa World Press, 2008.

Moore, Moses N. *Orishatukeh Faduma: Liberal Theology and Evangelical Pan-Africanism, 1857–1946.* Lanham, Md., and London: The American Theological Library Association and the Scarecrow Press, 1996.

Morgan, Philip, and Jack Greene, eds. *Atlantic History: A Critical Appraisal.* Oxford: Oxford University Press, 2009.

Mouser, Bruce L. "Théophilus Conneau: The Saga of a Tale." *History in Africa* 6 (1979): 97–107.

Mudimbe, V. Y. *The Invention of Africa: Gnosis, Philosophy, and the Order of Knowledge.* Bloomington: Indiana University Press, 1988.

Newell, Stephanie. *The Power to Name: A History of Anonymity in Colonial West Africa.* Athens, Ohio: Ohio University Press, 2013.

Okedara, J. T., and S. Ademola Ajayi. *Thomas Jefferson Bowen: Pioneer Baptist Missionary to Nigeria, 1850–1856.* Ibadan: John Archers Publishers, 2004.

Oladele, David Olusegun. *A Life for Freedom and Service: Dr. James Churchill Omosanya Vaughan (1893–1937).* Ibadan: Options Book and Information Services, 2000.

Omu, Fred I. A. "Journalism and the Rise of Nigerian Nationalism: John Payne Jackson, 1848–1915." *Journal of the Historical Society of Nigeria* 7, 3 (December 1974): 521–39.

Orr, Elaine Neill. *A Different Sun: A Novel of Africa.* New York: Berkley Books, 2013.

Osborne, Myles. "A Note on the Liberian Archives." *History in Africa* 36 (2009): 461–63.

Page, Jesse. *The Black Bishop: Samuel Adjai Crowther.* London: Hodder and Stoughton, 1908.

Painter, Nell Irvin. *Exodusters: Black Migration to Kansas after Reconstruction.* Lawrence: University Press of Kansas, 1986.

Palmer, Colin. "Defining and Studying the Modern African Diaspora." *Perspectives on History* 36, 6 (September 1998): 1, 22–25.

Patterson, Tiffany Ruby, and Robin D. G. Kelley. "Unfinished Migrations: Reflections on the African Diaspora and the Making of the Modern World." *African Studies Review* 43, 1 (2000): 11–45.

Peel, J. D. Y. *Ijeshas and Nigerians: The Incorporation of a Yoruba Kingdom, 1890s–1970s.* New York: Cambridge University Press, 1983.

———. *Religious Encounter and the Making of the Yoruba.* Bloomington: Indiana University Press, 2000.

Peffer, John, and Elisabeth L. Cameron, eds. *Portraiture and Photography in Africa.* Bloomington: Indiana University Press, 2013.

Peil, Margaret. *Lagos: The City Is the People.* Boston: G. K. Hall, 1991.

Perdue, Theda, and Michael D. Green. *The Columbia Guide to American Indians of the Southeast.* New York: Columbia University Press, 2001.

Peterson, John. *Province of Freedom: A History of Sierra Leone, 1787–1870.* London: Faber, 1969.

Phillips, Caryl. *The Atlantic Sound.* New York: Vintage Books, 2001.

Piot, Charles. "Atlantic Aporias: Africa and Gilroy's Black Atlantic." *South Atlantic Quarterly* 100, 1 (2001): 155–70.

Power-Greene, Ousmane K. *Against Wind and Tide: The African American Struggle against the Colonization Movement.* New York: New York University Press, 2014.

Pybus, Cassandra. *Epic Journeys of Freedom: Runaway Slaves of the American Revolution and Their Global Quest for Liberty.* Boston: Beacon, 2006.

Rediker, Marcus. *The Amistad Rebellion: An Atlantic Odyssey of Slavery and Freedom.* New York: Viking, 2012.

Roberson, Cecil F. *A History of Baptists in Nigeria, 1849–1935: with Appropriate Projections into Later Years.* Nashville: SBHLA, 1986.

———. *A History of the Baptists of Lagos, Nigeria, 1853–1935*. Meridian, Miss.: Cecil Roberson, 1990.

Rodney, Walter. *How Europe Underdeveloped Africa*. Washington, D.C.: Howard University Press, 1981.

Rosiji, Gbemi. *Lady Ademola: Portrait of a Pioneer; Biography of Lady Kofoworola Aina Ademola, MBE OFR*. Lagos: EnClair Publishers Ltd., 1996.

Rucker, Walter C. *The River Flows On: Black Resistance, Culture, and Identity Formation in Early America*. Baton Rouge: Louisiana State University Press, 2006.

Rydell, Robert W. *All the World's a Fair: Visions of Empire at American International Expositions, 1876–1916*. Chicago: University of Chicago Press, 1984.

Ryder, A. F. C. *Benin and the Europeans, 1485–1897*. New York: Humanities Press, 1969.

Safran, William. "Diasporas in Modern Societies: Myths of Homeland and Return." *Diaspora: A Journal of Transnational Studies* 1, 1 (1991): 83–99.

Sanneh, Lamin. *Abolitionists Abroad: American Blacks and the Making of Modern West Africa*. Cambridge, Mass.: Harvard University Press, 1999.

Sawada, Nozomi. "The Educated Elite and Associational Life in Early Lagos Newspapers: In Search of Unity for the Progress of Society." Ph.D. diss., University of Birmingham, 2011.

Schama, Simon. *Rough Crossings: Britain, the Slaves and the American Revolution*. London: BBC Books, 2005.

Scott, Rebecca J., and Jean M. Hébrard. *Freedom Papers: An Atlantic Odyssey in the Age of Emancipation*. Cambridge, Mass.: Harvard University Press, 2012.

Senshach, Jon F. *Rebecca's Revival: Creating Black Christianity in the Atlantic World*. Cambridge, Mass.: Harvard University Press, 2005.

Shepperson, George, and Thomas Price. *Independent African: John Chilembwe and the Origins, Setting, and Significance of the Nyasaland Native Rising of 1915*. Edinburgh: University Press, 1958.

Shick, Tom W. *Behold the Promised Land: A History of Afro-American Settler Society in Nineteenth-Century Liberia*. Baltimore: Johns Hopkins University Press, 1980.

———. *Emigrants to Liberia, 1820–1843: An Alphabetical Listing*. Newark, Del.: Dept. of Anthropology, University of Delaware, 1971.

Shillington, Kevin. *Encyclopedia of African History*. New York: Routledge, 2004.

Sickle, Eugene S. van. "Reluctant Imperialists: The U.S. Navy and Liberia, 1819–1845." *Journal of the Early Republic* 31 (2011): 107–34.

Sidbury, James. *Becoming African in America: Race and Nation in the Early Black Atlantic*. Oxford: Oxford University Press, 2007.

Sklar, Richard L. *Nigerian Political Parties: Power in an Emergent African Nation*. 1st Africa World Press, ed. Trenton, N.J.: Africa World Press, 2004 [orig. 1963].

Staudenraus, P. J. *The African Colonization Movement, 1816–1865*. New York: Columbia University Press, 1961.

Stepp, Eddie. "Interpreting a Forgotten Mission: African-American Missionaries of the Southern Baptist Convention in Liberia, West Africa 1846–1860." Ph.D. diss., Baylor University, 1999.

Stoler, Ann Laura. *Carnal Knowledge and Imperial Power: Race and the Intimate in Colonial Rule*. Berkeley: University of California Press, 2002.

Strobel, Margaret. *European Women and the Second British Empire*. Bloomington: Indiana University Press, 1991.

Sundiata, I. K. *Brothers and Strangers: Black Zion, Black Slavery, 1914–1940*. Durham: Duke University Press, 2003.

Sutherland, Bill, and Matt Meyer. *Guns and Gandhi in Africa: Pan-African Insights on Nonviolence, Armed Struggle and Liberation*. Trenton, N.J.: Africa World Press, 2000.

Sweet, James H. *Domingos Álvarez, African Healing, and the Intellectual History of the Atlantic World*. Chapel Hill: University of North Carolina Press, 2011.

————. *Recreating Africa: Culture, Kinship, and Religion in the African-Portuguese World, 1441–1770*. Chapel Hill: University of North Carolina Press, 2003.

Tallant, Harold D. *Evil Necessity: Slavery and Political Culture in Antebellum Kentucky*. Lexington: University Press of Kentucky, 2003.

Taylor, Alan. *The Internal Enemy: Slavery and War in Virginia, 1772–1832*. New York: Norton, 2013.

Taylor-Goins, Elsie, and Catherine Taylor-McConnell. *Naudin-Dibble Family: Selected South Carolina Historic Sites*. Columbia, S.C.: self-published, 1995.

Teal, Harvey. *Public Schools, 1868–1870: Education during Reconstruction in Kershaw County, S.C.* Columbia, S.C.: Pine Tree Publishing, 2004.

Thomas, Lamont D. *Rise to Be a People: A Biography of Paul Cuffe*. Urbana: University of Illinois Press, 1986.

Thomas, Lynn M. "Modernity's Failings, Political Claims, and Intermediate Concepts." *American Historical Review* 116, 3 (2011): 727–40.

Thompson, Era Bell. "The Vaughan Family: A Tale of Two Continents." *Ebony* 30, 2 (February 1975): 53–64.

Trelease, Allen W. *White Terror: The Ku Klux Klan Conspiracy and Southern Reconstruction*. Baton Rouge: Louisiana State University Press, 1995.

Tupper, H. A. *The Foreign Missions of the Southern Baptist Convention*. Philadelphia: American Baptist Publication Society, 1880.

Tuttle, William M. *Race Riot: Chicago in the Red Summer of 1919*. Champaign: University of Illinois Press, 1996 [1970].

Tyler-McGraw, Marie. *An African Republic: Black and White Virginians in the Making of Liberia*. Chapel Hill: University of North Carolina Press, 2007.

Ullman, Victor. *Martin R. Delany: The Beginnings of Black Nationalism*. Boston: Beacon, 1971.

Vaughan, Femi, et al. *The Making of the First Indigenous Church in Nigeria: An Abridged History of Ebenezer Baptist Church, Lagos, 1888–1999*. Lagos: Ebenezer Baptist Church, 2000.

Webster, James Bertin. *The African Churches among the Yoruba, 1888–1922*. Oxford: Clarendon Press, 1964.

Wikramanayake, Marina. *A World in Shadow: The Free Black in Antebellum South Carolina*. Columbia: University of South Carolina Press, 1973.

Wilkerson, Isabel. *The Warmth of Other Suns*. New York: Random House, 2010.

Williams, D. Newell, Douglas A. Foster, and Paul M. Blowers, eds. *The Stone-Campbell Movement: A Global History*. St. Louis: Chalice Press, 2012.

Williams, George W. *History of the Negro Race in America from 1619 to 1880*. 2 vols. New York: G. P. Putnam's Sons, 1883.

Williams, Lou Falkner. *The Great South Carolina Ku Klux Klan Trials, 1871–1872*. Athens: University of Georgia Press, 1996.

Williamson, Joel. *After Slavery: The Negro in South Carolina during Reconstruction, 1861–1877*. Chapel Hill: University of North Carolina Press, 1965.

Witt, John Fabian. *Patriots and Cosmopolitans: Hidden Histories of American Law*. Cambridge, Mass.: Harvard University Press, 2007.

Zachernuk, Philip S. *Colonial Subjects: An African Intelligentsia and Atlantic Ideas*. Charlottesville and London: University Press of Virginia, 2000.

Zinn, Howard. *A People's History of the United States*. New York: HarperPerennial, 1990.

Zuczek, Richard. *State of Rebellion: Reconstruction in South Carolina*. Columbia: University of South Carolina Press, 1996.

INDEX

Abeokuta, 110–11, 114, 119, 123–24, 194–95, 222, 224, 230–31; expulsion of Christians from, 3, 142–43, 145, 147; Church Vaughan in, 111, 113–14, 122, 136–38, 140–43, 182, 194, 213, 218; history of, 113–14; missionaries in, 113–14, 123–43 passim, 152, 188, 190, 197, 199; warfare involving, 113–14, 134–38, 140; as proposed African American settlement, 124, 129–31, 147, 170; cotton in, 191

Abolitionists, 51, 56–58, 64, 152

Abraham (S.C. slave), 29, 33

Adelu (Oyo Prince), 125

Ademola, Adetokunbo, 222, 230

Ademola, Kofoworola (Moore), 222, 224, 230–31, 234–35, 241 (n. 1)

Africa: as destination, 2–3, 7, 11–14, 42–51, 58, 62, 66–75, 87, 101, 106, 130, 133, 141, 170, 179, 219, 225, 232–33, 236; as origin of Scipio Vaughan, 4, 217, 224, 229, 236; connections with the U.S., 5, 217, 224, 232–33; politics in, 8; slavery and slaving in, 9, 87, 118; societies in, 10; history of, 11; as source of American slaves, 17–18; coast of, 48, 87–88, 105–8, 144, 148, 185, 195; colonization of, 58, 603, 124, 181, 193, 195; image of, 62, 94, 104, 120, 226, 229; as missionary field, 103–5, 120, 188–89, 193, 197; Atlantic, 111, 134;

Vaughan family in, 171, 236; colonial, 180; and the Bible, 181; writing about, 215; underdevelopment of, 236. *See also* West Africa

African Americans: in nineteenth century, 3, 9–10, 179, 182, 204; as slaves, 4, 101; in Africa, 7, 46, 204; migration of, 9–10, 49, 170, 225–26; interest in Africa, 9–10, 46–47, 225, 231; as settlers, 10–11, 45, 47–48, 58, 65, 85, 96, 108, 124, 129–31, 133; culture of, 12; in South Carolina, 13–14, 19, 23, 25, 27, 161–70, 228; as emigrants, 44, 49, 60, 71, 128–29, 226; views of Liberia and the ACS, 45, 47–48, 60, 71, 129, 226; political rights of, 47, 129, 159, 169, 235–36; in Liberia, 83, 87; as missionaries, 103, 183, 187–89, 195; Christianity of, 104; and genealogy, 215, 217, 231; in the 1920s, 225–29, 231

Africans: in South Carolina, 18–19, 23, 25, 35, 101; in Liberia, 85, 87, 89–92, 94, 97, 99–101, 103, 170; recaptured/liberated, 97, 185; diasporic, 111, 146, 182, 203–4; image of, 120–21, 182, 186, 191–92, 197, 208–9, 226, 228; educated, 147, 190, 192, 200; elite, 173–75, 181, 184–85, 190, 209; in Lagos, 179, 183, 198, 208

Agbebi, Mojola, 201, 207. *See also* Vincent, David Brown

Agriculture, 113. *See also* Farming

Akitoye (Lagos king), 110

Allen, Clara Zenobia (Vaughan), 209, 224, 271 (n. 110)

Allen, S. A., 192

Amazon warriors, 114

America. *See* United States of America

American Colonization Society, 44, 66, 77, 99, 129; and J. C. Vaughan, 2, 61–62, 64–65, 67, 77; records of, 7; ships, 43, 64, 71; agents, 44, 49, 61, 66–67, 80–82, 87, 95, 102; mission of, 45; origins of, 45, 47–48; black opposition to, 47–51, 65–66, 129; and Liberia colony, 48–50, 60, 76, 89, 98–99, 129, 170; support for settlers, 64, 68, 72–73, 80, 82, 95; recruitment, 66–67, 69–71, 83; receptacle, 84, 94

American Revolution, 18, 20, 23, 28, 46, 189

Americo-Liberians, 78, 106, 123, 258 (n. 71)

Ancestors, 56, 214–15, 217; in Vaughan family, 9, 25, 42, 133, 215, 225, 230–31, 236; continent of, 10, 13, 45, 111, 141; of African Americans, 48

Ancrum, Charlotte (Douglas), 61–62

Ancrum, William, 41, 55, 61

Anglican Church, 191. *See also* Church Missionary Society

Antislavery, 8, 9, 56–58, 88–89, 110, 119, 128, 153, 157, 182, 191, 193

Apprentices, of J. C. Vaughan, 150–51, 154, 157

Apprenticeship, 97–100, 103, 118, 234

Atadi, 138, 140, 218

Atiba (Oyo King), 125

Atlantic Ocean, 9–11, 43, 45, 80, 92, 96, 98, 108, 144, 230

Atlantic world, 5, 8, 11, 159, 170, 183, 233–34

Autonomy, 111, 124, 133–34, 140, 143, 154, 156, 180, 182–83, 206, 208–9

Ball, Charles, 19, 27, 32

Baltimore, Md., 17, 28, 43, 51, 64, 104

Baptism, 104, 122, 139, 156, 184, 186, 192

Baptist(s), 111, 144, 162; church(es), 44, 120, 148, 179, 182, 201, 208, 219; Liberia missions, 103, 105; faith, 104, 208; Lagos mission, 106, 150–51, 186, 192, 196, 198, 200, 202, 208; Yorubaland missions, 111, 115, 122, 136–43, 148, 182, 186; African, 139–40, 143, 156–57, 180–89 passim, 195, 198–99, 201, 203–8; Vaughan as, 148, 157, 180–81, 209, 213; principles, 180, 186, 200, 208. *See also* Missionaries: Baptist

Baptist Academy, Lagos, 198, 202

Barracoons, 87, 90, 97, 201, 204

Bassa, Liberia, 65, 87, 89, 91

Benin Kingdom, 1, 3, 126, 138–39, 141, 223

Berlin, Ira, 19

Berlin Conference (1884–85), 181, 195

Bible, 3, 4, 7, 22–23, 180–81, 196, 207, 212, 219

Bight of Benin, 18, 255 (n. 29)

Big Man, 154, 203, 211

Biography: genre of, 5; of Vaughan, 116, 217, 219

Black Atlantic, 10, 243 (n. 29)

Black Codes, 158

Blair, L. W. R., 169

Blaize, Richard Beale, 156, 193

Blanco, Pedro, 87–88

Blanding, Abram, 30, 34

Blanding, Rachel, 30, 34–35, 57, 60

Blanding, William, 35, 57, 60–61

Blyden, Edward Wilmot, 77, 91, 93–94, 97, 104, 195, 206–8

Bonetta, Sarah Forbes (Davies), 185

Boombo (African chief), 92–94

Boston, Mass., 46, 50–51, 234

Bowen, Lurana (Davis), 116, 118–20, 261 (n. 43)

Bowen, Thomas Jefferson, 79, 105–7, 113–21, 129, 186, 261 (n. 43)

Brazil, 9–10, 88, 90, 150, 182, 191, 234, 242 (n. 4)

Brazilians in Nigeria, 108–9, 147, 149–52, 155–56, 173, 207, 230, 255 (n. 29)

British Empire, 92, 153, 187, 193

"Cambellite" churches, 208, 213

Camden, S.C., 56, 115, 144, 234; Scipio Vaughan in, 1, 14–15, 19–23, 35, 40–42, 54; description, 14; African Americans in, 14, 37, 39–40, 160–63, 168–69, 228; history of, 14–17; slavery in, 19–20, 27–35; land in, 19–20, 34, 39–40, 145; J. C. Vaughan and, 25, 40–42, 44, 52–56, 60–67, 74, 157, 166, 218–19; migration from, 57–59; Vaughan relatives in, 144–45, 169, 176–78, 225, 227; Aida Moore visit to, 227–28

Camden Gazette, 20, 22, 31, 34

Camden Journal, 19, 33, 57, 160, 162, 166

Campbell, Robert, 124, 128–33, 147, 150, 155–56, 172, 174

Campos, Juan A., 209

Canada, 49, 57, 59, 164

Cane, George, 92–94

Cannon, James Churchwill Vaughan, 145

Cape Mesurado, 49, 85

Cape Mount, 78–79, 85, 87, 89, 91–94, 98–99

Cape Palmas, 50

Carpenter/carpentry, 40–43, 73–74, 113, 144, 183; J. C. Vaughan as, in Yorubaland, 3, 106, 108, 117–24, 134, 146–47, 218; Scipio Vaughan as, 13–14, 19–21, 34–35, 96; Bonds Conway as, 20; Denmark Vesey as, 35–36; Vaughan as, in Camden, 41, 53, 62–64, 96; Burrell Vaughan as, 41, 56, 63; Jacob Hammond as, 53; Vaughan as, in Liberia, 77, 80, 96, 103, 109, 233; Sewell Pettiford as, 83, 123; Vaughan as, in Lagos, 148, 150, 154–56, 203

Carter, Frank, 163, 165, 178

Carter, Harriet Josephine (McLaughlin), 165, 178

Carter, Nancy, 23–24, 53

Carter, William W., 178, 268 (n. 71)

Cason, John, 122

Catawba, 13–14, 16–17, 22–25, 41, 52–53, 55, 65

Cemeteries: in Camden, 14, 53, 59; in Lagos, 172, 213, 219

Census, U.S., 25, 38, 40, 55, 178

Chamberlain, Daniel H., 167–69

Champion, George Lloyd, 35

Champion, Richard, 16, 40–41

Champion, Richard Lloyd, 20, 244 (n. 20)

Chapel Hill, N.C., 43–44, 68–70, 73–74, 102

Charleston, S.C., 14–21 passim, 29, 35–36, 44, 56, 67, 74, 141, 161, 167, 170, 218

Charlotte, N.C., 44

Cherokee, 1, 17, 22–23, 46, 53, 116, 224

Chesapeake Bay, 17, 28

Chesnut, John, 18, 29–30, 33, 35, 39, 244 (n. 20)

Chesnut, Scipio, 33, 39

Chester County, S.C., 162–63

Chicago, Ill., 225–30

Children, 3, 20, 59, 140, 146, 152, 158, 164–65, 182, 191, 211, 219, 226–27; of Scipio Vaughan, 2, 14, 22, 24–25, 35, 38, 40–42, 51, 53, 55, 144; of J. C. Vaughan, 3, 13, 67, 171–76, 209, 213, 221–24, 230; of slaves, 19; of Native Americans, 23–24; enslaved, 34–35, 57, 94; of Liberian settlers, 43–44, 48, 64, 72–73, 83, 100; of Marshall Hooper, 68–72, 74, 82; as Liberian apprentices, 97; as pawns, 135; from Ijaye, 135–39, 143

Christianity, 113, 139; in Africa, 8, 105, 109, 115, 129, 181, 192, 194, 197, 207; of Church Vaughan, 10, 122, 146, 173, 181, 208; of S.C. slaves, 31; as part of "civilization," 46, 103; African American, 104

Christians: in Abeokuta, 3, 139–43, 230; and slavery, 51, 98, 116, 153; African, 139, 156–57, 180–84, 190–209; in Lagos, 143, 147

Churches: African American, 47, 160, 189, 204; independent African, 180–82, 221

Church Missionary Society (C.M.S.), 110, 114, 119, 130, 133, 139, 142–43, 181, 184–85,

187, 190–92, 195–96, 199–200, 203–7, 219, 230

Citizenship, 9, 12, 76–77, 85, 106, 158–59, 162–63, 169

Civilization, 46–47, 78, 98–99, 103–4, 182, 187, 208

Civil War, U.S., 9, 28, 57, 132, 137, 144–45, 148, 158–59, 166, 168, 170, 178, 187

Clarendon County, S.C., 56, 162

Clarke, William, 102, 105–7, 111–25 passim, 134, 141, 186, 259 (n. 100), 261 (n. 43)

Clay, Henry, 45, 47, 59, 94

Clothing, 103, 110, 123, 138, 176, 192, 196, 207

Clyburn, William Churchwill, 63

Coleman, Ellie, 20

Colley, William, 183–84, 186–89, 200–202

Colonialism, 233, 235–36; British, 3, 8–9, 46, 146–48, 190, 207–9, 227; in Nigeria, 10, 146, 154, 179; American, 24; in Liberia, 78

Colonization, 124; of Liberia, 47–51, 58–60, 65, 69, 99, 129; of Africa, 195

Columbia, S.C., 14, 16, 27, 32, 160, 176

Confederacy, 144, 158, 160, 169

Conneau, Theophilus, 87–88

Conway, Bonds, 20–25, 38–41, 52–53, 64–65, 176, 228

Conway, Dorcas, 39, 245 (n. 36)

Conway, Harriet, 20, 41, 54, 176, 225, 252 (n. 70), 269 (n. 78)

Conway, Maria Theresa Louisa Matilda (Vaughan), 4, 13, 22–24, 27, 35–41 passim, 53–55, 62–63, 269 (n. 78)

Conway, Peter, 20, 60

Cook, Strother Moses, 197–200, 208, 213

Cotton: in the U.S., 16, 18–20, 27, 38, 52, 56, 164; in Africa, 129–30, 148, 185, 191

Country marks, 3, 4, 10, 12, 19, 125, 215, 217, 224–25, 231–32, 236

Credit, 108, 154–55, 164, 198–200, 203, 205

Crowther, Josiah, 129, 191

Crowther, Samuel Ajayi, 130, 149, 174, 185, 190–91, 196, 199, 206, 229–30

Crowther, Samuel, Jr., 129–31

Cuba, 9–10, 87, 90, 109, 136, 226, 242 (n. 4)

Cubans in Nigeria, 149, 152, 155

Cuffe, Paul, 47

Cultural Nationalism, 182, 192, 207, 209, 217, 221, 233

Dahomey, 98, 113, 126, 136–38, 163

David, William, 180, 183–89, 196–205, 270 (n. 102)

Davies, James Pinson Labulo, 185–86

Day, John, 89–90, 98, 103, 105–6

Delany, Martin Robeson, 65–66, 99, 108, 124, 128–33, 147, 149, 159–61, 167, 170

Democratic Party/Democrats, 160, 167–69

Dennis, Henry, 80–84, 95

Dey (people), 49, 78, 81, 85, 87, 92

Diaspora, African, 10–11, 117, 157, 179, 206–7, 226, 234, 236, 242 (n. 21), 243 (nn. 22, 26)

Dibble, Eugene, 228, 230

Dibble family, 167, 271 (n. 117)

Dill, S. G. W., 161

Disease, 17–18, 25, 52–53, 108, 121, 144; in Liberia, 48–49, 61, 64, 83, 100, 104, 170, 233; in Nigeria, 126, 130, 132, 172, 175, 193, 201

Doby, T. W., 54–55

Dosunmu (Lagos king), 150

Douglas, James K., 61–66

Douglass, Frederick, 65, 128, 159, 277 (n. 3)

Dred Scott decision, 129

DuBois, W. E. B., 189

Ebenezer Baptist Church, 180, 205, 211–12, 217, 221–22. See also Native Baptist Church

Ebony magazine, 1, 7, 215–16, 224, 231

Ebute Metta (Lagos), 147–48, 150, 152, 156, 172, 209, 227

Education, 21, 234, 241 (n. 1); of Church Vaughan, 40, 103, 111, 120–21, 125, 204, 218; and civilization, 46, 103; African American, 50, 158, 164–65; S.C. public, 57, 158, 164–66; in Liberia, 97; and missionaries, 120, 199–200, 208; in

Nigeria, 133, 146, 171, 173–76, 184, 190, 192–93, 222, 234–35; in Sierra Leone, 149

Egba (Yoruba), 1, 113, 124, 130–31, 135–38, 140–43, 206

Ejiwunmi, Lande, 1, 241 (n. 1)

Elections: in Liberia, 76; in the U.S., 159, 161, 167–69

Emancipation, 9, 28, 34, 45–46, 51, 60, 132, 158–59, 166, 183, 193, 195

Emigrants: to Liberia, 44, 51, 61, 66–72, 74–75, 95, 164, 170; numbers of, 49–50, 60, 69; recruitment of, 67, 69–72, 102; from Liberia, 92–93

Emigration, 28, 34; of Church Vaughan, 9–10, 62–63, 72; for manumission, 44; ambiguities of, 45, 68, 103; early projects, 46–47; to Haiti, 49; to Liberia, 49–51, 60, 64–66, 72, 170; opposition to, 66, 129; to Yorubaland, 129–30, 160

England, 16, 46, 56, 99, 129, 138, 144, 175, 183, 185, 192–93, 222. See also United Kingdom

English language, 108, 113, 149, 175, 192–93, 196, 199, 226–27

Ethiopianism, 180–81

Eubank, Peyton, 196–98, 202

Europe, 8, 11, 46, 108–9, 148, 173, 195, 235

Europeans in Nigeria, 108, 143, 146, 149, 157, 181, 191, 206, 209

Examiner, 58

Exports, from Lagos, 149, 155–56

Faduma, Orishetuka, 176, 178–79

Fairfield County, S.C., 17, 22, 163

Family: of J. C. Vaughan, 3, 4, 8–9; African diaspora as, 10, 236; of Scipio Vaughan, 13, 27, 35, 38, 41–42; of J. C. Vaughan in S.C., 52–54, 56, 59–60, 63–64, 67, 73–74, 77, 123, 129, 144, 158, 178, 214, 219, 236; of J. C. Vaughan in Africa, 138, 140–41, 146, 150, 155, 157, 171–76, 182, 212, 214–15, 221–24, 230–31, 233, 235; reunions after slavery, 229–30

Farms/farming: in Liberia, 80–81, 94–97,

101; of Church Vaughan, 84, 126, 138; in Nigeria, 114, 119, 148, 152, 218

Fayetteville, N.C., 40, 43–44, 68–73, 83, 96

Ferrell, Joshua, 43, 72–73

Fever. See Disease

Fire, 152, 155, 171–72, 176

Fishtown, Liberia, 65, 91

Forbes, Frederick, 98–99

Foreign Mission Board, Southern Baptist Convention, 103–4, 122–23, 148, 156–58, 166, 183, 187–89, 194, 197–99, 201–3

Fourth of July, 30, 32, 162, 168–69

Fox, John, 29, 33

France, 85, 88, 90

Freedom, 25, 28, 31–32, 43, 102, 233; ambiguity of, 9, 11, 71, 75, 233–34; for African Americans, 13, 36, 46, 103, 145, 164; purchase of, 20, 36, 68; of Scipio Vaughan, 21, 24, 27, 35, 38, 42, 52; in Liberia, 77, 88, 97; meaning of, 111, 124, 133–34, 170, 179, 208; in Lagos, 143, 145, 153, 178–79, 186; struggles for, 159

Free people of color, 14; restrictions on, 9, 25, 33, 36–39, 41, 47, 49, 59–60, 65, 102, 165; population of, 20, 27, 36; in South Carolina, 21, 124; and Liberia, 45, 48–50, 61, 64

Fugitives. See Slaves: runaway

Fugitive Slave Act, 59–60

Gallinas, 87, 89, 98

Garrison, William Lloyd, 51, 57

Garvey, Marcus, 226

Genealogy, 3, 215–16, 232

Georgia, 16, 44, 46, 51, 57, 73, 84, 105, 116, 120

Ghana, 18, 232–33

Gilmor, Robert, 17–18

Glover, John, 141, 147–48

Golah (people), 78, 87, 92

Grando (African chief), 65, 91

Grant, Ulysses S., 164, 167–68

Great Britain. See United Kingdom

Great Migration, 170, 227. See also Migration

Green, Levi (Agbelusi), 189, 201–2
Greer, Justa (David), 201
Guardians, white, 37–40, 52, 54–56, 60

Haglar, 17, 25–26
Hahn, Steven, 170
Haiti, 35, 45, 49
Haitian Revolution, 28
Haley, Alex, 215, 217
Hall, Granderson, 41, 55
Hall, Henry, 63
Hall, Rebecca Ann, 63, 144
Hamite's General Economy, 193–95, 212
Hammond, Henrietta, 166
Hammond, William, 53–55, 63, 144–45, 166
Hammond(s), Jacob, 41, 53–55, 60, 63, 145
Hampton, Wade, 168–69
Harden, Joseph, 102–11 passim, 123, 146, 148, 150, 155, 183, 200–201
Harden, Samuel, 186, 188, 200, 202–4
Harden, Sarah, 146–48, 180, 183, 185–86, 188, 198–200, 202–3
Hardware business, Vaughan's, 155–56, 171, 175–76, 186, 198, 218, 221
Harlem, N.Y., 226–27
Harris, Sion, 95
Hartman, Saidiya, 229
Harvey, Wiley W., 197
Hathcock, Mary, 245 (n. 36)
Hayes, Rutherford B., 169
Hill, Elias, 162, 164, 170
Hinderer, Anna, 126, 128, 133
Hinderer, David, 121, 128, 133
Hirschman, Albert O., 232
Hooper, Allen, 96–97, 100
Hooper, Caroline Mallett, 68–71
Hooper, Emily, 44, 68–71, 73–74, 81, 102, 172
Hooper, Marshall, 44, 67–74, 81–83, 96, 102–3
Hooper, Rachel, 44, 68, 81
Hyde, Hodge, & Company, 92–93

Ibadan, Nigeria, 1, 120, 124–28, 131–42, 156, 174, 176, 200, 224

Ibadan-Ijaye War, 131, 134–38, 142, 143, 174, 218
Ibikunle, 126–28, 132
Identity, 55, 181, 186, 189, 209, 215, 235
Ido, 124–27, 134, 138
Ifole, 142, 147, 218
Ijaye, 105, 110–28 passim, 131–37, 141, 179, 182, 201, 213, 218, 260 (n. 23)
Ijebu, 137, 206
Ilorin, 125, 131
Imperialism, 206. *See also* Colonialism
Iwo, 119, 128

Jacobs, Arabella, 73–74, 84, 173
Jacobs, Benjamin, 43, 66–67
Jacobs, Peter, 43, 66, 84–84
Jefferson, Thomas, 46
Job (biblical figure), 219–20, 233
Johnson, Andrew, 158
Johnson, Henry, 133, 174, 192–93
Johnson, James (of Lagos), 191–92, 195–95, 206
Johnson, Samuel, 114, 133, 135, 207, 273 (n. 34)
Joseph Maxwell, 43–45, 67, 71–72, 74, 78, 80–84, 94–96, 103, 141
Joy, John R., 54–55, 145

Kentucky, 19, 57–58, 197–98, 208
Kershaw, John, 30
Kershaw County, S.C., 13–23 passim, 27, 29, 33, 39–40, 54–57, 60, 66, 109, 144, 161–63, 165–66
King Peter (Liberia), 49, 85
Kinship, 10–11, 23, 182. *See also* Family
Kru (people), 65, 80–81, 91
Ku Klux Klan, 160–63, 168–69, 178
Kurunmi, 114–19 passim, 124–27, 132, 135, 137

Labor, 16–18, 21–22, 25, 34, 92, 147, 152–55, 235; hired, 20, 34–36, 119, 153; forced, 40, 91, 99; in Liberia, 78, 94, 97–101, 170; in Nigeria, 119; in South Carolina, 160, 164

Lafontant, Jewel Stradford (Mankarious), 231, 234

Lagos, Nigeria, 113, 126, 132, 137–38, 176, 219, 222–24; J. C. Vaughan in, 3, 10–11, 108–11, 121, 123, 143, 49, 154–58, 171–88 passim, 193–94, 198–213 passim, 218, 233; economy of, 8, 146, 148–51; colonial government of, 9, 131, 141–42, 145–49, 153, 157, 179, 181, 209; slavery in, 9, 152–54, 157–58, 170, 179, 181, 234; missionaries in, 10, 105–6, 109, 142–48, 156–57, 180, 183–91, 197–204, 206, 233; British bombardment of, 106, 110, 185; description of, 108–10; population of, 109, 149, 152–53; as slaving port, 109–10, 136; "Victorian," 173–75, 182; African Christians in, 180–84, 188–207 passim; newspapers in, 191–93, 204, 213, 219–21, 231; Vaughan descendants in, 225, 230–31

Lancaster County, S.C., 19, 43, 66–67, 74, 163

Land, 14, 48–49, 57, 60, 116, 159, 164, 170; of Scipio Vaughan, 13, 40, 42, 53–54, 144; in South Carolina, 16–17, 25, 52–53, 106, 165–67; of Wylie Vaughan, 19–20, 34, 39; in Liberia, 49, 64, 68, 78, 81, 94–97, 100–101, 170; of J. C. Vaughan, 76–77, 84, 95–96, 124, 147–48, 150, 171, 175–76, 200, 209; in Yorubaland, 105, 114–15, 119, 131, 135; in Lagos, 147, 150, 154, 211, 227

Lang, Isaac, 29–33

Lang, Sarah, 29, 31, 33

Langley, William, 21–22, 30–31, 33–34

Lark, 89, 93

Lauly, Maria Sophronia (Vaughan), 3, 6, 55–56, 64, 144–45, 165, 178

Legislative Council, Lagos, 185, 222, 227

"Legitimate" trade, 110, 114, 119, 130, 152

Lee, Frances, 19, 30

Levy, Chapman, 29–33, 245 (n. 25)

Levy, March, 30

Lewis, John, 81, 83, 90, 93

Liberated Africans. See Recaptives

Liberia, 5, 119, 121–24, 132, 134, 160, 172–73, 195, 207; J. C. Vaughan in, 2–3, 7–8, 76–81, 84–85, 90–96, 100–103, 106–11, 117, 122, 147–48, 150, 170, 179, 188, 194, 206, 213, 218, 233; African American settlers in, 9–10, 48–50, 61, 64–67, 76–78, 81–86, 87, 89–91, 94–98, 100–108, 110, 170; emigration to, 43–44, 49–51, 60–72, 74–75, 81, 83, 164, 170, 226; origins of, 45–49, 101; colonization of, 49, 58, 78, 100, 129; independence of, 50, 58, 60, 65, 76, 89; missionaries in, 60–61, 81, 89, 98, 103–6, 109, 116, 157, 188–89; government of, 65, 76, 89, 92–94, 103, 170; relations between settlers and Africans, 65, 85, 87, 91–93; slavery in, 76, 78, 97–101, 106, 234; militia, 77, 85–93, 109, 127; civil war, 78; census of, 83; slave trade from, 85, 87–93

Liberia Herald, 76, 89, 92–95, 99

Lincoln, Abraham, 132, 159

Linda Stewart, 83–84, 94–95, 103

Literacy, 139; of Vaughan, 40, 63, 74, 111, 121, 125, 174

Lomax, Matilda, 84, 91, 101

Louisiana, 57, 97

Lugenbeel, J. W., 44, 61–62, 66–71, 82, 98

Lynching, 169

Macaulay, Herbert, 230

MacLaughlin, Harriet, 144, 165

Mallett, Sarah, 69–70, 102

Mann, Adolphus, 114–15, 133, 135–36, 259 (n. 100), 260 (n. 23)

Mann, Kristin, 153

Manumission, 27, 33–36, 38, 50–52, 68

Marriage, 22–24, 116, 138, 140, 154, 172, 175, 231

Maryland, 19, 27–28, 50, 52, 65

Masculinity, 64, 109, 179, 192, 195

Massachusetts, 34, 47, 57, 200, 204

Matilda Newport Day, 85

McLain, William, 62–63, 69–71

Mercer, Charles Fenton, 45, 48

Mercer University, 120–21

Merrell, James, 25

Methodists, 181–82, 205, 207. See also Missionaries: Methodist

Middle Passage, 18–19, 74, 224, 251 (n. 51)

Migration, 8–11, 19, 46, 57, 150, 225, 235–36

Militia, South Carolina, 21, 33, 35, 37, 161–62, 165, 167, 169. *See also* Liberia: militia

Millsburg, Liberia, 80–84, 94, 96, 100

Missionaries: Southern Baptist, 3, 7, 104–11, 115, 121–43 passim, 146, 148, 156–57, 172, 174, 180–89 passim, 196–208 passim, 233; Methodist, 110, 142, 183; C.M.S., 126, 128, 133, 142–43, 174, 191, 196, 206. *See also* Lagos, Nigeria: missionaries in; Liberia: missionaries in; Yorubaland: missionaries and

Mission, Anglican, 130, 138, 141–42. *See also* Missionaries: C.M.S.

Mission, Baptist in Nigeria, 111, 140–42, 150–51, 182, 186, 196, 198, 201, 204, 208, 218. *See also* Missionaries: Southern Baptist

Mobility, 5, 232, 235. *See also* Migration

Monrovia, Liberia, 49–50, 61–62, 65, 76–81, 83–103 passim, 109, 115, 148, 156, 170, 259 (n. 100)

Moore, Aida Arabella (Vaughan), 74, 173–75, 178, 208–9, 217, 222–23, 225–32

Moore, Eric, 222, 227

Murphy, Josephine (Dibble), 225, 228

Names, 25, 74, 141, 150, 154, 172–73, 192, 213

Nationalism, 10, 46, 181, 205. *See also* Cultural Nationalism

Native Americans, 13, 17, 22–25, 46–47, 57, 113, 117. *See also* Catawba; Cherokee

Native Baptist Church, 202–4, 206–8, 213. *See also* Ebenezer Baptist Church

Naudin, Moreau, 41, 54, 269 (n. 78)

Navy: British, 48, 88–90, 98, 106, 109–10, 185, 229; U.S., 48–49, 88–89, 97

Nesbit, William, 99–100

Networks, 10–11, 60, 69, 103, 230, 234

New Jersey, 178, 227, 232

Newton, C. C., 204, 206

New Virginia, Liberia, 68, 81–82, 84, 94, 97, 103, 105

New York, 50, 56, 58, 174, 178, 227

Niger Expedition (1841–42), 130, 190

Nigeria, 3–5, 7–8, 10, 105, 113, 181, 209, 214–15, 225, 230–32, 235

Nigerian National Democratic Party, 227, 230

Nigerian Youth Movement, 222–23, 234

Niger Mission (C.M.S.), 190–91, 206

North Carolina, 15, 28, 43–44, 49–50, 53, 55, 60, 67–71, 75, 82–83, 96, 101–2, 108, 117, 123

Ogbomosho, Nigeria, 117, 121–23, 128, 132, 186, 199–200

Ogundipe (Egba chief), 142–43

Ogunmola, 126, 132, 138, 140, 264 (n. 104)

Ogun River, 111

Ohio, 49, 56–58, 60, 197

Omotayo, Sarah (Vaughan), 139–43, 149, 172–74, 176, 194, 208–9, 223

Oriki, 223–24

Oriole, 83–84

Orline St. John, 58–59

Oshodi, Manly Ogunlana, 196–97

Owu, Nigeria, 231

Oyo, Nigeria (New), 122–23, 125, 127–28, 132

Oyo Empire, 110, 113, 115, 120, 125, 140, 224

Page, Solomon, 90–91

Palm oil, 108–9, 119, 142, 148, 152–53, 185, 191

Patronage: in S.C., 9, 21, 27, 38, 40, 45, 52, 60, 110; in Africa, 115, 118, 124, 133, 136, 152, 155, 179, 203, 235

Pawnship, 97–99, 135, 152

Pennsylvania, 15, 50, 99, 128

Pettiford, Henry Sewell, 83–85, 93, 123, 132, 135–36, 138, 141, 194–96, 212

Philadelphia, Pa., 15, 30, 47, 57–58, 65, 66, 91, 129

Phillips, A. D., 121, 123, 125, 127, 136–44, 148, 157, 260 (n. 22), 264 (n. 105)

Photography, 132, 138, 212

Plantations, 13–16, 19, 23, 29, 38, 57, 92, 97, 106, 116, 160, 166

Politics, 9–10, 155, 158–60, 222–23, 230, 234

Polygamy (polygyny), 193–94, 203, 211

Power, 9, 158–59

Priest, R. W., 122–23

Property, 35–36, 40, 51; of J. C. Vaughan, 3, 126, 134, 146–47, 150, 171, 209, 223; of African Americans, 9, 20, 39, 166–67, 168–69; of women, 16; slaves as, 24–25, 33; of Wylie Vaughan, 34; of Vaughan family, 52, 54, 59–60, 62, 145, 228; in Liberia, 76, 89; in Nigeria, 142, 146–47, 150, 154, 157, 235. *See also* Land

Race, 14, 21, 45–46, 62, 64, 122, 124, 127, 130, 143, 159–60, 162, 167, 186–87, 192–93, 206–7, 228

Racism, 8, 10, 49–50, 60, 128, 180–82, 189–93, 204–5, 207, 232–26, 268 (n. 51); "scientific," 187, 226. *See also* White supremacy

Raleigh, N.C., 69–71, 83

Ransom, 126, 133

Rayford, Bessie Boykin, 176–77

"Recaptives," 48, 84, 88, 97, 255 (n. 29)

Reconstruction, 9, 158–60, 164–67, 178, 189

Refugees, 174, 224; from slavery, 10, 12, 109–10, 208, 233–34; from warfare, 109–10, 113, 136, 141, 143, 201; from Abeokuta, 147

Reid, T. A., 122–23, 125, 131, 138, 144

Religion, 31, 41, 50, 104, 116, 120–21, 123, 133. *See also* Christianity

"Repatriates," 10, 109–10, 129–30, 133, 146, 149–50, 185, 190, 193, 201, 234

Republican Party/Republicans, 58, 159–69 passim, 178

Resistance, 25; to slavery, 28–29, 33; in Liberia, 91; to Reconstruction, 158–69

Richardson, James, 73, 84, 101

Richland County, S.C., 17, 22

Richmond, Va., 4, 14, 28, 105, 117, 122, 128, 136, 183, 186, 189, 198–99, 202

Richmond Institute, 183, 188, 200, 204

Roberts, Joseph J., 76–77, 84, 89–94, 99, 100

Rogers, John, Jr., 234

Roots (Haley), 215, 217

Russell, Richard, 123–24, 127–28, 132–34, 136

St. Paul's River, 80–81, 84, 94–97, 148

Salmond, Thomas, 30, 39

Saro (Sierra Leonians in Nigeria), 109, 117, 130, 141, 143, 147, 149–50, 153, 155–56, 173–74, 182, 191, 193–94, 203–4, 207, 222, 268 (n. 51)

Schools, 56, 60, 80, 167, 183, 204, 222; African American, 41, 47, 160, 169, 189, 204; public, 159, 164, 178, 228; in Lagos, 172, 174–75, 188, 193, 196, 198, 200, 206

Scott, Robert K., 163

Scramble for Africa, 181, 195

Segregation, 169, 228

Settlers, 28, 170; in South Carolina, 13, 15, 17, 22–25, 101; in Lagos, 110, 148–49; in Yorubaland, 129–32, 170. *See also* Liberia: African American settlers in

Sickness. *See* Disease

Sierra Leone, 10, 18, 46–49, 87–91, 105, 109, 117–18, 129–30, 133, 182–83, 185, 190–92, 200–201, 229–30, 234, 255 (n. 29), 271 (n. 114)

Skipwith, Peyton, 87–88, 100

Slave owners, 9, 24, 27, 45, 51, 58–59, 65, 103, 146, 154, 158, 183

Slave rebellion, 28; in Camden, 27, 29–35, 57, 162, 169; in Charleston, 35–36; in Virginia, 41, 49–50

Slavers, 9, 87–89

Slavery, 3, 7, 9–14, 17, 27, 36, 46, 51, 104, 106, 192–93, 201, 204, 208, 229; in the United States, 7–9, 17–19, 21–37 passim, 42, 45, 48–49, 56–58, 64–65, 72, 74, 87, 100, 102–3, 106, 115, 130, 158–59, 174, 186, 204, 236; in the Atlantic world, 8, 10–11, 110, 233–34; in Africa, 8, 111, 149–53, 179, 193–94; abolition of, 8–9, 92, 145–46, 153–54. *See also* Lagos: slavery in; Liberia: slavery in; South Carolina: slavery in; Yorubaland: slavery in

Slaves, 3, 4, 9, 88, 126–27, 137, 201; in
Yorubaland, 3, 9, 109, 115, 119, 147, 152–54,
157, 170, 179, 255 (n. 29); in the U.S., 8,
21–22, 28, 39, 42, 44–45, 50–53, 67, 69,
87, 116, 133, 161, 163, 186, 224; in South
Carolina, 13, 15–20, 24, 27, 29–31, 33,
35–37; of Wylie Vaughan, 15, 19–20, 24,
34–35, 41, 56; runaway, 29, 33–34, 37,
56–57, 59, 154; in Liberia, 87–90, 93–94,
97–100; as wives, 140
Slave trade: Atlantic, 3, 8, 17–18, 48, 74,
78, 85, 87–88, 90–93, 98–100, 106, 109,
113, 126, 133, 136, 141, 148–49, 153, 201,
208, 236, 255 (n. 29); within the U.S., 19,
52; suppression of, 47–48, 88–89, 114;
within Africa, 77, 111, 135; abolition of, 88.
See also Lagos, Nigeria: as slaving port;
Liberia: slave trade from
Smallpox, 17, 127, 137. *See also* Disease
Smith, Charles Edwin, 197–98, 202, 204
Smythe, Mabel Murphy, 225, 230, 234
Snowden, Muriel (Sutherland), 234
South Carolina, 3, 7, 14, 22–23, 25, 28–29,
44, 51, 53, 56–57, 143, 173, 178, 236; J. C.
Vaughan in, 3, 77–78, 91, 96, 101, 110, 121,
124, 177–78, 213, 215, 218–19; slavery in, 9,
13, 15, 17–20, 27, 29, 36, 57, 100, 106, 174,
233; upcountry, 9, 16–17, 158, 160–64;
Vaughan family in, 8, 63, 144, 146, 150,
158, 171, 174, 176, 177–78, 196, 225–26;
African Americans in, 9, 20–21, 36–42,
52, 65, 169, 171; population of, 20, 36, 57,
159; government of, 36, 158–61, 164–69;
Reconstruction in, 145, 158–61, 163–69.
See also Camden, S.C.
South Carolina General Assembly, 33, 36,
38, 161, 165–66, 168–69, 178
Southern Baptist Convention, 7, 98, 102–5,
115, 182. *See also* Foreign Mission Board
Spottswood (S.C. slave), 30–32
Steamships, 43–44, 58–59, 89–90, 101, 106,
108, 120
Stone, Moses Ladejo, 152, 157, 180, 183, 186,
196–97, 199–206, 208

Stone, Richard, 115, 118, 123, 127–28, 132–34,
146–37, 148, 150–51, 156, 182–83, 199
Stone, Sue, 123, 127–28, 132, 136
Stradford, Aida Arabella (Carter), 178, 215,
217, 224–30, 234
Stradford, C. Francis, 227, 229
Stradford, John B., 228–29
Sugar, 95–97, 138, 218
Sutherland, Bill, 232–34
Sutherland, James F., 56, 145, 165, 178, 257
(n. 66)
Sutherland, William, 178, 227

Taxes, 36, 38, 40, 54–56, 165–69
Tennessee, 19, 22, 50, 160
Thompson, Era Bell, 215, 217
Thompson, Sarah (Carter), 226–27
Townsend, Henry, 113, 130–31, 144, 261
(n. 28)
Trade, 8–9, 15, 17–19, 23, 129, 185, 234; in
Liberia, 68, 76–78, 81, 91, 101; in Nigeria,
113, 146, 148–51, 154–56, 157, 200
Trader(s): in South Carolina, 17, 22–23; in
Liberia, 77, 85, 87, 89–92; in Yorubaland,
106, 141–42, 206; in Lagos, 108–10, 149,
153–56, 175, 181, 223; Vaughan as, 155–56
"Tribal marks." *See* Country marks
Trimble, Selden, 122–23
Tulsa, Okla., 228–29
Turner, Nat, 41, 49

United Kingdom, 5, 7, 16, 28, 46, 85, 87–89,
92–93, 125, 129, 207
United Native African Church, 207, 221,
277 (n. 8)
United States of America, 5, 11, 39, 123–24,
158, 189, 209, 228, 233, 236; Vaughan
descendants in, 7–8, 214, 225, 227,
230–31, 234; African contacts with, 11,
49, 182; departure from, 43–44, 75, 77,
232, 236; Supreme Court, 45, 129, 163,
227; politics in, 45, 129, 168–69; removals
from, 46, 64; North, 46–49, 56, 60, 65,
225; government of, 87–89, 97, 145, 163;

Constitution, 158; Congress, 120, 129, 159, 163, 167; Army, 159. *See also* African Americans; Slavery: in the United States

U.S. South, 34, 51–52, 96–97, 114, 120, 144, 158, 162–63, 176, 179–80, 183, 189, 196, 234; oppression of African Americans in, 9, 11, 14, 67, 219, 236; after Reconstruction, 10, 170, 187, 225, 227–28; lawmakers in, 45, 47, 169; politics in, 158–60, 167, 169

Upper South, 19, 41, 50–52, 58, 60

Ussery, Dudley, 66–67

Vai (people), 78, 92, 106, 108, 111–12, 114, 117–18

Vaughan, Burrell Carter (of Lagos), 172, 174–76, 196, 205, 208–11, 219, 221–22, 227

Vaughan, Burrell Carter (of South Carolina), 25, 41, 55–56, 60, 62–63, 65, 144, 162, 165, 178, 224

Vaughan, Christopher B., 154, 209

Vaughan, Claiborne, 20

Vaughan, Elizabeth Margaret (Hall), 24, 41, 55, 63, 144, 165

Vaughan, Emily, 74, 172, 186

Vaughan, Harriet Amanda, 24, 41, 53, 55, 63, 67

Vaughan, James Churchwill: life story of, 2–4, 7–12, 224, 229, 231–36; death of, 213, 217, 219–20; memory of, 217–21, 224, 225. *See also references to J. C. Vaughan within individual entries*

Vaughan, James Churchwill Omosanya, 213, 222, 234

Vaughan, James Olabode, 231, 275 (n. 83)

Vaughan, James Richard Oladeinde, 223

Vaughan, James Wilson, 140, 143, 173–76, 202–3, 205, 208–10, 213, 219, 221–22, 224, 226–27

Vaughan, John Champion, 40, 56–59

Vaughan, Kitty Ann, 24, 41, 52–53, 63

Vaughan, (Maria) Virginia, 24, 41, 52, 63

Vaughan, Mary Elizabeth, 24, 41, 55, 63, 74, 145, 165, 178

Vaughan, Nancy Carter, 24, 41, 53, 63

Vaughan, Sarah, 172

Vaughan, Sarah (Champion), 16, 24–25, 35, 38, 40–41, 58–59

Vaughan, Sarah Ann, 24, 35, 41, 55, 61–63, 144, 162, 165, 177, 242 (n. 8)

Vaughan, Scipio, 1, 4, 7, 13–15, 19–27, 34–35, 38, 40–42, 51–53, 55–59, 63, 75, 96, 144, 215, 217, 224, 231, 242 (n. 8)

Vaughan, Virginia, 58–59

Vaughan, Wylie, 14–39 passim, 56, 58–59

Vaughan-Richards, Ayo, 230–31, 235, 277 (n. 16)

Vesey, Denmark, 35–36, 38

Victoria (queen of England), 89, 185

Vincent, David Brown, 192, 195, 200–202, 205–7. *See also* Agbebi, Mojola

Violence, 14, 27–28, 34–35, 78, 110, 143, 156, 161, 168–69, 188, 235

Virginia, 6, 13–15, 19–20, 24, 28–29, 41, 48–50, 71, 83, 87–88, 91, 101, 103, 106, 127, 183, 200, 204, 242 (n. 8)

Voting, 76–77, 109, 159, 169

Walker, David, 50–51

Warfare, 3, 9–10, 22, 28, 77, 91–92, 94, 106, 110, 124–26, 134, 137, 148–49, 199, 231; captives in, 110–11, 135, 137; Yoruba, 114, 130, 140

Warlords, 110–11, 125

War of 1812, 21, 28–29, 31, 33

Wateree River, 22–23, 33

Wealth, 101, 106, 146, 149–50, 152, 155, 171, 179, 221, 223, 232–33

Webster, Daniel, 60, 89

West Africa, 46, 97, 105, 108, 130, 144, 148, 180, 195, 206, 212; colonialism in, 8, 193; slavery in, 9; white supremacy in, 9; as destination, 10, 234; history of, 11; weather in, 79; missionary networks in, 103; geography of, 113; colonization in, 124. *See also* Africa

West Indies, 18, 28, 92

White Supremacy, 9–12, 42, 45–46, 106,

116, 124, 145–46, 169–70, 179, 183, 187, 189, 195–96, 198, 204, 206, 208–9, 228, 231. *See also* Racism

Williams, Samuel, 97, 100

Williamson, Joel, 166

Wills, 21, 27, 38–39, 209, 211

Wilmington, N.C., 43–44, 66–72, 109

Wilson, Ephraim, 44, 73, 141

Wives, 115, 140, 152, 194, 211, 234

Women, 39, 64, 135, 138, 229; Native American, 23–24; African American, 24, 62; as emigrants to Liberia, 73, 101; Yoruba, 110

Wright, Elijah, 66, 83

Yellow fever, 52–53. *See also* Disease

York County, S.C., 161–62

Yoruba (people), 1, 110, 113, 172, 182, 192–93, 196, 207–9, 211, 215, 217, 219, 224, 229–32

Yorubaland, 119, 159, 182, 185, 207; Vaughan in, 3, 7–8, 66, 85, 106, 108–11, 113–28, 132–43, 146–7, 150, 155, 180, 208, 214, 217–18, 223, 233; slavery in, 3, 9, 118–19, 229; as origin of Scipio Vaughan, 5; colonialism in, 10, 209; missionaries and, 105–6, 109, 113–44 passim, 153, 156–57, 181, 186, 193, 195, 197–98, 206; "age of confusion" in, 110, 143; repatriates in, 149, 152, 230; churches in, 180, 190

Yoruba language, 108–9, 111, 113, 116, 118, 123, 127, 140–41, 175, 192–93, 196, 199–200, 221, 226

H. EUGENE AND
LILLIAN YOUNGS LEHMAN SERIES

Lamar Cecil, *Wilhelm II: Prince and Emperor, 1859–1900* (1989).

Carolyn Merchant, *Ecological Revolutions: Nature, Gender, and Science in New England* (1989).

Gladys Engel Lang and Kurt Lang, *Etched in Memory: The Building and Survival of Artistic Reputation* (1990).

Howard Jones, *Union in Peril: The Crisis over British Intervention in the Civil War* (1992).

Robert L. Dorman, *Revolt of the Provinces: The Regionalist Movement in America* (1993).

Peter N. Stearns, *Meaning Over Memory: Recasting the Teaching of Culture and History* (1993).

Thomas Wolfe, *The Good Child's River*, edited with an introduction by Suzanne Stutman (1994).

Warren A. Nord, *Religion and American Education: Rethinking a National Dilemma* (1995).

David E. Whisnant, *Rascally Signs in Sacred Places: The Politics of Culture in Nicaragua* (1995).

Lamar Cecil, *Wilhelm II: Emperor and Exile, 1900–1941* (1996).

Jonathan Hartlyn, *The Struggle for Democratic Politics in the Dominican Republic* (1998).

Louis A. Pérez Jr., *On Becoming Cuban: Identity, Nationality, and Culture* (1999).

Yaakov Ariel, *Evangelizing the Chosen People: Missions to the Jews in America, 1880–2000* (2000).

Philip F. Gura, *C. F. Martin and His Guitars, 1796–1873* (2003).

Louis A. Pérez Jr., *To Die in Cuba: Suicide and Society* (2005).

Peter Filene, *The Joy of Teaching: A Practical Guide for New College Instructors* (2005).

John Charles Boger and Gary Orfield, eds., *School Resegregation: Must the South Turn Back?* (2005).

Jock Lauterer, *Community Journalism: Relentlessly Local* (2006).

Michael H. Hunt, *The American Ascendancy: How the United States Gained and Wielded Global Dominance* (2007).

Michael Lienesch, *In the Beginning: Fundamentalism, the Scopes Trial, and the Making of the Antievolution Movement* (2007).

Eric L. Muller, *American Inquisition: The Hunt for Japanese American Disloyalty in World War II* (2007).

John McGowan, *American Liberalism: An Interpretation for Our Time* (2007).

Nortin M. Hadler, M.D., *Worried Sick: A Prescription for Health in an Overtreated America* (2008).

William Ferris, *Give My Poor Heart Ease: Voices of the Mississippi Blues* (2009).

Colin A. Palmer, *Cheddi Jagan and the Politics of Power: British Guiana's Struggle for Independence* (2010).

W. Fitzhugh Brundage, *Beyond Blackface: African Americans and the Creation of American Mass Culture, 1890–1930* (2011).

Michael H. Hunt and Steven I. Levine, *Arc of Empire: America's Wars in Asia from the Philippines to Vietnam* (2012).

Nortin M. Hadler, M.D., *The Citizen Patient: Reforming Health Care for the Sake of the Patient, Not the System* (2013).

Louis A. Pérez Jr., *The Structure of Cuban History: Meanings and Purpose of the Past* (2013).

Jennifer Thigpen, *Island Queens and Mission Wives: How Gender and Empire Remade Hawai'i's Pacific World* (2014).

George W. Houston, *Inside Roman Libraries: Book Collections and Their Management in Antiquity* (2014).

Philip F. Gura, *The Life of William Apess, Pequot* (2015).

Daniel M. Cobb, ed., *Say We Are Nations: Documents of Politics and Protest in Indigenous America since 1887* (2015).

Daniel Maudlin and Bernard L. Herman, eds., *Building the British Atlantic World: Spaces, Places, and Material Culture, 1600–1850* (2016).

William Ferris, *The South in Color: A Visual Journal* (2016).

Lisa A. Lindsay, *Atlantic Bonds: A Nineteenth-Century Odyssey from America to Africa* (2017).

CPSIA information can be obtained
at www.ICGtesting.com
Printed in the USA
LVHW041415120123
736945LV00005B/361